The EASTERN FRONT

Day by Day, 1941–45

The EASTERN FRONT
Day by Day, 1941-45
A Photographic Chronology

STEVE CRAWFORD

SPELLMOUNT

British Library Cataloguing in Publication Data:
A catalogue record for this book is available from the British Library

First published in 2006 Great Britain by
SPELLMOUNT (PUBLISHERS) LTD
The Mill, Brimscombe Port, Stroud,
Gloucestershire GL5 2QG, UK
Tel: 0044 (0) 1453 883300
Fax: 0044 (0) 1453 883233
www.spellmount.com

ISBN 1-86227-359-6

Printed in China

Editorial and design
The Brown Reference Group plc
8 Chapel Place
Rivington Street
London
EC2A 3DQ
www.brownreference.com

Senior Editor: Peter Darman
Editor: Alan Marshall
Designer: Jerry Udall
Cartographer: Darren Awuah
Production: Beckie Sanderson
Picture Research: Andrew Webb
Index: Indexing Specialists (UK) Ltd

Pages 2–3: German panzers and infantry move forward to attack a Ukrainian village occupied by Red Army troops, January 1944.

CONTENTS

Key to maps	6
Introduction	7
1939	8
1940	14
1941	26
1942	74
1943	110
1944	144
1945	172
Conclusion	188
Bibliography	189
Index	190

Key to Maps

Military Units – Sizes

XXXXX Army group/front

XXXX Army

XXX Corps

XX Division

X Brigade

III Regiment

II Battalion

National Colours

German

Soviet

Romanian

Finnish

Italian

Polish

Hungarian

Army Movements

Attack/advance (in national colours)

Retreat (in national colours)

Frontline (in national colours)

Heavy defence line (in national colours)

Defence line (in national colours)

Military Units – Types

Infantry

Armoured/panzer

Panzergrenadier

Parachute

Cavalry

Mountain

General Military Symbols

Airfield

Parachute landing

Geographical Symbols

River

Road

Railroad

Urban area

Town or city

Capital city

Marsh

Trees

Bridge

Mountains

International border

INTRODUCTION

Nazi Germany's war against the USSR, which began on June 22, 1941, was one characterized by brutality, both in the way it was waged on the frontline and in the manner in which the conquered peoples were treated.

National Socialist ideology revolved around several key tenets, chief among them being anti-Semitism, anti-Bolshevism and the acquisition of *Lebensraum* (living space) to sustain a Thousand Year Reich populated by an Aryan *Herrenvolk* (master race), created at the expense of the "sub-human" Slav peoples in the East. Poland and the Soviet Union thus became the focus of Nazi fear and loathing. Fear because in the Nazi "worldview" the countless millions of Slavs east of the River Oder posed a threat to the Third Reich, much as the barbarian hordes had done to ancient Rome; loathing, because those countries were populated by the racial groups that the Nazis despised. For these reasons, Germany's war with the Soviet Union was inevitable and, for the same reasons, it would be conducted in a particularly brutal fashion.

Privately, Hitler saw it as a manifestation of history, being the merciless struggle of races. Indeed, the war of racial ideology and annihilation would be conducted with "unprecedented severity". Three days before Barbarossa, Hitler said to propaganda minister Goebbels: "Right or wrong we must win. And once we have won, who is going to question our methods?" As a result, the SS mobile killing squads (*Einsatzgruppen*) would follow the army groups into Russia to annihilate Jews and Communist Party members.

The Blitzkrieg that was unleashed against the USSR in the summer of 1941 almost succeeded in defeating Stalin's Bolshevik regime. As the veteran German Army smashed into a Soviet Red Army still undergoing reforms and emasculated by Stalin's purge of its leadership, the USSR suffered a series of catastrophic defeats. Hundreds of thousands of prisoners fell into German hands, most subsequently dying due to ill-treatment. Behind the lines, in German-occupied areas, the Nazis plundered the land "to procure as much food and mineral oil as possible for Germany". This resulted in death by starvation for millions of people as food was extracted from conquered areas. In addition, supply difficulties led some army units to plunder the land in order to survive, resulting in the devastation of entire regions, leading to more starvation.

The USSR was also plundered of people to work in Germany. Between November 1941 and June 1944, 2.8 million people from the German-occupied territories of the USSR were transported to Germany to serve as slave labour. In addition, when the German Army was forced to retreat west from mid-1943, it forced hundreds of thousands of civilians to accompany German forces, both to prevent them being recruited by the Red Army and to serve the Wehrmacht as slave labour. In response to the German occupation, partisan bands started to appear behind Wehrmacht lines. Small and militarily insignificant at first, from 1942 they began to have an impact on the occupiers' supply lines. Thus, the Germans adopted "collective reprisal methods" in an attempt to defeat them, which only resulted in aiding partisan recruitment. Hitler himself demanded that the war against the partisans be waged with the "most brutal methods", and so the occupiers resorted to transforming entire regions into desert zones. In such areas villages were burnt and civilians murdered or deported.

The following chapters record both the military operations that took place on the Eastern Front between 1941 and 1945, and the atrocities carried out against civilians in the rear areas. These include not only Nazi crimes but those committed by the Soviets as, perversely, Stalin was also waging a war against civilians he suspected of collaboration with the enemy, even as his regime was fighting for its life. The Soviet Union was a state ruled by Stalin's iron hand. While it is true that the country did become a major industrial nation by 1939, the 1930s themselves were a disaster for individual Russians. Millions had died in the famine that followed the failed experiment of collectivization, when small farms were merged to form one massive one. These bigger farms were called collectives. In Marxist thinking, large farms meant that more food could be grown and cities and factories could be fed. Villages that refused to join a collective had soldiers sent to them, and the villagers were usually shot as "enemies of the people". The net result was disaster, and Russia's agriculture was at the same level in 1939 as it had been in 1928, but with a 40 million increase in the population.

The secret police were omnipresent, actively encouraging people to inform on neighbours and work colleagues for any signs of seditious activities. The increasingly paranoid Stalin saw threats and rivals everywhere, an attitude that permeated downwards into all walks of life.

Throughout the following chapters, battlefield casualties have been listed to illustrate the scale of human and material losses in a merciless conflict between two totalitarian regimes.

This year saw the outbreak of World War II, with Hitler attacking Poland as part of his relentless drive for *Lebensraum* for the German people. Stalin, abandoning any hope of the USSR signing a formal alliance with Britain and France, readily agreed to Hitler's offer of a non-aggression treaty. And as Germany completed the conquest of Poland, the USSR, adhering to the secret clauses of the treaty, attacked Finland.

▲ *German Foreign Minister Joachim von Ribbentrop (centre) and Joseph Stalin (right) following the signing of the Nazi-Soviet Non-Aggression Treaty in Moscow in August.*

April 28

GERMANY, *DIPLOMACY*

In a speech to the German Parliament (Reichstag), Hitler repudiates the 10-year German-Polish Non-Aggression Pact to which he had put his signature in 1934. The pact had stated that neither signatory would "proceed to use force in order to settle" disputes. In his speech, Hitler states that the Polish Government has rejected several German proposals made earlier regarding the city of Danzig (under the terms of the Treaty of Versailles, a demilitarized Free City) and the Polish Corridor (a strip of land that gives Poland access to the Baltic and cuts off East Prussia from the rest of Germany). These proposals were the incorporation of Danzig as a free state "into the framework of the German Reich", and "a route through the Corridor and a railway line at her own disposal possessing the same extraterritorial status for Germany as the Corridor itself has for Poland". The reality is that the repudiation of the 1934 pact is part of Hitler's long-term goal of acquiring *Lebensraum* for Germany in the east, the achievement of which means Poland ceasing to exist as a state.

May 22

GERMANY, *DIPLOMACY*

Italian Foreign Minister Galeazzo Ciano and German Foreign Minister Joachim von Ribbentrop sign the Pact of Steel between Italy and Germany in Berlin. The pact guarantees that either country will come to the military aid of the other if attacked by another state, plus greater military collaboration between Italy and Germany. The pact will last for 10 years,

◀ ***The signatories of the Pact of Steel: Ribbentrop (left) and Italian Foreign Minister Galeazzo Ciano (centre).***

and though Ciano has grave doubts about the ramifications for Italy, Mussolini is delighted to be tied closely to his fascist ally. For his part, Hitler sees the pact as a means of isolating the Poles by weakening French and British resolve to come to Poland's aid in the event of a German attack. Hitler now only needs an assurance of non-interference from the USSR to clear the way for his campaign against Poland.

AUGUST 20

MONGOLIA, *LAND WAR*

The start of the Battle of Nomonhan, 24km (15 miles) east of the Halha River (also known as the Khalkhin Gol). The Soviets have been fighting the Japanese over disputed territory on the Manchukuo-Mongolia border since May (the Japanese instigated the war). The Japanese Sixth Army consists of 38,000 men, 130 tanks, 318 artillery pieces and 225 combat aircraft. Zhukov, the Soviet commander, has achieved superiority in numbers and firepower. His First Army Group has 57,000 men, 498 tanks, 515 aircraft and 542 artillery pieces. Zhukov's plan is to encircle the enemy with a three-pronged attack. After a massive artillery barrage, the 36th Motorized Rifle Division, 82nd Rifle Division and 5th Machine Gun Brigade advance straight into the centre of Japanese positions, pinning down Japanese troops while two larger motorized formations swing around both flanks. By August 24, the Japanese are encircled in a pocket that is pounded mercilessly by Soviet artillery and aircraft. Over the next six days, the Japanese 23rd Division is utterly destroyed.

▼ ***Polish prisoners go into captivity. Hitler had total contempt for the Poles, calling them "idle, stupid and vain".***

AUGUST 23

GERMANY, *DIPLOMACY*

Unable to reach agreement with either Britain or France, Soviet dictator Joseph Stalin, facing alone the prospect of resisting German aggression in Eastern Europe, concludes a treaty with Nazi Germany. Hitler sends Ribbentrop to Moscow where the Nazi-Soviet Non-Aggression Treaty is signed in the presence of Stalin.

The terms made public state that the two countries agree not to attack each other, either independently or in conjunction with other powers; not to support any third power that might attack the other party to the pact; to remain in consultation with each other upon questions touching their common interests; not to join any group of powers directly or indirectly threatening one of the two parties; and to solve all differences by negotiation or arbitration.

The pact is to last for 10 years, with automatic extension for another five years unless either party gives notice to terminate it one year before its expiry. The secret part of the pact divides the whole of Eastern Europe into German and Soviet spheres of influence: Poland will cease to exist and Lithuania, Latvia, Estonia and Finland are assigned to the Soviet sphere of influence. In addition, the treaty mentions the separation of Bessarabia from Romania, which the USSR covets, along with Northern Bukovino (the Soviets will seize both areas in June 1940).

▲ ***Polish troops surrender to a German officer at Lvov following the Blitzkrieg against Poland in September.***

AUGUST 25

BRITAIN, *DIPLOMACY*

The Anglo-Polish Agreement of Mutual Assistance is signed in London. It states that each government will undertake to give assistance to the other in the event of aggression

DECISIVE MOMENT

STALIN'S GREAT PURGES

Like most dictators, Stalin was continually fearful of coups, and was particularly suspicious of ambitious generals because they commanded large numbers of troops. Stalin's paranoia manifested itself in the Great Terror that began in 1937 and ended only in June 1941, on the eve of the German invasion. During this time, he purged old guard Bolsheviks, Communist Party bosses, military leaders, industrial managers and government officials. The first commander to be removed was Marshal Mikhail Tukhachevsky in June 1937, ostensibly on charges of conspiracy with Germany, but probably because he and Stalin had been "debating" for years which of them had been responsible for the Red Army's defeat before Moscow in 1920 (Stalin had been a party emissary, Tukhachevsky a front commander). The purge then took on a life of its own, with most of the military commanders arrested and shot – unknown to Stalin. These included three deputies of the people's commissar of defence, the people's commissar of the navy, 16 military district commanders, five fleet commanders, eight directors of military academies, 33 corps commanders, 76 division commanders, 40 brigade commanders, and 291 regimental commanders. In total, 35,000 officers of the armed forces were either dismissed, imprisoned or executed (hundreds of scientists and weapons designers were also arrested). Tens of thousands signed "confessions" to being party to non-existent conspiracies (as the arrested and subsequently executed Marshal Bliukher stated: "When they start twisting your arms and legs, you will sign anything").

The purges were to cause incalculable damage to the ability of the Red Army to resist the German invasion in June 1941. First, they removed experienced and bold commanders and replaced them with those who lacked experience and were noted for a distinct lack of initiative (which, in the Red Army, could shorten life quicker than the German invaders). Second, the command vacuum meant incompetent leaders were over-promoted, resulting in disaster on the battlefield.

Perversely, the purges were also advantageous for Stalin and his regime. The removal of potential opponents meant there was no popular revolt against him during the disasters that took place during Operation Barbarossa (in this way the Soviet system survived for another 50 years instead of collapsing in the summer of 1941). In addition, the purges led Hitler and his planners to underestimate Soviet military potential. Mesmerized by the spectre of emasculated armed forces, they failed to take account of Soviet industrial capacity and ignored the geography of the areas in which the German Army would be operating.

against either by any third power. In response, Hitler appeals to both Britain and France not to make the German-Polish dispute the cause of a general European war. Although France urges Poland to negotiate with Germany, Britain does not. Poland, meanwhile, calls up its reservists.

SEPTEMBER 1

POLAND, *LAND WAR*

German forces invade Poland. In total the Wehrmacht commits 1,512,000 men, 5805 artillery pieces, 4019 anti-tank guns, 2500 tanks, 713 bombers, 315 Junkers Ju 87 Stuka dive-bombers and 561 fighters to the attack, which is codenamed White. The strategy and dispositions of Poland's forces immediately prior to the German attack greatly aid the eventual outcome of the campaign. For example, one consequence of the September 1938 Munich Agreement (signed between Germany, Italy, France and Britain and ceding the German-speaking Sudetenland of Czechoslovakia to Germany) and Hitler's later takeover of the whole of Czechoslovakia in the spring of 1939 is that Poland shares a common border of 4800km (3000 miles) with Germany and German-occupied Czechoslovakia – in effect, the western half of Poland is surrounded by German-held territory.

The German invasion begins with heavy air attacks on Polish airfields, rail centres and communications links. Throughout the first few days of the campaign, German mobility and firepower has a catastrophic effect on Polish forces: first, by inflicting heavy casualties on Polish frontline units; second, by fracturing Polish communication and supply networks (roads and railways).

The Polish Army was able to mobilize 65 percent of its strength before the war broke out, with many reservists in transit as the Germans attacked. The speed and violence of the Blitzkrieg meant most reservists never reached their units, as the Luftwaffe was very effective in interdicting Polish troop movements. The Luftwaffe quickly gained air supremacy, making ground movements by any Polish forces during daylight hours extremely hazardous. Polish resistance ended on October 6, by which date the Polish Army had lost 123,000 killed and 133,700 wounded, with another 694,000 being taken prisoner by the Germans and a further 240,000 by the Russians. The Germans lost 8082 killed, 5029 missing and 27,278 wounded.

► Finnish troops examine Soviet dead during the Winter War. Note their winter clothing, which many Soviet troops lacked.

▼ A Red Army machine-gun team manhandle their Maxim Model 1910 machine gun in Finland.

SEPTEMBER 16

USSR, *DIPLOMACY*

The Soviet and Japanese governments sign a ceasefire treaty which brings the Mongolian conflict to a close. Japan has been bitterly stung by the 1939 war, and the militarists in the government will argue exclusively for campaigns in South-east Asia and the Pacific rather than into the bleak hinterlands of the USSR.

SEPTEMBER 17

POLAND, *LAND WAR*
In accordance with the secret clauses of the Nazi-Soviet Non-Aggression Treaty, the Red Army invades eastern Poland. Some 24 infantry divisions, 15 cavalry divisions and two tank corps smash west, stopping at the River Bug and effectively absorbing 200,000 square kilometres (125,000 square miles) of Polish territory and 13 million Polish citizens. Britain and France, having declared war on Germany for violating Polish territorial integrity, take no measures against the USSR.

POLAND, *SOVIET OCCUPATION*
As the Germans begin their campaign to reduce the Poles to slave status and annihilate Polish Jewry, so the Soviets bring their own brand of terror to eastern Poland. They immediately subjugate the population to communist misery as they steal Polish land and businesses, freeze bank accounts and currency, and treat the Poles with general contempt. They will also send 1.5 million Polish workers to the Soviet Union, fewer than half of whom will return. In the Kolyma gold mines, for example, the annual death rate of Polish slaves alone rose to more than 50 percent in 1940. After eight hours of inhumanly hard work, Polish workers received a bowl of potato soup and a slice of frozen black bread.

SEPTEMBER 19

POLAND, *ATROCITIES*
Lavrenti Beria, chief of the Soviet NKVD (People's Commissariat of Internal Affairs), sets up a Directorate for Prisoners of War and establishes camps for the 240,000 Polish prisoners of war in Soviet custody – 37,000 will become slave labourers.

SEPTEMBER 22

POLAND, *ATROCITIES*
The NKVD begins rounding up thousands of Polish officers and deporting them to the Soviet Union. Many will be executed at Katyn Wood in 1940.

SEPTEMBER 28

POLAND, *MILITARY PARADES*
At Brest-Litovsk, Red Army and German Army commanders hold a joint victory parade before German forces withdraw west behind the new demarcation line. Relations between the Red Army and the Wehrmacht at this time are genuinely friendly, being based on mutual hostility towards Poland. The parade has been organized by the Wehrmacht's General Heinz Guderian and the Red Army's Colonel Semyon Krivoschein. The Germans release no official photographs of the parade, as they wish to be seen as strongly anti-communist both at home and abroad. This 1939 encounter with Guderian almost cost Krivoschein his life when, in April 1945, a SMERSH (an abbreviation of its motto: *smert' shpionam* – death to spies) military counter-intelligence detachment scouring Nazi archives discovered a photograph of Krivoschein and Guderian shaking hands. The Soviet general was questioned but released, probably because he was Jewish and therefore viewed as an unlikely Nazi spy.

▲ ***Field Marshal Carl Mannerheim, the commander of the Finnish Army during the Winter War. He had been a cavalry officer in the Imperial Russian Army in the 1890s.***

SEPTEMBER 28

GERMANY, *DIPLOMACY*
In Moscow, Ribbentrop and Soviet Foreign Minister Vyacheslav Molotov put their signatures to the Soviet-German Treaty of Friendship. This ratifies the German-Soviet demarcation line in Poland. The treaty allows the repatriation of ethnic Germans to the Third Reich, and Ukrainians and Belorussians to the Soviet Union, and promises to suppress "Polish agitation" in both the German and Soviet areas of occupied Poland. The Soviet Union also agrees to deliver to Germany 304,800 tonnes (300,000 tons) of crude oil annually. In addition, Lithuania and Slovakia each receive small areas of Polish territory. A joint Soviet-German declaration states that Germany and the USSR have "definitively settled the problems arising from the collapse of the Polish state and have thereby created a sure foundation for a lasting peace in Eastern Europe".

OCTOBER 22

POLAND, *ELECTIONS*
Elections are held in eastern Poland for the selection of deputies to local Soviets. The electorate has no voice in the nomination of candidates, who come mostly from the Soviet Union and are thus complete strangers to the voters. Voting is permitted only for the one candidate whose name appears on the ballot paper (Red Army occupation troops are also given the right to vote). The "elected" deputies then proceed to pass resolutions providing for the "admission" of their territories into the

▶ ***A 203mm B-4 Model 1931 howitzer, one of the heaviest weapons in the Red Army's arsenal, during the Winter War. They were grouped in regiments, each one having 24 B-4 howitzers.***

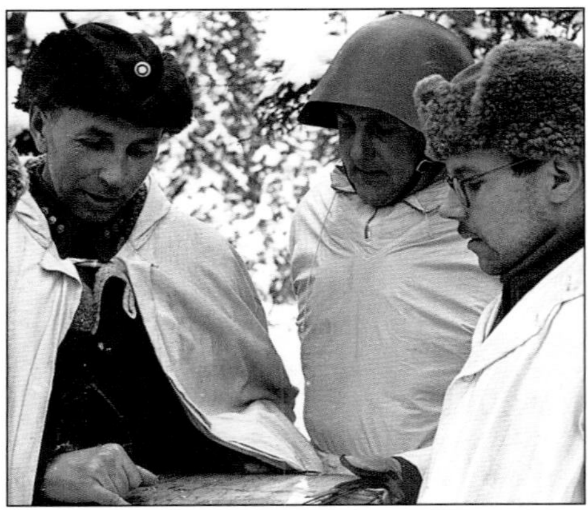

▲ ***Finnish troops in Karelia. Despite being outnumbered, the Finns were familiar with the local terrain and the short winter days limited the flight time of enemy aircraft.***

Soviet Union, for the confiscation of large estates, and for the nationalization of banks and industries. In addition, they also vote for the deportations of "undesirable" and "unreliable" elements from eastern Poland to the Soviet Gulag.

OCTOBER 30

USSR, *DIPLOMACY*

The USSR has imposed treaties of "mutual assistance" on each of three Baltic states, "allowing" the Soviets to establish military bases in Latvia, Estonia and Lithuania.

FINLAND, *GROUND WAR*

The Winter War begins. With Finland a Soviet sphere of influence under the terms of the Nazi-Soviet Non-Aggression Treaty, Stalin is determined to impose his will on the Finnish state and people: Stalin wants Finnish islands in the Gulf of Finland, including Suursaari Island, handed over to the USSR, to defend the approach to Leningrad; he wants to lease Hanko as a military base and to establish a garrison of 5000 men there; and he demands more Finnish land on the Soviet border to be ceded to the USSR. In return, he has offered land in Soviet Karelia to Finland, and the right to fortify the Aaland Islands. These terms are rejected by the Finns.

Stalin has thus decided to resolve the matter by force, and has assembled 600,000 troops, 1500 tanks and 300 aircraft, under the command of General Kirill Meretskov, to crush the Finns. Meretskov has boasted that his troops will be in the capital, Helsinki, in 10 days. The Finnish Army totals 30,000 men, and the air force can muster barely 100 aircraft. The Red Army, though, enters the war with a number of major disadvantages. It has been trained to fight on large expanses of open, treeless terrain, not the snow-covered forests of Finland. And the Red Army will be forced to fight on a narrow front because large parts of the 960km (600 mile) border are impassable.

The Finnish commander-in-chief, Field Marshal Carl Mannerheim, has massed his meagre forces on the Karelian Isthmus, southwest of Lake Ladoga. This area contains the Mannerheim Line. It is imperative that the Finns hold the Karelian Isthmus as its loss would give the Red Army a direct line to Helsinki, less than 320km (200 miles) to the west.

With reservists, there are 133,000 Finns defending the Karelian Isthmus, divided between II and III Corps. Facing them are 19th and 50th Corps of the Soviet Seventh Army, supported by 10th Tank Corps and four independent artillery regiments – in all, 190,000 men, 900 artillery pieces and 1400 tanks.

The Finns have deployed IV Corps in the Ladoga-Karelia region, the North Finland Group (two battalions), the Northern Karelia Group (three battalions) and the Lapland Group (one battalion) in the far north. There are an additional seven battalions deployed along the southern coastline, with the 6th and 9th Divisions in reserve. North of Lake Ladoga is the Soviet Eighth Army (1st, 56th Corps and the army reserve); to its north is the Soviet Ninth Army (47th and Special Corps); and in northern Lapland the Soviet

Fourteenth Army (14th and 52nd Rifle Divisions and 104th Mountain Division).

OCTOBER 30

USSR, *DIPLOMACY*

The Soviet Union creates a puppet Finnish government in Moscow under the leadership of a Finnish communist exile, Otto Kuusinen. Kuusinen hates Finland, even the Finnish language, and wants to see the country under Soviet rule. This so-called "People's Government" has been created to assist Stalin's political and military goals in his attempt to conquer Finland.

DECEMBER 2

FINLAND, *LAND WAR*

Advancing from Murmansk, the Red Army captures the ice-free port of Petsamo and clears Finnish forces from the Sredny and Rybachy peninsulas.

▼ ***Finnish troops digging in on the Mannerheim LIne, a belt of trenches, barbed wire, minefield and obstacles.***

▲ ***A knocked-out Soviet T-26 tank in Karelia during the Winter War. This is a commander's tank, as indicated by the frame aerial round the turret.***

DECEMBER 6

FINLAND, *LAND WAR*

Red Army attacks against the Mannerheim Line are beaten back. Battalion- and regiment-sized Soviet attacks across frozen lakes are costly as the dark Russian uniforms stand out against the white background. Finnish machine-gun and rifle positions are taking a terrible toll on the attackers. It is estimated that the Red Army is losing an average of 10,000 troops killed and wounded a day, compared with Finnish casualties of 250 a day.

DECEMBER 8

FINLAND, *LAND WAR*

The start of the Battle of Suomussalmi. A key element of Soviet strategy is to cut Finland in half by striking across country to Oulu. To this end, the Soviet 44th Motorized Rifle Division advances along the Raate Road from the south; and the 163rd Rifle Division marches from Juntusranta from the north. The plan is to link up at Suomussalmi and then drive west to Oulu. Soviet strength is 48,000 men, 335 artillery pieces, 10 tanks and 11 armoured cars. Finnish forces comprise the 9th Division under the command of Colonel Hjalmar Siilasvuo (11,500 men).

Siilasvuo first attacks the 163rd Division in Suomussalmi. He cuts the Soviet division's supply line (the Raate Road) and places a blocking force in position to prevent the 163rd from being relieved. The Red Army's 44th Division tries such a relief on December 25, and the 163rd attempts a link-up as well, but Siilasvuo's force holds. On December 30 the depleted 163rd Division again attempts to escape from Suomussalmi, but is cut to pieces by Siilasvuo's ski troops and Finnish aircraft.

While these events are taking place, the 44th Division digs in along the Raate Road, but the Soviet troops are harassed mercilessly by Finnish snipers. Siilasvuo launches his main attack on January 5, and by January 9 the 44th has been destroyed.

The Battle of Suomussalmi cost the Red Army 22,500 men killed and wounded. More importantly, it ended the Soviet threat in central Finland.

DECEMBER 23

FINLAND, *LAND WAR*

In the Ilomantsi region, a Finnish counterattack inflicts heavy losses on the Soviet 139th and 75th Rifle Divisions. This action halts the Red Army advance in this region and establishes a static frontline.

Germany experienced a string of stunning military victories this year, the Wehrmacht conquering Denmark, Norway, the Low Countries and France within the space of four months. With Germany's armed forces at their zenith, Hitler made plans for the attack on the USSR, confident that he could easily defeat the Red Army in a short Blitzkrieg campaign, a view reinforced by the Soviets' poor performance in the Winter War against Finland.

JANUARY 7

USSR, *ARMED FORCES*

Stalin, exasperated over the lack of progress in the Winter War, replaces Meretskov with General Semyon Timoshenko, who becomes commander of the Northwest Front and instigates a large build-up of forces in Karelia. Other Soviet leaders have paid with their lives for failure in battle. The commander of the 44th Division, Vinogradov, plus all his staff, have been executed for their failure at the Battle of Suomussalmi.

During January, the Red Army trained for new offensives, coordinating tanks, infantry and artillery to take Finnish positions. Mass attacks would henceforth not be used. Instead, large-scale artillery barrages would destroy enemy strongpoints before attacks took place.

JANUARY 29

USSR, *DIPLOMACY*

With little progress in the Winter War, the Soviet Government sends a note via Sweden stating that the "USSR has no objection in principle to concluding an agreement" with the Finnish Government. This indicates that Moscow is prepared to drop the Kuusinen government idea. However, the Soviets still want Hanko, which Helsinki will not relinquish. In

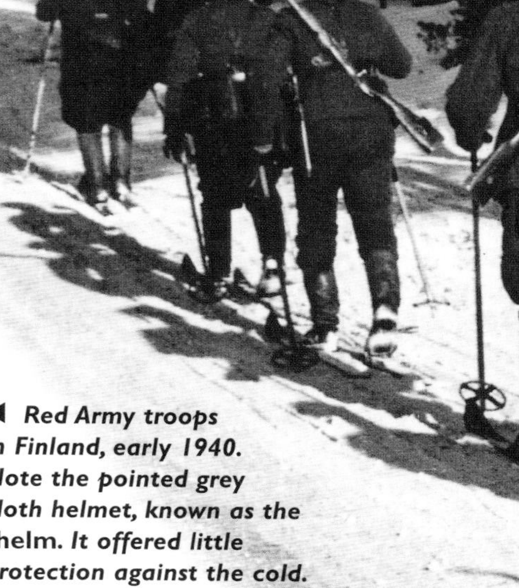

◀ *Red Army troops in Finland, early 1940. Note the pointed grey cloth helmet, known as the shelm. It offered little protection against the cold.*

▶ *Finnish ski troops retreat from the Vyborg area following the Soviet February offensive in Karelia.*

▲ ***The price of the Treaty of Moscow. Finnish civilians prepare to leave Vyborg rather than live under Bolshevik rule.***

▲ ***The victor of the Winter War: Semyon Timoshenko. He was made a marshal and Hero of the Soviet Union on May 7, 1940.***

addition, the excellent performance of the Finnish Army in the war thus far, plus the offer, albeit vague, of French and British help, has emboldened the Finns to hold out for better terms.

FEBRUARY 1

FINLAND, *GROUND WAR*
The Red Army begins its offensive in Karelia. The Soviet Thirteenth Army (nine infantry divisions, a tank brigade and two tank battalions) attacks between Taipale and Lake Muolaanjarvi, while the Seventh Army (twelve infantry divisions, five tank brigades and two tank battalions) assaults the Summa sector. In all, some 600,000 men are committed to the attack. The Finns have six divisions in line and a further three in reserve. Finnish positions are pounded by 300,000 artillery shells on the first day, with Soviet artillery mustering 440 guns in the Summa sector alone. The Soviets also deploy close air support all along the front. The Red Army attacks for three days non-stop, pauses for a day, then resumes the offensive for a further three days. Finnish forces are gradually worn down by the onslaught.

FEBRUARY 11

GERMANY, *DIPLOMACY*
Germany and the USSR agree a new trade pact. Under the terms of the agreement, which covers a period of 27 months, the Soviets have promised to deliver the following goods in the first 12-month period: 1,016,000 tonnes (1,000,000 tons) of vegetables and grain for cattle; 914,000 tonnes (900,000 tons) of mineral oil; 101,600 tonnes (100,000 tons) of cotton; 508,000 tonnes (500,000 tons) of phosphates; 101,600 tonnes (100,000 tons) of chrome ore; 508,000 tonnes (500,000 tons) of iron ore; 304,800 tonnes (300,000 tons) of scrap iron and pig iron; and 2400kg (5280lb) of platinum. In return, the Germans will deliver to the Soviets industrial products, industrial processes and installations as well as war material. Furthermore, the Soviet Union has declared her willingness to act as a buyer of metals and raw materials in third-party countries for the German war effort. Ironically, Soviet metal ore will be used to produce bombs that will be used in the Battle of Britain.

KEY PERSONALITIES

ADOLF HITLER

Hitler's aim in the East was very clear: acquiring *Lebensraum* in the East up to the Ural Mountains. These lands were occupied by groups that Hitler and Nazism despised: Bolsheviks, Slavs and Jews. Under the New Order, these peoples would either become slaves under German overlords or would be exterminated. He was to state in 1942: "If we do not complete the conquest of the East utterly and irrevocably, each successive generation will have war on its hands". For him the war in Russia was a racial conflict, in which the racially superior German Aryan race was locked in a struggle with the "sub-human" Slavs. This made retreat in the face of "inferior" peoples unimaginable, for the Führer could not conceive of the racially inferior Slavs being able to defeat a superior race. As he stated on the eve of Kursk: "Germany needs the conquered territories or she will not exist for long. She will win hegemony over the rest of Europe. Where we are – we stay."

The racial dimension to the war on the Eastern Front would adversely affect his strategic decisions, but Hitler was not a military imbecile. During the inter-war years he had read a great deal of military history and had acquired a deep knowledge of the theory of war. He was certainly intelligent, bold, creative and genuinely indifferent to human suffering, all the attributes needed in a capable commander. He had fought in the trenches in World War I, and this experience gave him, he believed, an insight into warfare that many of the army generals lacked. In the first three years of the war he conquered Poland, Norway, the Low Countries, France, the Balkans and most of European Russia. These outstanding successes gave him an inflated view of his own abilities. The early war years of World War II had seemingly proved this when, often against the advice of his senior commanders, he had taken decisions that had proved correct. The best example was in December 1941, when the Germans faced defeat before the gates of Moscow. His generals urged retreat; the Führer demanded that the troops stand and fight where they were. The front held – just – thus vindicating his decision.

Two things resulted from Hitler's disagreements with his generals at the end of 1941. First, his mistrust of the professional officer class increased; second, he came to believe that "National Socialist will" alone could turn military defeat into victory. Thus, when the Sixth Army was surrounded in Stalingrad, he refused to order it to break out to the west, believing that if his troops stood where they were he could organize a relief operation. All they needed was the will to stand and fight. Things were very different for the half-starved and battered troops in the city, of course, who faced the reality of being trapped with little hope of relief. The result was inevitable: Stalingrad fell.

Stalingrad made Hitler even more determined to run the war in the East the way he wanted, and increased further his mistrust of his "defeatist generals". Before the war, he appointed himself supreme commander of the armed forces and, through the Armed Forces High Command (*Oberkommando der Wehrmacht*), imposed his will on the army, navy and air force. In the early war years, his senior officers were glad to go along with the Führer's wishes; after all, they had shared in his victories and been showered with honours and riches. It was only after Stalingrad that many generals came to see the negative side of Hitler's obstinacy. Those who disagreed with him were sacked, which cost the army such capable commanders as Manstein and Guderian. As defeat followed defeat on the Eastern Front, Hitler increasingly withdrew into a fantasy world, trusting in the ability of "wonder weapons" to reverse the situation. By the time the Red Army reached Berlin in 1945, Hitler was a physical and mental wreck. Absolving himself of all responsibility for the outbreak of war and Nazi Germany's impending defeat, he shot himself on April 30, 1945.

FEBRUARY 12

FINLAND, *GROUND WAR*

The Red Army pierces the Mannerheim Line in the Summa sector. This is the turning point in the war because Finnish units, exhausted and short of ammunition, are unable to retake positions once they have been lost. By February 21, the Finns had abandoned the Mannerheim Line and retreated to an intermediate position, which had already been breached in two places.

MARCH 3

FINLAND, *GROUND WAR*

Red Army troops reach the outskirts of Viipuri. The Soviets have thus all but broken through the Finnish rear positions in the Tali sector. By March 13 the Red Army offensive was still continuing, with the result that the Finnish Army was so exhausted that its units were losing fighting value. For example, in the Vuosalmi sector the Russians had penetrated into the rear of the Finnish position. The only option was to abandon Viipuri and retreat to a line connecting the Gulf of Finland at Vilajoki, Lake Saimaa and Lake Ladoga. However, such a move would only give Helsinki a temporary reprieve as the army badly needed reinforcements of troops, artillery and anti-tank guns.

▲ *The Blitzkrieg smashes west. French troops surrender as German forces pour through northern France in late May.*

▲ *Integral to the success of the Blitzkrieg was German aerial supremacy. This Dutch aircraft was destroyed on the ground.*

MARCH 5

FINLAND, *DIPLOMACY*

With Finland on the verge of defeat and Allied help no nearer (the British and French moved the deadline for Finland to invite them to intervene in the war from March 5 to March 12 - and they did not say what their action would be in the event of a Swedish refusal to permit transit rights), a Finnish delegation led by Prime Minister Ryti leaves for Moscow to request an armistice.

MARCH 13

USSR, *DIPLOMACY*

The Treaty of Moscow is signed in the Soviet capital, bringing the Winter War to an end. The conditions are harsh on the Finns, who lose the entire Karelian Isthmus with the city of Viipuri; the whole of Viipuri Bay with its islands; as well as the territory west and north of Lake Ladoga (including the cities of Kakisalmi and Sortavala); part of the area near Salla and Kuusamo; Finnish islands in the eastern part of the Gulf of Finland; and the western part of the Rybachy Peninsula near Petsamo. In addition, Hanko and the surrounding area is leased to the USSR for 30 years. Finland has lost 10 percent of her land containing 450,000 citizens (all of whom decide to leave their homes and move to Finnish territory), plus the industry and agriculture contained therein.

Casualties in the war were heavy on both sides. In total, the USSR had committed 1,200,000 men, 1500 tanks and 3000 aircraft to the campaign, truly colossal numbers against a nation of 4 million Finns. Red Army losses were 126,875 dead and 391,783 wounded. The Finnish Army lost 25,000 dead and 45,500 wounded out of a force that never exceeded 200,000.

The Red Army learns some valuable lessons from the Winter War: infantry tactics need to be flexible; there needs to be greater coordination between different units; battle training should be realistic; and winter clothing is imperative for winter warfare. Absorbing these lessons, the Red Army would become a more effective force in the run-up to Barbarossa.

In Berlin, different conclusions were drawn. The performance of the Red Army did little to lessen the disdain with which Hitler and the Nazis viewed the Soviet regime. Indeed, the fact that a small "Nordic" country had withstood the onslaught of a nation of 180 million Slavs further convinced Hitler of the overall superiority of the Aryan race. How much worse would the Red Army fare against the mighty Wehrmacht?

▼ *German troops in a burning village during the invasion of Norway. This operation was notable for being under the direction of OKW, and not of OKH.*

APRIL 9

NORWAY AND DENMARK, *AIR AND SEA WAR*

German forces commence the invasion of Norway and Denmark, codenamed Operation Weserubung. Denmark is overrun in a matter of hours. Using paratroopers, in Norway the Germans will secure their initial objectives by April 14, notwithstanding the landing of an Allied expeditionary force of

10,000 men at Narvik on the same day. The campaign will continue until June 8, by which time German troops will have overrun France and the Low Countries. Norwegian bases will prove useful against the USSR after Operation Barbarossa is launched, although Norway will also become a drain on German resources as Hitler will continually reinforce the garrison in the years to come.

During the invasion, the Norwegian Communist Party, under orders from Moscow through the Comintern, issues an appeal to Norwegian workers blaming Britain for the "imperialist war" and calling for an end to hostilities, i.e. the war between Germany and the Western Allies is a war over colonial booty and one in which working people have no interest. The war is caused by the British, not by the Axis powers. The social democrats are "lackeys" of the imperialists and must be excised from the working-class organizations. Peace with Germany serves the interests of the working people.

ARMED FORCES

GERMAN INFANTRY DIVISION

A German infantry division had a paper strength of 17,000 men, although most divisions were well below this figure following the close of Barbarossa. For example, by the end of December 1941 the average infantry company (official strength 120 troops) was down to 60 men. A typical infantry division consisted of a headquarters, three rifle regiments, an artillery regiment, a reconnaissance battalion, an anti-tank battalion, an engineer battalion (engineers were actually pioneers trained in the use of explosives and mines rather than construction or bridging), a signals battalion and support units. The attrition in infantry divisions was recognized in the 1944 reorganization, which reduced the number of battalions in each rifle regiment from three to two, and the artillery regiment to two field and one medium battalions.

It was the job of the infantry to hold ground, reduce enemy pockets and generally mop up – a thankless, arduous but necessary job. These tasks required large amounts of ammunition and hand grenades. To reflect these mission requirements, each infantry division had an abundance of firepower, and much more than a Red Army rifle division. Each infantry division had more than 500 machine guns, and the pre-1944 artillery regiment deployed three field artillery battalions (each one with 12 105mm gun-howitzers) and a medium battalion that possessed eight 150mm howitzers and four 100mm guns. Although German infantry divisions relied on feet for their motive power, their training emphasized the infiltration of enemy lines and the exploitation of opportunities, and commanders at all levels were expected to display initiative to take advantage of potentially advantageous situations.

MAY 10

FRANCE AND THE LOW COUNTRIES, *LAND WAR*

The Germans launch Case Yellow, the codename for their invasion of France and the Low Countries. In the space of six weeks the Wehrmacht defeats the French, Dutch and Belgian Armies and the British Expeditionary Force in a Blitzkrieg campaign. The campaign is a stunning example of German military might, and specifically the power of the German air force (Luftwaffe), the effectiveness of the concentrated use of panzer tank divisions and the fighting power and stamina of German infantry divisions – some of which cover distances of up to 56km (35 miles) a day in France.

The overall effectiveness of the Wehrmacht is increasing substantially, with panzers and motorized infantry working closely on the battlefield. German night-time combat skills have increased greatly (one example being the 7th Panzer Division's crossing of the La Basée Canal in the dark). Once again the Luftwaffe has been crucial to this success, first by destroying dozens of enemy aircraft on the ground during the first hours of the offensive, and then by providing close air support to ground units. The German battle of annihilation (*Vernichtungsschlacht*) in the West alarms Stalin, who had not reckoned on such a speedy German victory.

▼ ***While the world watched events in France, the Soviets tightened their grip on the Poles. OT-26A tanks in eastern Poland.***

JUNE 14

USSR, *AGGRESSION*

The Soviet Government delivers an ultimatum to Lithuania, accusing it of conspiracy against the USSR. The Red Army begins to occupy Lithuania the next day using 300,000 troops.

JUNE 16

USSR, *AGGRESSION*

Moscow issue ultimatums to Latvia and Estonia, demanding the establishment of Soviet-approved governments in their countries and the right of passage for Soviet troops. The ultimatums state that both countries have six hours to reply. Being isolated, both states have no choice but to agree, and the Red Army begins to occupy them the next day. Stalin immediately installs puppet governments in all three states. President Ulmanis of Latvia and President Pats of Estonia are deported to the USSR, while President Smetona of Lithuania goes into voluntary exile. The banking systems, transportation system, all industry and mines are seized as property of the state. No one is allowed to own property. In January 1941, the Soviet rouble becomes the only legal tender in the Baltic.

The Catholic Church is persecuted by the Soviets and is forced to hand over all churches and property; seminaries and monasteries are converted into garrisons for the Red Army; and religion is eliminated from the curriculum of local schools.

Following the Red Army is the NKVD, which begins operations immediately. On average, 200–300 people a month disappear without trace. By June 22, 1941, civilian losses due to deportations and massacres stood at 60,000 in Estonia, 35,000 in Latvia and 34,000 in Lithuania. Following the occupation, "elections" were held in all three republics, which returned communist governments that immediately passed resolutions applying for membership of the USSR. Between August 3 and August 6 the USSR annexed all three states. Stalin had thus absorbed the Baltic states to create a buffer zone against German aggression.

JUNE 26

USSR, *AGGRESSION*

Stalin demands that Romania surrenders Bessarabia and Northern Bukovino to the USSR within four days (Soviet claims on Bessarabia are recognized under the secret terms of the Nazi-Soviet Non-Aggression Treaty). After World War I, Romania was given the former Russian regions of Bessarabia and Transylvania. The country was ruled by a parliamentary democracy during the 1920s and 1930s. A combination of external menace (from Hungary and Bulgaria), the world economic collapse (causing a drop in agricultural prices and widespread unemployment, in turn undermining confidence in democratic government) and the activities of the Romanian fascist Iron Guard movement (which exploited nationalism, fear of communism and resentment of alleged foreign and Jewish domination of the economy) led to the creation of a royal dictatorship in 1938 under King Carol II.

▼ Hitler with General Halder, his Chief of the Army General Staff. A conservative, it was not unknown for Halder to burst into tears.

JUNE 28

USSR, *AGGRESSION*

Having no support from Germany, Romania is forced to give in to Moscow, and the Red Army occupies Bessarabia and Northern Bukovino. Romanian impotence will encourage Hungary to seize northern Transylvania and Bulgaria to take the southern Dobruja (a region located between the lower River Danube and the Black Sea) during the next few weeks.

▲ Hitler with Romanian dictator Ion Antonescu (left). Nicknamed "Red Dog" because of his hair colour, Antonescu called the Nazi invasion of the USSR a "holy war".

JULY 21

GERMANY, *STRATEGY*

Following an order from Hitler on the 21st to Field Marshal Walter von Brauchitsch (Army Commander-in-Chief), General Franz Halder (Chief of the Army General Staff) begins to study the problems of an offensive against the Soviet Union. Halder favours a simple, direct attack against the USSR: an assault concentrated on narrow fronts and launched from assembly areas in East Prussia and northern Poland towards Moscow. After destroying the Soviet armies defending Moscow and seizing the city, the attacking German field armies would destroy Soviet formations trapped in the Ukraine. The stalemate with Britain has brought the problem of the USSR to the forefront of the Führer's mind. He believes an attack against the Soviet Union will remove the last barrier to German hegemony on the continent and will secure the *Lebensraum* for which the war is being fought.

JULY 31

GERMANY, *STRATEGY*

At the Berghof, his retreat in the Bavarian Alps, Hitler presents his plans for the invasion of the USSR to the OKH (*Oberkommando des Heeres* – German Army High Command) and OKW (*Oberkommando der Wehrmacht* – Armed Forces

KEY PERSONALITIES

JOSEPH STALIN

The dictator of the Soviet Union was not radically different from Adolf Hitler. Both men shared a dislike of liberalism and weakness, and both saw treason and incompetence everywhere. Unlike Hitler, Stalin had not seen war service (he was found to be unfit for military service by the Russian authorities). This put him at a disadvantage when it came to conferences with senior Red Army commanders during the war, due to his lack of practical military knowledge. However, he was quite happy to give a certain latitude to his generals, secure in the knowledge that his secret police maintained an iron grip over the Soviet people and that he could always have incompetent officers shot or sent to the Gulag if they failed in their duty to Mother Russia.

Born in 1879, Stalin was exiled to Siberia several times for Bolshevik activity before World War I. The first editor of *Pravda* in May 1912, he took part in the revolution that deposed the tsar in 1917, the Civil War (organizing the defence of Tsaritsyn and Petrograd) and became de facto dictator of the Soviet Union from 1927 (Lenin had him appointed secretary general of the Central Committee in 1922, a position from which he removed rivals and consolidated his power). Like Hitler, he was utterly indifferent to human suffering, once stating: "One death is a tragedy, one million is a statistic". When his beloved wife Ekaterina died of typhus in 1908 he reportedly said, "and with her died my last warm feelings for all human beings". His brutality was legendary: in the 1930s his efforts at collectivization resulted in the deaths of up to 10 million peasants through starvation; the Great Purge of the Red Army between 1937 and 1941 resulted in the deaths of 35,000 officers and men executed on suspicion of being "counter-revolutionaries", although they were in fact killed because they represented a potential threat to Stalin's rule.

A political realist, Stalin entered into a secret non-aggression treaty with Hitler, his supposed ideological enemy, in 1939 on the eve of World War II. And, when German forces unleashed the Blitzkrieg on Poland, Red Army units invaded Polish territory from the east as part of Stalin's share of the spoils. When Germany invaded the Soviet Union in June 1941, Stalin was initially stunned, but quickly recovered to direct the Russian war effort. Abandoning the conflict as a defence of international communism, the wily dictator instead issued a call to arms for the defence of Mother Russia. To ensure that the patriotism of the Russian people did not falter, Stalin's secret police and Communist Party commissars maintained rigid control over the Red Army. Supposed defeatism and cowardice were crushed ruthlessly. Between 1941 and 1942, for example, 157,593 men were executed for cowardice. But Stalin himself was no coward: when German troops approached Moscow in late 1941 and the government was evacuated to the Urals, he stayed in the city.

Stalin directed the war through the Headquarters of the Main Command (*Shtab vierhovnogo komandovani* – Stavka) as commander-in-chief, supported by army officers and commissars. Stalin rarely left the Kremlin or ventured outside the USSR (he had a fear of flying). His only visits to the war zone, to the Western and Kalinin Fronts, were made on August 3 and 5, 1943, apparently for use in propaganda films. In common with Hitler, Stalin was loathe to sanction retreats (his refusal to pull back from Kiev in 1941 resulted in 660,000 Russians becoming prisoners of the Germans), but he did come to listen to commanders such as Zhukov about how battles and campaigns should be conducted. For example, in April 1943 Zhukov reported to Stalin concerning the situation in the Kursk salient: "I consider that it would be pointless for our forces to go over to the offensive in the near future in order to pre-empt the enemy. It would be better for us to wear out the enemy on our defences, to smash his tanks and then, by introducing fresh reserves and going over to a general offensive, to beat the main enemy force once and for all." Stalin took this advice, and the Battle of Kursk was fought Zhukov's way.

He viewed the Western Allies with suspicion, often accusing them of postponing the second front because they wanted to see the USSR bled white. Always putting his own interests first, he made exorbitant demands when it came to Lend-Lease supplies, and planned the final offensives of the war with a Russian-dominated post-war Europe in mind. After the war he quickly moved to consolidate his position by removing famous wartime commanders, and so figures such as Zhukov, Rokossovsky, Meretskov, Vatutin and Konev disappeared from public view. He also did not forget those Russian nationals who, in his view, had collaborated with the enemy. He insisted that the British and Americans adhere strictly to the terms of the Yalta Agreement, which they did, even though they knew that repatriation would mean death or imprisonment for those returned. Thus, between 1945 and 1947, 2,272,000 Soviet citizens were returned by the Western Allies to the USSR. One-fifth of these were either shot or given 25-year sentences in the Gulag. Stalin's paranoia grew as he instigated fresh repressions against peasants, intellectuals and Jews, hundreds of the latter being shot between 1951 and 1953. Stalin died from a stroke in March 1953.

High Command). Speaking of increased Soviet strength along the eastern frontier, Hitler believes that Stalin has further territorial ambitions in the Balkans, namely the Romanian oil fields. Hitler then expands by claiming that Stalin's aims are no different from those of Peter the Great two centuries earlier, namely the conquest of Poland, Bulgaria, Finland and the Dardanelles. War with the USSR is thus inevitable. In addition, he believes that defeating the Soviet Union will further weaken Britain because, with the Soviet Union laid low, Japan will be able to gain hegemony in the Far East. This in turn will focus the United States' attention on the Pacific region to the detriment of Britain. "If Russia is laid low, then Britain's last hope is wiped out, and Germany will be master of Europe and the Balkans."

Accepting that an attack cannot now take place before spring 1941, Hitler states that the army will be expanded to 180 divisions, 120 of which will be in the East by the spring. Neither Brauchitsch nor Halder offer any objections to these plans.

SEPTEMBER 6

ROMANIA, *POLITICS*

Following the loss of the northeastern part of Transylvania to Hungary (an attempt to pacify the territorial claims of Hungary under the German- and Italian-sponsored Vienna Award of August 30) and the south of Dobruja to Bulgaria, there is a political crisis in Romania. This leads to the abdication of the pro-Western King Carol II in favour of his son, Michael I. However, Prime Minister Ion Antonescu forms a right-wing government called the "National Legionary State" with the cooperation of the Iron Guard.

▲ ***German "advisors" instruct Romanian troops. The Italian invasion of Greece in October gave Hitler an excuse to send more troops to Romania on the pretext of deterring Britain's Balkan ambitions.***

SEPTEMBER 17

ROMANIA, *ARMED FORCES*

Antonescu requests a Germany Military Mission in Romania for the purpose of modernizing the Romanian Army, specifically with tanks and artillery. In return he promises Hitler that his forces will be deployed on the Russian, not the Hungarian, border.

The first German units arrive in the country on October 7 (in total 22,430 military personnel will be deployed to Romania, of whom 17,561 will be from the army). By mid-November the 13th Motorized Infantry Division, 4th Panzer Regiment, engineers, signal troops and anti-aircraft detachments, plus six fighter and two reconnaissance Luftwaffe squadrons, had arrived in the country.

Unknown to either Antonescu or the mission members, on September 19 the OKW issued a statement detailing the specific tasks of the mission in Romania: to protect the Ploesti oil fields from a third party, to enable Romania's armed forces to undertake specific missions according to German interests, and to prepare for operations by Axis forces from Romanian territory in the event of a war against the USSR.

SEPTEMBER 21

FINLAND, *ALLIES*

The first German troops arrive in the country, at the port of Vaasa. Their arrival is generally welcomed by the Finns, who see them as a deterrent against further Soviet threats. Over the

▼ ***Part of the German Military Mission to Romania, ostensibly sent to organize and train Romania's armed forces but in reality to protect the Ploesti oil fields and prepare for the launch of Barbarossa.***

next few months more German troops will arrive and establish quarters, depots and bases along the rail lines from Vaasa and Oulu to Kolari and Rovaniemi, and from there along the roads via Kilpisjärvi or Ivalo to northern Norway.

OCTOBER 28

ITALY, *AGGRESSION*
Mussolini launches an invasion of Greece from Italian-occupied Albania. Heralded as the beginning of a glorious episode in Italy's history, it is a complete debacle. For Hitler, the campaign threatens German interests in Southeast Europe. The Führer had hoped to bring Greece into the Axis alliance, but the invasion has made this unlikely (although Germany has not severed diplomatic relations with Greece).

During the following months the Italians were unable to defeat the Greeks, and in February 1941 Britain promised to send 100,000 troops to help them. With British troops arriving on Greek soil in early March 1941, Hitler was therefore forced to plan the conquest of Greece to secure his Balkan flank.

NOVEMBER 12

GERMANY, *STRATEGY*
Hitler issues a secret directive to his commanders. It states: "Russia. Political discussions have been initiated with the aim of establishing what Russia's posture will be over the coming period. Irrespective of the outcome of these discussions, all the preparations orally ordered for the East are to continue."

USSR, *DIPLOMACY*
Soviet Foreign Minister Molotov arrives in Germany to discuss German and Soviet mutual spheres of interest. The trip is a disaster. The Soviet delegation is suspicious of its German hosts, and Molotov issues a series of demands to Hitler: the USSR wishes to conquer the whole of Finland, and Moscow is going to "invite" Bulgaria to sign a non-aggression pact that will permit the establishment of a Soviet naval base near the Dardanelles.

Hitler is unwilling to sanction the loss of Finland as he needs the country's timber and nickel supplies. In addition, the Führer requires the USSR to declare solidarity with the Tripartite Pact powers if Moscow wants a share of the spoils when the British Empire falls apart. However, it is clear that Soviet and German interests are now incompatible. Molotov returns home empty handed.

NOVEMBER 20

HUNGARY, *DIPLOMACY*
Hungary signs the Tripartite Pact. Under a right-wing government headed by the regent, Admiral Nicholas Horthy,

Hungary has profited from close relations with Nazi Germany. For example, a trade agreement with Germany pulled Hungary's economy out of depression but made her dependent on the German economy for both raw materials and markets. In 1928, Germany accounted for 19.5 percent of Hungary's imports and for 11.7 percent of its exports; by 1939 the figures were 52.5 percent and 52.2 percent, respectively (Hungary's annual rate of economic growth from 1934 to

▼ ***Admiral Horthy (centre, in black greatcoat), regent of Hungary, on a state visit to Germany before the war. To Horthy's right is Deputy Führer Rudolf Hess.***

▲ ***Italian troops in Greece in late 1940. Hitler was appalled that Mussolini had launched an attack in the Balkan autumn rains and winter snows. He was also angry because it destabilized his southern flank.***

1940 averaged 10.8 percent). In addition, with the assistance of Hitler, Hungary has made territorial gains: parts of southern Slovakia in 1938; Carpatho-Ukraine in 1939; and northeastern Transylvania in 1940. Hitler's help has come at a price, however, and Hungary has been forced to implement anti-Jewish legislation. In addition, two months ago the Hungarian Government allowed German troops to transit the country on their way to Romania.

NOVEMBER 23

ROMANIA, *DIPLOMACY*

Romania signs the Tripartite Pact. Hitler informs Antonescu of his plans against Greece. Romania will not be required to lend active assistance in the attack on Greece (Operation Marita), but is to permit the assembly of German forces on its territory.

On the 24th, Antonescu holds a conference with Field Marshal Wilhelm Keitel, the chief of OKW, and explains the Romanian plan of defence against an attack by the USSR. Keitel assures him that the German Army will lend immediate assistance in the event of a Soviet invasion, which he considers highly unlikely.

As a result of this conversation, the German Military Mission will be reinforced by the transfer of the 16th Panzer Division to Romania during the second half of December.

SLOVAKIA, *DIPLOMACY*

As part of Germany's efforts to develop an anti-Soviet alliance, the puppet state of Slovakia signs the Tripartite Pact.

STRATEGY & TACTICS

BLITZKRIEG

Blitzkrieg (Lightning War) was the doctrine employed by the German Army in World War II. Used to devastating effect in Poland in 1939, in France and the Low Countries in 1940 and in the USSR in 1941, it harnessed the firepower and mobility of the panzer divisions with aggressive leadership at both the strategic and tactical level. Each campaign was complicated and unique but, in general, a Blitzkrieg campaign was made up of the following phases:

Planning: First the Germans selected the point or points where they would launch their attack, each point of main effort being called the *Schwerpunkt*. A weak point was always preferable, or a place where an attack was least expected by the enemy.

Reconnaissance: Once the attack plans had been finalized, next came the reconnaissance phase to determine the location and strength of the enemy at the point of main effort.

Surprise: Great efforts were made to keep the precise time and date of the attack from the enemy, so as to achieve maximum surprise when the operation was launched (although often, as with Operation Barbarossa, the sheer size of the attacking forces involved made this all but impossible).

The role of the Luftwaffe: Air superiority was crucial to the success of the Blitzkrieg. The role of the Luftwaffe during the first few days of the Blitzkrieg was: 1) to destroy the enemy's air force – preferably on the ground during the first 24 hours; and 2) to provide close air support for ground units, which included interdicting enemy supplies and communications to bring about enemy paralysis.

The ground attack: The Blitzkrieg was launched after a brief artillery bombardment. Panzers, mechanized infantry and mobile artillery poured through the breach made in the enemy line. Speed was of the essence to maintain the advance and keep the enemy off balance. Enemy strongpoints were bypassed (attritional frontal attacks were to be avoided) as the German armoured columns punched deep into enemy territory. The panzers' flanks were vulnerable but, since the Germans usually had total air superiority and the enemy high command was paralyzed like a rabbit caught in a car's headlights, German commanders did not worry unduly.

A demoralized enemy: As the panzers drove deep into enemy territory and German bombers and dive-bombers destroyed road convoys, trains and strafed refugee columns, morale among enemy units was severely affected. This in turn led to indecision, inertia and defeatism, the very opposite of the emotions that German commanders were experiencing. Generals such as Rommel and Guderian, always at the front, were quick to spot opportunities and exploit them to the full.

The final phase: The panzer pincers gradually encircled whole enemy armies in giant pockets, and then held the perimeter until the slower-moving infantry divisions moved up to reduce the pockets. By this time, enemy units inside the pockets were totally demoralized and short of supplies and ammunition. Their defeat was inevitable.

DECEMBER 5

GERMANY, *STRATEGY*

The Wehrmacht High Command gathers in the Reich Chancellery to hear the proposals for the attack on the USSR. Halder's OKH draft emphasizes a powerful main drive towards Moscow. The OKW study, prepared by Lieutenant-Colonel Lossberg, gives more weight to the attack of the northern army group and the occupation of the Baltic coast. Hitler, while not detracting from a main assault on Moscow, wants Soviet forces in the Baltic states to be encircled and destroyed, together with a huge encirclement operation to the south of the Pripet Marshes that will annihilate Red Army forces in the Ukraine. For Hitler, securing the Baltic region is imperative, because Germany's

▲ ***A Panzer 35(t) in Romania in 1940. This Czech-built tank was taken into German service following the annexation of Czechoslovakia in 1939. It also equipped the armies of Romania and Bulgaria.***

iron ore supplies from Scandinavia are routed through the Baltic Sea. In addition, after destroying Soviet forces in the Baltic the Wehrmacht will be free to undertake further operations. The plan for the offensive is re-worked according to Hitler's wishes.

DECEMBER 18

GERMANY, *STRATEGY*

Hitler issues Directive No 21, confirming plans for the attack on the USSR, code-named Operation Barbarossa. Only nine copies of the order are made. It states: "The German Armed Forces must be prepared, even before the conclusion of the war against England, to crush Soviet Russia in a rapid campaign (Operation Barbarossa). The Army will have to employ all available formations to this end, with the reservation that occupied territories must be insured against surprise attacks.

The Luftwaffe will have to make available for this Eastern campaign supporting forces of such strength that the Army will be able to bring land operations to a speedy conclusion and that eastern Germany will be as little damaged as possible by enemy air attack.

The main efforts of the Navy will continue to be directed against England even during the Eastern campaign. In certain circumstances, I shall issue orders for the deployment against Soviet Russia eight weeks before the operation is timed to begin.

Preparations which require more time than this will be put in hand now, in so far as this has not already been done, and will be concluded by May 15, 1941.

▲ ***Romanian troops on the march. In his memoirs, Field Marshal Manstein described the Romanian soldier as being brave but almost impossible to train to think for himself due to his poor education.***

It is of decisive importance that our intention to attack should not be known. The preparations of the High Commands will be made on the following basis:

I. GENERAL INTENTION

The bulk of the Russian Army stationed in western Russia will be destroyed by daring operations led by deeply penetrating armoured spearheads. Russian forces still capable of giving battle will be prevented from withdrawing into the depths of Russia.

The enemy will then be energetically pursued and a line will be reached from which the Russian Air Force can no longer attack German territory. The final objective of the operation is to erect a barrier against Asiatic Russia on the general line Volga–Archangel. The last surviving industrial area of Russia in the Urals can then, if necessary, be eliminated by the Luftwaffe.

In the course of these operations the Russian Baltic Fleet will quickly lose its bases and will then no longer be capable of action.

The effective operation of the Russian Air Force is to be prevented from the beginning of the attack by powerful blows.

II. PROBABLE ALLIES AND THEIR TASKS

1. On the flanks of our operations we can count on the active support of Romania and Finland in the war against Soviet Russia. The High Command of the Armed Forces will decide and lay down in due time the manner in which the forces of these two countries will be brought under German command.
2. It will be the task of Romania to support the attack of the German southern flank, at least at the outset, with its best troops; to hold down the enemy where German forces are not engaged; and to provide auxiliary services in the rear areas.
3. Finland will cover the advance of the Northern Group of German forces moving from Norway (detachments of Group XXI) and will operate in conjunction with them. Finland will also be responsible for eliminating Hanko.
4. It is possible that Swedish railways and roads may be available for the movement of the German Northern Group, by the beginning of the operation at the latest.

III. CONDUCT OF OPERATIONS

A. ARMY

In the theatre of operations, which is divided by the Pripet Marshes into a Southern and a Northern sector, the main weight of attack will be delivered in the Northern area.

The more southerly of these two Army Groups (in the centre of the whole front) will have the task of

▼ ***German Ju 87 Stuka dive-bombers, which played a crucial part in the first phase of Barbarossa. For example, Ju 87s supported the Second Panzer Group's crossing of the River Bug in June.***

advancing with powerful armoured and motorized formations from the area about and north of Warsaw, and routing the enemy forces in White Russia [Belorussia]. This will make it possible for strong mobile forces to advance northwards and, in conjunction with the Northern Army Group operating out of East Prussia in the general direction of Leningrad, to destroy the enemy forces operating in the Baltic area. Only after the fulfilment of this first essential task, which must include the occupation of Leningrad and Kronstadt, will the attack be continued with the intention of occupying Moscow, an important centre of communications and of the armaments industry.

Only a surprisingly rapid collapse of Russian resistance could justify the simultaneous pursuit of both objectives.

The most important task of Group XXI, even during these operations, remains the protection of Norway.

Any forces available after carrying out this task will be employed in the North (Mountain Corps), at first to protect the Petsamo area and its iron ore mines and the Arctic highway, then to advance with Finnish forces against the Murmansk railway and thus prevent the passage of supplies to Murmansk by land.

It will be the duty of the main body of the Finnish Army, in conjunction with the advance of the German North flank, to hold down the strongest possible Russian forces by an attack to the West, or on both sides of Lake Ladoga, and to occupy Hanko.

The Army Group operating south of the Pripet Marshes will also seek, in a concentric operation with strong forces on either flank, to destroy all Russian forces west of the Dnieper in the Ukraine. The main attack will be carried out from the Lublin area in the general direction of Kiev, while forces in Romania will carry out a wide enclosing movement across the lower Prut. It will be the task of the Romanian Army to hold down Russian forces in the intervening area. When the battles north and south of the Pripet Marshes are ended the pursuit of the enemy will have the following aims:

In the South the early capture of the Donets Basin, important for war industry; in the North a quick advance to Moscow. The capture of this city would represent a decisive political and economic success and would also bring about the capture of the most important railway junctions.

B. LUFTWAFFE

It will be the duty of the Luftwaffe to paralyze and eliminate the effectiveness of the Russian Air Force as far as possible. It will also support the main operations of the Army, i.e. those of the central Army Group and of the vital flank of the Southern Army Group. Russian railways will either be destroyed or, in accordance with operational requirements, captured at their most important points (river crossings) by the bold employment of parachute and airborne troops.

In order that we may concentrate all our strength against the enemy air force and for the immediate support of land operations, the Russian armaments industry will not be attacked during the main operations. Such attacks will be made only after the conclusion of mobile warfare, and they will be concentrated first on the Urals area.

C. NAVY

It will be the duty of the Navy during the attack on Soviet Russia to protect our own coasts and to prevent the breakout of enemy naval units from the Baltic. As the Russian Baltic Fleet will, with the capture of Leningrad, lose its last base and will then be in a hopeless position, major naval action will be avoided until this occurs.

After the elimination of the Russian fleet the duty of the Navy will be to protect the entire maritime traffic in the Baltic and the transport of supplies by sea to the Northern flank (clearing of minefields!).

All steps taken by Commanders-in-Chief on the basis of this directive must be phrased on the unambiguous assumption that they are precautionary measures undertaken in case Russia should alter its present attitude towards us."

▲ ***Luftwaffe He 111 bombers. According to Hitler's Directive No 21, the initial tasks of the air force was to destroy the Soviet Air Force and support the advance of the army groups.***

DECEMBER 20

GERMANY, *STRATEGY*

A series of OKH war games and independent studies regarding a German war in the East, conducted under the direction of Head Quartermaster of the General Staff, Major-General Friedrich Paulus, come to an end. Paulus' conclusions are that German forces are "barely sufficient for the purpose" assigned to them. In addition, the Wehrmacht will have no reserves left by the time it reaches Moscow, forcing the army to undertake an attack against the city with no reinforcements. And the Volga–Archangel line is a target that will be beyond the reach of the Wehrmacht. More worryingly, the studies revealed that in a campaign area the size of the western USSR, the panzer columns and slower-moving infantry would quickly become separated, leaving the flanks of the panzer forces dangerously exposed.

1941

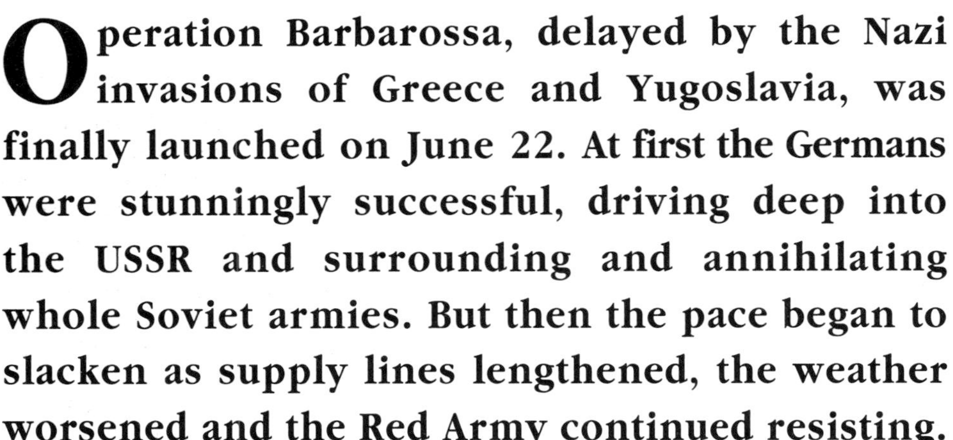

Operation Barbarossa, delayed by the Nazi invasions of Greece and Yugoslavia, was finally launched on June 22. At first the Germans were stunningly successful, driving deep into the USSR and surrounding and annihilating whole Soviet armies. But then the pace began to slacken as supply lines lengthened, the weather worsened and the Red Army continued resisting.

▲ *King Boris of Bulgaria (left) with young Bulgarian Army recruits. As Bulgaria was not on the Soviet frontier, it played little part in German plans for Operation Barbarossa.*

▲ *Alfred Rosenberg, Reich Commissioner for the Eastern Territories. Born in Tallinn, Estonia, in 1893, he was convicted of war crimes after the war and executed in 1946.*

JANUARY 10

USSR, *DIPLOMACY*

A secret protocol between Germany and the USSR is signed in Moscow by Foreign Minister Molotov and the German ambassador, Count von der Schulenburg. By this protocol Germany renounces her claim to the "Suwalki Strip" of Lithuanian territory. In return the USSR will pay 31.5 million Reichmarks to Germany in compensation.

JANUARY 20

ROMANIA, *POLITICS*

The simmering power struggle between Ion Antonescu and the Vice-Premier of Romania and leader of The Iron Guard, Horia Sima, erupts into violence.

During three days of violence in the country, Antonescu suppresses the Iron Guard with the help of the army. Hitler offers German troops to help crush the rebellion, which Antonescu declines. Thereafter, German troops in Romania help to smuggle Iron Guard members, including Sima, out of the country.

JANUARY 31

GERMANY, *STRATEGY*

Halder and Brauchitsch present the Deployment Directive Barbarossa to Hitler, which outlines the basic areas of deployment and operational objectives for the German army groups, panzer groups and armies in the forthcoming attack on the USSR. Army Group Centre with "a strong portion of its mobile strength should cooperate with Army Group North in order to destroy the enemy forces along the Baltic and in the area of Leningrad". An assault on Moscow would take place only if "an unexpected and total collapse of enemy resistance in northern Russia" negated the need to turn armoured forces towards the north.

FEBRUARY 3

GERMANY, *STRATEGY*
At a meeting at the Berghof, Halder informs Hitler of increased military activity in the Ukraine and Baltic. He states that, according to German intelligence estimates, there are 155 Red Army divisions deployed in the western USSR against just 116 German and Axis divisions. The Führer insists that Red Army forces must be destroyed and not driven back during the German attack. He believes the best way to achieve this is by placing strong German forces on the flanks. In this way once the flanks are secure, Soviet forces in the centre can then be destroyed.

FEBRUARY 15

BRITAIN, *DIPLOMACY*
Britain breaks off diplomatic relations with Romania.

MARCH 1

GERMANY, *DIPLOMACY*
Bulgaria signs the Tripartite Pact. The government of the country, including the German-speaking King Boris, had been worried that if Bulgaria joined the pact Soviet troops would invade. Having already profited from German friendship by being given southern Dobruja from Romania, in the coming weeks Bulgaria will gain Greek Thrace, Yugoslav Macedonia and part of Serbia in return for allowing German troops to use Bulgarian territory as a jumping-off point for the invasion of Greece.

▲ ***Yugoslav fighters ablaze on the ground following a Luftwaffe raid. The Yugoslav Air Force was destroyed in a matter of hours.***

◄ ***Waffen-SS troops in Belgrade in mid-April 1941. The city was actually captured by* SS-Hauptsturmführer *Fritz Klingenberg and 10 men of the* Das Reich *Division on April 12.***

MARCH 25

GERMANY, *DIPLOMACY*
Following intense German diplomatic pressure, Yugoslav Prime Minister Cvetkovic and the Foreign Minister Cincar-Markovic sign the Tripartite Pact in Vienna. Yugoslavia has had little choice in the matter, as a refusal to sign the agreement would have led to war with Germany. Yugoslavia has no allies, and her armed forces are in a poor state compared with those of the Wehrmacht.

To buy time, the government had proposed the substitution of a simple non-aggression pact instead of the Tripartite Pact. Berlin, however, remained adamant, insisting on outright Yugoslav adherence to the Axis camp. Some concessions were offered. For example, when objections were made to Article III of the treaty, which might have obligated Yugoslavia to fight the United States or perhaps even the USSR, the Germans agreed not to insist upon this stipulation. Also, Germany agreed to respect Yugoslav sovereignty and not to demand passage for troops earmarked for the invasion of Greece. In Belgrade there are disturbances when it becomes known that Yugoslavia has signed the pact.

MARCH 27

YUGOSLAVIA, *DIPLOMACY*
A coup overthrows the government that had signed the Tripartite Pact. The Yugoslav military, led by General Dusan Simovic, revolts, the government falls and the 17-year-old Peter II is proclaimed king. A new anti-German government is then formed in Belgrade. Hitler hears the

◀ A German 150mm FH 36 howitzer in Yugoslavia. Note the mats beneath the wheels, which were designed to prevent the gun sinking in soft ground. This gun was usually horse drawn.

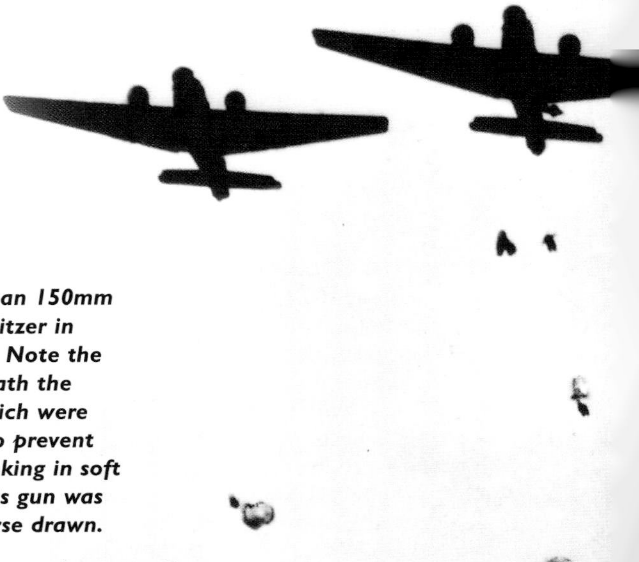

news and flies into a rage, taking the coup as a personal affront. He orders that Operation Marita be expanded to include an invasion of Yugoslavia, codenamed "Punishment", stating: "Politically it is especially important that the blow against Yugoslavia is carried out with pitiless harshness and that the military destruction is done with lightning rapidity."

APRIL 2

GERMANY, *POLITICS*

Hitler appoints Nazi ideologist Alfred Rosenberg to be Reich Commissioner for the Eastern Territories. A firm believer in the policy of *Lebensraum*, he wrote in 1932: "The understanding that the German nation, if it is not to perish in the truest sense of the word, needs ground and soil for itself and its future generations, and the second sober perception that this soil can no more be conquered in Africa, but in Europe and first of all in the East – these organically determine the German foreign policy for centuries." His published works include *The Myth of the Twentieth Century*, which declares the existence of two opposing races: the Aryan race, creator of all values and culture; and the Jewish race, the agent of cultural corruption.

Just prior to the invasion of the USSR, he stated that the job of feeding Germans was at the top of Germany's claim on the East; that there was no obligation to feed the Russian people; and that the Russians were in for many hard years. Rosenberg would be hanged by the Allies at Nuremberg in October 1946.

APRIL 5

USSR, *DIPLOMACY*

The Soviet-Yugoslav Non-Aggression Treaty is signed in Moscow. It pledges war materials to Yugoslavia in the event of a German attack, though not outright military support. The treaty is an attempt to form a barrier against further German aggression in the Balkans and to maintain Soviet interests in the region.

APRIL 6

YUGOSLAVIA AND GREECE, *GROUND WAR*

The German invasion of Greece and Yugoslavia begins. Hitler's Order of the Day issued from Berlin states: "Since early this morning the German people are at war with the Belgrade government of

▶ A column of Panzer IIIs of the 2nd Panzer Division roll through the port of Thessalonika, Greece, signalling the outflanking of the Allied Metaxas Line.

▲ German paratroopers drop on the Corinth Canal on April 26, 1941, to interdict the withdrawal of British forces from Greece.

▲ Hitler, Field Marshal von Leeb (right) and Field Marshal Keitel (second from left) ponder the Barbarossa objectives.

intrigue. We shall only lay down arms when this band of ruffians has been definitely and most emphatically eliminated, and the last Briton has left this part of the European Continent, and that these misled people realize that they must thank Britain for this situation, they must thank England, the greatest warmonger of all time. The German people can enter into this new struggle with the inner satisfaction that its leaders have done everything to bring about a peaceful settlement."

Under relentless aerial and ground assaults the Yugoslav Army disintegrates rapidly. On April 17, an armistice between the Yugoslavs and Germans is signed in Belgrade. Stalin does not criticize the invasion and sends no help to his new ally. In Greece resistance is stiffer, but by May 3 the Germans have conquered the Greek mainland. The subsequent German airborne invasion of Crete on May 20 heralds another German victory, although with heavy losses in paratroopers (one in four are casualties). Hitler has thus secured his southern flank in preparation for Operation Barbarossa.

Field Marshal von Brauchitsch has estimated that the Balkan campaign has delayed the start of Barbarossa by between four and six weeks. The new start date for the invasion of the USSR will be June 22. This delay is due to the commitment of panzer and mechanized divisions in the Balkans, which are crucial to Barbarossa and which will have to be re-deployed back to their jump-off positions. Also, the 2nd and 5th Panzer Divisions are in southern Greece by the end of the campaign and will not be available for the start of Barbarossa. The losses suffered by the Luftwaffe during the seizure of Crete, especially transport aircraft, will also affect the strength of German air power available at the start of the Russian campaign.

APRIL 7

BRITAIN, *DIPLOMACY*

Britain severs diplomatic relations with Hungary.

APRIL 13

USSR, *DIPLOMACY*

The Soviet-Japanese Neutrality Pact is signed in Moscow. The pact states that each party will "respect the territorial integrity and inviolability of the other party; and should one of the Contracting Parties become the object of hostilities on the part of one or several third powers, the other Contracting Party will observe neutrality throughout the duration of the conflict". The pact will initially last for five years.

The pact frees up Red Army divisions facing the Japanese in the East for deployment elsewhere and allows Japan to concentrate on its ambitions in China and Southeast Asia.

APRIL 23

GERMANY, *STRATEGY*

There are now 59 German divisions deployed along the Soviet border.

▶ A Red Army commissar. According to Hitler's Directive for the Treatment of Political Commissars, any commissars captured by German troops were to be shot.

MAY 13

USSR, *ARMED FORCES*

A General Staff directive is issued that orders the movement of several Soviet armies from the interior to the western USSR. The Twenty-Second Army is moved from the Urals to Velikiye Luki north of the River Dvina, the Twenty-First Army from the Volga district to Gomel, the Nineteenth Army from the north Caucasus to Belaia Tserkv south of Kiev, the Sixteenth Army from the Transbaikal District to Shepetovka in the Ukraine, and the 25th Rifle Corps from the Kharkov District to the River Dvina area.

▶ ***German infantry at rest in the early hours of June 22, the start date of Hitler's anti-Bolshevik crusade in the East.***

JUNE 5

GERMANY, *STRATEGY*

More than 100 German divisions have now been assembled along the frontier with the USSR.

JUNE 6

GERMANY, *STRATEGY*

Hitler's Directive for the Treatment of Political Commissars is issued by the High Command of the Armed Forces under Field Marshal Keitel's signature. Every Soviet military unit has a political officer, a commissar, who has as much power as the commander. This "dual command" structure is militarily disastrous, as most commissars are uneducated and have little or no military knowledge.

The directive sets the tone for the conduct of the war against the USSR: "The war against Russia cannot be fought in a knightly fashion. The struggle is one of ideologies and racial differences and will have to be waged with unprecedented, unmerciful and unrelenting hardness. All officers will have to get rid of any old-fashioned ideas they may have. I realize that the necessity for conducting such warfare is beyond the comprehension of you generals, but I must insist that my orders be followed without complaint. The commissars hold views directly opposite to those of National Socialism. Hence these commissars must be eliminated. Any German soldier who breaks international law will be pardoned. Russia did not take part in the Hague Convention and, therefore, has no rights under it.

"In the struggle against Bolshevism, we must not assume that the enemy's conduct will be based on principles of humanity or international law. Political commissars have initiated barbaric, Asiatic methods of warfare. Consequently, they will be dealt with immediately and with maximum severity. As a matter of principle they will be shot at once, whether captured during operations or otherwise showing resistance. The following regulations will apply: on capture they will be immediately separated from other prisoners on the field of battle. After they have been separated they will be liquidated."

JUNE 13

USSR, *MEDIA*

TASS, the Soviet news agency, issues a communique stating that the USSR has no intention of attacking Germany and that the massive movements of troops are just military exercises. By this time the Red Army has 170 divisions deployed in the western USSR west of Moscow and east of Kiev.

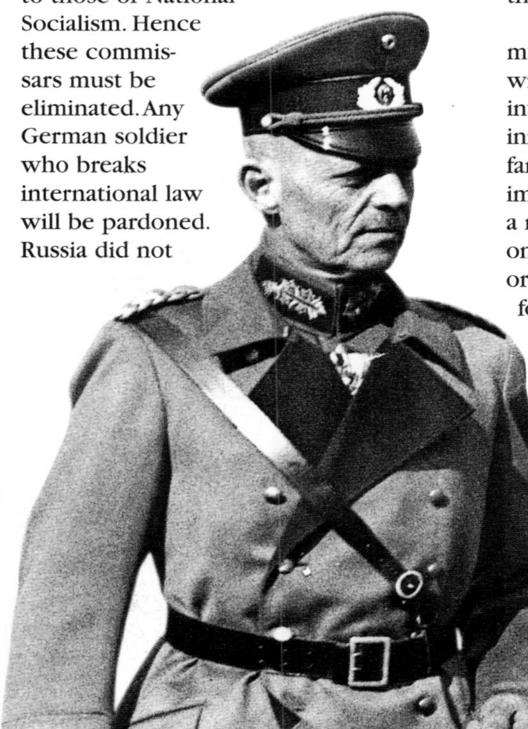

◀ ***Field Marshal von Rundstedt, head of Army Group South. He believed that the USSR could not be conquered in a quick campaign.***

JUNE 14

USSR, *ESPIONAGE*

The Lucy Spy Ring informs Moscow that the German attack on the USSR will begin on June 22. The Lucy Ring is part of the so-called Red Orchestra spy ring that has three main branches: in France, Belgium and Holland; in Berlin; and in relatively safe neutral Switzerland. The Lucy Ring contains some high-level German officers, including Lieutenant-General Fritz Theile, a senior officer in the Wehrmacht's communications branch; and Colonel Freiherr Rudolf von Gersdorff, who will be the intelligence officer of Army Group Centre on the Eastern Front. The Berlin-based Red Orchestra agents include Harro Schulze-Boysen, an intelligence officer assigned to the German Air Ministry; and Arvid von Harnack, an employee of the German Ministry of Economics.

ARMED FORCES

PANZER DIVISION

Originally each panzer division possessed two panzer regiments, comprising 400 tanks in total. This was unwieldy, and the division lacked motorized infantry to support the tanks. Thus, in late 1940, the panzer division was reorganized. The authorized organization now comprised: a divisional headquarters (with its own armoured support company); armoured reconnaissance battalion; a tank regiment (originally three battalions, later reduced to two comprising one of 96 Panzer IVs and one of 96 Panzer V Panthers, often with an additional company of Tiger tanks or assault guns – the Tigers were later organized into their own independent battalions); two panzergrenadier regiments; an anti-tank battalion (later equipped with 75mm long-barrelled assault guns, while some divisions also had some self-propelled or towed 88mm guns); anti-aircraft battalion (two heavy batteries, each with 4–6 towed 88mm guns, plus a battery of 12 20mm guns); artillery regiment (three battalions, one with 18 Wespe and Hummel self-propelled guns, plus one with 12 105mm gun-howitzers and another with 12 150mm gun-howitzers); armoured signals battalion; armoured engineer battalion; and divisional services.

The average manpower strength of a panzer division was around 15,000, but this could vary according to battle losses and the speed of replacements. Tank strength per panzer division varied wildly. From 1943, for example, it was rare for a panzer division to have more than 100 operational tanks at any one time. The panzer divisions retained a high combat efficiency throughout the war, despite falling tank inventories. This was because each division usually had a core of veteran tankers (often including an "ace") able to maintain a high level of combat proficiency and combat "kills". Tank crews were not necessarily killed when their vehicles were knocked out. In addition, German tanks – the Panzer IV, Panther and Tiger – were qualitatively better than those of their opponents, and far more lethal when fighting from prepared defensive positions, as was the case on the Eastern Front from the autumn of 1943.

JUNE 17

FINLAND, *ARMED FORCES*

Finland begins mobilizing its forces. A partial mobilization had been ordered on June 9, and the northern Finnish air defence troops (30,000 men) had been placed under German command, although in reality the Wehrmacht already held the northern half of the border with the USSR. On June 14, the Finnish III Army Corps had been mobilized and put under German command.

JUNE 18

TURKEY, *DIPLOMACY*

Turkey signs a 10-year Non-Aggression Pact with Germany. Despite German pressure on Turkey to side with the Axis powers, President Inönü has always been of the opinion that the Axis powers cannot win the war. And despite German pressure, Turkey will at no time permit the future passage of Axis troops, ships or aircraft through or over Turkey and its territorial waters.

JUNE 19

BALTIC, *NAVAL WAR*

German warships begin laying mines in the Baltic, and German U-boats move to their war stations.

USSR, *STRATEGY*

The Soviets order a black-out of all major cities and towns near the border.

JUNE 21

GERMANY AND USSR, *ARMED FORCES*

On the eve of Operation Barbarossa, the order of battle for each side is as follows:

GERMAN AND AXIS

German Army in Norway

Mountain Corps Norway (2nd and 3rd Mountain Divisions); XXXVI Corps (169th Infantry Division, SS Group *Nord*). Finnish III Army Corps (3rd and 6th Divisions)

▲ *Field Marshal von Leeb, whose Army Group North targeted Leningrad.*

Finnish Army

14th Division

Karelian Army: Group Oinonen (three brigades); VI Corps (5th, 11th Divisions); VII Corps (1st, 7th, 19th Divisions); II Corps (2nd, 10th, 15th, 18th Divisions); IV Corps (4th, 8th, 12th, 17th Divisions)

Army Group North

Eighteenth Army: XXVI Corps (61st, 217th, 291st Infantry Divisions); XXXVIII Corps (58th Infantry Division); I Corps (1st, 11th, 12th Infantry Divisions)

Fourth Panzer Group: XXXXI Panzer Corps (1st, 6th Panzer Divisions, 269th Infantry Division, 36th Motorized Division); LVI Panzer Corps (290th Infantry Division, 8th Panzer Division, 3rd Motorized Division); SS *Totenkopf* Division

Sixteenth Army: X Corps (30th, 126th Infantry Divisions); XXVIII Corps (122nd, 123rd Infantry Divisions); II Corps (12th, 32nd, 121st, 253rd Infantry Divisions)

Army Group Reserve: 251st, 254th, 206th Infantry Divisions

OKH Reserve (in Army Group North): L Corps (86th Infantry Division, SS *Polizei* Division)

Rear area security: 207th, 281st, 285th Security Divisions

Army Group Centre

Third Panzer Group: VI Corps (6th, 26th Infantry Divisions); XXXIX Panzer Corps (14th, 20th Motorized Divisions, 7th, 20th Panzer Divisions); V Corps (5th, 35th Infantry Divisions); LVII Panzer Corps (18th Motorized Division, 12th, 19th Panzer Divisions)

Ninth Army: VIII Corps (8th, 28th, 161st Infantry Divisions); XX Corps (162nd, 256th Infantry Divisions); XXXXII Corps

▲ *The Prussian Field Marshal von Bock commanded Army Group Centre.*

▲ ***At the beginning of Barbarossa, Luftwaffe bombs and cannon found their targets with deadly precision.***

(87th, 102nd, 129th Infantry Divisions)
Fourth Army: VII Corps (7th, 23rd, 258th, 268th Infantry Divisions); XIII Corps (17th, 78th Infantry Divisions); IX Corps (137th, 263rd, 292nd Infantry Divisions); XXXXIII Corps (131st, 134th, 252nd Infantry Divisions)
Second Panzer Group: XXXXVI Panzer Corps (*Grossdeutschland* Infantry Regiment, SS *Das Reich* Motorized Division, 10th Panzer Division); XXXXVII Panzer Corps (29th Motorized Division, 167th Infantry Division, 17th, 18th Panzer Divisions); XII Corps (31st, 34th, 45th Infantry Divisions); XXIV Panzer Corps (10th Motorized Division, 3rd, 4th Panzer Divisions, 267th Infantry Division); Reserve 255th Infantry Division
Army Group Reserve: LIII Corps (293rd Infantry Division)
OKH Reserve (in Army Group Centre): XXXV Corps (15th, 52nd, 112th, 197th Infantry Divisions); XXXXII Corps (106th, 110th Infantry Divisions, 900th Motorized Brigade)
Rear area security: 221st, 286th, 403rd Security Divisions

Army Group South
First Panzer Group: XIV Panzer Corps (SS *Wiking* Motorized Division, 9th, 16th Panzer Divisions); III Panzer Corps (14th Panzer Division, 44th, 298th Infantry Divisions); XXIX Corps (111th, 299th Infantry Divisions); XXXXVIII Panzer Corps (11th Panzer Division, 57th, 75th Infantry Divisions); reserve (16th, 25th SS *Leibstandarte* Motorized Divisions, 13th Panzer Division)
Sixth Army: XVII Corps: (56th, 62nd Infantry Divisions); XXXXIV Corps (9th, 297th Infantry Divisions); LV Corps (168th Infantry Division)
Seventeenth Army: IV Corps (24th, 71st, 262nd, 295th, 296th Infantry Divisions); XXXXIX Mountain Corps (1st Mountain Division, 68th, 257th Infantry Divisions); LII Corps (101st Jäger Division); reserve (97th, 100th Jäger Divisions)
Eleventh Army: Romanian Mountain Corps (1st, 2nd, 4th Mountain Brigades, 8th Cavalry Brigade, 7th Infantry Division); XI Corps (76th, 239th infantry divisions, 6th, 8th Romanian Infantry Divisions, 6th Romanian Cavalry Brigade); XXX Corps (5th Romanian Cavalry Brigade, 14th Romanian Infantry Division, 198th Infantry Division); LIV Corps (50th, 170th Infantry Divisions); reserve (Romanian cavalry HQ, 22nd Infantry Division)
Army Group Reserve: 99th Jäger Division
OKH Reserve (in Army Group South): XXXIV Corps HQ; 4th Mountain Division, 113th, 125th, 132nd Infantry Divisions; LI Corps (79th, 95th Infantry Divisions)
Rear area security: 213th, 444th, 454th Security Divisions

OKH reserve
XXXX Panzer Corps: 60th Motorized Division; 46th, 73rd, 93rd, 94th, 96th, 98th, 183rd, 260th, 294th Infantry Divisions; 2nd, 5th Panzer Divisions; 707th, 713th Security Divisions; Romanina Third and Fourth Armies (four corps, nine divisions, two brigades)

German Army divisional strengths:
Panzer division (late war): 13,700 men, 100 tanks
Mountain division: 13,100 men
Panzergrenadier division: 13,900 men, 48 tanks/assault guns
Infantry division (early war): 17,000 men; infantry division (1944): 12,500 men
Volksgrenadier division: 10,100 men
Jäger division: 13,000 men
Waffen-SS panzer division: 19,500 men, 160 tanks
Waffen-SS panzergrenadier division: 18,000 men, 70–76 armoured fighting vehicles
Waffen-SS infantry division: 14,000 men
Waffen-SS mountain division: 16,000 men
Waffen-SS cavalry division: 12,900 men
Luftwaffe field division: 12,500 men
Luftwaffe parachute division: 12,500 men

The Luftwaffe element of Barbarossa comprises the 1st Air Fleet (379 aircraft), which will support Army Group North; 2nd Air Fleet (1223 aircraft), which will support Army Group Centre; and 4th Air Fleet (630 aircraft), which will support Army Group South. Crucially, German doctrine demands close cooperation between the Luftwaffe and the army. To this end staff officers were regularly exchanged between the two services, resulting in an excellent working relationship between ground and air staff.

German combat effectiveness
After nearly two years of unbroken success, the Wehrmacht began Barbarossa with high morale and the expectation of an easy victory. The Blitzkrieg had been astonishingly successful in Poland in 1939 and in the West in 1940. Germany's leaders and soldiers believed it would be equally successful in Russia. More than three million German and Axis troops began the invasion of the USSR, accompanied by 3330 tanks, 600,000 motor vehicles and 750,000 horses. The Luftwaffe deployed 2232 aircraft to take part in Barbarossa, approximately 65 percent of its frontline strength.

The German Army was at its peak, its ranks filled with veterans of the Polish and French campaigns. At the start of Barbarossa nearly all of its 120 infantry divisions were at their full offensive power. German divisions usually recruited from a single geographic area, thus many soldiers began military service having already known each other for years (often having served in the Hitler Youth together as boys). Each division had a training battalion in Germany to train replacements. Noncommissioned officers (NCOs) were rotated from the front to the training battalion. Thus the trainees were taught the latest battle tactics by combat soldiers.

Junior and middle-grade officers (lieutenants to colonels) were excellent, being well trained and expertly evaluated for specific command posts. Officers were selected on the basis of their suitability for command, and promotion was on merit. Senior commanders were even better, the restrictions of the post-World War I Versailles Treaty resulting in only the best being retained. Their only drawback, and one that often infuriated Hitler, was their Prussian conservatism regarding how to conduct a war.

The army did have its weak spots, such as the artillery arm, which was mostly horsedrawn and had a shortage of radios and spotter aircraft. However, the guns themselves were reliable, the crews were well trained and fire-control techniques were excellent.

◀ ***A Ju 87 Stuka in a dive on the first day of Barbarossa. On June 22, the Soviets were given no time to recover between air and artillery strikes.***

ARMED FORCES

RED ARMY RIFLE DIVISIONS

The infantry units of the Red Army were in a constant state of flux during the first two years of the war on the Eastern Front. Huge losses required constant reorganization to keep the units in some sort of fighting order. The reasons for these massive losses are not hard to find: during 1941–42, units were quickly formed and often thrown into battle with little or no training. Stalin's purges in the 1930s meant that thousands of inexperienced officers were promoted beyond their level of competence. This resulted in poor leadership on the battlefield. To compound problems, each rifle division had an inadequate number of radios, which made coordinating artillery support all but impossible (German commentators during Barbarossa noted the almost total absence of artillery support for attacking Red Army infantry units).

On the eve of Barbarossa, the Red Army had 200 rifle and mountain rifle divisions; by the end of December 1941 this had risen to 400, peaking at 430 in July 1943. Of these, 216 were reformed at least once due to battle losses, and 52 were reformed three or four times! Some 117 rifle divisions earned the Guards distinction for outstanding performance on the battlefield.

A rifle division was divided into three infantry regiments, an artillery regiment, headquarters company, reconnaissance battalion, anti-tank battalion, engineer battalion, signals battalion and services. A rifle division numbered approximately 9400 troops which, like many wartime establishments, could fluctuate wildly. Guards rifle divisions numbered 10,700 troops.

When it came to mobility and firepower, rifle divisions were at a disadvantage compared with their German rivals. A December 1941 rifle division had 213 trucks and 1613 horses, but by July 1942 these had dropped to 117 trucks and 601 horses. The December 1941 rifle division could deploy 120 machine guns, 184 submachine guns and 24 artillery pieces, but by July 1942 these had dropped to 41 machine guns, 164 submachine guns and 16 artillery pieces.

SOVIET
Northern Front
Fourteenth Army: 42nd Rifle Corps (104th, 122nd Rifle Divisions); 14th, 52nd Rifle Divisions; 23rd Fortified Region; 104th High Command Reserve Artillery Regiment; 1st Tank Division; 1st Mixed Aviation Division; 42nd Corrective Aviation Squadron; 31st Separate Sapper Battalion
Seventh Army: 54th, 71st, 168th, 237th Rifle Divisions; 26th Fortified Region; 208th Separate Anti-Aircraft Battalion; 55th Mixed Aviation Division; 184th Separate Sapper Battalion
Twenty-Third Army: 19th Rifle Corps (115th, 122nd Rifle Divisions); 50th Rifle Corps (43rd, 70th, 123rd Rifle Divisions); 27th, 28th Fortified Regions; 24th, 28th, 43rd Corps Artillery Regiments; 573rd Gun Artillery Regiment; 101st Howitzer Artillery Regiment; 519th High-Power Howitzer Artillery Regiment; 20th Separate Mortar Battalion; 27th, 241st Separate Anti-Aircraft Battalions; 10th Mechanized Corps (21st, 24th Tank Divisions, 198th Motorized Division, 7th Motorcycle Regiment); 5th Mixed Aviation Division; 41st Bomber Aviation Division; 15th, 19th Corrective Aviation Squadrons; 109th Motorized Engineer Battalion; 153rd Separate Engineer Battalion
Front Units: 177th, 191st Rifle Divisions; 8th Rifle Brigade; 21st, 22nd, 25th, 19th Fortified Regions; 541st, 577th Howitzer Artillery Regiments; 2nd Corps PVO [National Air Defence] (115th, 169th, 189th, 192nd, 194th, 351st Anti-Aircraft Artillery Regiments, five brigade PVO regions); 1st Mechanized Corps (3rd Tank Division, 5th Motorcycle Regiment, 163rd Motorized Division); 2nd Mixed Aviation Division; 3rd, 39th, 54th Fighter Aviation Divisions; 311th Reconnaissance Aviation Regiment; 103rd Corrective Aviation Squadron; 12th, 29th Engineer Regiments; 6th Pontoon Bridge Regiment

▲ ***Soviet aircraft destroyed on June 22. In Belorussia alone, 66 airfields were attacked simultaneously by the Luftwaffe.***

Northwestern Front
Eighth Army: 10th Rifle Corps (10th, 48th, 50th Rifle Divisions); 11th Rifle Corps (11th, 125th Rifle Divisions); 44th, 48th Fortified Regions; 9th Anti-Tank Artillery Brigade; 47th, 51st, 73rd Corps Artillery Regiments; 39th Separate Anti-Aircraft Battalion; 12th Mechanized Corps (23rd Tank Division, 202nd Motorized Division, 10th Motorcycle Regiment); 25th Engineer Regiment
Eleventh Army: 16th Rifle Corps (5th, 33rd, 188th Rifle Divisions); 29th Rifle Corps (179th, 184th Rifle Divisions); 23rd, 126th, 128th Rifle Divisions; 42nd, 45th, 46th Fortified Regions; 10th Anti-Tank Artillery Brigade; 270th, 448th, 615th Corps Artillery Regiments; 110th High-Power Howitzer Artillery Regiment; 429th Howitzer Artillery Regiment; 19th, 247th Separate Anti-Aircraft Battalions; 3rd Mechanized Corps (2nd, 5th Tank Divisions, 84th Motorized Division, 5th Motorcycle Regiment); 38th Separate Engineer Battalion
Twenty-Seventh Army: 22nd Rifle Corps (180th, 182nd Rifle Divisions); 24th Rifle Corps (181st, 183rd Rifle Divisions); 16th, 67th Rifle Divisions; 3rd Rifle Brigade; 613th, 614th Corps Artillery Regiments; 103rd, 111th Separate Anti-Aircraft Artillery Regiments
Front Units: 65th Rifle Corps HQ; 5th Airborne Corps (9th, 10th, 214th Airborne Brigades); 41st Fortified Region; 402nd High-Power Howitzer Artillery Regiment; 11th Separate Anti-Aircraft Artillery Battalion; 10th, 12th, 14th PVO brigades; three PVO regions; 57th Fighter Aviation Division; 4th, 6th, 7th, 8th Mixed Aviation Divisions; 21st Fighter Aviation Regiment PVO; 312th Reconnaissance Aviation Regiment; 4th, 30th Pontoon Bridge Regiments

▶ ***A German section waits for supporting artillery fire to halt before advancing on the first day of Barbarossa.***

Western Front
Third Army: (largely destroyed during the border battles in June 1941): 4th Rifle Corps (27th, 56th, 85th Rifle Divisions); 68th Fortified Region; 7th Anti-Tank Artillery Brigade; 152nd, 444th Corps Artillery Regiments; 16th Separate Anti-Aircraft Artillery Battalion; 11th Mechanized Corps (29th, 33rd Tank Divisions, 204th Motorized Division, 16th Motorcycle Regiment)
Fourth Army: (disbanded due to losses in July 1941): 28th Rifle Corps (6th, 49th, 42nd, 75th Rifle Divisions); 62nd Fortified Region; 447th, 455th, 462nd Corps Artillery Regiments; 120th High-Power Howitzer Artillery Regiment; 12th Separate Anti-Aircraft Artillery Regiment; 14th Mechanized Corps (22nd, 30th Tank Divisions, 205th Motorized Division, 20th Motorcycle Regiment)
Tenth Army: (destroyed/reformed October 1941): 1st Rifle Corps (2nd, 8th Rifle Divisions); 5th Rifle Corps (13th, 85th, 113th Rifle Divisions); 6th Cavalry Corps (6th, 36th Cavalry Divisions); 155th Rifle Division; 66th Fortified Region; 6th Anti-Tank Artillery Brigade; 130th, 156th, 262nd, 315th Corps Artillery Regiments; 311th Gun Artillery Regiment; 124th, 375th Howitzer Artillery Regiments; 38th, 71st Separate Anti-Aircraft Battalions; 6th Mechanized Corps (4th, 7th Tank Divisions, 29th Motorized Division, 4th Motorcycle Regiment); 13th Mechanized Corps (25th, 31st Tank Divisions, 208th Motorized Division, 18th Motorcycle Regiment)
Thirteenth Army HQ
Front Units: 2nd Rifle Corps (100th, 161st Rifle Divisions); 21st Rifle Corps (17th, 24th, 37th Rifle Divisions); 44th Rifle Corps (64th, 108th Rifle Divisions); 47th Rifle Corps (55th, 121st, 143rd Rifle Divisions); 50th Rifle Division; 4th Airborne Corps (7th, 8th, 214th Airborne Brigades); 58th, 61st, 63rd, 64th, 65th Fortified Regions; 8th Anti-Tank Artillery Brigade; 293rd, 611th Gun Artillery Regiments; 360th Howitzer Artillery Regiment; 5th, 318th, 612th High-Power Howitzer Artillery Regiments; 29th, 49th, 56th, 151st, 467th, 587th Corps Artillery Regiments; 32nd Separate Special-Power Artillery Battalion; 24th Separate Mortar Battalion; 86th Separate Anti-Aircraft Artillery Battalion; 4th, 7th PVO brigades; five PVO brigade regions; 17th Mechanized Corps (27th, 36th Tank Divisions, 209th Motorized Division, 22nd Motorcycle Regiment); 20th Mechanized Corps (26th, 38th Tank Divisions, 210th Motorized Division, 24th Motorcycle Regiment); 43rd Fighter Aviation Division; 12th, 13th Bomber Aviation Divisions; 9th, 10th, 11th Mixed Aviation Divisions; 184th

KEY WEAPONS

MP38

The 9mm MP38 was the standard German submachine gun of World War II. As its designation suggests, it was first issued in 1938. Two years later it was replaced by the MP40, which was similar except it utilized less expensive stamped metal for certain parts, which was more cost effective for a mass-produced weapon. The MP38/40 was a very successful firearm, and even Allied forces preferred it to their own submachine guns and scavenged MP38/40s whenever possible.

Between 1939 and 1945, the German Army received 689,403 MP38/40 guns, most of which went to frontline units, especially panzergrenadier formations (its folding stock made it an ideal weapon when troops were being transported in trucks and armoured personnel carriers). Both the MP38 and MP40 fired full-automatic only, having a cyclic rate of fire of 500 rounds per minute.

Calibre: 9mm
Magazine capacity: 32 rounds
Length: 833mm (32.8in), stock extended; 630mm (24.8in), stock folded
Weight: 4.3kg (9.5lb)
Muzzle velocity: 396mps (1300fps)

Fighter Aviation Regiment PVO; 313th, 314th Reconnaissance Aviation Regiments; 59th, 60th Fighter Aviation Divisions; 10th, 23rd, 33rd Engineer Regiments; 34th, 35th Pontoon Bridge Regiments; 275th Separate Sapper Battalion

Southwestern Front
Fifth Army: (destroyed September 1941, reformed October 1941): 15th Rifle Corps (45th, 62nd Rifle Divisions); 27th Rifle Corps (87th, 124th, 135th Rifle Divisions); 2nd Fortified Region; 1st Anti-Tank Artillery Brigade; 21st, 231st, 264th, 460th Corps Artillery Regiments; 23rd, 243rd Separate Anti-Aircraft Artillery Battalions; 9th Mechanized Corps (20th, 35th Tank Divisions, 131st Motorized Division, 32nd Motorcycle Regiment); 22nd Mechanized Corps (19th, 41st Tank Divisions, 215th Motorized Division, 23rd Motorcycle Regiment); 5th Pontoon Bridge Regiment
Sixth Army: (disbanded in August 1941 due to losses, then reformed): 6th Rifle Corps (41st, 97th, 159th Rifle Divisions); 37th Rifle Corps (80th, 139th, 141st Rifle Divisions); 5th Cavalry Corps (3rd, 14th Cavalry Divisions); 4th, 6th Fortified Regions; 3rd Anti-Tank Artillery Brigade; 209th, 229th, 441st, 445th Corps Artillery Regiments; 135th Gun Artillery Regiment; 17th, 307th Separate Anti-Aircraft Artillery Battalions; 4th Mechanized Corps (8th, 32nd Tank Divisions, 81st Motorized Division, 3rd Motorcycle Regiment); 15th Mechanized Corps (10th, 37th Tank Divisions, 212th Motorized Division); 9th Pontoon Bridge Regiment
Twelfth Army: 13th Rifle Corps (44th, 58th, 192nd Mountain Rifle Divisions); 17th Rifle Corps (60th, 96th Mountain Rifle Divisions, 164th Rifle Division); 10th, 11th, 12th Fortified Regions; 4th Anti-Tank Artillery Brigade; 269th, 274th, 283rd, 468th Corps Artillery Regiments; 20th, 30th Separate Anti-Aircraft Artillery Battalions; 16th Mechanized Corps (15th, 39th Tank Divisions, 240th Motorized Division, 19th Motorcycle Regiment); 37th Engineer Regiment; 19th Pontoon Bridge Regiment
Twenty-Sixth Army: (destroyed September 1941, reformed November 1941): 8th Rifle Corps (99th, 173rd Rifle Divisions, 72nd Mountain Rifle Division); 8th Fortified Region; 2nd Anti-Tank Artillery Brigade; 233rd, 236th Corps Artillery Regiments; 28th Separate Anti-Aircraft Artillery Battalion; 8th Mechanized Corps (12th, 34th Tank Divisions, 7th Motorized Division, 2nd Motorcycle Regiment); 17th Pontoon Bridge Regiment
Front Units: 31st Rifle Corps (193rd, 195th, 200th Rifle Divisions); 36th Rifle Corps (140th, 146th, 228th Rifle Divisions); 49th Rifle Corps (190th, 197th, 199th Rifle Divisions); 55th Rifle Corps (130th, 169th, 189th Rifle Divisions); 1st Airborne Corps (1st, 204th, 211th Airborne Brigades); 1st, 3rd, 5th, 7th, 13th, 15th, 17th Fortified Regions; 5th Anti-Tank Artillery Brigade; 205th, 207th, 368th, 437th, 458th, 507th, 543rd, 646th Corps Artillery Regiments; 305th, 555th Gun Artillery Regiments; 4th, 168th, 324th, 330th, 526th High-Power Artillery Regiments; 331st, 376th, 529th, 538th, 589th Howitzer Artillery Regiments; 34th, 245th, 315th, 316th Separate Special-Power Artillery Battalions; 263rd Separate Anti-Aircraft Artillery Battalion; 3rd, 4th, 11th PVO Brigades; five PVO brigade regions; 19th Mechanized Corps (40th, 43rd Tank Divisions, 213th Motorized Division, 21st Motorcycle Regiment); 24th Mechanized Corps (45th, 49th Tank Divisions, 216th Motorized Division, 17th Motorcycle Regiment); 44th, 64th Fighter Aviation Divisions; 19th, 62nd Bomber Aviation Divisions; 14th, 15th, 16th, 17th, 63rd Mixed Aviation Divisions; 315th, 316th Reconnaissance Aviation Regiments; 45th Engineer Regiment; 1st Pontoon Bridge Regiment
Ninth Separate Army: 14th Rifle Corps (25th, 51st Rifle Divisions); 35th Rifle Corps (95th, 176th Rifle Divisions); 48th Rifle Corps (74th, 150th Rifle Divisions, 30th Mountain Rifle Division); 2nd Cavalry Corps (5th, 9th Cavalry Divisions); 80th, 81st, 82nd, 84th, 86th Fortified Regions; 320th Gun Artillery Regiments; 430th High-Power Howitzer Artillery Regiment; 265th, 266th, 374th, 648th Corps Artillery

▶ ***As the Germans advanced (seen here) Red Army formations on the border began to fall apart: the Eleventh Army was shattered in a few hours.***

▲ ***In many Ukrainian towns and villages the Germans were welcomed as liberators from the Bolshevik yoke.***

DECISIVE MOMENT

DELAYING BARBAROSSA

There is little doubt that the German campaign in the Balkans in the spring of 1941 had a detrimental effect on the outcome of Barbarossa. The decision to invade Yugoslavia and Greece was made on March 27, postponing the start of Barbarossa from mid-May. On April 7, OKH delayed Barbarossa again, by four weeks, thus putting the start date in mid-June. Only on June 17 did Hitler set the start date for the invasion of the USSR for June 22. However, even without the "Balkan interlude", the Germans would have faced difficulties in launching Barbarossa in mid-May. The spring of 1941 had been especially wet. General Greiffenberg, Chief of Staff to the German Twelfth Army, had this to say of the effects that heavy rains had on the ground: "East of the Bug-San line in Poland, ground operations are always very restricted until May, because most roads are muddy and the country generally is a morass. But 1941 was an exceptional year. The winter had lasted longer. As late as the beginning of June, the Bug in front of our army was over its banks for miles." In the north, moreover, heavy rain continued to fall until early June.

The Balkan campaign adversely affected German preparations in other ways. First, divisions that had taken part had to be re-deployed to the east. Thus, there was great wear and tear on engines, especially those of the panzers, which contributed to the high rate of mechanical failure experienced during Barbarossa. Second, when Barbarossa was launched, several divisions were still in transit from the southeast (Army Group South was lacking a third of its armoured strength at the start of Barbarossa). Third, the high losses in airborne forces on Crete meant Hitler would sanction no further large-scale airborne operations. Therefore, the Wehrmacht was denied the use of a highly effective part of its inventory.

Regiments; 317th Separate Special-Power Artillery Battalion; 26th, 268th Separate Anti-Aircraft Artillery Battalions; one brigade PVO region; 2nd Mechanized Corps (11th, 16th Tank Divisions, 15th Motorized Division, 6th Motorcycle Regiment); 18th Mechanized Corps (44th, 47th Tank Divisions, 218th Motorized Division, 26th Motorcycle Regiment); 20th, 21st, 45th Mixed Aviation Divisions; 131st Fighter Aviation Division PVO; 317th Reconnaissance Aviation Regiment; 65th, 66th Fighter Aviation Divisions; 8th, 16th Separate Engineer Battalions; 121st Motorized Engineer Battalion

Stavka Reserve

Sixteenth Army: 32nd Rifle Corps (46th, 152nd Rifle Divisions); 126th Corps Artillery Regiment; 112th Separate Anti-Aircraft Artillery Battalion; 5th Mechanized Corps (13th, 17th Tank Divisions, 109th Motorized Division, 8th Motorcycle Regiment)

Nineteenth Army: 25th Rifle Corps (127th, 134th, 162nd Rifle Divisions); 34th Rifle Corps (129th, 158th, 171st Rifle Divisions); 38th Rifle Division; 442nd, 471st Corps Artillery Regiments; 26th Mechanized Corps (52nd, 56th Tank Divisions, 103rd Motorized Division, 27th Motorcycle Regiment); 111th Engineer Battalion; 238th, 321st Separate Sapper Battalions

Twentieth Army: (destroyed October 1941, reformed November 1941): 61st Rifle Corps (110th, 144th, 172nd Rifle Divisions); 69th Rifle Corps (73rd, 229th, 233rd Rifle Divisions); 18th Rifle Division; 301st Howitzer Artillery Regiment; 537th High-Power Howitzer Artillery Regiment; 438th Corps Artillery Regiment; 7th Mechanized Corps (14th, 18th Tank Divisions, 1st Motorized Division, 9th Motorcycle Regiment); 60th Pontoon Bridge Battalion

Twenty-First Army: 63rd Rifle Corps (53rd, 148th, 167th Rifle Divisions); 66th Rifle Corps (61st, 117th, 154th Rifle Divisions); 387th Howitzer Artillery Regiment; 420th, 546th Corps Artillery Regiments; 25th Mechanized Corps (50th, 55th Tank Divisions, 219th Motorized Division, 12th Motorcycle Regiment)

Twenty-Second Army: 51st Rifle Corps (98th, 112th, 153rd Rifle Divisions); 62nd Rifle Corps (170th, 174th, 186th Rifle Divisions); 336th, 545th Corps Artillery Regiments

Twenty-Fourth Army: (destroyed October 1941, reformed December 1941): 52nd Rifle Corps (91st, 119th, 166th Rifle Divisions); 53rd Rifle Corps (107th, 133rd, 178th Rifle Divisions); 524th Heavy Gun Artillery Regiment; 392nd, 542nd, 685th Corps Artillery Regiments

Separate formations: 20th Rifle Corps (137th, 160th Rifle Divisions); 45th Rifle Corps (187th, 227th, 232nd Rifle Divisions); 67th Rifle Corps (102nd, 132nd, 151st Rifle Divisions); 267th, 390th Corps Artillery Regiments; 21st Mechanized Corps (42nd, 46th Tank Divisions, 18th Motorized Division, 11th Motorcycle Regiment)

Red Army unit strengths:

Cavalry corps: 21,000 men
Cavalry division: 6000 men
Tank army: 45,000 men, 450–560 tanks

▶ ***A Panzer IV motors east in late June. Dirt tracks that were marked as roads on maps came as a nasty surprise to the Germans.***

Tank corps: 7800 men, 168 tanks; tank corps (January 1944): 11,000 men
Tank brigade (November 1943): 1400 men, 53 tanks
Mechanized corps (January 1944): 16,500 men, 246 tanks and self-propelled guns
Motorized rifle brigade (November 1943): 3500 men
Rifle corps: 40,000 men
Guards rifle and rifle divisions: 10,700 men (guards), 9400 (rifle)
Mountain rifle division: 9400 men
Destroyer division: 4000 men
Ski brigade: 3800 men
Airborne brigade: 3600 men
Naval infantry brigade: 4300 men
Artillery division: 9200 men

Red Army combat effectiveness

Although massive - 5.5 million men - the Red Army had serious problems at the start of Barbarossa. The purges of the 1930s resulted in a severe shortage of experienced commanders, and those who survived were loathe to show any initiative lest they be accused of insubordination. Tactics were unimaginative. SS-Oberführer Max Simon, commander of the SS *Totenkopf* Division, witnessed many Soviet infantry attacks during Operation Barbarossa: "They were rule of thumb, cooperation with the heavy weapons was lacking and one could sense the absence of flexible leadership. Attacks against our good infantry regiments, still intact and firm in well-prepared positions, met with virtually no success. Usually the main Russian attack was preceded by an artillery preparation that lasted several hours. As soon as the artillery fire lengthened, the infantry attack began, supported by armour and snipers, and to the accompaniment of fighter aircraft. If our infantry held its positions until the enemy artillery fire had passed over it, then it could always beat off the first attack."

The new Soviet border in Poland required the building of fresh fortifications. However, although 2500 fortified positions had been built by June 1941, some 1500 were equipped only with machine guns. The army's rifle divisions were also under strength, having 8000–9000 men, or even 5000–6000 men, as opposed to the authorized strength of 9500 (and many rifle divisions in the western military districts had only 50 percent of their vehicle allocation). One reason for their poor performance was a dire lack of radios. Indeed, the divisions relied mainly on cable for communications which, especially during Barbarossa, was often cut by German infiltration squads, Luftwaffe bombs or German Army artillery. Very quickly, regiments, divisions, even armies, became "blind", a situation made worse by German aerial superiority which acted as the "eyes and ears" of army units, pinpointing stranded Red Army infantry formations.

The Red Army had no answer to the panzer group. Its mechanized corps, each one numbering 36,000 men and 1031 tanks, were scattered along the frontier – not concentrated, as they were in Wehrmacht army groups. On paper the armoured force in 1941 was impressive: 29,484 vehicles. However, of this number, 29 percent of the tanks required a major overhaul; 44 percent required a rebuild. This left 7000 as combat worthy. Tank crew training was poor, leadership was even worse and the tanks themselves were mechanically unreliable. A lack of radios in individual tanks meant it was impossible to coordinate tank units on the battlefield. In addition, at the start of Barbarossa there was a shortage of 76.2mm ammunition, which adversely affected the performance of the Red Army's two best tanks, the KV-1 and T-34. The result was that by the end of 1941 the German offensive had destroyed 90 percent of the USSR's tank force.

On paper the Red Air Force was impressive, with 19,533 aircraft, 7133 of which were located in the western USSR. However, many of its aircraft were obsolete, its pilots lacked flying experience, few aircraft had radios, and three successive air force commanders plus many senior officers had been shot in the

KEY PERSONALITIES

HEINZ GUDERIAN

Born in Chelmno in 1888, Guderian became a communications specialist in the German Army and then, after World War I, an advocate of mechanized warfare. In 1934, now a colonel, he became Chief of Staff of the Motorized Troops Command Staff, and in October 1935 assumed command of one of the first three panzer divisions, the 2nd. Guderian stayed with his division until February 1938, thereafter heading XVI Corps headquarters and taking part in the takeover of Austria in March 1938. Hitler was impressed by Guderian and made him Chief of Mobile Troops with the rank of General of Panzer Troops.

Guderian was a gifted panzer commander, as shown by his successes in Poland and France. He stressed to his tank commanders the importance of maintaining attacking momentum and encouraged them not to worry about their exposed flanks, but he was also headstrong and unyielding in his views, which meant he often clashed with his superiors. His arguments over maintaining the advance in northern France in May 1940, for example, brought him into conflict with Kleist, and Guderian threatened to resign (he could also be petulant).

Operation Barbarossa was Guderian's finest hour, when he led his Second Panzer Group east and achieved stunning victories at Minsk, Smolensk and Kiev. Failure before Moscow during Operation Typhoon, however, brought him into conflict with Hitler over the Führer's refusal to sanction withdrawals. A further clash with the commander of Army Group Centre, Kluge, in late December 1941 resulted in Guderian's dismissal.

Guderian was recalled in March 1943 and created Inspector General of Armoured Troops, tasked with rebuilding the shattered panzer arm. On July 21, 1944, he was made Chief of the General Staff, which resulted in more clashes with Hitler over strategy, particularly on the Eastern Front. The result was inevitable: Hitler sent Guderian on six weeks' sick leave on March 28, 1945. After the war he was a prisoner of the Americans until June 1948, thereafter living in retirement in West Germany until his death in May 1954. His memoirs, *Panzer Commander*, became a seminal work on the theory and practice of armoured warfare.

purges, which further diluted its effectiveness. The losses suffered by the air force during the first week of Barbarossa resulted in the Germans retaining air superiority in Russia until the end of 1942!

▲ ***German infantry fire on a Soviet bunker beside a burning Red Army improvised armoured scout car.***

JUNE 22

FINLAND, *LAND WAR*
Elements of Dietl's Mountain Corps move into the Petsamo area.

FINLAND, *AIR WAR*
The Luftwaffe bombs targets on the Kola Peninsula.

FINLAND, *POLITICS*
Finland declares its neutrality, but this does not prevent the Soviets attacking Finnish shipping in the Gulf of Finland.

BALTIC, *SEA WAR*
German torpedo boats *S59* and *S60* sink a Soviet steamer off the Gotland coast.

USSR, *AIR WAR*
In the first Luftwaffe strike, an estimated 1800 Soviet aircraft are destroyed on the ground (two German aircraft are lost). In the second strike a few hours later, a further 700 Soviet aircraft are destroyed for the loss of 37 aircraft.

NORTHERN USSR, *LAND WAR*
The Fourth Panzer Group makes good progress against the Northwest Front, especially LVI Panzer Corps, which smashes the Soviet Eighth Army's left flank and heads towards the River Dvina. The German Eighteenth Army advances along the coast while the Sixteenth Army heads for the River Niemen, forcing apart the Soviet Eighth and Eleventh Armies. Heavy German artillery barrages and Luftwaffe attacks hinder Red Army movements.

CENTRAL USSR, *LAND WAR*
The Fourth Panzer Group pierces the front between the Northwest and Western Fronts. Reinforcements from the 3rd and 12th Mechanized Corps come under sustained Luftwaffe attack, and the German Ninth Army inflicts heavy casualties on the Soviet Third Army. Meanwhile, the Second Panzer Group attacks Brest-Litovsk, whose garrison withdraws into the citadel. Under relentless attacks the Soviet Third, Fourth and Tenth Armies begin to fall apart, compounded by Luftwaffe strikes against troop concentrations at Bialystok, Grodno, Lida, Volkovsky, Brest-Litovsk; and against airfields, and fuel and ammunition dumps. As the German Ninth and Fourth Armies maul the Soviet Tenth Army, the Russian 6th Cavalry Corps is virtually wiped out. The Tenth Army begins to withdraw, while the 14th Mechanized Corps begins a day-long battle with the 18th Panzer Division. By evening the Soviet Tenth Army has suffered severe casualties.

SOUTHERN USSR, *LAND WAR*
The Luftwaffe achieves almost immediate air superiority, destroying more than 300 aircraft in the first three hours of operations. The First Panzer Group and Sixth Army attack the Soviet Third, Fourteenth and Sixth Armies as the Germans cross the River Bug. The Seventeenth Army attacks towards Lvov. As the day wears on, the Soviet 15th Rifle Corps disintegrates at the junction of the Fourth and Fifth Armies. General Mikhail Kirponos, Southern Front commander, counterattacks with the 4th and 22nd Mechanized Corps but fails to halt the panzers.

MOSCOW, *MEDIA*
Molotov makes a broadcast to the Soviet people: "Today at 4 o'clock am, without any claims having been presented to the Soviet Union, without a declaration of war, German troops attacked our country, attacked our borders at many points and bombed from their airplanes our cities Zhitomir, Kiev, Sevastopol, Kaunas and some others." He ends his statement with the following words: "The government calls upon you, citizens of the Soviet Union, to rally still more closely around our glorious Bolshevist party, around our Soviet government, around our great leader and comrade, Stalin. Ours is a righteous cause. The enemy shall be defeated. Victory will be ours."

JUNE 23

NORTHERN USSR, *LAND WAR*
The Soviet 3rd Mechanized Corps launches a counterattack

▼ ***A horse-drawn German 75mm le IG 18 infantry gun on the move into the USSR. This gun was first issued in 1927 and remained in service until 1945.***

KEY WEAPONS

PPSH-41 SUBMACHINE GUN

Designed by George Shpagin, the PPSh-41 entered service shortly before the German invasion of the Soviet Union in June 1941. The PPSh-41 was designed to be as simple as possible. It used a minimum number of parts, a simple blow-back action and fired from the open bolt position. It soon proved itself to be effective as a weapon as well as easy to manufacture, and became one of the most famous small arms of World War II. Factories and workshops throughout the Soviet Union began turning out this reliable weapon, and more than five million were produced by 1945.

The Germans were also impressed with the weapon, particularly the large ammunition supply. This was either a 71-round drum or a 35-round box. The high capacity of the drum magazine increased firepower, but the magazines were too slow to refill and not entirely reliable. In 1942, the Soviets developed a curved box magazine. Large numbers of captured PPSh-41s were issued to German troops on the Eastern Front, including some re-chambered for the 9mm parabellum round. The PPSh-41 had a cyclic rate of fire of 900 rounds per minute (this is the rate of fire with a continuous supply of ammunition, and does not take into account the need to change magazines).

Calibre: 7.62mm
Magazine capacity: 71 (drum) or 35 (box)
Length: 838mm (33in)
Weight: 3.64kg (8lb)
Muzzle velocity: 488mps (1600fps)

against LVI Panzer Corps but only succeeds in losing 70 tanks. The panzers reach Kedainiai towards evening. An attack by the 3rd and 12th Mechanized Corps against XXXXI Panzer Corps near Rasainiai is equally disastrous, with the panzers and Luftwaffe taking a heavy toll of Soviet vehicles. Meanwhile, the infantry of the German Sixteenth Army continue their march towards the Niemen unopposed.

CENTRAL USSR, *LAND WAR*
The German XXXIX and LVII Panzer Corps, heavily supported by the Luftwaffe, reach the Niemen while VIII Corps captures Grodno. The Soviet Third and Eighth Armies withdraw, creating a gap through which the panzers pour. Farther south, Heinz Guderian's Second Panzer Group advances towards Slutsk. General Pavlov, commander of the Western Front, orders up his reserve, the Thirteenth Army, in an effort to stabilize the front.

SOUTHERN USSR, *LAND WAR*
The 11th Panzer Division captures Berestechko, splitting the Soviet Fifth and Sixth Armies. Kirponos orders an immediate attack by the 4th, 9th and 19th Mechanized Corps in an effort to slow the Germans.

USSR, *ARMED FORCES*
The Stavka (*Shtab vierhovnogo komandovani* – Headquarters of the Main Command) and Industrial Evacuation Group, tasked with relocating plants out of the range of the enemy, are formed in Moscow.

SLOVAKIA, *DIPLOMACY*
Slovakia declares war on the USSR.

JUNE 24

FINLAND, *LAND WAR*
German units advance towards Murmansk, and the Finns capture Aaland.

NORTHERN USSR, *GROUND WAR*
Despite fierce, albeit fragmented, resistance by the Red Army, LVI Panzer Corps continues the advance towards the Dvina, cutting the road to Daugavpils. The German X Corps takes Kaunas and then holds it in the face of a Soviet counterattack by the 23rd Rifle Division.

CENTRAL USSR, *LAND WAR*
The German LVII Panzer Corps captures Vilnius, and XXXIX Panzer Corps advances east towards Minsk. The Soviet Third Army has been bypassed and is being reduced by ground and air attacks. The Second Panzer Group captures Slonim.

SOUTHERN USSR, *LAND WAR*
The German XIV Panzer Corps reaches Lutsk, but on this front Soviet resistance is intensifying as the 22nd Mechanized Corps attacks the 13th and 14th Panzer Divisions east of Vladimir Volynsky and the 15th Mechanized Corps tries unsuccessfully to halt the 11th Panzer Division. To the south, the Seventeenth Army captures Nemirov. As elsewhere, Luftwaffe activity is severely hampering Soviet movements. However, Kirponos is attempting to gather a large armoured force to strike the flanks of the First Panzer Group and Sixth Army.

HUNGARY, *DIPLOMACY*
Hungary breaks off diplomatic relations with the USSR.

USA, *DIPLOMACY*
President Roosevelt extends Lend-Lease aid to the USSR.

JUNE 25

FINLAND, *AIR WAR*
A force of 500 Soviet bombers attacks cities and airfields in Finland. Finnish Prime Minister Rangell announces that as a result Finland is at war with the USSR.

▶ ***The troops of Leeb's Army Group North found northern Russia crisscrossed by a network of rivers and streams.***

KEY WEAPONS

KV-1

This Soviet heavy tank shared many components with the T-34 tank, such as the engine and 76.2mm main gun. Although unreliable (in 1941 many of the 639 KV-1s broke down on the way to the battlefield), it was continually upgraded throughout the war. Design "features" included transmission gears that were so difficult to shift that drivers were issued with a hammer to knock them into place!

In early 1943, a decision was made to redesign the KV-1. Soviet tank designers wanted to develop a new KV with lighter armour and a higher speed, similar to the T-34/76 medium tank. The new tank was named KV-1S, the "s" meaning *skorostnoy* (speed). The thickness of the frontal armour was reduced, the rear hull was redesigned, and the existing road wheels were replaced with newer, lighter ones. The KV-1's transmission was also redesigned and wider tracks were fitted for increased cross-country mobility. In addition, the new tank was armed with four machine guns: a coaxial machine gun; a bow machine gun; an anti-aircraft machine gun; and a machine gun in the rear of the turret. A total of 130 KV-1S models were built, with 6160 KV-1s of all variants being produced during the war.

Weight: 47,500kg (104,500lb)
Crew: 5
Speed: 35kmh (21.8mph)
Range: 180km (112 miles)
Dimensions: length: 6.9m (22.63ft); width: 3.32m (10.9ft); height: 2.71m (8.9ft)
Armament: 1 x 76.2mm cannon, 3 x 7.62mm machine gun
Ammunition: 114 x 76.2mm, 3000 x 7.62mm
Armour: front (maximum): 110mm (4.33in); side (maximum): 77mm (3in)

◀ ***Ukrainians greet German troops in the summer of 1941. Seven million Ukrainians would die during the next four years.***

The attack was designed to destroy German aircraft that the Soviets believed were stationed in Finland.

BALTIC, *AIR WAR*
Four Junkers Ju 88 bombers, operating from Malmi airfield, bomb the Soviet heavy cruiser *Kirov* at Kronstadt but fail to hit the target.

USSR, *AIR WAR*
The Luftwaffe has established air superiority over the whole of the Eastern Front. It can now focus on providing air support for the army.

NORTHERN USSR, *LAND WAR*
The 21st Mechanized Corps tries to hold LVI Panzer Corps west of the Dvina as the 12th Mechanized Corps employs KV-1 and T-34 tanks against XXXXI Panzer Corps around Rasainiai, causing the Germans some disquiet. The German advance towards Riga prompts the building of siege lines around the port. The Soviet Eighth and Twenty-Seventh Armies are ordered to establish a defensive line from Riga to Kraslava.

CENTRAL USSR, *LAND WAR*
The speed of the Blitzkrieg has resulted in the Soviet Tenth and Third Armies being isolated around Bialystok and Volkovsky. XXXIX Panzer Corps captures Molodechno and Lida while XXIV Panzer Corps races towards the Dnieper. Seeing the Western Front under threat of collapse, Timoshenko orders the Twenty-Second Army to deploy on the front's northern wing.

SOUTHERN USSR, *LAND WAR*
As Kirponos prepares his armoured counterattack, the 11th Panzer Division enters Dubno and Lutsk falls to the Germans. There is heavy fighting around Lvov between the Seventeenth Army and the Soviet Twenty-Sixth Army.

JUNE 26

FINLAND, *LAND WAR*
The Soviets launch an abortive attack from the Murmansk area.

NORTHERN USSR, *LAND WAR*
The Soviet 3rd and 12th Mechanized Corps are destroyed between Siauliai and Rasainiai. As Manstein's panzers race ahead, the infantry of the Eighteenth and Sixteenth Armies struggle to keep up with the armoured units.

CENTRAL USSR, *LAND WAR*
The lead elements of the Third Panzer Group are now only 29km (18 miles) north of Minsk and the Second Panzer Group is approaching from the south. The jaws are closing on Soviet units around the city. The Soviet Tenth Army begins to fall apart and the Fourth Army struggles to extricate itself. The Western Front is collapsing, and in desperation Timoshenko decides to build a second defence line east of Minsk.

SOUTHERN USSR, *LAND WAR*
Kirponos launches his counterattack against the Sixth Army and First Panzer Group. However, the attacks by the 15th, 22nd, 19th and 9th Mechanized Corps fail. The Soviet Sixth and Twenty-Sixth Armies are ordered to retire through Lvov, while the Sixteenth Army struggles to hold Shepetovka from attacks by XIV Panzer Corps (the town is a major Red Army supply base).

JUNE 27

NORTHERN USSR, *LAND WAR*
As the tanks of XXXXI and LVI Panzer Corps near the Dvina, Timoshenko orders Red Army units to muster on the river line. The German Eighteenth Army encounters heavy resistance as it pushes into the Baltic states, and the Sixteenth Army is mopping up in the wake of the Fourth Panzer Group.

CENTRAL USSR, *LAND WAR*
The Second and Third Panzer Groups link up at Minsk, trapping the Soviet Third, Fourth, Tenth and Thirteenth Armies.

SOUTHERN USSR, *LAND WAR*
Counterattacks by the Soviet 19th, 9th and 8th Mechanized Corps and 36th Rifle Corps are disrupted by Luftwaffe attacks.

The Sixteenth Army continues to defend Shepetovka as the Seventeenth Army forces the Red Army to abandon Lvov.

HUNGARY, *DIPLOMACY*
Hungary declares war on the USSR.

JUNE 28

NORTHERN USSR, *LAND WAR*
Fierce Red Army counterattacks against Daugavpils fail after savage fighting in the town. The Red Air Force fails to destroy the bridges over the Dvina. To date the Northwest Front has lost 400 tanks and 200 artillery pieces.

CENTRAL USSR, *LAND WAR*
As the Minsk Pocket is reduced, XXIV Panzer Corps reaches Bobruisk. Stalin removes Pavlov and replaces him with General Andrei Eremenko.

SOUTHERN USSR, *LAND WAR*
Kirponos' armoured attack has failed and he tries to withdraw his forces. The 9th Mechanized Corps does manage to inflict heavy casualties on the 13th Panzer Division near Rovno.

JUNE 29

FINLAND, *LAND WAR*
Dietl's Operation Silverfox (the attack on Murmansk) gets under way. The 2nd and 3rd Mountain Divisions launch their attack against Soviet positions. However, the terrain is inhospitable and the Germans make slow progress against determined opposition. Silverfox starts to stall.

NORTHERN USSR, *LAND WAR*
As the Germans breach the Dvina river line, the 21st Mechanized Corps is reduced to 7 tanks, 74 guns and 4000 men. Libau falls to the German 291st Infantry Division.

CENTRAL USSR, *LAND WAR*
Brest-Litovsk falls to the Germans. The Stavka orders a scorched earth policy in an effort to slow the German advance.

SOUTHERN USSR, *LAND WAR*
The German Seventeenth Army enters Lvov.

USSR, ARMED *FORCES*
The Central Committee of the Communist Party issues a directive that establishes partisan groups to fight the Germans.

POLAND, *ATROCITIES*
As the Red Army withdraws through Lvov, the NKVD kills more than 3000 Polish political prisoners.

JUNE 30

NORTHERN USSR, *ARMED FORCES*
General Fedor Kuznetsov is replaced by General Petr Sobennikov as commander of the Northwest Front.

▲ ***The aftermath of a Luftwaffe air strike. In the first phase of Barbarossa German air crews flew up to eight sorties a day.***

CENTRAL USSR, *LAND WAR*
XXIV Panzer Corps captures Bobruisk and establishes a crossing point over the River Berezina as General Pavlov is shot in Moscow for incompetence.

SOUTHERN USSR, *LAND WAR*
Rovno, Ostrog and Lvov fall to the Germans. To date the Southwest Front has lost 2600 tanks.

USSR, *ARMED FORCES*
The State Committee for Defence (*Gosudarstvennyi Komit Oborony* – GKO) is set up, comprising army, air force, navy and party representatives, including Molotov, Voroshilov, Malenkov and Beria.

GERMANY, *ARMED FORCES*
The Second and Third Panzer Groups are brought under the overall command of Field Marshal Günther von Kluge's Fourth Army, which is to be renamed the Fourth Panzer Army. OKH hopes this will facilitate the speedy seizure of the crossing points over the River Dnieper.

▼ ***A Panzer 38(t) light tank on an improvised bridge. The sterling efforts of Germans engineers ensured that the panzers were able to maintain their momentum in June and July.***

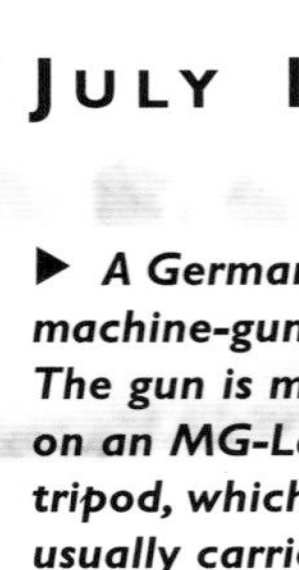

▶ ***A German MG34 machine-gun team. The gun is mounted on an MG-Lafette 34 tripod, which was not usually carried as a field item. It was usually deployed in formally prepared firing positions.***

JULY 1

FINLAND, *LAND WAR*
The German XXXVI Corps attacks the Soviet 42nd Rifle Corps in the Salla region, although the terrain hampers progress. The Finnish III Corps advances from Uhtua.

USSR, *AIR WAR*
Total Soviet losses in aircraft now stand at 4900.

NORTHERN USSR, *LAND WAR*
The German XXVI Corps captures Riga, and the army group approaches Pskov. Of the Northwest Front's 31 divisions, 22 are now below half-strength.

SOUTHERN USSR, *LAND WAR*
The First Panzer Group advances around Rovno, Dubno and Kremenets, its northern flank protected by the Sixth Army, which is fending off spirited resistance from the Soviet Fifth Army. Meanwhile, the Southern Front is attacked by LIV, XXX, XI Corps and the Third and Fourth Romanian Armies.

JULY 2

FINLAND, *LAND WAR*
An attack by the Soviet 10th Mechanized Corps in front of Vyborg is stopped by the Finnish IV Corps.

NORTHERN USSR, *LAND WAR*
The Soviet 12th Mechanized Corps is forced to retreat by XXXXI Panzer Corps as the 21st Mechanized Corps tries to hold off LVI Panzer Corps.

CENTRAL USSR, *LAND WAR*
Timoshenko takes direct control of the Western Front and brings the Nineteenth, Twentieth, Twenty-First and Twenty-Second Armies from the reserve into the line. The 19th Panzer Division reaches the River Disna but is stopped by resistance, and the 18th Panzer Division farther south establishes a bridgehead over the River Berezina. XXXXVII Panzer Corps is also approaching the Berezina to the south.

SOUTHERN USSR, *LAND WAR*
The First Panzer Group advances on the road to Kiev, heading for Radomyshl and Zhitomir. The Seventeenth Army advancing from Lvov continues to meet fierce resistance from the retreating Twenty-Sixth Army. Two other Soviet armies, the Ninth and Eighteenth, also slow the advance of the German Eleventh Army, which is attacking from Moldavia.

JULY 3

NORTHERN USSR, *LAND WAR*
The marshy and woody terrain is hindering the advance of the panzers, but the Soviet Eighth, Eleventh and Twenty-Seventh Armies are falling apart under the relentless German assault.

▲ ***Hitler's racial warriors on the Eastern Front. Men of the Waffen-SS* Leibstandarte *Division with a war trophy. The division was a component of Army Group South.***

CENTRAL USSR, *LAND WAR*
Resistance in the Bialystok Pocket ends. The Soviet Third and Tenth Armies have been destroyed, the Fourth and Thirteenth Armies reduced to remnants. The Germans have taken 290,000 prisoners, 2500 tanks and 1500 artillery pieces. Meanwhile, the 19th Panzer Division forces a crossing of the Disna.

SOUTHERN USSR, *LAND WAR*
The Soviets suffer heavy losses attempting to destroy Axis bridgeheads on the River Prut. The 48th Rifle and 2nd Mechanized Corps in particular incur severe losses.

USSR, *POLITICS*
Stalin, having recovered from the shock of the German attack on June 22, makes a radio broadcast to the Soviet people. His address makes an appeal to the Soviet people to rally to the defence of the homeland, saying that the "issue is one of life or death for the Soviet state, for the peoples of the USSR; the issue is whether the peoples of the Soviet Union shall remain free or fall into slavery". He further calls for a scorched earth policy and promises a "ruthless fight against all disorganizers of the rear, deserters, panic-mongers and rumour-mongers".

JULY 4

FINLAND, *LAND WAR*
The Finnish 14th Infantry Division makes good progress along the Repola axis against sparse resistance.

NORTHERN USSR, *LAND WAR*
The 6th Panzer Division easily penetrates the Stalin Line as the 1st Panzer Division

◀ *German troops in Lvov. Before the Red Army fled from the city, NKVD units massacred many of its Ukrainian prisoners and herded others east in long columns.*

enters Ostrov. The Stavka orders the fortification of the River Luga line to stop the German advance on Leningrad. However, General Markian Popov's Northern Front is short of men and equipment and is having to commit forces to fend off Finnish attacks in Karelia. The German Sixteenth Army, covering the army group's southern flank, is being held back by Hitler's insistence that it protect the junction with Army Group Centre.

CENTRAL USSR, *LAND WAR*
Timoshenko organizes a counterattack using the Twenty-Second Army at Polotsk against LVII Panzer Corps; the Twentieth Army, with the 5th and 7th Mechanized Corps in support (1000 tanks each), against XXXIX Panzer Corps at Lepel; and the Twenty-First Army in the south near the Pripet Marshes.

SOUTHERN USSR, *LAND WAR*
The Third Panzer Group continues the advance on Kiev as the Soviet Eighteenth Army manages to escape across the River Dniester, being subjected to Luftwaffe attack as it does so. The German Sixth Army is divided into two groups: the northern group supports the Third Panzer Group for the drive on Kiev; the southern group will link up with XIV and XXXXVIII Panzer Corps and will swing south to join up with the Eleventh Army to encircle the Soviet Sixth, Twelfth, Eighteenth and Twenty-Sixth Armies.

JULY 6

FINLAND, *LAND WAR*
The Soviet 52nd and 14th Rifle Divisions withdraw to the River Litsa. The German advance towards Salla grinds to a halt in the face of Soviet resistance.

NORTHERN USSR, *AIR WAR*
The Luftwaffe's Fighter Wing 54 shoots down 65 of 73 Soviet bombers that attacked the German bridgehead at Ostrov.

NORTHERN USSR, *LAND WAR*
The German Eighteenth Army completes the occupation of Latvia and Lithuania and advances into Estonia, its XXVI Corps then engaging the Soviet Eighth Army. There is heavy fighting at Ostrov as the Eleventh and Twenty-Seventh Armies try to halt XXXXI Panzer Corps, the Soviets losing 140 tanks in the process.

CENTRAL USSR, *LAND WAR*
As LVII Panzer Corps holds off an assault by the Twenty-Second Army at the Disna, Timoshenko launches his counterattack. The Twentieth Army stops XXXIX Panzer Corps from taking Vitebsk, and XXIV Panzer Corps is attacked by the Twenty-First Army from Zhlobin. The 5th and 7th Mechanized Corps also engage XXXIX and XXXXVII Panzer Corps.

SOUTHERN USSR, *LAND WAR*
With Red Army forces disintegrating, III, XIV and XXXXVIII Panzer Corps approach Kiev. To the south, the

KEY WEAPONS

PANZER IV

The Panzer IV became the backbone of the German panzer arm on the Eastern Front. Continually upgraded in terms of armament and armour throughout the war, the Panzer IV soldiered on until the surrender of Germany in 1945, by which time 8600 of all variants had been built. Originally armed with the short-barrelled 75mm gun, experience in Russia revealed this weapon to be totally inadequate against Soviet T-34 and KV-1 tanks. The Panzer IV had originally been designed to destroy "soft" targets such as infantry, soft-skinned vehicles and anti-tank emplacements, while the Panzer IIIs were for tank-versus-tank combat. Therefore, the long-barrelled 75mm L/43 or L/48 guns were installed in Panzer IVs to enable them to knock out Soviet tanks. The Panzer IV was not an ideal design, having relatively thin, non-sloping armour that produced many shot traps and a high, box shape. However, it was a platform where the guns and armour could be upgraded. The most numerous version of the Panzer IV (3774 built) was the Ausf H (specifications below), which had a maximum armour thickness of 100mm (3.93in). To the left is the Ausf H version.

Weight: 25,000kg (55,000lb)
Crew: 5
Speed: 38kmh (23.75mph)
Range: 166km (104 miles)
Dimensions: length: 7m (22.9ft); width: 3.3m (10.8ft); height: 2.68m (8.79ft)
Armament: 1 x 75mm cannon, 3 x 7.92mm machine gun
Ammunition: 87 x 75mm, 3150 x 7.92mm
Armour: front (maximum): 100mm (3.93in); side (maximum): 30mm (1.18in)

Seventeenth Army pushes back the Soviet Twenty-Sixth Army, which forces the Twelfth Army to retreat in Moldavia. To date the Southwestern Front has lost 165,400 killed or missing, 65,700 wounded, 4400 tanks, 5800 artillery pieces and 1200 aircraft.

July 8

NORTHERN USSR, *LAND WAR*
XXXXI Panzer Corps enters Pskov.

CENTRAL USSR, *LAND WAR*
Timoshenko's counterattack fails to stop the German advance as XXXIX Panzer Corps attacks the flanks of the Twentieth and Twenty-Second Armies near Vitebsk, and then becomes involved in heavy street fighting with Konev's Nineteenth Army in Vitebsk itself. The 5th and 7th Mechanized Corps fail to smash through at the juncture of the Second and Third Panzer Groups, LVII Panzer Corps advances from the Dvina and the Germans take Polotsk.

SOUTHERN USSR, *LAND WAR*
In an effort to halt the German advance towards Kiev, Kirponos commits the 9th, 15th, 19th and 22nd Mechanized and 31st Rifle Corps to a counterattack northwest of the city. However, it is stopped by III Panzer Corps and infantry from the Sixth Army.

July 9

NORTHERN USSR, *LAND WAR*
OKH issues new orders to Army Group North regarding objectives: XXXXI Panzer Corps will advance to the River Luga prior to an assault against Leningrad, and LVI Panzer Corps will mount a flanking attack towards Lake Ilmen. Trying to stop them is the Northwestern Front, which to date has lost 73,900 troops killed or missing, 13,300 wounded, 2520 tanks, 3500 artillery pieces and 990 aircraft.

CENTRAL USSR, *LAND WAR*
Resistance in the Minsk Pocket ends, signalling the destruction of the Soviet Third, Fourth, Tenth and part of the Thirteenth Armies. The ruins of Vitebsk fall to XXXIX Panzer Corps although the Soviet Nineteenth Army continues to counterattack. To date the Western Front has lost 418,000 killed, wounded and missing; 4800 tanks; 9427 artillery pieces; and 1777 aircraft. However, it has received reinforcements totalling 45 divisions, giving it a strength of 579,000 troops by early July.

▲ A Panzer 35(t) of the 6th Panzer Division. The division had 155 Panzer 35(t)s in June; most were lost by December.

SOUTHERN USSR, *LAND WAR*
XIV Panzer Corps captures Zhitomir as the Soviet 4th Mechanized Corps and units of the Sixth Army batter the 11th Panzer Division at Berdichev. However, it is a temporary reprieve for the front, and Kirponos orders a further retreat. Losses among the Southwestern and Southern Fronts have been huge: 242,000 troops, 4400 tanks, 5800 artillery pieces and 1200 aircraft.

July 10

FINLAND, *LAND WAR*
The Finnish Karelian Army begins its offensive, advancing southeast to clear

▼ A German 50mm Pak 38 anti-tank gun in action against Soviet armour. Designed to replace the lighter 37mm Pak 36, it was issued to units in late 1940.

ARMED FORCES

THE EINSATZGRUPPEN

The Einsatzgruppen (Special Action Groups) were formed by the SS in 1939, being attached to Amt (Office) IV of the RSHA (Reichssicherheitshauptamt – Reich Central Security Office). Their task was to follow immediately behind the German armies as they advanced into the USSR, and round up Jews, gypsies, political commissars and anyone else who was perceived by the Nazis as being a real or potential threat to the "New Order" being established in the East. All persons thus taken were to be executed immediately.

There were four Einsatzgruppen, each one containing a mixture of Waffen-SS, Gestapo, Kripo (Criminal Police), SD (Security Police) and regular uniformed police personnel. Einsatzgruppe A, commanded by SS-Brigadeführer Franz Stahlecker, was attached to Army Group North. Einsatzgruppe B, commanded by SS-Gruppenführer Arthur Nebe, was attached to Army Group Centre. Einsatzgruppen C (commanded by SS-Oberführer Dr Otto Rasch) and D (commanded by SS-Gruppenführer Otto Ohlendorf) were attached to Army Group South. The combined strength of the Einsatzgruppen was 3000 men.

During Barbarossa, their activities turned into a mass hunt for Jews waged from the Baltic to the Black Sea. The method of murder was quite simple. Jews and communists (but mainly Jews) were rounded up in towns and cities (often duped into presenting themselves by promises of safe passage). They were then marched to nearby woods and ravines, made to hand over any valuables, forced to undress, then conducted in single file to long ditches that had been dug earlier. Once there, they would be shot by Einsatzgruppen personnel armed with rifles and machine guns. SS Chief Himmler attended such an execution near Minsk in early August 1941, during which he commended the firing squad on their professionalism and reminded them of the "sacred duty of their task".

As they advanced into the USSR, the Einsatzgruppen were able to enlist the help of thousands of the indigenous population to aid them. Thus, Lithuanians, Latvians, Estonians, Ukrainians and even Poles assisted the Einsatzgruppen as willing executioners. They did so for many reasons: hostility towards the Soviets (especially among the previously independent Baltic states); deep-rooted anti-Semitic sentiments that the Nazis were able to exploit; the prospect of loot; the desire of individuals to ingratiate themselves with the occupiers; and, for a few, the attraction of murder with impunity. It is estimated that the Einsatzgruppen murdered 730,000 Jews during their killing spree in the USSR between 1941 and 1944, plus tens of thousands of non-Jews.

the Karelian Isthmus. IV Corps breaks through Soviet positions at Korpiselka.

NORTHERN USSR, *LAND WAR*

XXXXI Panzer Corps fails to take Luga but LVI Panzer Corps captures Porkhov after heavy fighting. The Soviet Northern Front totals 153,000 troops, and the Northwestern Front 272,000 troops.

CENTRAL USSR, *LAND WAR*

As the Nineteenth Army continues to battle at Vitebsk, XXIV Panzer Corps crosses the River Dnieper and pushes back the Thirteenth Army.

SOUTHERN USSR, *LAND WAR*

The German Sixth Army is attacked by the 31st Rifle, 9th, 19th and 22nd Mechanized Corps near Korosten, although the Soviet assaults make little headway. Meanwhile, Kirponos mounts desperate attacks against enemy positions at Berdichev, Zhitomir and Fastov in an effort to protect Kiev.

USSR, *ARMED FORCES*

Several theatre commands (*glavkom*) are established to coordinate front defences more effectively. *Glavkom* Northwest is headed by Marshal Voroshilov (Northern and Northwest Fronts and Baltic and Northern Fleets), Marshal Timoshenko commands *Glavkom* West (Western Front and Pinsk Flotilla), and *Glavkom* Southwest is under Marshal Budenny (Southwestern and Southern Fronts and the Black Sea Fleet).

JULY 11

FINLAND, *LAND WAR*

The Soviet 52nd Rifle Division holds a German assault on the Litsa line.

CENTRAL USSR, *LAND WAR*

LVII Panzer Corps attacks towards Velikiye Luki, XXXIX Panzer Corps strikes from Vitebsk towards Smolensk, and the Second Panzer Group pushes the Thirteenth Army back from the Dnieper.

SOUTHERN USSR, *LAND WAR*

The Soviet Fifth, Sixth, Twelfth and Twenty-Sixth Armies continue in their efforts to hold the German advance, but the tanks of the First Panzer Group are pouring through a 64km (40-mile) gap between the Soviet Fifth and Sixth Armies.

JULY 12

SOUTHERN USSR, *LAND WAR*

III Panzer Corps is ready to strike at Kiev but is prevented from doing so by Hitler. The Soviet Fifth, Twenty-Sixth and Thirty-Seventh Armies are re-deployed to protect the city. In the extreme south, Romanian forces capture Balti.

USSR, *ARMED FORCES*

The Supreme Soviet orders Gulag camps to free certain categories of prisoners directly into the Red Army. Prisoners to be released for military service include those imprisoned for missing work, and those found guilty of ordinary and insignificant administrative and economic crimes.

USSR, *DIPLOMACY*

A Mutual Assistance Agreement is signed in Moscow between the Soviets and the British. It states: "The two Governments mutually undertake to render each other assistance and support of all kinds in the present war against Hitlerite Germany. They further undertake that during this war they will neither negotiate nor conclude an armistice or treaty of peace except by mutual agreement."

JULY 14

GERMANY, *STRATEGY*

Anticipating victory in the USSR, Hitler orders war production away from guns and vehicles to U-boats and aircraft.

NORTHERN USSR, *LAND WAR*

XXXXI Panzer Corps approaches the mouth of the Luga, and the 8th Panzer Division captures Soltsy.

▶ ***A welcome for the Germans in Riga, capital of Latvia, on July 7. Troops of the Eighteenth Army had reached the city on June 29.***

JULY 15

CENTRAL USSR, *LAND WAR*
Although the German panzers are advancing north and south of Smolensk, the infantry of their Second and Ninth Armies are struggling to keep up with the armoured units and are marching up to 48km (30 miles) a day. The Soviet Thirteenth Army engages in heavy combat with the enemy at Gorki and Mstislavl. Multiple rocket salvos are fired against the German 5th Infantry Division by the Twentieth Army.

SOUTHERN USSR, *LAND WAR*
The Soviet 3rd Airborne Corps is deployed to Borispol in anticipation of a German airborne assault across the Dnieper.

JULY 15

NORTHERN USSR, *LAND WAR*
As XXXXI Panzer Corps approaches Leningrad, thousands of the city's civilians begin to build a cordon of pillboxes, trenches and artillery positions. Near Lake Ilmen, LVI Panzer Corps is surrounded by the Soviet Eleventh Army.

CENTRAL USSR, *LAND WAR*
The 19th Panzer Division captures Nevel, and XXXIX Panzer Corps swings south to take Yartsevo and threaten the rear of the Western Front. As XXXXVII Panzer Corps bulls its way into Orsha it becomes apparent that the panzer pincers are closing around Smolensk.

SOUTHERN USSR, *LAND WAR*
The southern flank of the Soviet Southwestern Front is being encircled as the Seventeenth Army breaks through the Stalin Line near Bar. Meanwhile, the Romanian V Corps is marching towards Kishinev, the capital of Bessarabia.

▲ ***Some of the tens of thousands of prisoners captured by the Germans during the first two months of Barbarossa.***

JULY 17

NORTHERN USSR, *LAND WAR*
Soviet forces attacking LVI Panzer Corps are now exhausted by their efforts.

CENTRAL USSR, *LAND WAR*
The 19th Panzer Division captures Velikiye Luki but XXXIX Panzer Corps has difficulty in advancing due to Soviet resistance.

SOUTHERN USSR, *LAND WAR*
As the Germans cross the Dniester at Dubossary and threaten the rear of the Southern Front, the Romanian Fourth Army marches towards Odessa.

SOUTHERN USSR, *ATROCITIES*
When Romanian and German units enter Kishinev, many Jews are slaughtered in the streets and in their homes. In total, around 10,000 Jews are killed (Einsatzgruppe D is active in this part of the USSR). In addition, Antonescu, dictator of Romania, issued a secret order before Operation Barbarossa that all Jews in Bessarabian villages were to be murdered on the spot, Jews in the towns were to be removed to ghettos, and anyone who served the Soviets during their rule was to be executed after being found guilty. Following this murder spree the occupiers established a ghetto in the town that held 11,000 Jews.

▼ ***Panzer IIs and IIIs on the steppe. The vehicle in the foreground is an SdKfz 250 semi-tracked armoured personnel carrier.***

GERMANY, *ARMED FORCES*
The Gestapo issues an order providing for the killing of all Soviet prisoners of war who are, or might be, dangerous to National Socialism. The order states: "Above all, the following must be discovered: all important functionaries of State and Party, especially professional revolutionaries ... all People's Commissars in the Red Army, leading personalities of the State ... leading personalities of the business world, members of the Soviet Russian Intelligence, all Jews, all persons who are found to be agitators or fanatical Communists".

JULY 18

NORTHERN USSR, *LAND WAR*
The Soviet Eleventh and Twenty-Seventh Armies launch attacks against the Germans, with little success.
CENTRAL USSR, *LAND WAR*
The Second and Third Panzer Groups struggle to contain trapped Red Army units in the Smolensk Pocket. The 7th Panzer Division is halted near Yartsevo.
SOUTHERN USSR, *LAND WAR*
The Soviet Thirty-Seventh Army prepares to defend Kiev as the German Seventeenth Army crosses the River Bug and establishes a bridgehead around Vinnitsa. The Stavka orders a partial withdrawal of the Sixth, Twelfth and Eighteenth Armies.

▼ ***German DKW NZ350 motorcycle, car and captured Morris Commercial Artillery Tractor in the Ukraine. It is still dry, but the dirt tracks quickly wore out axles and suspensions of vehicles designed for use on tarmac roads.***

JULY 19

GERMANY, *STRATEGY*
Hitler issues Directive No 33 regarding the future direction of the war against the USSR. Regarding the war in the south, German forces are "to destroy the enemy Sixth and Twelfth Armies while they are still west of the Dnieper", plus the Fifth Army. In the centre, "Army Group Centre, while continuing to advance to Moscow with infantry formations, will use those motorized units which are not employed in the rear of the Dnieper line to cut communications between Moscow and Leningrad, and so cover the right flank of the advance on Leningrad by Army Group North". In the north, "the advance on Leningrad will be resumed only when Eighteenth Army has made contact with Panzer Group Four and the extensive flank in the east is adequately protected by Sixteenth Army. At the same time Army Group North must endeavour to prevent Russian forces still in action in Estonia from withdrawing to Leningrad." Forces are also to advance on the Finnish Front north of Lake Ladoga, and the Luftwaffe is ordered to undertake an air raid against Moscow.

JULY 20

CENTRAL USSR, *LAND WAR*
XXIV Panzer Corps establishes a firm position between Krichev and Mstislavl. The Stavka, in an effort to shore up the front, orders the Twenty-Fourth, Twenty-Eighth, Twenty-Ninth and Thirtieth Armies to advance west to support the Sixteenth and Twentieth Armies. Bock orders Guderian to encircle enemy forces around Smolensk before any further advances east.
SOUTHERN USSR, *LAND WAR*
XXXXVIII Panzer Corps advances towards Uman, endangering the Soviet Sixth and Twelfth Armies, which are threatened with encirclement by the panzer corps and the German Seventeenth Army.

▲ ***German troops in a captured trench. The weapons stuck in the ground are abandoned Soviet Model 1891/30 rifles.***

JULY 21

FINLAND, *LAND WAR*
The Army of Karelia reaches the eastern shore of Lake Ladoga around Salmy.
CENTRAL USSR, *AIR WAR*
Further to Hitler's Directive No 33, and specifically his desire to "burn the Kremlin to ashes", the Luftwaffe mounts its first air raid against Moscow. Some 195 bombers are involved: Junkers Ju 88s from KG 3 and KG 54; Heinkel He 111s from KG 53, KG 55, KG 28, III/KG 26 and K.Gr. 100; and Dornier Do 17s from KG 2 and KG 3. They are met by 170 Soviet fighters and heavy anti-aircraft fire over the city. In total, Soviet anti-aircraft guns fire 29,000 artillery shells and 130,000 machine-gun bullets during the raid. The Luftwaffe loses four aircraft shot down and drops 106 tonnes (104

▲ ***German troops crossing the River Luga at the end of July. The buildings on the far bank burn after a Luftwaffe attack.***

tons) of high explosives and 46,000 incendiaries on the city. The Kremlin survives.

CENTRAL USSR, *LAND WAR*
There is fierce fighting around the Smolensk Pocket, with Red Army attacks near Velikiye Luki and at Yelnya.

SOUTHERN USSR, *LAND WAR*
The panzers begin to close the pincers around Uman, trapping the Soviet Sixth and Twelfth Armies (130,00 men, 1000 artillery pieces and 384 tanks). Kirponos commits the Twenty-Sixth Army in an effort to save the trapped formations.

USSR, *ARMED FORCES*
Stalin appoints himself Defence Commissar.

JULY 23

NORTHERN USSR, *LAND WAR*
The Fourth Panzer Group engages in heavy fighting on the Luga Line.

GERMANY, *STRATEGY*
Keitel orders the Third Panzer Group north to assist in the capture of Leningrad and then move back to the centre to take part in an advance to the Volga. The Fourth Panzer Group will be withdrawn back to Germany, and the Second Panzer Group is to link up with Kleist in the Ukraine to assist in the occupation of the Donbas and Caucasus. Halder, however, wants an autumn attack against Moscow.

USSR, *ARMED FORCES*
The Stavka creates a new Central Front between the Western and Southwestern Fronts. The new front comprises the Third and Twenty-First Armies.

JULY 25

NORTHERN USSR, *LAND WAR*
The German Eighteenth Army pushes back the Soviet Eighth Army in Estonia.

SOUTHERN USSR, *LAND WAR*
The Southwestern Front withdraws on Uman as III Panzer Corps moves east along the Dnieper, and XIV and XXXXVIII Panzer Corps advance south towards Pervomaisk to link up with the Eleventh and Seventeenth Armies and trap the Sixth and Twelfth Armies around Uman (these formations have now been assigned to the Southern Front).

POLAND, *ATROCITIES*
Anti-Jewish pogrom in Lvov. With German encouragement, and working from prepared lists, civilians and police assault with clubs, knives and axes any Jew whom they encounter. Over the next three days 2000 Jews will be murdered in a pogrom known as the "Petliura Days", in commemoration of Simon (Semyon) Petliura, the Ukrainian premier who organized massive pogroms against the Jews in 1919 and was murdered in exile by a Jew in 1926.

JULY 26

FINLAND, *LAND WAR*
The Army of Karelia reaches Lake Onega at Petrozavodsk, but the Red Army is putting up heavy resistance at Suoyarve and around Lake Yanisyarve.

USSR, *AIR WAR*
The Luftwaffe's Dive-Bomber Wing 210 has completed 1574 sorties since the beginning of Barbarossa. Its aircraft have thus far destroyed 915 enemy aircraft (823 on the ground), 165 tanks, 2136 vehicles and 60 trains.

CENTRAL USSR, *LAND WAR*
The Germans seal the Smolensk Pocket, trapping 700,000 Red Army troops. The Soviets mount a series of desperate attacks to break out from the encirclement, with particularly heavy fighting at Yelnya and in the Yartsevo corridor. In addition, the Soviet Thirteenth, Twenty-First and Twenty-Eighth Armies launch assaults at Gomel, Rudnya and Roslavl against the German Second Army, which is holding the southern wing of the pocket.

LITHUANIA, *ATROCITIES*
With German encouragement, the local militia murders 1500 Jews in Kovno. A report by Einsatzgruppe A states: "To our surprise it was not easy at first to set any large-scale anti-Jewish pogrom in motion there [in Lithuania]. Klimatis, the leader of the partisan group referred to above ... succeeded in starting a pogrom with the aid of instructions given him by a small advance detachment operating in Kovno, in such a way that no German orders or instructions could be observed by outsiders. In the course of the first pogrom during the night of June 25/26, the Lithuanian partisans eliminated more than 1500 Jews, set fire to several synagogues or destroyed them by other means, and burned down an area consisting of about 60 houses inhabited by Jews. During the nights that followed, 2300 Jews were eliminated in the same way. In other parts of Lithuania similar *Aktionen* followed the example set in Kovno, but on a smaller scale, and including some Communists who had been left behind."

JULY 27

NORTHERN USSR, *LAND WAR*
As XXXXI Panzer Corps crosses the Luga at Kingisepp, the remnants of the Soviet Eighth Army dig in at Tallinn and Narva.

CENTRAL USSR, *LAND WAR*
The Soviet 61st Rifle Corps attempts to break out of Mogilev, and the 45th Rifle Corps fights its way east across the Sozh.

SOUTHERN USSR, *LAND WAR*
The Soviet Twenty-Sixth Army counter-attacks against the flank of the First Panzer Group between Kiev and Cherkassy. Despite heroic but foolhardy mass infantry attacks, the Germans break up the assault. On the southern flank of the Southwestern Front, the German Seventeenth Army launches an assault against Red Army units in the Uman area.

GERMANY, *ARMED FORCES*
Kluge's Fourth Panzer Army is disbanded, with the Fourth Army becoming an infantry force once again. Guderian's Second Panzer Group is thus removed from under Kluge's command and is placed directly under the control of Army Group Centre. This is due to disagreements between Guderian and Kluge regarding strategy and objectives, which were having an adverse effect on operations.

▼ Uman sector, July 1941. Under the gaze of advancing German troops, wounded Red Army prisoners trudge to the rear.

JULY 29

CENTRAL USSR, *LAND WAR*
In an effort to seal the Smolensk Pocket, XXXXVIII Panzer Corps is ordered to advance on Pervomaisk. In Moldavia, XXX Corps forces a gap between the Soviet Ninth and Eighteenth Armies.

USSR, *ARMED FORCES*
Following his suggestion that Kiev be abandoned, Zhukov resigns as Chief of Staff after Stalin rejects the idea.

JULY 30

GERMANY, *STRATEGY*
Hitler issues Führer Directive No 34 regarding the progress of Barbarossa: "In the Northern Sector of the Eastern front the main attack will continue between Lake Ilmen and Narva towards Leningrad, with the aim of encircling Leningrad and making contact with the Finnish Army. North of Lake Ilmen this attack will be covered in the Volkhov sector; south of Lake Ilmen it will be carried northeastwards only so far as is required to protect the right flank of the attack north of the lake. The situation around Velikiye Luki will have been previously cleared up. All forces not required for these operations will be transferred to take part in the flank attacking north of Lake Ilmen. The intended thrust by Panzer Group Three against the high ground around Valdai will be postponed until armoured formations are fully ready for action. Instead, the left flank of Army Group Centre will advance sufficiently far northeastwards to afford protection to the right flank of Army Group North.

"Estonia must first of all be mopped up by all the forces of the Eighteenth Army; only then may divisions advance towards Leningrad. Army Group Centre will go over to the defensive. Panzer Groups Two and Three will be withdrawn from the front-line for quick rehabilitation as soon as the situation allows.

"Operations on the Southeastern front will ... be conducted only by formations of Army Group South. Their objective must be to destroy the strong enemy forces west of the Dnieper and ... to establish the conditions necessary for bringing Panzer Group One later to the eastern bank of the Dnieper. The Fifth Red Army, fighting in the marshland northwest of Kiev, must be brought to battle west and annihilated.

"Finnish Front: The attack in the direction of Kandalaksha will be halted.

"Luftwaffe. Northeastern Front: The Luftwaffe will switch the main weight of air attack to the Northeastern front by attaching the bulk of VIII Air Corps to the 1st Air Fleet.

"Centre: The task of such units of the Luftwaffe with Army Group Centre is to afford such fighter cover as is absolutely necessary on the 2nd and 9th Army fronts.

"Finland: The main task of 5th Air Fleet is to support the Mountain Corps. The offensive by III Finnish Corps will also be supported at favourable points."

▶ The racial war against Jews began from the start of Operation Barbarossa. This is a German Army execution of Jews.

JULY 31

FINLAND, *LAND WAR*
The Finnish assault towards Leningrad commences as the Southeastern Army assaults the Soviet Twenty-Third Army. Meanwhile, Finnish forces continue to attack Vyborg and Vousalmi.

NORTHERN USSR, *LAND WAR*
The German X Corps reaches the southern shore of Lake Ladoga.

CENTRAL USSR, *LAND WAR*
The Second Panzer Group finishes its redeployment to the southern flank of Army Group Centre along with the Second Army. XXIV Panzer Corps attacks Group Kachalov south of Smolensk.

USSR, *GERMAN FORCES*
By the end of July German losses on the Eastern Front total 213,000 men. The army has also lost 863 tanks.

► *A Red Army 76mm Zis-3 divisional gun on the Karelian Front. This artillery piece entered service in 1941 and was still being exported by the Soviets in the 1980s.*

AUGUST 1

CENTRAL USSR, *LAND WAR*
The Soviet Twenty-Fourth, Twenty-Ninth and Thirtieth Armies mount desperate assaults in an effort to relieve those forces trapped in the Smolensk Pocket. To the south, the Soviet Twenty-First Army counterattacks near Gomel against the Second Army. However, the Second Panzer Group pierces the Red Army's front to the north, with XXIV Panzer Corps capturing Roslavl.

SOUTHERN USSR, *LAND WAR*
Despite the Soviet Fifth Army attacking the flank of the German Sixth Army from the Pripet Marshes, the German line holds. Meanwhile, Red Army units in the Uman Pocket are running out of fuel and ammunition. To the south the Soviet Ninth Army goes on the defensive. The prospects of relief for those units trapped at Uman are evaporating quickly.

AUGUST 3

CENTRAL USSR, *LAND WAR*
The German IX Corps links up with XXIV Panzer Corps south of Roslavl, trapping 70,000 troops of the Soviet Twenty-Eighth Army.

SOUTHERN USSR, *LAND WAR*
The Germans have encircled the Soviet Sixth, Twelfth and part of the Eighteenth Armies between Uman and Pervomaisk, a total of more than 200,000 men. Marshal Semyon Budenny orders the Twenty-Sixth Army to attack from the Dnieper to relieve the trapped armies, but this formation is in a weakened state.

AUGUST 5

CENTRAL USSR, *LAND WAR*
Soviet resistance ends in the Smolensk Pocket. Red Army losses are 309,000 prisoners, 3200 tanks, 3100 artillery pieces and 1000 aircraft.

SOUTHERN USSR, *LAND WAR*
As fighting continues around Malin, the Romanian Fourth Army commences the siege of Odessa.

AUGUST 6

FINLAND, *LAND WAR*
Finnish forces battle their way through to Lake Ladoga near Khitola.

NORTHERN USSR, *LAND WAR*
The German Sixteenth Army captures Cholm and Staraya Russa.

CENTRAL USSR, *LAND WAR*
The 3rd and 4th Panzer Divisions, part of the Second Panzer Group, launch fresh assaults against Gomel.

SOUTHERN USSR, *LAND WAR*
The Soviet 9th and 22nd Mechanized Corps and 1st Airborne Corps make little headway against the enemy around Malin as the Thirty-Seventh Army stalls the German XXIX Corps in Kiev's suburbs. Red Army troops begin surrendering in the Uman Pocket as units from XIV Panzer Corps capture Voznesensk to the south.

◄ *Soviet infantry await the next German assault. The soldier on the left has a 7.62mm SVT-40 automatic rifle, a complex and unreliable weapon.*

AUGUST 8

FINLAND, *LAND WAR*
To destroy Soviet units around Lake Ladoga, the Finns form I Corps, comprising the 2nd, 7th and 19th Infantry Divisions.

NORTHERN USSR, *LAND WAR*
Army Group North launches a fresh assault on Leningrad. XXXXI Panzer and XXXVIII Corps attack from the Kingisepp bridgehead, LVI Panzer Corps starts from Luga, and I and XXVIII Corps attack from the Schimsk-Novgorod-Chudovo axis. The Eighteenth Army is ordered to complete the conquest of Estonia, and the Sixteenth Army is detailed to advance into the Valdai Hills.

CENTRAL USSR, *LAND WAR*
The Second Panzer Group reduces the surrounded elements of the Soviet Twenty-Eighth Army around Roslavl, taking 38,000 prisoners, 200 tanks and 200 artillery pieces. Farther south, the Second Army commences an attack around Gomel against the Soviet Twenty-First Army.

SOUTHERN USSR, *LAND WAR*
Fighting in the Uman Pocket comes to an end with a further 103,000 Red Army troops being captured, along with 300 tanks and 800 artillery pieces.

AUGUST 11

GERMANY, *AIR WAR*
A Soviet air raid against Berlin is mounted by the newly formed 81st Long-Range Bombing Aviation Division, commanded by Major-General Mikhail Vassilievich Vodopyanov. Flying from

Pushkin near Leningrad, the Soviet bombers fly along the coastlines of Estonia and Latvia, then across the Baltic to a landfall north of Stettin, before heading for Berlin. The forces comprise 14 Petlyakov Pe-8s from Pushkin, two squadrons of Ilyushin Il-4s and a squadron of Yermolayev Yer-2s. Only 11 Pe-8s and three Il-4s reach Berlin to bomb the city, causing little damage.

August 12

NORTHERN USSR, *LAND WAR*
As the German offensive grinds forward, the Soviets counterattack with the Eleventh, Thirty-Fourth and Forty-Eighth Armies. The Thirty-Fourth is ordered to trap the German X Corps against the southern shores of Lake Ladoga and annihilate it.

◀ ***A captured Soviet train. The conversion of the railway system to the European gauge had barely started by early August.***

CENTRAL USSR, *LAND WAR*
XXIV Panzer Corps encircles elements of the Soviet Thirteenth and Twenty-Eighth Armies near Krichev.

SOUTHERN USSR, *LAND WAR*
The Soviet Thirty-Seventh Army manages to stabilize the situation around Kiev following a counterattack.

GERMANY, *STRATEGY*
Hitler issues a supplement to Directive No 34, laying down objectives for the various army groups. Army Group North: "The attack which is now in progress should result in the encirclement of Leningrad and a junction with the Finnish forces."
Army Group Centre: "The most important task here is to eliminate the enemy flanking positions, projecting deeply to the west, with which he is holding down large forces of infantry on both flanks of Army Group Centre. For this purpose close cooperation in timing and direction on the southern flank, between the adjoining flanks of Army Group South and Army Group Centre, is particularly important. The Russian Fifth Army must be deprived of any further power to operate by cutting the roads to Ovruch and Mozyr, by which it obtains supplies and reinforcements, and then finally annihilated. On the northern flank the enemy must be defeated as soon as possible by the employment of mobile forces west of Toropets. The left flank of Army Group Centre will then be moved as far northwards as is necessary to relieve Army Group North of anxiety about its right flank, and to enable it to transfer infantry divisions to take part in the attack on Leningrad. Only after these threats to our flanks have been entirely overcome and armoured formations have been rehabilitated will it be possible to continue the offensive, on a wide front and with echeloning of both flanks, against the strong enemy forces which have been concentrated for the defence

▲ ***A German motorized column on the move following the reduction of the Uman Pocket. On the right is an SdKfz 10 half-track, which was issued to panzer units.***

of Moscow. Before the beginning of this attack on Moscow operations against Leningrad must be concluded."

Army Group South: "The largest possible portion of enemy forces still west of the Dnieper must be destroyed, and bridgeheads across the Dnieper won as soon as possible. To occupy the Crimean peninsula, which is particularly dangerous as an enemy air base against the Romanian oil fields. To occupy the Donets area and the industrial area of Kharkov."

AUGUST 16

NORTHERN USSR, *LAND WAR*
The Soviet Luga line has been shattered by XXXXI and LVI Panzer Corps, forcing the Red Army to abandon Kingisepp and retreat to Gatchina. The German I and XXVIII Corps force the Forty-Eighth Army out of Novgorod.

CENTRAL USSR, *LAND WAR*
The newly formed Soviet Bryansk Front engages in heavy fighting with the Second Panzer Group and Second Army at Konotop and Chernigov.

USSR, *STRATEGY*
On receiving news from Budenny about his perilous position, Stalin orders the Southwestern Front to withdraw behind the Dnieper, except the Thirty-Seventh Army, which will protect the approaches to Kiev.

AUGUST 19

NORTHERN USSR, *LAND WAR*
The Soviet Forty-Eighth Army is forced back from Novgorod, and the Thirty-Fourth Army is mauled by LVI Panzer Corps and X Corps.

CENTRAL USSR, *LAND WAR*
The German Second Army and Second Panzer Group force the Central and Southwestern Fronts apart.

SOUTHERN USSR, *LAND WAR*
As it attempts to withdraw, the Soviet Fifth Army is attacked by the Sixth Army. Meanwhile, XIV Panzer Corps enters Dnepropetrovsk and reaches Zaporozhye. The Stavka reacts by ordering the Fifth Army across the Dnieper and the Fortieth Army to hold the Desna near Novgorod Seversky.

▲ ***Two members of the German 68th Infantry Division, which was assigned to Army Group South. At the end of 1941 it was deployed in the Poltava sector.***

AUGUST 20

NORTHERN USSR, *LAND WAR*
The German XXXXI and LVI Panzer Corps advance nearer to Leningrad. In

◄ ***A German panzer reconnaissance unit in the Ukraine. Note the Zundapp KS750 motorcycles with sidecars. Each panzer division had dozens of motorcycles, but they proved useless on soft ground and vulnerable in battle. They were thus soon phased out of service.***

the process they destroy one tank, six rifle and two militia divisions – 30,000 Red Army troops, 120 tanks and 400 artillery pieces. The Soviet Forty-Eighth Army, having been overcome by the 21st Infantry Division, is forced to give up Chudovo, meaning the Germans have now severed the Moscow–Leningrad railway line. The Forty-Eighth, now an "army" of only 6200 men, is given the ludicrous order to halt the German advance along the River Volkhov.

AUGUST 21

FINLAND, *LAND WAR*
The Finnish II Corps captures Kexholm and advances into the rear of the Soviet Twenty-Third Army.

NORTHERN USSR, *LAND WAR*
The German X and LVI Panzer Corps continue to bludgeon the Thirty-Fourth Army around Lake Ilmen.

CENTRAL USSR, *LAND WAR*
The Second Panzer Group continues its offensive operations, XXIV Panzer Corps taking Kostobobr and XXXXVII Panzer Corps lunging towards Pochep. The German Second Army forces the Soviet Twenty-First Army out of Gomel.

SOUTHERN USSR, *LAND WAR*
As the Soviet Fifth Army withdraws to the Dnieper, the SS *Leibstandarte* Division captures Kherson.

GERMANY, *STRATEGY*
Hitler revises his Directive 34, giving priority to economic objectives. Army Group South will now capture Kharkov and the Donbas region after capturing Kiev, prior to seizing the Caucasus oil fields at Maikop and Grozny. But the logistics of such an enterprise are vast and daunting.

KEY WEAPONS

KATYUSHA

The Katyusha multiple rocket launcher was better known as "Stalin's Organ", named thus by German troops due to its resemblance to a pipe organ. Stalin's Organ was seen in many forms during World War II, the rockets being mounted on various trucks (often American Lend-Lease Studebaker US6 vehicles, as shown at right), tanks and even on farm tractors.

Before the German invasion, the Red Army's artillery branch was unimpressed by the Katyusha because it took up to 50 minutes to load and fire the rockets in one salvo (a howitzer could fire up to 150 rounds in the same time). However, the great attribute of the Katyusha was its simplicity. It comprised a rack of parallel rails on which 16 or more rockets were mounted, with a folding frame to raise the rails to launch position.

The rocket itself was 1.8m (5.9ft) long and had a 22kg (48lb) explosive warhead. Katyushas were first used in July 1941 against the Germans at Orsha, and on August 8, 1941, the first eight regiments of missile artillery (36 launchers in each unit) were created. Thereafter, Katyusha batteries were often used in large numbers to create a shock effect.

Crew: 3
Range: 5km (3.1 miles)

AUGUST 22

NORTHERN USSR, *LAND WAR*
The retreating Soviet Eighth Army comes under sustained attacks from XXVI and XXXVIII Corps. Farther south, LVI Panzer and X Corps defeat the Soviet Thirty-Fourth Army and reach the River Lovat. In this engagement the Soviet formation loses 12,000 troops captured and 140 tanks and 240 artillery pieces destroyed. To date Army Group North has lost 80,000 men since June 22. Since July 10, the Soviet Northern Front has lost 40,500 killed and missing, and a further 15,000 wounded.

CENTRAL USSR, *LAND WAR*
The German 19th and 20th Panzer and 110th and 121st Infantry Divisions begin the attack against Velikiye Luki.

SOUTHERN USSR, *LAND WAR*
As the Soviet Ninth and Eighteenth Armies withdraw across the River Dnieper, the German Sixth Army launches a major assault against Red Army defences before Kiev.

USSR, *ARMED FORCES*
The ongoing disasters that are befalling the Red Army force the Stavka to reorganize its forces yet again. *Glavkom* Northwest is disbanded, as is the Northern Front. Two new fronts are created: Karelian and Leningrad.

AUGUST 24

FINLAND, *LAND WAR*
The Karelian Front fails to stop the Finnish Southeastern Army from isolating Vyborg and three Soviet rifle divisions. The Finnish 12th and 18th Divisions, of IV Corps, inflict substantial casualties on the Soviets.

NORTHERN USSR, *LAND WAR*
German forces are now within 9.6km (six miles) of Tallinn, and XXXXI Panzer Corps is only 32km (20 miles) from Leningrad, although the Soviet 41st Rifle

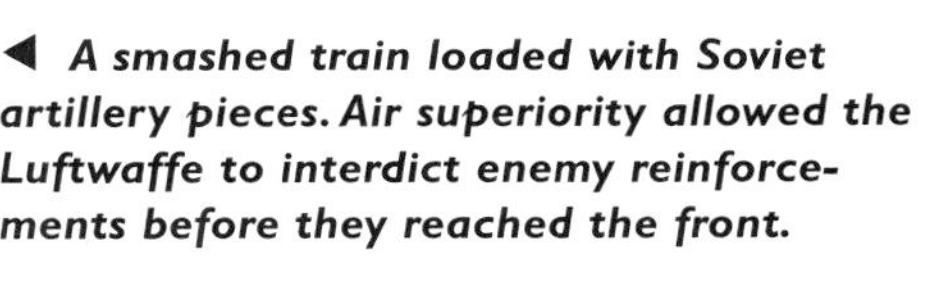

◀ ***A smashed train loaded with Soviet artillery pieces. Air superiority allowed the Luftwaffe to interdict enemy reinforcements before they reached the front.***

AUGUST 25

▶ ***German forces east of Minsk on the highway to Moscow. By this time the advance was slowing as supply lines became longer and vehicles broke down.***

Corps is fighting hard to halt its progress. XXXIX Panzer Corps, meanwhile, completes its deployment alongside I and XXVIII Corps for the investment of Leningrad from the southeast.

CENTRAL USSR, *LAND WAR*

The German LVII Panzer Corps continues to batter Velikiye Luki. Farther south, XXIV Panzer Corps captures Novo Sybkov. In an effort to slow the German advance, the Soviet Twenty-First Army launches a counterattack against the Second Army near Gomel.

AUGUST 25

NORTHERN USSR, *LAND WAR*

XXXIX Panzer Corps forces back the Soviet Forty-Eighth Army and captures Lyuban. Volkhov is now threatened by the German 20th Motorized Division.

CENTRAL USSR, *LAND WAR*

LVI Panzer Corps begins the final reduction of what is left of the Soviet Twenty-Second Army in Velikiye Luki. The Red Army in the centre is now in danger of collapse, with XXXXVII Panzer Corps capturing Trubchevsk and threatening the rear of the Soviet Twenty-First and Fortieth Armies. In response, the Stavka disbands the Central Front and transfers the Third and Twenty-First Armies to the Bryansk Front. It also orders a counterattack by the Western, Reserve and Bryansk Fronts against the Second Panzer Group to halt the German tanks.

SOUTHERN USSR, *LAND WAR*

In a further reorganization the Stavka deploys the newly formed Fortieth Army on the northern flank of the Southwestern Front, and the Southern Front is allocated the Sixth and Twelfth Armies.

AUGUST 26

FINLAND, *LAND WAR*

Finish forces are now only 11.2km (seven miles) from Viipuri.

NORTHERN USSR, *LAND WAR*

As the Red Army retreats from Tallinn, German troops come under heavy fire from Soviet ships in the harbour, causing many casualties. Meanwhile, the German Eighteenth Army and Fourth Panzer Group begin their assault on Leningrad.

CENTRAL USSR, *LAND WAR*

The German LVII Panzer Corps continues to mop up in Velikiye Luki, taking 34,000 prisoners and 300 artillery pieces. XXIV Panzer Corps and the Second Army reach the Desna, trapping the Soviet Fifth Army west of the river. Though XXXXVII Panzer Corps is overextended and its flanks threatened, the advance of the German tanks is endangering the northern flank of the whole Southwestern Front.

SOUTHERN USSR, *LAND WAR*

The Soviet Sixth Army assaults the 13th Panzer Division at Dnepropetrovsk.

IRAN, *LAND WAR*

Because of the British and American need to transport war materials across Iran to the Soviet Union, which would violate Iranian neutrality, Britain and the Soviet Union simultaneously invade Iran. The Red Army strikes from the northwest and the British across the Iraqi frontier from the west and at the head of the Persian Gulf in the south. Resistance quickly collapses. The occupation of Iran will be vital to the Allied cause: Britain, the USSR and the United States together will move more than 5.08 million tonnes (5 million tons) of munitions and other war material across Iran to the USSR during the next four years.

▼ ***German infantry near Novgorod, northern Russia, at the end of August. Advance Wehrmacht units had entered this ancient Russian city on August 16.***

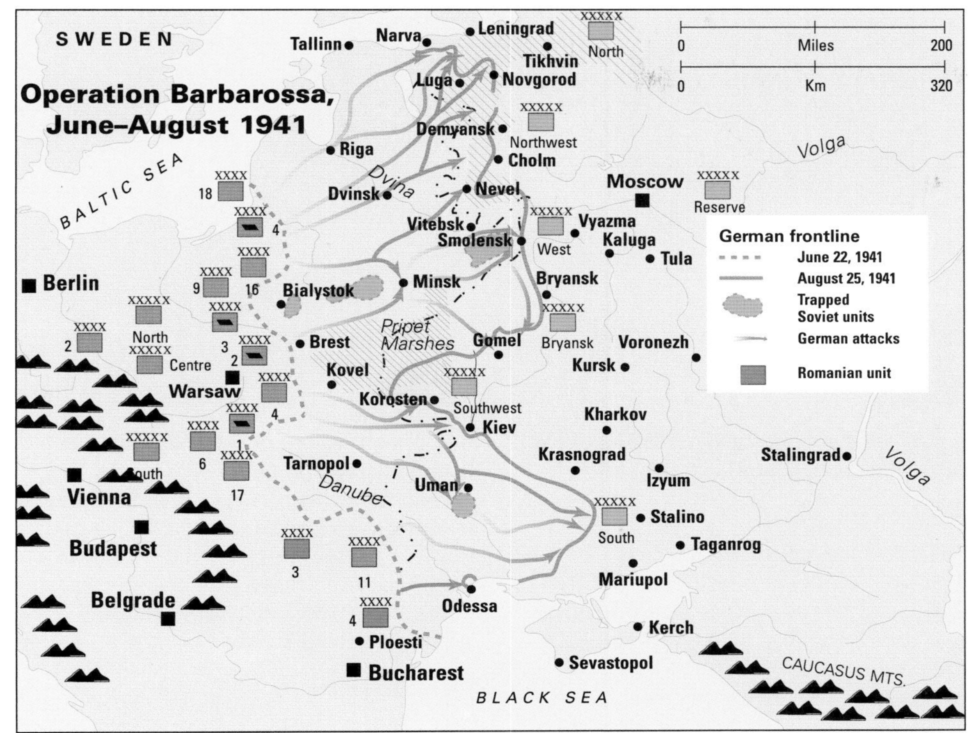

USSR, *ATROCITIES*
Hungarian forces take over Kamenets-Podolsk, arrest 14,000 Jews and turn them over to SS-Obergruppenführer Friedrich Jeckeln, Higher SS and Police Leader in the south, who promises to kill by September all the Jews whom the Hungarians have turned over. During the next two days the SS will murder all those arrested in Kamenets-Podolsk.

AUGUST 27

FINLAND, *STRATEGY*
As a sign of things to come, Mannerheim refuses to act in direct cooperation with Army Group North, signalling a divergence in the war aims of Finland and Germany.

NORTHERN USSR, *LAND WAR*
The Stavka commences the deployment of the Fourth, Fifty-Second and Fifty-Fourth Armies along the Volkhov.

CENTRAL USSR, *LAND WAR*
The Third Panzer Group pushes the Soviet Twenty-Second and Twenty-Ninth Armies across the River Dvina.

AUGUST 29

FINLAND, *LAND WAR*
The Finnish Southeastern Army recaptures Viipuri and Kivennapa as the German XXXVI Corps reaches the old Russo-Finnish border in the Salla region.

NORTHERN USSR, *LAND WAR*
Tallinn falls to the Germans. For the assault on Leningrad, Leeb organizes his forces into two groups: the Krasnogverdievsk Group (XXXXI Panzer, XXXVIII and L Corps); and the Slutsk-Kolpino Group (XXVIII Corps). In addition, Leeb deploys XXXIX Panzer Corps to the east and holds the 8th Panzer Division in reserve.

CENTRAL USSR, *LAND WAR*
Soviet attacks continue, with the Thirtieth Army trying to relieve the Twenty-Second Army; and the Sixteenth, Nineteenth and Twentieth Armies launching assaults between Dukhovschina and Yartsevo.

AUGUST 30

FINLAND, *LAND WAR*
The Finns capture Raivola.

NORTHERN USSR, *LAND WAR*
The 20th Panzer Division captures Mga and shatters the Soviet Forty-Eighth Army; the last rail link out of Leningrad to the rest of the USSR has been severed.

CENTRAL USSR, *LAND WAR*
In an effort to destroy the German Fourth Army in the Yelnya salient, Zhukov launches the Twenty-Fourth Army against the enemy position. Another Red Army assault commences against the Second Panzer Group. The Third and Fiftieth Armies attack near Roslavl, supported by the Forty-Third Army; and the Thirteenth and Twenty-First Armies are ordered to destroy the panzer group.

SOUTHERN USSR, *LAND WAR*
The German Sixth Army grinds its way into Kiev in the face of heavy resistance.

AUGUST 31

NORTHERN USSR, *ALLIED AID*
The first convoy with aid from Britain, codenamed Dervish, docks at the port of Archangel, a total of seven merchant ships escorted by the carrier HMS *Argus*.

▶ ***A panzer column passes Red Army prisoners, who, by the expression of the soldier leading the group, seem glad to be out of the fighting.***

SEPTEMBER 1

FINLAND, *LAND WAR*
The Soviet Twenty-Third Army withdraws to the old Russo-Finnish border to hold the Finns on the Sestra Line.

NORTHERN USSR, *LAND WAR*
Having lost Mga on August 31, the Germans retake the town. Leningrad comes under German artillery fire from Wehrmacht units south of the city.

CENTRAL USSR, *LAND WAR*
There is fierce fighting as the Soviet Sixteenth, Nineteenth and Twentieth Armies try to reach Smolensk. Guderian commits his reserve as the Bryansk Front attacks XXXXVII Panzer Corps.

USSR, *ATROCITIES*
The mass deportation of 440,000 Volga Germans to Kazakhstan and Siberia begins. Many will be forced to work as slave labour in Gulag camps such as Kolyma. They will then be stripped of their citizenship and will not regain their civil rights until after Stalin's death. There are 151 train convoys departing from 19 stations, with 20,000 NKVD troops and large amounts of rolling stock and other resources being diverted from the war effort. Around 50–60 people, including the young, old, women and children, are packed into each freight car and given water only when the train stops every three or four days. Food, when provided, is salted herring, which only makes the prisoners' thirst even greater. The journey will take many weeks and will result in 40 percent of those being moved dying from either cold or malnutrition.

SEPTEMBER 6

NORTHERN USSR, *AIR WAR*
The 1st NKVD Division is bombed by 300 Luftwaffe aircraft at Schlusselburg and then assaulted by XXVIII and XXXIX Panzer Corps. Hitler orders that Leningrad is to be starved into submission and its population removed by any means (there is only a month's supply of food in the city).

CENTRAL USSR, *LAND WAR*
Yelnya is recaptured by the Soviet Twenty-Fourth Army, a rare victory for the Red Army since the beginning of Barbarossa. This victory prompts the start of the Soviet practice of creating guards units. The price has been high, however, with the Twenty-Fourth Army losing 10,000 dead and 21,000 missing. Of the 103,000 troops committed to the offensive 32,000 have become casualties, reflecting the poor tactics and leadership of the Red Army.

▲ ***German troops in Finland. Note the mosquito nets the men are wearing. The many lakes in the country meant millions of biting mosquitoes.***

GERMANY, *STRATEGY*
Hitler issues the order for Operation Typhoon, the attack on Moscow.

SEPTEMBER 8

NORTHERN USSR, *LAND WAR*
Dietl's attack against Murmansk grinds to a halt. Finnish forces capture Lodenoye Pole and sever the Leningrad to Murmansk rail line. The Soviet Forty-Eighth Army is shattered around Lake Ladoga, allowing the 20th Motorized and 12th Panzer Divisions to capture Schlusselburg and sever the last link out of Leningrad.

BALTIC, *SEA WAR*
The Germans launch Operation Beowulf, an amphibious assault against the Estonian islands, which are defended by 23,600 troops and 140 artillery pieces of the Eighth Army. In the first part of the

▼ ***German artillery at the River Lovat on September 18. The Soviet Thirty-Fourth and Eleventh Armies had been unable to hold the river line.***

operation the 389th Infantry Regiment attacks the island of Vormsi, taking 200 Soviet prisoners in the process. However, it will take until October 21 before all the Estonian Islands are in German hands. They will remain so until November 1944.

CENTRAL USSR, *LAND WAR*
The German XIII Corps captures Chernigov, and the Soviet Western Front ceases offensive operations and goes over to the defensive.

GERMANY, *ARMED FORCES*
An OKW directive on the treatment of Red Army prisoners of war declares that they have forfeited every claim to be treated as an honourable enemy, and that the most ruthless measures are justified in dealing with them.

September 10

NORTHERN USSR, *LAND WAR*
Fierce fighting rages around Sinyavino as the Soviet Fifty-Fourth Army attempts to relieve the pressure on Leningrad. Meanwhile, OKH orders XXXXI Panzer Corps to Army Group Centre.

CENTRAL USSR, *LAND WAR*
XXIV Panzer Corps captures Konotop and Romny as the Soviet Reserve Front assumes a defensive posture.

SOUTHERN USSR, *LAND WAR*
Disaster is looming in the south for the Red Army: the Fifth Army is cut off on the Desna and the Thirty-Eighth Army cannot dislodge the Germans from Kremenchug. To compound problems, Stalin forbids any withdrawal of Budenny's Southwestern Front.

September 11

FINLAND, *LAND WAR*
The Soviet Seventh Army retreats behind the River Svir and digs in.

NORTHERN USSR, *LAND WAR*
The Germans close in on Leningrad, capturing Slutsk, Pushkin and battling for control of Krasnoye Selo. The Stavka takes measures to strengthen the Red Army defence, appointing Zhukov commander of the Leningrad Front, which has a strength of 425,000 troops. There are a further 85,000 men of the Fifty-Fourth Army around Volkhov plus the shattered remnants of the Forty-Eighth Army.

CENTRAL USSR, *LAND WAR*
XXXXVII Panzer Corps captures Glukhov.

SOUTHERN USSR, *LAND WAR*
With Stalin insistent that Kiev be held, the Germans move XXXXVIII Panzer Corps into the Kremenchug bridgehead as part of their plan to encircle the city.

September 12

FINLAND, *LAND WAR*
Although they capture Podporogye, the Finns are unable to make any further progress across the Svir.

NORTHERN USSR, *LAND WAR*
As the bloodletting increases around Leningrad, the 1st Panzer Division captures Krasnoye Selo and XXXXI Panzer Corps threatens to outflank the Soviet Forty-Second Army's defences at Krasnogvardievsk. The German XXVIII Corps launches an assault towards Slutsk and Pushkin. The Stavka disbands the Forty-Eighth Army and allocates its units to the Fifty-Fourth Army. The Fourth, Fifty-Second and Fifty-Fourth Armies are ordered to muster along the Volkhov. German losses reinforce Hitler's desire to starve Leningrad into submission rather than take the city by force.

CENTRAL USSR, *LAND WAR*
XXIV Panzer Corps continues to drive south. Realizing the danger to Kiev, the Stavka orders the Bryansk Front to organize an attack against the Second Panzer Group's left flank.

SOUTHERN USSR, *LAND WAR*
For advocating a withdrawal, Marshal Budenny is sacked and replaced by Timoshenko as commander of the Red Army in the south. But Stalin's obstinacy is about to spell disaster as the First Panzer Group strikes from the Kremenchug bridgehead. The German Second and Sixth Armies continue their remorseless drive against the west of the forming Kiev Pocket. The pincers are about to close around Kiev.

▼ ***The sinews of war: a German wagon loaded with ammunition moves through a burning Soviet town on September 19.***

September 14

SOUTHERN USSR, *LAND WAR*
The 3rd and 16th Panzer Divisions link up at Lokhvitsa, thus beginning the encirclement of the Southwestern Front in the Kiev Pocket. Yet another major disaster is unfolding for the Red Army.

September 16

NORTHERN USSR, *LAND WAR*
XXXXI Panzer and XXXVIII Corps resume their assaults, isolating the Soviet Eighth Army in the Oranienbaum Pocket, and XXVIII Corps then pierces Soviet defences.

CENTRAL USSR, *LAND WAR*
The German Second Army begins to redeploy along the Moscow axis.

SOUTHERN USSR, *LAND WAR*
The Soviet Fifth, Twenty-First, Twenty-Sixth, Thirty-Seventh and Thirty-Eighth Armies are cut off in the Kiev Pocket and face annihilation.

YUGOSLAVIA, *INSURGENCY WAR*
Hitler issues a directive to Field Marshal Wilhelm List, Commander-in-Chief South-east, ordering him to suppress a partisan revolt in Serbia. List will appoint General Boehme to this task. Boehme succeeded in putting down the revolt in western Serbia and inflicting more than 2000 casualties on the partisans by mid-December. His forces included the 113th, 125th and 342nd Infantry Divisions that arrived from Germany late in November, and the 704th and 714th Infantry Divisions. Unfortunately for the Germans, and a portent of things to come, large numbers of partisans fled into Croatia where a new centre of open revolt was formed.

▲ *Red Army soldiers of the Southwestern Front surrender as the Germans tighten their grip on the Kiev Pocket.*

SEPTEMBER 17

NORTHERN USSR, *LAND WAR*
The German Eighteenth Army attempts to bludgeon its way into Leningrad but is stopped by the Forty-Second and Fifty-Fifth Armies. Meanwhile, XXXXI, LVI and LVII Panzer Corps begin to redeploy south for the attack on Moscow.

SOUTHERN USSR, *LAND WAR*
The Southwestern Front begins to fragment under repeated German assaults. Stalin at last authorizes an evacuation east. The German Eleventh Army crosses the Dnieper at Berislav. The aim of its leader, Manstein, is to cut off the Crimea by seizing the Perekop Isthmus. His LIV Corps is directed to Perekop. The Romanian Third Army is advancing behind Manstein's army.

SEPTEMBER 18

NORTHERN USSR, *LAND WAR*
The Germans make more gains around Leningrad, the 1st Panzer and SS *Polizei* Divisions capturing Pushkin and XXVIII Corps taking Slutsk.

SOUTHERN USSR, *LAND WAR*
In Kiev the Soviet Thirty-Seventh Army is being ground down by the German Sixth Army. Kirponos orders all units trapped in the Kiev Pocket to battle their way east.

USSR, *ARMED FORCES*
The Soviets issue an order for the conscription of all men between the ages of 16 and 50.

SEPTEMBER 20

NORTHERN USSR, *LAND WAR*
The Soviet Eighth Army launches an attack from the Oranienbaum bridgehead in an effort to relieve the pressure on the southern part of Leningrad's defences.

SOUTHERN USSR, *LAND WAR*
As Red Army units try to escape from Kiev, Kirponos and his staff are ambushed near Lokhvitsa. Kirponos is killed.

SEPTEMBER 22

FINLAND, *LAND WAR*
Hitler halts the assault on Murmansk.

SOUTHERN USSR, *LAND WAR*
Red Army units in the Kiev Pocket are now a leaderless mob. The German Eleventh Army reaches the entrance to the Crimea, with LIV Corps assaulting the Perekop Isthmus. For the moment, however, the Red Army manages to hold

DECISIVE MOMENT

DELAYING OPERATION TYPHOON

Timing had a critical influence on the outcome of the Moscow attack, codenamed Typhoon, but there were other factors that influenced its course. First, although Army Group North had succeeded in encircling Leningrad in early September, the fact that the city was still in Soviet hands meant that Army Group North could not contribute to Operation Typhoon by mounting a flanking attack against the Soviet capital from the northwest. In addition, Hitler's insistence that Army Group South should direct its combat strength towards the conquest of the Donets basin, Rostov and the Crimea meant it could not participate directly in Typhoon. Nevertheless, both Hitler and OKH believed that Army Group Centre, suitably reinforced, could defeat Red Army forces in front of Moscow and capture the city before the end of the year. Thus, on September 15, OKH ordered the Fourth Panzer Group to withdraw half its armour and transfer it to Army Group Centre. This transfer began two days later. Unfortunately for Army Group Centre, the late conclusion of the Battle of Kiev and the time-consuming regrouping of reinforcements from the north and south meant that preparations for Typhoon were concluded only by the end of September. In addition, the panzer divisions involved were only 40–50 percent of their original combat strength.

As Typhoon got under way, the Germans were in a race against time before the autumn rains turned the ground into a sea of mud. It was a race they lost. From October 10, as reported by Guderian: "The next few weeks were dominated by the mud. Wheeled vehicles could only advance with the help of tracked vehicles. These latter, having to perform tasks for which they were not intended, rapidly wore out." There were no chains for towing, so ropes had to be air-dropped. Furthermore, mud restricted the Germans to movement by roads, along which Zhukov could concentrate his forces and form defensive strongpoints.

The cauldron battles at Bryansk and Vyazma were massive tactical successes but, ironically, they lessened the chances of strategic success. Some German spearheads were only 100km (62 miles) from Moscow by the middle of October, but the mud restricted movement to 5–10km (3–6 miles) a day (a situation that did not improve with the arrival of snow and ice). In addition, by the end of October, Zhukov had received reinforcements of at least 13 infantry divisions and 5 armoured brigades from the Far East to bolster his forces before Moscow.

The final German push for Moscow began on November 15–19, when sub-zero temperatures had firmed up the ground, but the condition of the attacking units was poor. Army Group Centre had suffered losses of 87,400 since October 2, and the combat strength of the infantry averaged 50 men per company (frostbite accounted for 500 men per infantry regiment). With no air support, bottlenecks in supply and lack of winter clothing and equipment, the chances of Typhoon succeeding were almost nil. Some panzer divisions were down to 17 operational tanks each, the moving parts of small arms froze solid, 37mm anti-tank guns were useless against the increasing numbers of T-34 tanks (causing near panic in some German units), and mechanized units became stranded due to lack of fuel. At one time, 40 degrees of frost reduced XXIV Panzer Corps' artillery to just 11 working pieces. Operation Typhoon died in the snows before Moscow.

The German failure to capture Moscow saved Stalin and his Bolshevik regime, and defeat before the gates of Moscow also dealt a massive psychological blow to the hitherto invincible Wehrmacht. Guderian again: "Only he who saw the endless expanse of Russian snow during this winter of our misery and felt the icy wind that blew across it ... and who also saw by contrast the well-fed, warmly clad and fresh Siberians, fully equipped for winter fighting – only a man who knew all that can truly judge the events which now occurred."

◀ *Some of Kiev's Jews at Babi Yar. They were forced to hand over any valuables, undress and then walk to the ravine's edge, where they were machine-gunned.*

the enemy. At Odessa, the Romanians are pushed back from the city by a Soviet counterattack.

USSR, *ATROCITIES*

Ukrainian militia, under SS orders, kill 6000 Jews in Vinnitsa. This is the finale of a killing spree that has seen a further 24,000 Jews killed in the past few days. A German eyewitness reported: "Ukrainian militia on horseback, armed with pistols, rifles and long, straight cavalry swords, were riding wildly inside and around the town park. As far as we could make out, they were driving people along from their horses – men, women and children. A shower of bullets was then fired at this human mass. Those not hit outright were struck down with swords. Like a ghostly apparition, this horde of Ukrainians, let loose and commanded by SS officers, trampled over human bodies, ruthlessly killing innocent children, mothers and old people whose only crime was that they had escaped a great mass murder, so as eventually to be shot or beaten to death like wild animals."

SEPTEMBER 23

NORTHERN USSR, *AIR WAR*

Luftwaffe ace Hans-Ulrich Rudel, piloting a Ju 87 Stuka, sinks the Soviet battleship *Marat* in shallow water in Kronstadt harbour (she is hit by bombs that detonate the forward magazines).

SEPTEMBER 26

SOUTHERN USSR, *LAND WAR*

All Soviet resistance in the Kiev Pocket ends. The Germans have taken an estimated 665,000 prisoners, killed a further 100,000 and captured or destroyed 400 tanks, 28,400 artillery pieces and 340 aircraft. It is a major disaster for the Red Army, whose Fifth, Twenty-First, Twenty-Sixth and Thirty-Seventh Armies have ceased to exist, and the Thirty-Eighth and Fortieth Armies have taken fearful losses. In total, the entire Soviet Southwestern Front now numbers only 150,000 troops. To the south the German LIV Corps captures Perekop. However, the dubious fighting qualities of the Romanians are revealed when a counterattack by the Soviet Ninth and Eighteenth Armies penetrates their lines with ease.

SEPTEMBER 29

CENTRAL USSR, *LAND WAR*

German forces are almost ready to start Operation Typhoon. The Ninth Army and Third Panzer Group will drive to the north of the city, and the Second Panzer Group and Second Army will attack from the south. In this way Moscow will be enveloped by a double pincer movement, with the panzer formations forming the outer pincers. In the centre the Fourth Army and Fourth Panzer Group will prevent Soviet units striking the flanks.

The composition of the German forces is as follows: Third Panzer Group – XXXXI and LVI Panzer Corps and Ninth Army; Fourth Panzer Group – XXXX, XXXXVI and LVII Panzer Corps and Fourth Army; Second Panzer Group – XXIV, XXXXVII and XXXXVIII Panzer Corps, XXXIV and XXXV Corps and Second Army, and Second Air Fleet and VIII Air Corps of the Fourth Air Fleet. This force numbers 1,929,000 troops, 14,000 artillery pieces, 1000 tanks and 1390 aircraft.

Opposing this juggernaut are Konev's Western Front: Sixteenth, Nineteenth, Twentieth, Twenty-Second, Twenty-Ninth and Thirtieth Armies (558,000 troops); Budenny's Reserve Front: Twenty-Fourth, Thirty-First, Thirty-Second, Thirty-Third and Forty-Ninth Armies (448,000 troops); and Eremenko's Bryansk Front: Third, Thirteenth and Fiftieth Armies (244,000 troops). In total, the Red Army musters 1,250,000 troops, 7600 artillery pieces, 990 tanks and 670 aircraft for the defence of Moscow.

USSR, *ATROCITIES*

A German SS unit, Sonderkommando 4a, working in conjunction with Ukrainian auxiliary police, begins the mass murder of Kiev's Jews at Babi Yar ravine. At the end of the day the bodies are covered by a thin layer of soil. In two days of shooting, 33,771 Jews are murdered. Tens of thousands of others will be slaughtered at Babi Yar during the coming months.

▼ *A 105mm le FH 18, the standard German divisional field howitzer, in action in the Kiev Pocket. The barrel elevation suggests an anti-tank role.*

OCTOBER 2

CENTRAL USSR, *GROUND WAR*
Operation Typhoon begins at 05:30 hours with the German Fourth and Ninth Armies, Third and Fourth Panzer Groups and VIII Air Corps attacking. The Soviet Nineteenth and Thirtieth Armies are shattered, and a 48km (30-mile) gap opens up between them. The German Fourth Army attacks at Roslavl against the Forty-Third Army, and the Fourth Panzer Group smashes into the juncture of the Forty-Third and Twenty-Fourth Armies. The Second Panzer Group and Second Army force the Bryansk and Southwestern Fronts apart.

SOUTHERN USSR, *LAND WAR*
The German Sixth and Seventeenth Armies attack the northern flank of the Southwestern Front as the First Panzer Group lances into the rear of the Southern Front. The German Eleventh Army forces the Soviet XXX Corps back along the Sea of Azov coast.

OCTOBER 3

CENTRAL USSR, *GROUND WAR*
It is becoming apparent that the Red Army is having difficulty containing the impetus of Typhoon as the Third Panzer Group and Ninth Army reach the River Dnieper and XXIV Panzer Corps rumbles into Orel. A counterattack by the Soviet Thirtieth Army fails, as does an attack against XXXXVII Panzer Corps at Seredina Buda. Eremenko requests permission to withdraw but is refused.

▲ ***German infantry in a slit trench. The heavy fluted steel canister strapped to the soldier in the foreground carries his gas mask.***

OCTOBER 5

CENTRAL USSR, *GROUND WAR*
German forces continue to make gains on the road to Moscow, the Fourth Panzer Group capturing Yukhnov and Mosalsk, XXXXVII Panzer Corps taking Karachev and XXXXVIII Panzer Corps capturing Rylsk. With yet another disaster unfolding, the Stavka orders a withdrawal of the Western, Bryansk and Reserve Fronts, with Stalin deciding to rally his forces on the Mozhaisk Line. However, this defensive line consists in the main of field fortifications and is only 50 percent complete.

SOUTHERN USSR, *LAND WAR*
With the Southern Front suffering numerous defeats, its commander, Ivan Tyulenev, is replaced by Yakov Cherevichenko. The latter immediately orders his command – Ninth, Twelfth and Eighteenth Armies – to stand firm, which means they will soon be surrounded by the First Panzer Group advancing towards the Azov coast.

OCTOBER 7

CENTRAL USSR, *GROUND WAR*
As LVI Panzer Corps advancing from the north links up with XXXX and XXXXVI Panzer Corps moving from the south near Vyazma, the Germans create another pocket, inside of which are trapped the Soviet Sixteenth, Nineteenth, Twentieth, Twenty-Fourth and part of the Thirty-Second Armies. And the Second Army links up with the 18th Panzer Division (XXXXVII Panzer Corps) east of Bryansk, isolating the Soviet Third, Thirteenth and Fiftieth Armies. The Luftwaffe flies 800 bomber sorties against the pocket.

SOUTHERN USSR, *GROUND WAR*
With the German Eleventh Army and First Panzer Group having surrounded much of the Southern Front, the Red Army units try to fight their way out of the pocket, suffering heavy casualties in the process.

USSR, *ARMED FORCES*
Zhukov is given command of the Soviet capital. In a desperate attempt to boost

DECISIVE MOMENT

MOVING SOVIET INDUSTRY EAST

The invasion of the USSR by Nazi Germany was a disaster for the Soviet economy. By the end of 1941, for example, the USSR had lost the grain lands of Belorussia and the Ukraine; one-third of its rail network; three-quarters of its iron ore, coal and steel supply; and 40 percent of its electricity generating capacity. This catastrophe would have been much worse had it not have been for the evacuation of hundreds of factories and tens of thousands of workers east to the Urals, to the Volga region, to Kazakhstan and to eastern Siberia.

The scale of the movement was astounding: between July and December 1941, 1523 enterprises, the majority steel, iron and engineering plants, were transported east. That so many could be moved was in large part due to the Soviet economy being centrally planned. Thus, before the war broke out, economists and bureaucrats had experience of building plants on greenfield sites and organizing the large-scale movements of workers. The hasty relocation was still a rushed and brutal affair. Boxcars were converted for the long journeys, each one being equipped with bunk beds, an iron stove and a paraffin lamp. A workshop superintendent was put in charge of each train, whose job it was to supervise the loading and unloading of the plant and equipment at the destination. When they arrived in the east, the workers and their families were housed in wooden barracks, and then the plant had to be re-assembled, often in sub-zero temperatures.

Despite the conditions, production was soon restarted – in the case of the Yakovlev aircraft factory, within six days of arrival in western Siberia. Once in the east, factories often had to improvise. For example, wood or peat was burnt when there were no coal supplies. Such measures saved the Soviet war economy in 1941.

morale, Stalin lifts the ban on religion throughout the USSR.

OCTOBER 8

CENTRAL USSR, *GROUND WAR*
The Soviet Third and Fiftieth Armies come under heavy and sustained attacks mounted by the Second Panzer Group and Second Army.

SOUTHERN USSR, *GROUND WAR*
The First Panzer Group begins to pummel the Soviet Ninth and Eighteenth Armies. The Germans capture Mariupol in the face of deteriorating weather conditions.

USSR, *ATROCITIES*
The liquidation of the Vitebsk Ghetto begins, the Germans using the pretext that epidemics have allegedly emanated from the place. Over the next three days 16,000 Jews will be taken to the Vitbe River, where they will be shot and their bodies thrown into the water.

OCTOBER 10

FINLAND, *LAND WAR*
Since August 23 the Soviet Karelian Front has lost 30,000 killed and missing and 32,000 wounded.

NORTHERN USSR, *LAND WAR*
The 250th "Blue" Division, made up of Spanish volunteers and formed within days of the German attack on the USSR, goes into action against the Russians for the first time in the sector between Lake Ilmen and the west bank of the Volkhov.

CENTRAL USSR, *LAND WAR*
Zhukov is given command of the Western Front as the Germans tighten their grip around the Vyazma and Bryansk Pockets. XXIV Panzer Corps reaches Mtsensk, and the German XIII Corps crosses the River Ugra. Zhukov moves up the Twenty-Sixth, Sixteenth, Fifth, Forty-Third and Thirty-Third Armies to plug the gap in the line.

SOUTHERN USSR, *LAND WAR*
The battle along the Sea of Azov is nearly over. The First Panzer Group has all but annihilated the Soviet Ninth and Eighteenth Armies, with III Panzer Corps fighting its way into Taganrog. In addition, the German Sixth Army captures Sumy. Despite these successes, Hitler is worried that there is a dangerous gap opening between Army Groups Centre and South.

GERMANY, *STRATEGY*
In the light of its success OKH expands its offensive, the Third Panzer Group being ordered to advance to Kalinin and link up with Army Group North. In the centre, the Fourth Panzer Group and Fourth Army will lunge for Moscow, while the Second Panzer Group and Second Army will assault the city on the southern flank.

OCTOBER 11

CENTRAL USSR, *LAND WAR*
As Soviet forces attempt to break out of the Vyazma Pocket, the Third Panzer Group and Fourth and Ninth Armies run into heavy Red Army resistance, which slows their progress. At Mtsensk the 1st Guards Corps sacrifices itself to slow the progress of XXIV Panzer Corps. In Moscow, orders are given to prepare 1119 factories, schools and public buildings for demolition before the Germans can capture them.

SOUTHERN USSR, *LAND WAR*
The battles along the Sea of Azov end as the Soviet Ninth and Eighteenth Armies surrender: 106,000 prisoners, 210 tanks and 670 artillery pieces. The road is now clear for the First Panzer Group to advance on Rostov.

OCTOBER 12

CENTRAL USSR, *LAND WAR*
With Kalinin under threat, the Stavka forms the Kalinin Group under Konev, though it comprises only one tank brigade and three understrength rifle divisions. The Germans continue to inch their way forward, the SS *Das Reich* Division capturing Gzhatsk and the 36th Motorized Division taking Pogoreloye. With Moscow under direct threat, 440,000 of its citizens, mostly women, children and old men, are mobilized to build defences in and around the city. In four days they will dig 96km (60 miles) of anti-tank ditches, 8000km (5000 miles) of troop trenches and lay 283km (177 miles) of barbed wire.

▲ ***Troops of the Spanish "Blue" Division on the Eastern Front. Hitler admired the Spaniards' fighting qualities but thought they were a "crew of ragamuffins".***

OCTOBER 15

CENTRAL USSR, *LAND WAR*
Fierce fighting goes on around Kalinin as the Soviet Twenty-Ninth Army

▼ ***A panzer regiment of Army Group South on the outskirts of a Russian village. The vehicles on the left and right are Panzer III medium tanks.***

launches a series of counterattacks. The Germans capture Borovsk, and resistance ends in the Vyazma Pocket. It is another colossal loss for the Red Army, with the Germans taking 650,000 prisoners, 1200 tanks and 5400 artillery pieces, thus almost annihilating the Western Front.

SOUTHERN USSR, *LAND WAR*
The Red Army continues the evacuation of Odessa. To date they have withdrawn 86,000 troops, and tonight they will pull out a further 35,000. The Southwestern Front is conducting a capable retreat in the face of faltering German advances, which are being hampered by the deteriorating weather conditions.

OCTOBER 16

NORTHERN USSR, *LAND WAR*
A new offensive begins on the Volkhov involving XXXIX Panzer and XXXVIII Corps, hitting the junction of the Soviet Fourth and Fifty-Second Armies. Heavy snow is now falling in this sector.

SOUTHERN USSR, *LAND WAR*
The Soviets have completed their evacuation of Odessa, the Romanians taking possession of the port. The latter have suffered 98,000 casualties in the siege.

OCTOBER 18

CENTRAL USSR, *LAND WAR*
XXXX Panzer Corps enters Mozhaisk against heavy resistance, and LVII Panzer Corps pierces the Soviet defence line, which is held by 90,000 troops. The Germans are also making steady progress to the southwest of Moscow.

SOUTHERN USSR, *LAND WAR*
As the German Sixth Army captures Grayvoron, the Eleventh Army's LIV Corps launches an assault designed to lance through the Perekop Isthmus into the Crimea, which is held by 200,000 Red Army troops.

OCTOBER 20

NORTHERN USSR, *LAND WAR*
In an effort to break the siege of Leningrad, the Red Army prepares to launch the Second Sinyavino Offensive. For this assault the Leningrad Front has assembled 63,000 troops, 475 artillery pieces and 97 tanks. The intention is to link up with the Fifty-Fourth Army near Sinyavino. The obstacle to this objective is a force of 54,000 German troops deployed in strong defensive positions.

CENTRAL USSR, *LAND WAR*
Combat continues to rage along the Mozhaisk axis as the German V Corps crosses the River Ruza.

SOUTHERN USSR, *LAND WAR*
The SS *Leibstandarte* Division enters Stalino but has to fight for every inch of ground as it does so.

◄ ***Troops of the SS* Leibstandarte *Division head for Stalino. The Soviets have fired this village as part of their scorched earth policy.***

DECISIVE MOMENT

THE FINNS REFUSE TO ATTACK LENINGRAD

Following the Winter War of 1939–40, Finland was eager to get back the territory she had lost to the USSR. As early as December 5, 1940, the Germans had stated that they expected the Finns to cooperate with their plans for military operations against the Soviets in the Arctic, and Hitler's Directive No 21 of December 18 included the Finns cooperating with Army Group North in an assault against Leningrad. Finland's aims were, however, different from those of Nazi Germany. In February 1941, the Finnish General Staff informed Colonel Buschenhagen, Chief of Staff of the German Army of Norway, that Finland's strategic aims were limited to liberating Soviet-occupied Karelia. President Ryti believed Finland should stay out of any Russo-German war. And when Operation Barbarossa was launched, the Finns were quick to point out that they were participating only to retake the territory lost in 1940 (they had only joined the offensive following Soviet air raids on June 25). Indeed, when the Germans requested Finnish aid against Leningrad, Marshal Mannerheim, Finnish Commander-in-Chief, answered on August 27 that Finland had no interest in capturing the city. By December 1941, the Finns had advanced to the outskirts of Leningrad and the River Svir, but there they halted and dug in, making no attempt to take part in the siege of the city.

▲ ***German troops on the outskirts of Kharkov in late October. To their front is a StuG III assault gun, a vehicle specifically designed for infantry support.***

OCTOBER 23

USSR, *ATROCITIES*
In retaliation for a bomb attack against the Romanian garrison in Odessa, 34,000 of the city's Jews are murdered either by shooting or being herded into buildings which are then set on fire. Odessa is now the administrative seat of Transnistria (the Ukraine between the Bug and Dniester) under Romanian control.

OCTOBER 24

NORTHERN USSR, *LAND WAR*
The Second Sinyavino Offensive commences but fails to dislodge the Germans from their defensive positions.

CENTRAL USSR, *LAND WAR*
The city of Torzok becomes the focus of intense fighting between the Third Panzer Group and Soviet Kalinin Front in the battle for Moscow. As XXIV Panzer Corps

▲ ***On the way to Moscow. German troops hitch a lift on Panzer IIIs during Operation Typhoon. Note the greatcoats, a sign that winter was not far away.***

captures Chern, and LIII Corps takes Belev, the battered Bryansk Front is ordered to withdraw to cover the southern approaches to Moscow. The German Ninth Army, having taken part in the reduction of the Vyazma Pocket, redeploys to join the Third Panzer Group's efforts around Kalinin.

SOUTHERN USSR, *LAND WAR*
The German Sixth and Seventeenth Armies enter Kharkov, and the Sixth takes Belgorod. The First Panzer Group enters the Donbas to capture the area's industry, but the Soviets have evacuated or destroyed the mines and factories.

OCTOBER 25

CENTRAL USSR, *LAND WAR*
Resistance ends in the Bryansk Pocket. Yet again the Red Army suffers grievous losses with the Third, Thirteenth and units of the Fiftieth Armies being wiped out – 50,000 troops killed. Operation Typhoon continues to grind forward, with the 10th Panzer Division capturing Ruza.

SOUTHERN USSR, *LAND WAR*
Following heavy battles in the city, Kharkov falls to the Germans.

OCTOBER 31

CENTRAL USSR, *LAND WAR*
Typhoon begins to falter as the German Ninth Army gets embroiled in combat around Kalinin, the Third Panzer Group is locked in combat with the Soviet Nineteenth and Thirtieth Armies, and the Fourth Panzer Group and Fourth Army are held up on the River Nara.

SOUTHERN USSR, *LAND WAR*
As the Soviet Fifty-First Army retreats in the Crimea, the Germans capture 65,000 prisoners. Heavy snow begins to fall at the front, slowing the German advance.

GERMAN ARMY, *EASTERN FRONT*
To date the German Army has incurred 686,000 casualties on the Eastern Front, including 145,000 killed (41,000 have been killed in October). Wehrmacht strength stands at 2.7 million men.

◄ ***German troops advancing in southern Russia. Despite its losses, by the end of October the Red Army still had 2.2 million troops fighting on the Eastern Front.***

NOVEMBER 2

SOUTHERN USSR, *LAND WAR*
The German Eleventh Army captures Simferopol, capital of the Crimea. Two days later the Eleventh also captures Feodosia.

NOVEMBER 7

NORTHERN USSR, *LAND WAR*
XXXIX Panzer Corps closes in on Tikhvin as the Red Army struggles to contain the German advance. Leningrad itself comes under Luftwaffe attack.

CENTRAL USSR, *LAND WAR*
Army Group Centre redeploys for the next stage of Operation Typhoon. The Third Panzer Group will deploy between the Ninth Army and Fourth Panzer Group with the aim of reaching Moscow from the north. However, the temperature is dropping and the Germans have no winter uniforms. As a result, cases of frostbite are appearing among the ranks.

SOUTHERN USSR, *LAND WAR*
The First Panzer Group continues its advance towards Rostov, the German plan being to drive straight into the city.

USSR, *STRATEGY*
On the anniversary of the October Revolution, Stalin makes a speech in Moscow's Red Square predicting a German disaster. Among the gross distortions and lies, Stalin makes an accurate assessment of Operation Typhoon: "The German invaders are straining their last forces. There is no doubt that Germany cannot keep up such an effort for any long time."

NOVEMBER 9

NORTHERN USSR, *LAND WAR*
In freezing temperatures, XXXIX Panzer Corps captures Tikhvin and pushes on towards the Svir. The Soviet Fourth Army fights to prevent a German link-up with the Finns. The Fourth numbers just 62,700 troops, the Fifty-Second Army 42,000 and the Fifty-Fourth 55,600. However, they are holding the Germans.

SOUTHERN USSR, *LAND WAR*
As the First Panzer Group nears Rostov, Timoshenko organizes a counterattack using the Ninth, Twelfth, Eighteenth and Thirty-Seventh Armies. The Fifty-Sixth Independent Army will pin the panzer group with a frontal assault.

NOVEMBER 11

CENTRAL USSR, *LAND WAR*
The Soviet Fortieth and Forty-Ninth Armies counterattack the German XXXXIII Corps north of Tula, heralding five days of heavy fighting.

SOUTHERN USSR, *LAND WAR*
The First Panzer Group rests for refitting, and temporarily halts its attack on Rostov.

NOVEMBER 12

NORTHERN USSR, *LAND WAR*
The Soviets counterattack at Tikhvin with the Fourth Army, and the Soviet Fifty-Second Army attacks at Malaya Vyshera.

GERMANY, *STRATEGY*
A conference of army group and army commanders at Orsha decides that Army Group North will assume a defensive posture while Army Group Centre will continue the attack against Moscow. Army Group South will capture Rostov and then drive into the Caucasus.

USSR, *STRATEGY*
Zhukov, realizing that Moscow is still in danger, places the Western Front on high alert. This formation has lost 750,000 troops since October and numbers only 250,000 men. It comprises the Thirtieth,

▶ *German trucks during Operation Typhoon. Winter conditions put a strain on mechanical parts, forcing the Germans to cannibalize broken-down vehicles for spares.*

▲ ***German forces suffered many cases of frostbite during Typhoon, especially when troops overheated from combat were forced to spend the night in the open.***

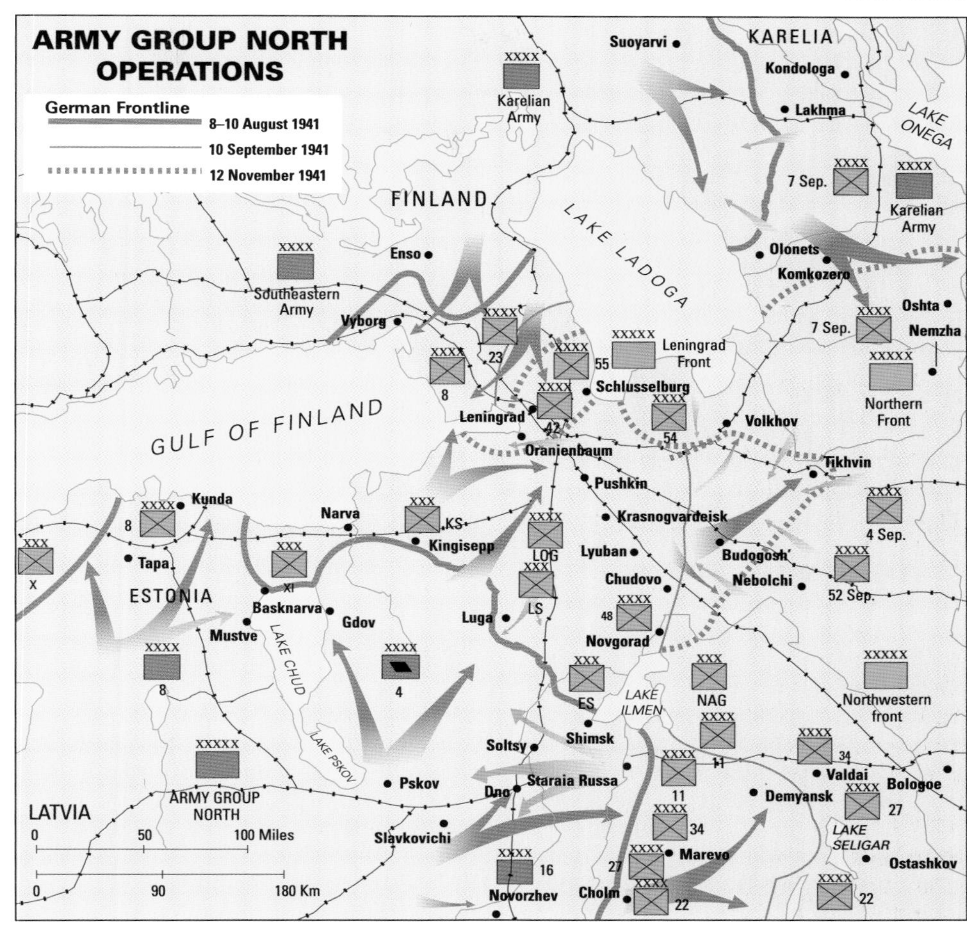

Sixteenth, Fifth, Thirty-Third, Forty-Ninth and Fiftieth Armies. To the front's north is Konev's Kalinin Front (Twenty-Second, Twenty-Ninth and Thirty-First Armies).

NOVEMBER 15

NORTHERN USSR, *LAND WAR*
The Red Army withdraws from Volkhov.

CENTRAL USSR, *LAND WAR*
The Germans commence the second phase of Operation Typhoon. The Third Panzer Group, supported by the Ninth Army, attacks the Thirtieth Army around Kalinin and heads for Klin. The Fourth Panzer Group tears into the Sixteenth Army in front of Istra. However, the Soviet Forty-Ninth and Fiftieth Armies halt the tanks of the Second Panzer Group north of Tula.

SOUTHERN USSR, *LAND WAR*
The German Eleventh Army continues its success in the Crimea, and is now in control of most of the peninsula, aside from Sevastopol and Kerch.

NOVEMBER 16

CENTRAL USSR, *LAND WAR*
A Soviet spoiling attack by the Soviet Sixteenth Army against units of the Ninth Army and Third Panzer Group fails. The Germans then counterattack, forcing a crossing of the River Lama. The Fourth Panzer Group then attacks the Sixteenth Army, tearing it to pieces and also mauling the Thirtieth Army to the north. The only success for the Red Army is its attacks against XIII Corps, which suffers heavily.

SOUTHERN USSR, *LAND WAR*
The First Panzer Group resumes its drive to Rostov. Soviet losses in the battle for the city thus far have been high: Southwestern Front, 11,200 killed and missing; Southern Front, 132,000 killed and missing. In the Crimea the Germans take Kerch, capturing 100,000 troops as they do so. During the Crimea battles, the Red Army has lost 48,000 killed and missing, 15,000 wounded, plus 700 artillery pieces and 160 tanks captured or destroyed.

NOVEMBER 17

CENTRAL USSR, *LAND WAR*
The Soviet Thirtieth Army is transferred to the Western Front to support the hard-pressed Sixteenth Army.

◀ ***German troops clearing the aftermath of a heavy snowfall in November. They also hired civilians for shovelling and for driving horse-drawn snow ploughs.***

NOVEMBER 18

SOUTHERN USSR, *LAND WAR*
To support the assault against Rostov, the German Eleventh Army transfers the 73rd Infantry Division to the First Panzer Group, which is pinning down the Soviet Eighteenth Army as it strikes towards the city. The Soviet Thirty-Seventh Army has also hit the flanks of the panzer group, although without much success thus far. Rostov is defended by the Fifty-Sixth Independent Army, which is being attacked by III Panzer Corps.

NOVEMBER 18

NORTHERN USSR, *LAND WAR*
The Soviet Fifty-Second Army encircles units of XXXVIII Corps at Malaya Vyshera. German counterattacks fail to dislodge the Soviets from the town.

CENTRAL USSR, *LAND WAR*
The Third and Fourth Panzer Groups and Ninth Army continue to grind into Soviet defences north of Moscow. The German Fourth Army, however, fails to cross the River Oka due to Red Army resistance. To the south, XXIV Panzer Corps attacks the Fiftieth Army, but then a counterattack from Venev causes panic among German units. To avoid this sector crumbling altogether, Guderian is forced to counter-attack with XXXXVII Panzer Corps into the right flank of the Western Front.

SOUTHERN USSR, *LAND WAR*
The Soviet Thirty-Seventh Army continues to attack the First Panzer Group.

NOVEMBER 20

NORTHERN USSR, *LAND WAR*
The Soviet Fifty-Second Army continues its actions at Malaya Vyshera, as the Germans feed troops into Tikhvin in the face of the Fourth Army's assaults.

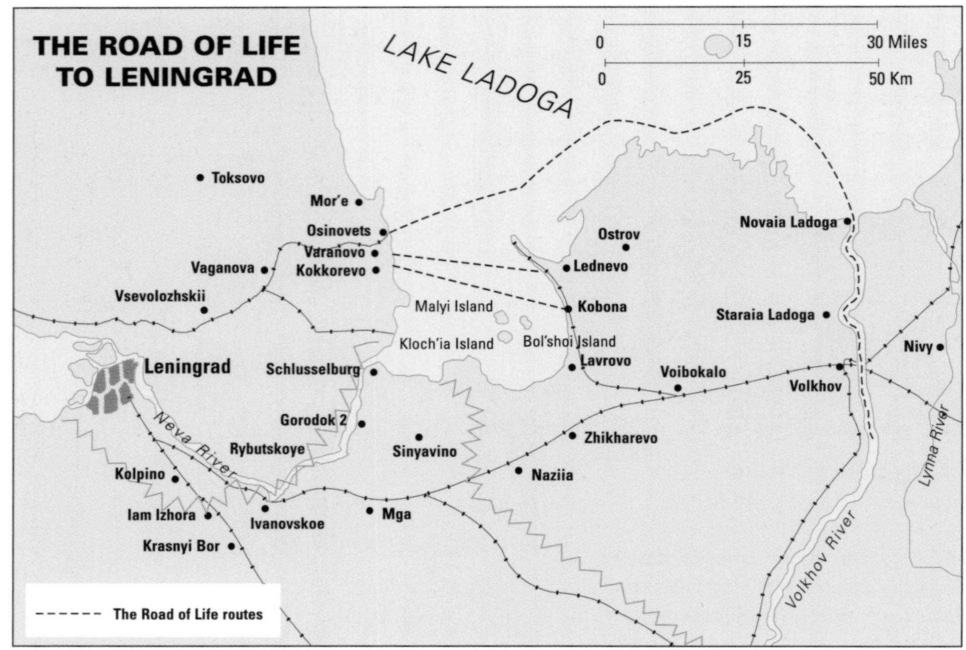

CENTRAL USSR, *LAND WAR*
The Germans inflict major casualties on the Soviet Fifth, Sixteenth, Thirtieth and Fiftieth Armies. The Third Panzer Group makes good progress, although the Fourth Panzer Group is suffering losses. XXIV Panzer Corps captures Tim.

SOUTHERN USSR, *LAND WAR*
Most of Rostov has fallen to the Germans, together with 10,000 prisoners. But the Soviet Fifty-Sixth Independent Army continues to launch attacks, and there now exists a gap between the First Panzer Group and the German Seventeenth Army. In addition, III Panzer Corps has to switch the 13th and 14th Panzer Divisions to Tuslov to counter the continuing attacks by the Soviet Thirty-Seventh Army.

NOVEMBER 22

CENTRAL USSR, *LAND WAR*
The spearhead units of the Third Panzer Group are now only 48km (30 miles) north of Moscow. Zhukov commits the 2nd Cavalry Corps at Kashira to block the Second Panzer Group's advance, and XXXXVIII Panzer Corps is attacked near Tim by Timoshenko's forces.

NOVEMBER 24

CENTRAL USSR, *LAND WAR*
The 7th Panzer Division captures Klin, the 2nd Panzer Division takes Solnechnogorsk and the 10th Motorized Division enters Michailov. Meanwhile, the 78th Rifle Division, a Siberian unit, prepares to defend Istra, the linchpin of the Soviet defences in front of Moscow.

SOUTHERN USSR, *LAND WAR*
Under frontal and flank attacks, the First Panzer Group withdraws from Rostov to the River Mius. Rundstedt is determined to prevent his units from being encircled.

NOVEMBER 26

CENTRAL USSR, *LAND WAR*
The 7th Panzer Division is now at the Moscow–Volga Canal as the 78th Rifle Division defends Istra against the SS *Das Reich* Division and 10th Panzer Division. What is left of the Soviet 2nd Cavalry Corps continues to engage the advancing 17th Panzer Division on the road to

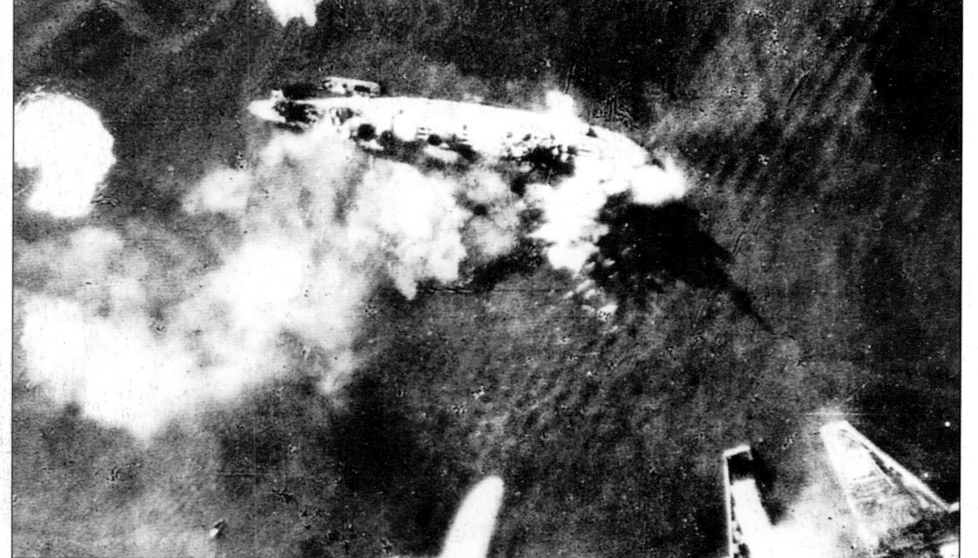

◀ Kronstadt naval base under Luftwaffe attack on November 29. The Stavka moved the bulk of the Baltic Fleet from Kronstadt to Leningrad during the winter of 1941–42.

▲ *As German armies advanced east, the Einsatzgruppen carried on their murderous work as part of Himmler's plan to clear the conquered areas of "undesirables".*

Kashira. In recognition of its efforts, it has been renamed 1st Guards Cavalry Corps.

NOVEMBER 28

NORTHERN USSR, *LAND WAR*
The German Eighteenth Army is being pushed back west under relentless pressure from the Soviet Fourth, Fifty-Second and Fifty-Fourth Armies.

CENTRAL USSR, *LAND WAR*
The 7th Panzer and 14th Motorized Divisions roll into Yakhroma, 32km (20 miles) north of Moscow. After fierce fighting, the *Das Reich* and 10th Panzer Divisions have captured Istra. However, the Western Front is attacking XXXXIII Corps, and the Soviet command has the First Shock and Tenth Armies just behind the line ready to commit to the fighting.

SOUTHERN USSR, *LAND WAR*
As most of the First Panzer Group pulls back to the Mius, the Red Army recaptures Rostov. An irritated Hitler orders Rundstedt to hold on to all his positions.

NOVEMBER 29

USSR, *ATROCITIES*
Near Riga, the massacre of 38,000 Jews by the Germans begins.

NOVEMBER 30

CENTRAL USSR, *LAND WAR*
XXXXVI and XXXX Panzer Corps and V Corps tighten their grip around the Soviet Fifth and Sixteenth Armies. However, the Stavka releases the First Shock and Twentieth Armies from the reserve to relieve the pressure on the hard-pressed Soviet armies. Zhukov intends to destroy the whole of Army Group Centre in front of Moscow. To achieve this he will attack on three axes: northern flank – First Shock, Sixteenth, Twentieth and Thirtieth Armies; centre – Fifth, Thirty-Third, Forty-Third and Forty-Ninth Armies; and southern flank – Tenth and Fiftieth Armies. These forces total 718,000 troops, 7985 artillery pieces and 720 tanks. Facing them are 801,000 troops, 14,000 artillery pieces and 1000 tanks of Army Group Centre, which is now in a parlous state.

SOUTHERN USSR, *LAND WAR*
Rundstedt pulls his forces back to the Mius. The Führer accuses the field marshal of defeatism, sacks him and appoints Walter von Reichenau in his place.

▲ *Field Marshal von Rundstedt was the scapegoat for the setback at Rostov. Hitler was to sack this most loyal of generals no less than three times during the war.*

▼ *The winter proved problematic for the panzers: their narrow tracks and low ground clearance meant they sank deep into the snow.*

December 1

December 1

NORTHERN USSR, *LAND WAR*
The German I Corps at Tikhvin continues to hold out against concentrated assaults by the Leningrad Front seeking to relieve the city.

CENTRAL USSR, *LAND WAR*
The German Fourth Army grinds forward towards Naro-Fominsk, with Zhukov feeding reserves into the line to halt the enemy. The Stavka commits the Tenth Army, threatening the southern flank of the Second Panzer Group and stalling Guderian's further advance. It is becoming obvious that Army Group Centre is at the end of its endurance, which Bock states to Hitler. The Führer, however, insists on continuing Operation Typhoon.

SOUTHERN USSR, *LAND WAR*
As the First Panzer Group and the Seventeenth Army continue their fighting withdrawal, Hitler at last permits his forces to pull back to the Mius river line.

USSR, *ATROCITIES*
The commander of Einsatzkommando 3, Karl Jaeger, reports to his superiors on the killing of Jews in Lithuania.
"I can confirm today that Einsatzkommando 3 has achieved the goal of solving the Jewish problem in Lithuania. There are no more Jews in Lithuania, apart from working Jews and their families. These number: in Shavli, about 4500; in Kovno, about 15,000; in Vilna, about 15,000."

He provides details of the murders, carried out with the cooperation of local units: "The carrying out of such *Aktionen* is first of all an organizational problem. The decision to clear each sub-district systematically of Jews called for a thorough preparation for each *Aktion* and the study of local conditions. The Jews had to be concentrated in one or more localities and, in accordance with their numbers, a site had to be selected and pits dug. The marching distance from the concentration points to the pits averaged 4–5km [2.5–3.1 miles]. The Jews were brought to the place of execution in groups of 500, with at least 2km [1.25 miles] distance between groups. All the officers and men of my command in Kovno took an active part in the *Grossaktionen* in Kovno."

But he complains: "I wanted to eliminate the working Jews and their families as well, but the Reichskommissar [Civil Administration] and the Wehrmacht attacked me most sharply and issued a prohibition against having these Jews and their families shot."

▲ ***Troops of Major-General L M Dovator's 2nd Guards Cavalry Corps, which took part in Zhukov's counteroffensive. The Jewish Dovator was killed on December 20.***

▼ ***The fate of thousands of German troops during Typhoon: death in the snow. Most German troops had only overcoats, sweaters and hoods to combat the cold.***

December 4

CENTRAL USSR, *LAND WAR*
Operation Typhoon finally splutters to a halt. The Third and Fourth Panzer Groups can go no farther, and the Fourth Army withdraws back to the Nara. Zhukov prepares to unleash his offensive: 100,000 troops of the Kalinin Front, 558,000 troops of the Western Front and 60,000 troops of the Southwestern Front.

December 5

USSR, *AIR WAR*
Since September 28, the Luftwaffe has lost 489 aircraft destroyed and 333 damaged on the Eastern Front.

CENTRAL USSR, *LAND WAR*
Zhukov's counteroffensive begins in the early morning with the Thirty-First Army attacking the German Ninth Army south of Kalinin, followed by offensives by the Soviet Fifth and Twenty-Ninth Armies.

December 6

NORTHERN USSR, *LAND WAR*
The Soviet Fourth Army continues to hammer away at Tikhvin, and the Fifty-Second Army mounts attacks against the Germans at Malaya Vyshera.

CENTRAL USSR, *LAND WAR*
The Soviet First Shock, Twentieth and Thirtieth Armies begin their assaults along the Moscow–Volga Canal and at Krasnaya Polyana. The Third Panzer Group is forced to conduct a fighting retreat to Klin. The Tenth Army ploughs into the southern flank of the Second Panzer Group, forcing Guderian to order a withdrawal to the Don, Shat and Upa Rivers. The German Second Army at Yelets also comes under pressure from the Thirteenth Army.

December 7

CENTRAL USSR, *LAND WAR*
The Soviet Thirtieth Army breaks through the Third Panzer Group's lines northeast

of Klin. The First Shock, Sixteenth and Twentieth Armies continue their attacks, their main objective being the destruction of enemy forces at Krasnaya Polyana. The Second Panzer Group is pushed back by the Tenth and Fiftieth Armies, the Tenth recapturing Michailov and the Fiftieth nearing Tula to cut off the Second Panzer Group.

GERMANY, *ARMED FORCES*
After suffering a heart attack, Brauchitsch, Chief of the Army General Staff, tenders his resignation, an offer that is not immediately accepted by Hitler.

DECEMBER 8

NORTHERN USSR, *LAND WAR*
The German Eighteenth Army is under severe pressure at Tikhvin and is on the verge of losing the town.

CENTRAL USSR, *LAND WAR*
The Thirtieth Army passes Klin in the north, and the First Shock Army is approaching the town. These moves threaten the Third Panzer Group. The Soviet Sixteenth and Twentieth Armies continue to make steady gains, although to the south the Fiftieth Army is held up before Tula by the 3rd Panzer and 296th Infantry Divisions. The Soviet Third Army batters the German Second Army, and Soviet horsemen of the 55th Cavalry Division pour into the German rear.

GERMANY, *STRATEGY*
Hitler issues Directive No 39. As the Wehrmacht fights for its life on the Eastern Front, Hitler dictates that:
"The severe winter weather which has come surprisingly early in the East, and the consequent difficulties in bringing up supplies, compel us to abandon immediately all major offensive operations and to go over to the defensive. The way in which these defensive operations are to be carried out will be decided in accordance with the purpose which they are intended to serve, viz:
"(a) To hold areas which are of great operational or economic importance to the enemy.
"(b) To enable forces in the East to rest and recuperate as much as possible.
"(c) Thus to establish conditions suitable for the resumption of large-scale offensive operations in 1942."

In an oblique admission of the losses incurred in Russia, the directive ends with measures to supply fresh manpower to the Eastern Front: "The replacement of personnel of the Armed Forces for 1942 must be ensured even in the event of heavy casualties. As the Class of 1922 will not be sufficient alone for this purpose, drastic steps are necessary."

DECEMBER 9

NORTHERN USSR, *LAND WAR*
The Red Army recaptures Tikhvin after bitter fighting, allowing supplies into Leningrad. The German Eighteenth Army retreats to the Volkhov.

CENTRAL USSR, *LAND WAR*
The Soviet First Shock Army recaptures Fedorovka and the Sixteenth and Twentieth Army continue to push west. Kleist reinforces the threatened Third Panzer Group with the 10th Panzer Division. XXXXVII Panzer Corps retreats from east of Tula, and XXIV Panzer Corps is hit by the Fiftieth Army. The German Second Army is forced to retire, creating a gap between it and the Second Panzer Group, through which the Soviet 5th Cavalry Corps and 121st Rifle Division pour.

▲ ***Field Marshal von Brauchitsch, head of the army, whose health collapsed as Hitler sought scapegoats in late 1941. The Führer accepted his resignation on December 19.***

DECEMBER 11

CENTRAL USSR, *LAND WAR*
In an effort to slow the Soviet advance, the Germans blow up the Istra dam, which halts the progress of the Soviet Sixteenth Army. The Fiftieth Army is also slowed. Nevertheless, the gap between the Second Panzer Group and Second Army could lead to the encirclement of Army Group Centre.

SOUTHERN USSR, *LAND WAR*
The German First Panzer Group, Sixth and Seventeenth Armies are now on the

▼ ***A German artillery column withdraws west from Moscow. The head of Army Group Centre, Bock, believed that his command was in danger of collapsing "in ruins" in the face of Zhukov's assault.***

▲ *Well-dressed and equipped Siberian troops of the Red Army march past a destroyed German vehicle column in mid-December.*

defensive and are fighting to stop enemy incursions into the Donbas and eastern Ukraine. Red Army units are massing to cross both the Mius and Donets Rivers.

DECEMBER 12

TURKEY, *ATROCITIES*
The *Struma*, an old cattle boat built in 1867, leaves Romania for Palestine. On board are 769 Jews who have spent their savings to escape persecution. Their plan is to sail to Istanbul and there obtain immigration visas for Palestine.

At Istanbul the passengers were confined to the ship for 10 weeks, with the British refusing to accept the Jews into Palestine. The Turkish authorities also refused to transfer the Jews to a transit camp on land. Finally, on February 23, 1942, the Turkish police towed the ship into the open sea, although it had no water, food or fuel on board. Within a few hours it was sunk, struck by a torpedo apparently launched from a Soviet submarine. Only one person survived.

DECISIVE MOMENT

HITLER'S "NO RETREAT" ORDER

The failure of Operation Typhoon and the subsequent Soviet counteroffensive had sparked a crisis for the German Army on the Eastern Front in December 1941. With troops suffering from a lack of winter clothing, weapons, fuel and reserves, plus a fear of being taken prisoner by the Russians, German commanders all along the front were requesting permission to withdraw, particularly Bock, commander of Army Group Centre; Leeb, who headed Army Group North; and Kluge, commander of the Fourth Army under Bock. Hitler's response to any request to retreat was to refuse permission. For example, when Bock stated that his front might collapse at any moment, Hitler replied: "That is a risk I must just take".

On December 17, 1941, Hitler issued an order to all German soldiers on the Eastern Front: "Major withdrawal movements cannot be made. They will result in the complete loss of heavy weapons and equipment. Under the personal leadership of commanders and officers alike, the troops are to be forced to put up a fanatical resistance in their lines, regardless of any enemy breakthrough in their flanks and rear. Only this kind of fighting will win the time we need to move up the reinforcements I have ordered from the home country and the west."

As the Soviet counteroffensive gathered momentum, German forces suffered horrendous equipment losses. Still Hitler forbade any withdrawals, believing, probably correctly, that any strategic retreat would spark a general collapse. On December 31, for example, he argued with Field Marshal Kluge for three hours over the telephone regarding a request to pull back. And those commanders who disobeyed him – Guderian, Reichenau, Sponeck and Hoepner – were dismissed. The troops stayed in their positions, and the Eastern Front was saved from collapse.

DECEMBER 13

CENTRAL USSR, *LAND WAR*
The Soviet Twenty-Ninth and Thirty-First Armies cut the German line of retreat from Kalinin as the Fifth and Sixteenth Armies approach Istra. Red Army tanks and cavalry continue to pour through gaps in the German line. More worrying for the Wehrmacht is the growing vulnerability of the Second Panzer Group, which is now without flank cover.

USSR, *ATROCITIES*
Men of Einsatzgruppe D and German police finish the execution of 12,500 Jews who had been held in Simferopol. The victims had been transported out of the town in trucks, unloaded and then shot.

DECEMBER 15

NORTHERN USSR, *LAND WAR*
The German I and XXXVIII Corps, on the Volkhov, fail to prevent the Red Army from establishing a bridgehead on the river south of Lake Ladoga. This threatens the German investment of Leningrad.

CENTRAL USSR, *LAND WAR*
The Soviet offensive before Moscow continues to pay dividends, the Twenty-Ninth

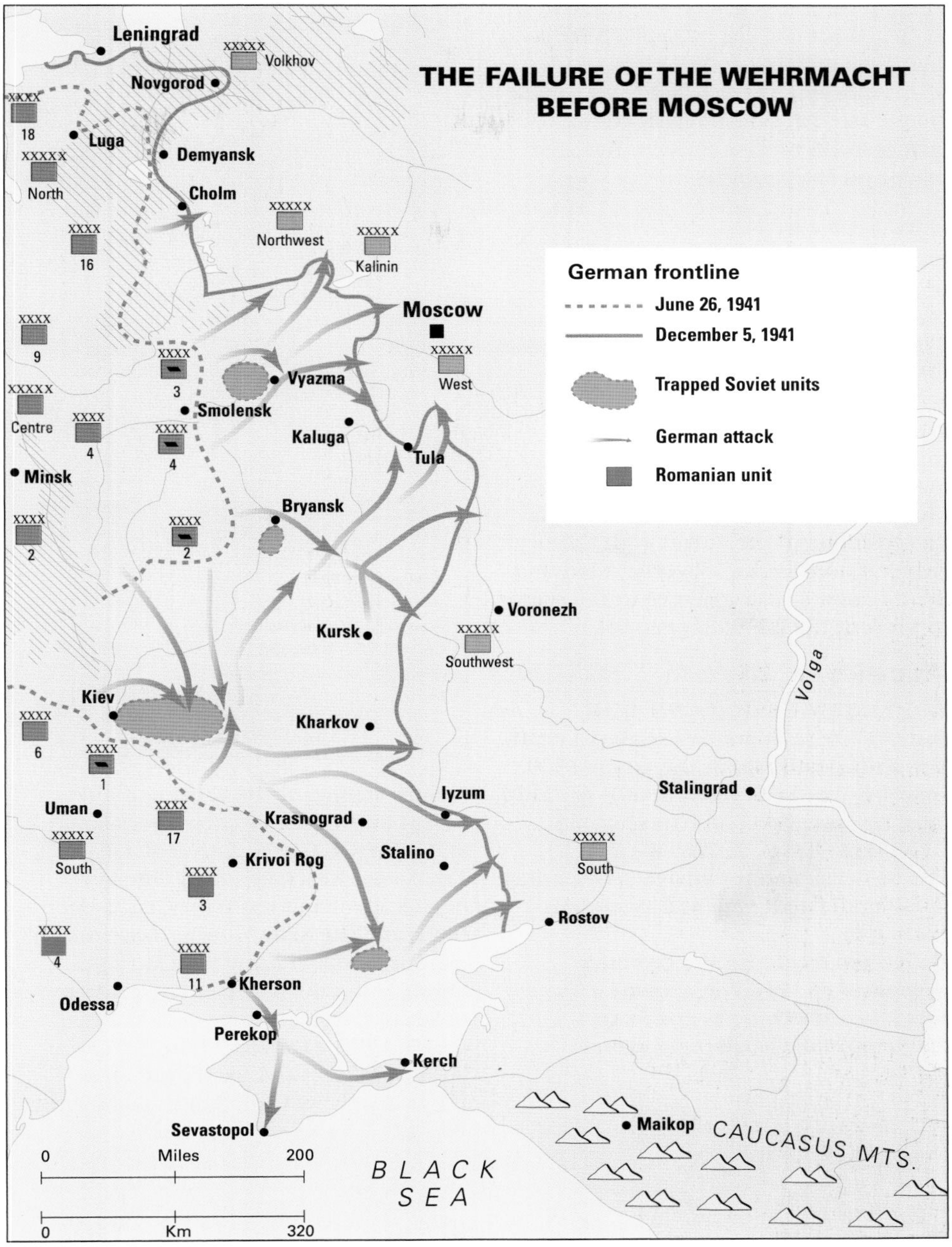

and Thirty-First Armies battling their way into the suburbs of Kalinin. The town falls during the night with the help of units from the Soviet First Shock Army. The German front is in danger of falling apart as the Third Panzer Group withdraws in confusion, and the advance of the Soviet Fifth Army hastens the retreat of the Fourth Panzer Group lest it be cut off.

USSR, *STRATEGY*

Stalin, convinced that the offensive has saved Moscow, orders all functions of the Soviet state to relocate back to the city.

DECEMBER 17

NORTHERN USSR, *LAND WAR*

Two new Soviet fronts are activated in the Leningrad sector: Volkhov Front (Fourth, Fifty-Second, Fifty-Ninth and Second Shock Armies) under Meretskov; and Northwestern Front (Eleventh, Thirty-Fourth and Third and Fourth Shock Armies) under General Pavel Kurochkin.

CENTRAL USSR, *LAND WAR*

The German Eleventh Army resumes its assault upon Sevastopol, with supporting heavy artillery and air strikes. Although the Germans make minor gains, XXX and LIV Corps are soon bogged down in the face of Red Army firepower.

DECEMBER 19

CENTRAL USSR, *LAND WAR*

Army Group Centre is still in grave danger as the flanks of its Fourth Army are on the verge of collapse and its rear is threatened by the 2nd Guards Cavalry Corps, supported by the Tenth Army. In addition, XXXXVII Panzer and LIII Corps are thrown back across the River Plava.

SOUTHERN USSR, *LAND WAR*

Sevastopol continues to hold out against heavy assaults.

GERMANY, *ARMED FORCES*

Hitler relieves Brauchitsch of his post and assumes command of the army on the Eastern Front. In his proclamation to the troops, he announces: "Soldiers, I know war from four years of the gigantic struggle in the West from 1914 to 1918. I lived through the horrors of nearly all the great battles as a common soldier. Twice I was wounded, and I was threatened with becoming blind. Therefore, nothing that is

▲ *A Soviet photograph of German graves taken during the Red Army's December counteroffensive, some of the 743,000 Germans lost since the start of Barbarossa.*

tormenting and troubling you is unknown to me...What you can and will do for me, I know. You will follow me loyally and obediently until the Reich and our German people are safe. God Almighty will not deny victory to His bravest soldiers." But there will be no more retreats.

DECEMBER 21

CENTRAL USSR, *GROUND WAR*
With typhus reportedly sweeping through the German Army, the Soviet 31st Cavalry Division battles its way into Kaluga but is then thrown out by the 137th Infantry Division. The Germans also prevent the Soviet Fiftieth Army from advancing to Kaluga.
SOUTHERN USSR, *LAND WAR*
The Germans grind their way through the positions of the Soviet 40th Cavalry Division northeast of Severnaya Bay, but the defenders rush reserves to the sector to prevent the fall of Sevastopol.

RED ARMY OFFENSIVES SOUTH OF LENINGRAD

Soviet Frontlines
12 Nov 1941
11–15 Dec 1941
31 Dec 1941

DECEMBER 25

NORTHERN USSR, *LAND WAR*
Today 3700 Leningraders starve to death. The daily death rate in the city is 1500, very few due to German bombs or shells; most to starvation and hypothermia.
CENTRAL USSR, *LAND WAR*
The Soviet counteroffensive is beginning to falter, the Sixteenth and Twentieth Armies stalling at the Lama and Ruza Rivers in the face of enemy resistance.
SOUTHERN USSR, *LAND WAR*
The Soviet Kerch-Feodosia Offensive begins, involving the Trans-Caucasian Front and the Azov Flotilla. Elements of the Forty-Fourth Army land at Cape Opuk; and units of the Fifty-First Army north of Kerch.
GERMANY, *ARMED FORCES*
For his retreats and insubordination, Hitler dismisses Guderian as commander of the Second Panzer Group. He is replaced by General Rudolf Schmidt.

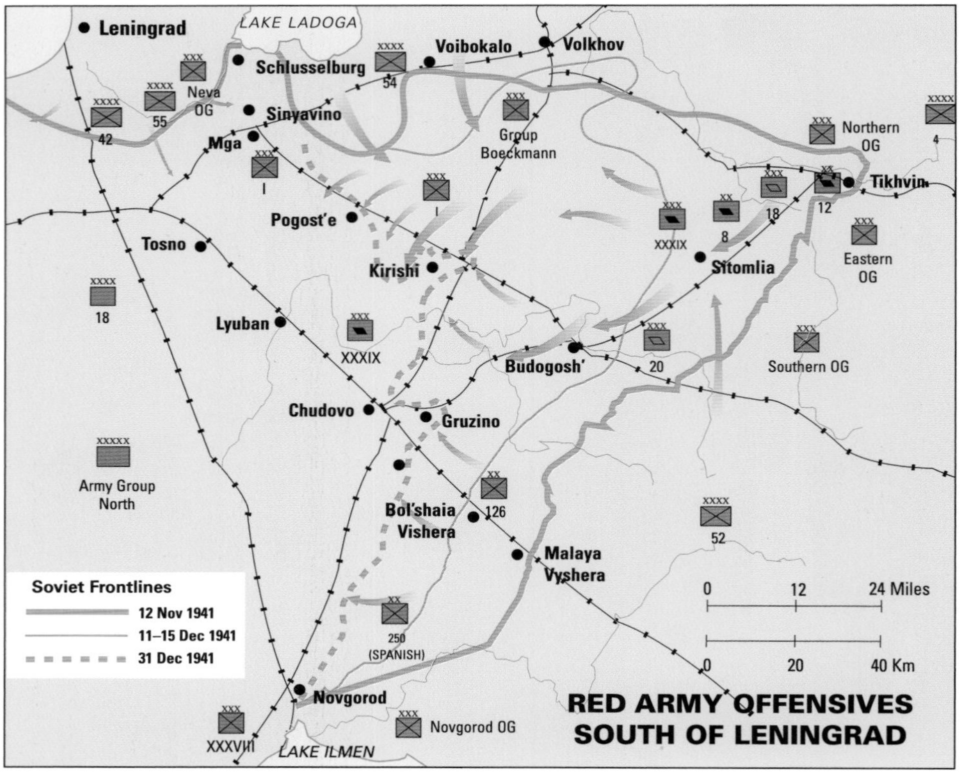

DECEMBER 26

CENTRAL USSR, *LAND WAR*
The Soviet Forty-Ninth Army attacks in the Rzhev sector with the aim of fracturing the Ninth Army's lines. Meanwhile, the Second Panzer Group gives up Kaluga to the Soviet Fiftieth Army.
SOUTHERN USSR, *LAND WAR*
The German Eleventh Army continues its attacks against Sevastopol, though with little success.

▼ German troops on the defensive at the end of 1941. The extreme cold jammed rifle bolts and froze the recoil liquid in machine guns.

▲ ***Heinz Guderian (second from left) was relieved of his command on December 25. Hitler believed he was too preoccupied "by the sufferings of the soldiers. You feel too much pity for them".***

DECEMBER 29

SOUTHERN USSR, *LAND WAR*

With the fighting continuing around Sevastopol, 23,000 troops of the Soviet Forty-Fourth Army land in the Crimea at Feodosia. They quickly brush aside the Romanian troops in the area and establish a bridgehead. This threatens the German XXXXII Corps, which is forced to withdraw. This in turn forces Manstein to divert XXX Corps east to support the threatened corps.

DECEMBER 31

CENTRAL USSR, *LAND WAR*

The Soviet Tenth Army recaptures Kozelsk. However, the Red Army offensive is running out of steam due to losses in men and equipment. The Third Army, for example, totals only 16,000 troops and 138 artillery pieces.

SOUTHERN USSR, *LAND WAR*

The German XXXXII Corps comes under pressure at Feodosia from the 40,000 troops that the Red Army has landed. Manstein is thus forced to halt attacks against Sevastopol until this threat has been dealt with.

GERMANY, *ARMED FORCES*

The Wehrmacht has suffered major losses on the Eastern Front during its first campaign against the Soviet Union. The Luftwaffe has lost 2100 aircraft destroyed and 1300 badly damaged (Luftwaffe monthly losses in November and December were 741 aircraft and 318 air crews), while the army has lost 302,000 troops killed.

USSR, *ARMED FORCES*

Soviet losses thus far have been colossal. During the last three months the army and navy combined has lost 1,007,996 killed and missing and 648,521 wounded.

USSR, *LEND-LEASE AID*

Allied convoy aid to the USSR thus far amounts to 750 tanks, 800 fighters, 1400 other vehicles and more than 101,600 tonnes (100,000 tons) of other stores. This is most welcome, because Soviet equipment losses to date have been huge: 56 percent of all small-arms and machine guns; 69 percent of all anti-tank guns; 59 percent of all field guns and mortars; 72 percent of all tanks; and 34 percent of all combat aircraft (around 20,000 tanks and 10,000 combat aircraft have been lost between June and the end of December).

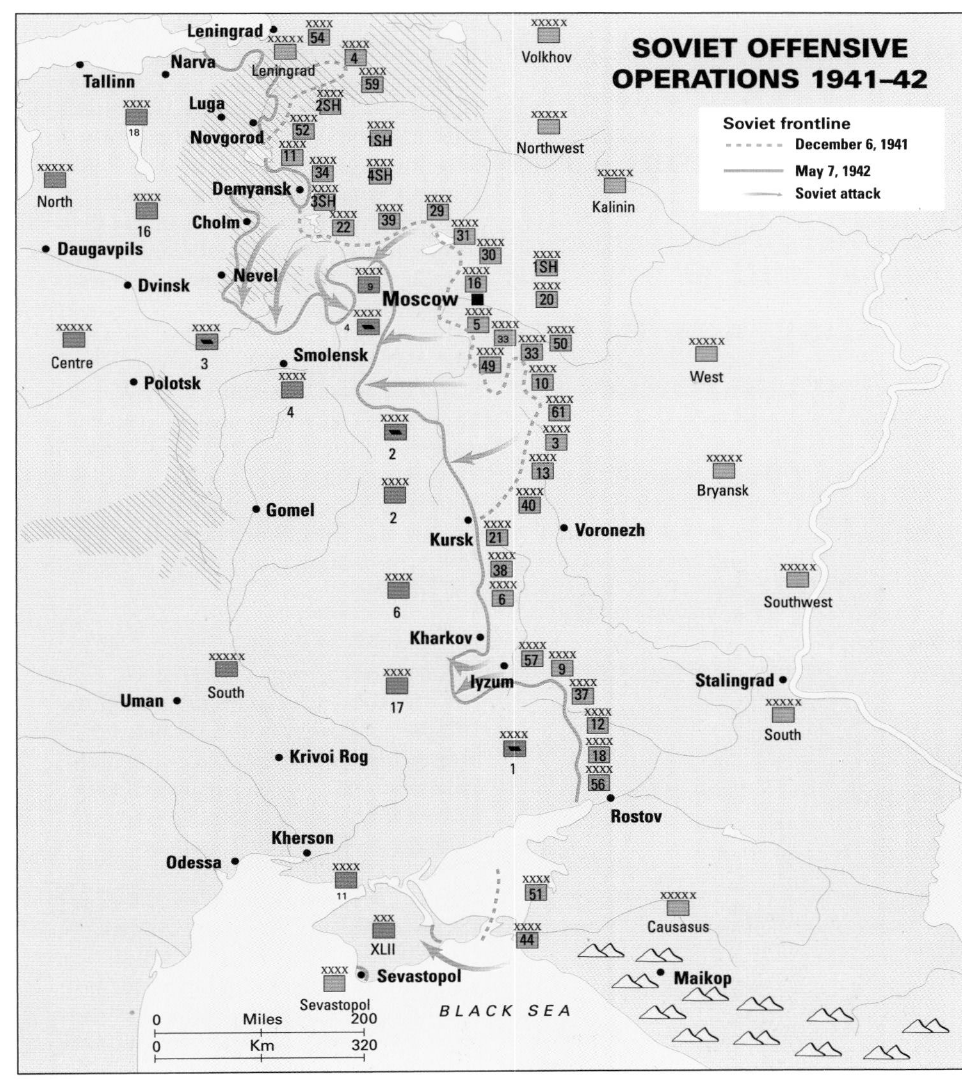

▲ ***"I believe that I am entitled to ask any German soldier to lay down his life." Adolf Hitler to Heinz Guderian, December 20.***

▲ *Germans taken prisoner by the Red Army near Klin, northeast of Moscow. Note their lack of winter clothing.*

Operation Blue, the German offensive launched this year, was designed to seize the vital Caucasus oil fields. This would both provide the Germans with oil supplies and deny them to the Soviets, thus fatally wounding their defence potential. At first Blue was successful, the panzer columns ranging at will across the open steppe. But the Red Army was trading space for time, and when the Germans reached the city of Stalingrad they became embroiled in a long, bloody battle of attrition.

▼ *Troops of the SS* Das Reich *Division in early January. The division had begun Barbarossa with 19,000 men, but by the end of 1941 it had lost 7000 troops.*

JANUARY 1

SOUTHERN USSR, *LAND WAR*
A Red Army offensive in the Ukraine begins involving the Bryansk Front (Third, Thirteenth and Sixty-First Armies), Southwestern Front (Sixth, Twenty-First, Thirty-Eighth and Fortieth Armies) and Southern Front (Ninth, Thirty-Seventh and Fifty-Seventh Armies). The Twenty-First and Fortieth Armies begin their advance towards Oboyan and Kursk. In the Crimea, the weak German XXXXII Corps is unable to make any headway against the Soviet Feodosia bridgehead.

JANUARY 3

SOUTHERN USSR, *LAND WAR*
The Soviet Sixth Army makes little progress at Kharkov. The Twenty-First and Thirty-Eighth Armies have been ordered to recapture Belgorod by January 5. In the Crimea, the Soviet Forty-Fourth and Fifty-First Armies launch offensives at Feodosia and Kerch.

JANUARY 5

SOUTHERN USSR, *LAND WAR*
The Germans are counterattacking the Twenty-First Army around Belgorod, prompting Timoshenko to commit the Thirty-Eighth Army in this area. In the Crimea, the Germans repel Red Army landings at Sudak and Evatoria.

USSR, *STRATEGY*
Buoyed by the success of the Moscow counteroffensive, Stalin decides to expand the offensive to the whole front. Zhukov wants to maintain the focus against Army Group Centre but is overruled. The Soviet dictator has failed to take into account the losses sustained by

south the offensive by the Northwestern Front is also faltering, with the Third and Fourth Shock Armies making slow progress north of Lake Seligar.

CENTRAL USSR, *LAND WAR*
Although the Soviet Thirty-Ninth Army has advanced past Rzhev, the Twenty-Ninth Army is still held up in front of the town.

SOUTHERN USSR, *LAND WAR*
The German Sixth Army counterattacks around Kharkov, hitting the junction of the Soviet Twenty-First and Fortieth Armies.

JANUARY 12

GERMANY, *ARMED FORCES*
As Red Army units threaten to cut off 100,000 troops around Demyansk, the commander of Army Group North, Leeb, requests permission to retreat. Hitler refuses, whereupon Leeb resigns. He is replaced by Georg von Küchler.

JANUARY 13

NORTHERN USSR, *LAND WAR*
The Leningrad and Volkhov Fronts commence their combined offensive. The Fifty-Fourth, Fourth, Second Shock, Fifty-Second and Fifty-Ninth Armies assault German positions. Though fierce fighting erupts all along the line, it soon becomes apparent that German defences are very strong. Soon the attacks by the Fourth, Fifty-Second and Fifty-Ninth Armies peter out; only the Second Shock and elements of the Fifty-Second establish small bridgeheads across the Volkhov. The Red Army has more success south of Lake Ilmen, with the Third and Fourth Shock Armies threatening the German Sixteenth Army.

CENTRAL USSR, *LAND WAR*
Although the German Ninth Army still holds Rzhev, the Fourth Panzer Army is pushed back and loses contact with the Fourth Army to the south as the Soviet Thirty-Third Army nears Vyazma.

▲ Red Army troops of the Fifth Army approach the great monastery at Mozhaisk. The Fifth was part of the Western Front.

his forces during the Moscow Offensive, which amount to 140,000 troops killed, and 429 tanks, 13,000 artillery pieces and 140 aircraft destroyed.

JANUARY 7

NORTHERN USSR, *LAND WAR*
The Volkhov Front opens the Demyansk Offensive with the Second Shock and Fifty-Ninth Armies smashing into the German I and XXXVIII Corps, with little success. The Northwestern Front, located south of Lake Ilmen, also attacks, inflicting heavy losses on the SS *Totenkopf*, 30th and 290th Infantry Divisions.

CENTRAL USSR, *LAND WAR*
The Soviet Kalinin Front advances to the River Volga near Rzhev.

JANUARY 8

NORTHERN USSR, *LAND WAR*
The Soviet Second Shock, Fifty-Second and Fifty-Ninth Armies continue their offensive, although the Germans maintain a solid defence. The Northwestern Front launches more assaults against the German Sixteenth Army, inflicting heavy casualties on II Corps.

CENTRAL USSR, *LAND WAR*
The German Ninth Army at Rzhev and Fourth Army at Mozhaisk continue to repel Red Army attacks. In response, the Stavka reinforces the Kalinin Front, bringing its strength up to 346,000 troops. The Western Front is ordered to achieve breakthroughs at Volokolamsk and Rzhev and reach Vyazma, thus separating and isolating the German Fourth Army and Second Panzer Army. For these tasks it has 713,000 troops. To the south the Bryansk Front (317,000 troops) starts its offensive. These attacks are grouped under the Moscow Offensive.

SOUTHERN USSR, *LAND WAR*
Repeated attacks against Kharkov by the Soviet Twenty-First, Thirty-Eighth and Fortieth Armies are having no success.

JANUARY 9

NORTHERN USSR, *LAND WAR*
The Soviet Third and Fourth Shock Armies attack across the frozen Lake Seligar, hoping to punch a hole in the German Sixteenth Army's line. The Twenty-Second Army lends its support to the attack from the south. Under pressure the Sixteenth Army's defences at Peno begin to disintegrate. Meanwhile, the Northwestern Front's Eleventh Army has broken into the enemy's rear and is nearing Staraya Russa.

CENTRAL USSR, *LAND WAR*
The dogged defence of the Ninth Army at Rzhev continues. To the south the Red Army has more success, the Tenth Army recapturing Lyudinovo and the Forty-Ninth Army grinding its way towards Vyazma.

JANUARY 10

NORTHERN USSR, *LAND WAR*
The attacks by the Soviet Second Shock and Fifty-Ninth Armies along the Volkhov have failed. The Red Army will thus try a new tactic: a combined offensive by the Leningrad and Volkhov Fronts. To the

▶ Soviet ski troops, supported by T-26 tanks, during Zhukov's counteroffensive. Note the soldiers riding on the front tank.

STRATEGY & TACTICS

GERMAN HEDGEHOGS

The failure of Operation Typhoon heralded a crisis for the German Army on the Eastern Front at the end of 1941. Understrength and exhausted divisions lacked the manpower with which to defend every mile of the front, especially in the face of the Red Army counter-offensive that began in early December. To compound the problem, pre-war training had largely shunned anything to do with defensive operations in winter conditions. Individual commanders and units therefore had to learn fast if they were to avoid being annihilated by the more numerical and often better equipped enemy. In response, the Germans adopted so-called hedgehog tactics to beat off Red Army attacks and preserve their lines.

German forces grouped around towns and villages, which they fortified as best they could. Any buildings that were superfluous to the defence were destroyed, both to deny them to the enemy and to aid German observation and fields of fire. Houses earmarked as fighting positions were reinforced by packing snow against the outer walls, with overhead cover being strengthened and firing embrasures being cut and camouflaged. Some houses had their roofs removed and quad 20mm flak guns installed for anti-aircraft defence. Known as "flak nests", the flak guns could also be used against enemy infantry. Artillery and air strikes (when available) were usually directed against enemy assembly areas, with the anti-tank guns, mortars and machine guns in the hedgehog opening fire when the enemy approached the settlement. All buildings had interlocking fields of fire, and even if Red Army infantry got among them they would be counterattacked immediately by reserves armed with submachine guns and grenades.

Hedgehog positions, especially the smaller ones, had several disadvantages. Usually situated on hills and ridges, they were vulnerable to tank and artillery fire, and encirclement, especially at night. In response, the Germans were forced to extend defensive perimeters beyond village limits, thus reducing the distance between individual hedgehogs. The extended perimeter comprised infantry fighting positions, living quarters, minefields and communications paths (the lavish firepower of infantry divisions – more than 500 machine guns – allowed even understrength squads to cover long frontages). Fighting positions had thick ice walls, which were reinforced by pouring water over poncho-covered bundles of sticks and logs, but they were not covered (allowing men to throw stick grenades in all directions). There were separate bombardment shelters with overhead cover. Because of the extreme cold, the Germans favoured tripwire-detonated mines (heavy accumulations of snow and low temperatures made pressure-activated mines unreliable), with anti-tank mines being laid on roads and other obvious avenues of approach.

To break up enemy infantry attacks before they reached the hedgehogs, the Germans used local agricultural tools to fashion "knife rest obstacles", on which enemy soldiers injured themselves when wading through deep snow. Trees were felled to create barriers, and snow walls up to 3m (9.84ft) high were built to impede enemy tanks (deep snow on its own restricted the movement of enemy infantry lacking skis or snow shoes).

Despite these measures, there were always large gaps in the German lines, through which the Soviets could infiltrate substantial forces. In response, the Germans built forward hedgehogs in checkerboard fashion to provide a modicum of defensive depth. They also converted rear area logistical installations into hedgehogs and arranged their heavy weapons so that enemy breakthrough forces would be under continuous artillery fire to a certain depth. More importantly, the Germans always launched aggressive counterattacks whenever possible to defeat penetrations. For example, the 97th Light Infantry Division beat off 300 separate Soviet attacks between January and March 1942, launching more than 100 counter-attacks during the same period. With such tactics, the German Army saved itself during the winter of 1941–42 on the Eastern Front.

JANUARY 16

NORTHERN USSR, *LAND WAR*

The German Sixteenth Army is forced to retreat from north of Lake Seligar, thus exposing the rear of Army Group Centre. The Soviet Eleventh Army is pushing into the German rear at Pskov.

CENTRAL USSR, *LAND WAR*

The Third Panzer Army is redeployed from the Rzhev salient to take up position between the Sixteenth and Ninth Armies in an effort to shore up the front.

SOUTHERN USSR, *LAND WAR*

The German Eleventh Army captures Feodosia, together with 10,000 prisoners. This prompts Hitler to order the arrest of General von Sponek, commander of XXXXII Corps, who had retreated in December.

JANUARY 18

NORTHERN USSR, *LAND WAR*

The German Eighteenth Army is forced out of Schlusselburg, which allows the Red Army to establish a narrow link with Leningrad. Farther south, the Sixteenth Army continues to be battered by the enemy and falls back to Toropets. As the Soviet Third and Fourth Shock Armies continue to drive into the German lines, the main supply route for the German II and X Corps at Demyansk is severed.

CENTRAL USSR, *LAND WAR*

The Soviets attempt an airborne drop into the rear of Army Group Centre, with 2000 men of the 201st Airborne Brigade dropping between Yukhnov and Vyazma. It is a fiasco: around 1600 are lost.

SOUTHERN USSR, *LAND WAR*

The Soviet Barvenkovo-Lozavaia Offensive begins as the Southwestern and Southern Fronts attack into the Ukraine, aiming to recapture Kharkov, Krasnograd and Pavlograd.

GERMANY, *ARMED FORCES*

Field Marshal von Bock replaces the recently deceased Reichenau as commander of Army Group South.

JANUARY 20

NORTHERN USSR, *LAND WAR*

The German hold on Staraya Russa is helped by counterattacks by the Eleventh Army mounted by the German SS *Totenkopf* and 18th Motorized Divisions. Farther south, the Soviet Fourth Shock

▲ *Well-equipped soldiers of the SS Totenkopf Division near Staraya Russa. SS units were supplied with winter clothing from a depot in Riga.*

Army recaptures Toropets together with much ammunition and other supplies.

CENTRAL USSR, *LAND WAR*
The German Fourth Army is forced out of Mozhaisk, prompting Hitler to replace its commander, Kubler, with Heinrici.

JANUARY 22

NORTHERN USSR, *LAND WAR*
The Soviet Third Shock Army increases its pressure on Cholm in an effort to take the town.

CENTRAL USSR, *LAND WAR*
The Stavka has withdrawn the First Shock and Sixteenth Armies from this sector for redeployment, thus relieving the pressure on the Ninth Army. Although the Thirty-Ninth Army continues to attack the Ninth's positions, it is unable to break through. Indeed, a counter-attack by XXXXVI Panzer Corps manages to stabilize the German frontline.

SOUTHERN USSR, *LAND WAR*
The Soviet Sixth and Fifty-Seventh Armies lance 32km (20 miles) into the German front, heading for Barvenkovo.

JANUARY 24

NORTHERN USSR, *LAND WAR*
Three Soviet armies attack on the Volkhov: the Second Shock, Fifty-Second and Fifty-Ninth. Of these, only the Second Shock manages to break through the German lines. Fighting continues at Cholm as the Third Shock Army continues to attack the German defenders.

CENTRAL USSR, *LAND WAR*
The German Ninth Army is attacking the isolated Soviet Twenty-Ninth and Thirty-Ninth Armies, with few results. The reconstituted Soviet Sixteenth Army is ordered to strike the southern flank of the German Fourth Army and advance northwest to link up with the Kalinin Front near Smolensk.

SOUTHERN USSR, *LAND WAR*
The Soviet Ninth Army recaptures Barvenkovo. To reinforce this success the Stavka reinforces the Southern Front with more than 300 tanks.

▲ *The new commander of Army Group North, General Georg von Küchler, favoured using prisoners to clear mines.*

JANUARY 28

CENTRAL USSR, *LAND WAR*
XXXXVI Panzer Corps mounts a counter-attack in an effort to stabilize German positions around Rzhev.

SOUTHERN USSR, *LAND WAR*
The Stavka activates the new Crimean Front under General Dmitriy Kozlov in the Crimea. This is in advance of a Red Army assault against German forces around Sevastopol.

JANUARY 30

NORTHERN USSR, *LAND WAR*
The Soviet Third Shock and Thirty-Fourth Armies smash into the flank of the German Sixteenth Army south of Lake Ilmen.

CENTRAL USSR, *LAND WAR*
With the northern flank of Army Group North in grave danger, LIX Corps spreads its units thin to prevent a Soviet breakthrough. At Velizh, 3000 German defenders hold out against 30,000 troops of the Soviet Fourth Shock Army.

JANUARY 31

SOUTHERN USSR, *LAND WAR*
The Barvenkovo Offensive has cost the Southern and Southwestern Fronts dear, with at least 11,095 killed and 29,786 wounded. The Red Army offensive around Kharkov has now run out of steam.

GERMANY, *ARMED FORCES*
The German Army on the Eastern Front can now deploy only 4241 tanks and self-propelled guns.

◀ *As the Germans withdrew, they destroyed anything that could be of use to the advancing Red Army, such as this village.*

▲ ***A sign celebrates the fact that this German howitzer has fired 10,000 shells thus far on the Eastern Front.***

FEBRUARY 1

CENTRAL USSR, *LAND WAR*

The German Third Panzer Army, reinforced with LIX Corps, holds all Red Army attacks in front of Vitebsk; and the Fourth and Ninth Armies restore their lines between Rzhev and Vyazma. Indeed, around Rzhev the Ninth Army has managed to surround the Soviet Twenty-Ninth and Thirty-Ninth Armies.

FEBRUARY 3

NORTHERN USSR, *LAND WAR*

The Soviet First Shock Army deploys east of Staraya Russa, threatening German units around Demyansk.

CENTRAL USSR, *LAND WAR*

The Red Army increases its efforts to take Velizh, Demidov and Velikiye Luki, although thus far the Germans are holding on to all three places. The Fourth Panzer Army counterattacks to tighten the line between it and the Fourth Army, in the process cutting off the Soviet Thirty-Third Army.

FEBRUARY 8

NORTHERN USSR, *LAND WAR*

The jaws snap shut on 90,000 German troops around Demyansk as the Soviet First Shock and Eleventh Armies link up on the River Lovat. Inside the German pocket are the 12th, 30th, 123rd and 290th Infantry Divisions and the 3rd SS *Totenkopf* Division. These units will have to rely on the Luftwaffe for supplies of food and ammunition. Fighting continues at Cholm as the Soviet Third Shock Army launches attacks against the town.

CENTRAL USSR, *LAND WAR*

The German LIX Corps comes under heavy attack as the Soviets intensify their efforts to take Velizh, Demidov and Velikiye Luki.

FEBRUARY 10

NORTHERN USSR, *AIR WAR*

Colonel Fritz Morzik is the Luftwaffe chief of air transport responsible for supplying the troops inside the Demyansk Pocket. He has estimated that, to deliver 305 tonnes (300 tons) daily, he will need at least 150 operational aircraft. The commander of the First Air Fleet, General Alfred Keller, is cooperating fully with Morzik. Inside the pocket the landing airfields are Demyansk, Pieski (which will be completed in March), Supply Drop Area Demyansk (a marked, open area used to drop supplies during the coming muddy season) and Cholm. Unfortunately, the Junkers Ju 52 transport aircraft earmarked for the supply operation will have little fighter support. The air fleet staff urge Morzik to "select that route which offers the best chance of avoiding losses". In response to this and growing losses, Morzik will order his planes to fly at an altitude of 2500m (8200ft) and in groups of 20–30 aircraft to battle enemy fighters with concentrated fire.

CENTRAL USSR, *LAND WAR*

The Soviet Fourth Shock Army penetrates into Velizh, but its units are repelled by counterattacks. The Third Panzer Army is now approaching the town, albeit slowly.

FEBRUARY 12

NORTHERN USSR, *LAND WAR*

The Luftwaffe's Demyansk airlift begins as the Soviets launch attacks against the pocket's perimeter, which are held.

CENTRAL USSR, *LAND WAR*

The Soviet Fourth Shock Army continues its efforts against Velizh as the Third

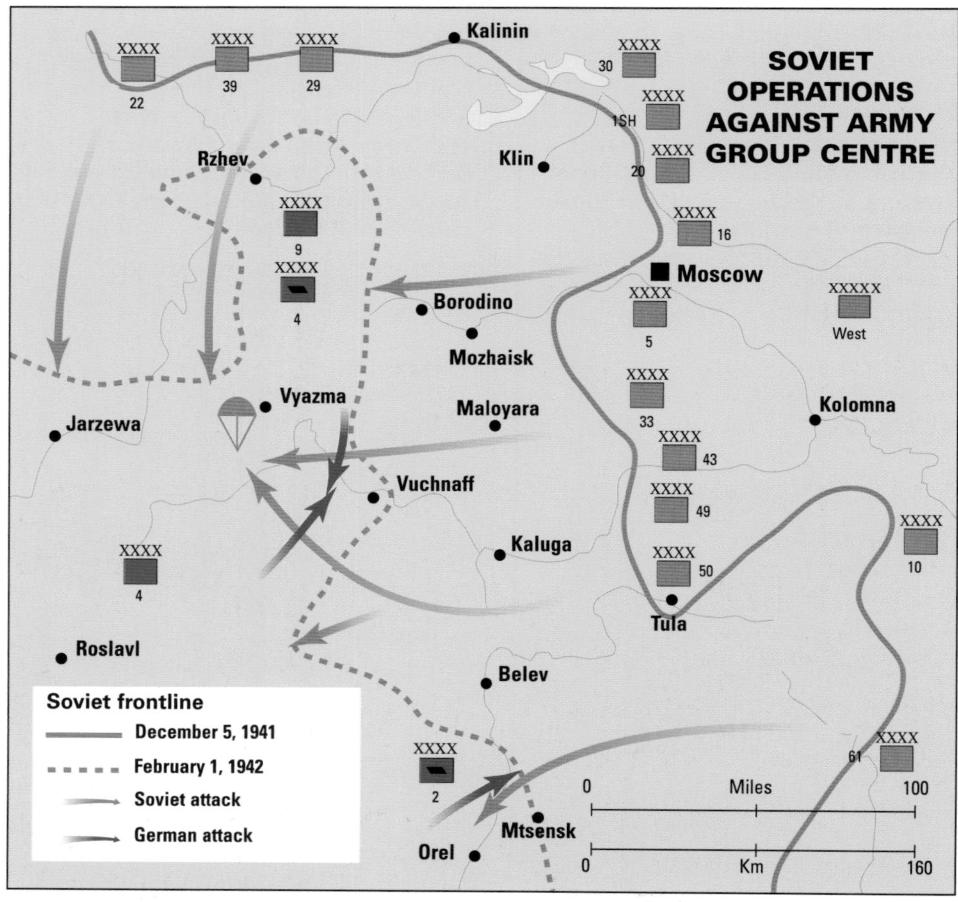

Panzer Army inches its way towards the town (it is also under Red Army attack). The German Ninth Army continues to defend Rzhev, and the encircled Soviet Twenty-Ninth and Thirty-Ninth Armies continue to suffer attacks.

FEBRUARY 15

NORTHERN USSR, *LAND WAR*
The Soviets drop paratroopers into the Demyansk Pocket. Failing to realize that airborne troops on the ground are very vulnerable unless they can be speedily relieved, the Red Army has condemned these men to death: the entire force is virtually wiped out.

CENTRAL USSR, *LAND WAR*
Having reinforced his forces in front of Moscow, Zhukov issues new orders. The Kalinin Front is to destroy the German Ninth Army and seize the Olenino region. For this task it has the Twenty-Second, Thirtieth and Thirty-Ninth Armies. The Western Front is ordered to take Yukhnov and Bryansk, its forces for doing so comprising the Sixteenth, Forty-Third, Forty-Ninth, Fiftieth and Sixty-First Armies (with the 4th Airborne Corps dropping near Yukhnov).

▼ A Red Army tank-hunting unit marches out of Leningrad towards the front armed with 14.5mm PTRD anti-tank rifles.

FEBRUARY 17

CENTRAL USSR, *LAND WAR*
The German relief force reaches Velizh at last, although the Soviet Fourth Shock Army is still before the town. Near Rzhev the Soviet Thirty and Thirty-Ninth Armies attempt to relieve the Twenty-Ninth Army, although the 1st Panzer Division counterattacks and again traps the Twenty-Ninth, which is fast crumbling. The Red Army penchant for frittering away its airborne forces continues as the 14th Airborne Brigade is dropped west of Yukhnov, and then suffers heavy losses.

▲ The aerial workhorse on the Eastern Front: the Ju 52. This one is being readied to supply the Demyansk Pocket.

FEBRUARY 27

SOUTHERN USSR, *LAND WAR*
The Red Army begins a new offensive in the Crimea against the Eleventh Army. It is a disaster, with the Fifty-First Army on the Kerch Peninsula suffering high losses in men and tanks at the hands of German artillery and Luftwaffe attacks. The Red Army will persist in these attacks for the next two weeks. At Sevastopol the garrison fails to breach the besiegers' lines.

FEBRUARY 28

NORTHERN USSR, *LAND WAR*
The Stavka orders the Second Shock and Fifty-Fourth Armies to link up and surround enemy forces near Lubansk.

CENTRAL USSR, *LAND WAR*
German units push back the Soviet Fourth Shock Army in the Demidov area.

SOUTHERN USSR, *LAND WAR*
The Soviet Fifty-First Army again attacks the Kerch Peninsula, but the assault is cut to pieces by German artillery.

GERMANY, *ARMED FORCES*
To date the army on the Eastern Front has lost 394,000 killed, 725,000 wounded, 414,000 captured, 46,000 missing and 112,000 injured through illnesses.

MARCH 13

SOUTHERN USSR, *LAND WAR*

The senseless attacks by the Red Army on the Kerch Peninsula continue, the Soviet Forty-Fourth and Fifty-First Armies seeking to overwhelm the German Eleventh Army by sheer mass alone. In three days the Red Army loses 130 tanks for no results.

MARCH 19

NORTHERN USSR, *LAND WAR*

The German Eighteenth Army attacks on the River Volkhov and surrounds 130,000 troops of the Soviet Second Shock Army, which is commanded by General Vlassov. At Staraya Russa the Germans organize a force to relieve those units trapped in the Demyansk Pocket. It consists of the 5th and 8th Light and 122nd, 127th and 329th Infantry Divisions.

USSR, *PARTISAN WAR*

Operation Munich is launched. Joined by a Luftwaffe detachment, German troops attack partisan bases around Yelnya and Dorogobuzh. Another anti-partisan sweep, Operation Bamberg, commences near Bobruisk. In these actions SS police troops attack Russian villages and German security forces burn many dwellings, killing 3500 people. Both operations succeed only in alienating the local population and swelling the ranks of the partisans. The diary of the Third Panzer Army records: "There are indications that the partisan movement in the region of Velikiye Luki, Vitebsk,

◀ ***A German machine-gun position in northern Russia, an image that conveys the terrible conditions in which German troops lived during the winter of 1941–42.***

▲ ***Panzer IIIs of Army Group Centre in winter camouflage. They are probably the Ausf G model, which was armed with a 50mm main gun. Secondary armament comprised two 7.92mm machine guns.***

Rudnya and Velizh is now being organized on a large scale. The fighting strength of the partisans, hitherto active, is being bolstered by individual units of regular Red Army troops."

MARCH 20

SOUTHERN USSR, *LAND WAR*
The German 22nd Panzer Division is deployed on the Kerch Peninsula, and receives a bloody nose in the subsequent fighting, though alleviating the pressure on XXXXI Corps.

MARCH 21

NORTHERN USSR, *LAND WAR*
The German ground effort to relieve the Demyansk Pocket begins. The Germans have to battle through the entrenched positions of the Soviet First Shock and Eleventh Armies.

MARCH 31

NORTHERN USSR, *LAND WAR*
A narrow corridor is created through to the isolated Second Shock Army, but the Red Army cannot free Vlassov's force.

USSR, *ARMED FORCES*
To date the Red Army and Navy have suffered 675,315 killed and missing and a staggering 1,179,457 wounded.

▲ Red Army troops and T-40 Light Tanks advance as part of the abortive Soviet attempt to relieve General Vlassov's trapped Second Shock Army.

APRIL 1

▶ *German troops of Army Group Centre take cover during a Red Army artillery barrage. By late April, the Soviet offensives in central Russia were petering out.*

APRIL 1

SOUTHERN USSR, *LAND WAR*

The Red Army musters its units for an offensive near Izyum. For this operation the Southwestern Front has the Twenty-First, Sixth, Thirty-Eighth, Fifty-Seventh, Ninth and Twenty-Eighth Armies. The Southern Front deploys the Thirty-Seventh, Twelfth, Eighteenth and Fifty-Sixth Armies. Facing these formations are the German Sixth, Seventeenth and First Panzer Armies.

APRIL 5

GERMANY, *STRATEGY*

Hitler issues Directive No 41 outlining the aims of the forthcoming summer offensive on the Eastern Front. "In pursuit of the original plan for the Eastern campaign, the armies of the Central sector will stand fast, those in the North will capture Leningrad and link up with the Finns, while those on the southern flank will break through into the Caucasus."

The Wehrmacht is tasked with "destroying the enemy before the Don, in order to secure the Caucasian oil fields and the passes through the Caucasus mountains". To create favourable conditions, Hitler orders "mopping up and consolidation on the whole Eastern front and in the rear areas so that the greatest possible forces may be released for the main operation". Also, the Kerch Peninsula is to be cleared and Sevastopol captured.

APRIL 9

SOUTHERN USSR, *LAND WAR*

Another Red Army attack on the Kerch Peninsula achieves little.

April 14

CENTRAL USSR, *AIR WAR*
The Luftwaffe stops an attack by the Soviet Fiftieth Army aimed at relieving the encircled Thirty-Third Army. The Fiftieth is forced to retire with loss.

April 19

CENTRAL USSR, *LAND WAR*
The Soviet Thirty-Third Army is wiped out and its commander, General Efremov, is killed in the fighting.

April 20

NORTHERN USSR, *LAND WAR*
The Demyansk relief force links up with the 3rd SS *Totenkopf* Division on the River Lovat, though the rescue corridor is very fragile.

CENTRAL USSR, *LAND WAR*
Bryansk Front losses thus far in 1942 amount to 21,319 killed and missing and 39,807 wounded.

YUGOSLAVIA, *PARTISAN WAR*
A combined German-Italian-Croatian operation to clear eastern Bosnia, led by General Bader and under the operational control of the Italian Second Army, begins. The force consists of three Italian divisions: the German 718th Infantry Division, German units from Serbia, and Croatian national troops. It will last until May 3, by which time the partisans will have suffered 168 dead, 1309 prisoners taken and stocks of weapons, ammunition and other equipment captured. Unfortunately for the Germans, large numbers of guerrillas escape through Italian lines and make their way to Croatia.

April 24

FINLAND, *LAND WAR*
The Finnish III Corps defeats a major assault by three rifle divisions of the Soviet Twenty-Sixth Army in the Kastenga area. Combat will continue for the next six days.

April 30

NORTHERN USSR, *LAND WAR*
The Lyuban Offensive conducted by the Volkhov and Leningrad Fronts comes to an ignominious end. It has cost the Red Army 95,064 killed and missing and 213,303 wounded. The Second Shock Army has also been annihilated.

CENTRAL USSR, *LAND WAR*
Red Army losses in the central sector of the front since the beginning of the year have been massive, with the Kalinin Front having lost 123,400 killed and missing and another 217,800 wounded. The Western Front has lost 149,000 killed and missing and 286,000 wounded.

GERMANY, *ARMED FORCES*
The Fourth Panzer Army has relocated to the south to be deployed on the northern flank of Army Group South.

USSR, *ATROCITIES*
An Einsatzgruppen report states with satisfaction that there are no longer any Jews in the Crimea. The Jewish population in the area had numbered up to 60,000 men, women and children, but they have all been liquidated by SS squads assisted by local militias.

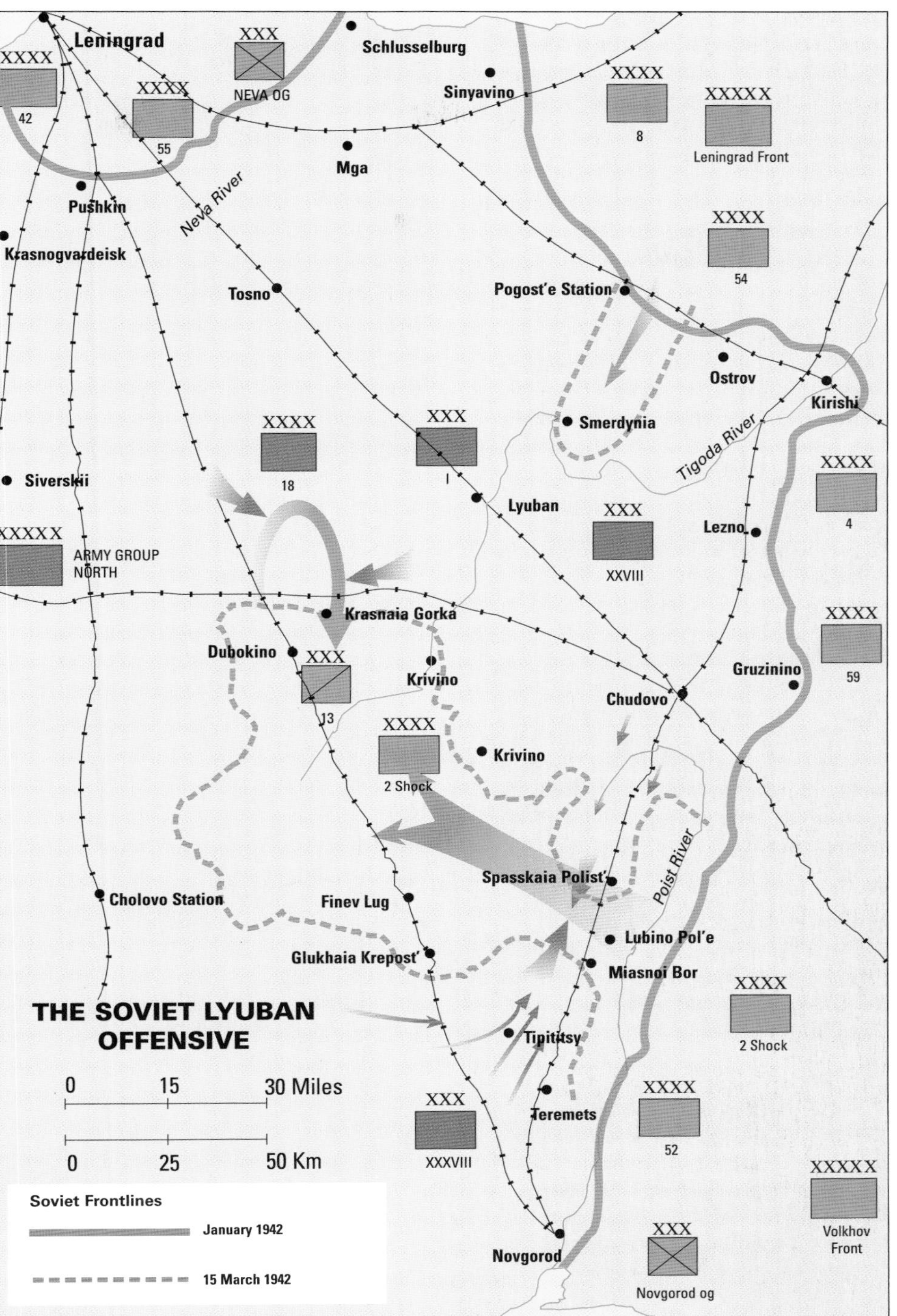

◀ ***German troops in the siege lines before Leningrad. Hitler had told his propaganda minister, Goebbels, that the city should "disappear completely". In any case, the Führer remarked, it would be impossible to feed its population of five million. Once taken, the cradle of Bolshevism was to be razed to the ground – a "hard but justifiable nemesis of history", wrote Goebbels.***

▲ ***Troops of the Soviet Southwestern Front attack during the Kharkov Offensive. Designed to weaken any German attack against Moscow, it was a total disaster.***

MAY 5

NORTHERN USSR, *LAND WAR*
XXXIX Panzer Corps relieves the garrison of Cholm after fighting off the Soviet Third Shock Army, thus bringing to an end the 103-day siege. The defenders have lost 1500 troops killed and 2200 wounded. In addition, in its effort to keep the garrison supplied the Luftwaffe has lost 252 Ju 52 transport aircraft.

MAY 8

SOUTHERN USSR, *LAND WAR*
The German Eleventh Army launches Operation Bustard to destroy enemy forces in the Kerch Peninsula. For this task it deploys XXXII, VII Romanian and XXX Corps (LIV Corps covers Sevastopol). The attack makes a good start with XXX Corps attacking the Forty-Fourth Army in its front, whose southern flank soon collapses.

MAY 9

SOUTHERN USSR, *LAND WAR*
XXX Corps continues to cut through the Forty-Fourth Army's flank as the 22nd Panzer Division throws back the Soviet Fifty-First Army farther north. Though heavy rain allows some Red Army units to escape, the bulk of the two Soviet armies are surrounded by the 10th.

MAY 10

USSR, *ATROCITIES*
The Germans open a new death camp at Maly Trostenets, a small village outside the Belorussian city of Minsk. Some 250,000 Jews will be deported from Western Europe to the camp, where they will be killed in gas vans similar to those used at Chelmno and Riga.

MAY 11

The 22nd Panzer Division arrives at the northern coast of the Kerch Peninsula, thus achieving the encirclement of the Soviet Fifty-First Army. The Soviet Forty-Fourth Army has by this time been almost destroyed in the fighting.

MAY 12

The Soviet Southwestern Front launches the Kharkov Offensive designed to push German forces back to the River Dnieper from the Barvenkovo salient. To achieve this it has Group Bobkin and the Sixth, Twenty-First, Twenty-Eighth and Thirty-Eighth Armies. In addition, the Southern Front (Ninth and Fifty-Seventh Armies) will attack from the south. Total Red Army forces for the offensive are 765,000 troops, 1200 tanks, 13,000 artillery pieces

▼ ***Soviet cavalry in action during the Kharkov Offensive. This is probably a propaganda shot, for mounted cavalry charges were rare on the Eastern Front. The Red Army used horses for mobility, with troopers conducting combat dismounted.***

and 900 aircraft. Following lengthy artillery barrages the Twenty-First, Twenty-Eighth and Thirty-Eighth Armies attack, to achieve advances of only 9.6km (6 miles).

Despite taking heavy casualties, the German XVII and LI Corps hold their positions. To the south the Soviet Group Bobkin and the Sixth Army make better progress, advancing up to 16km (10 miles) on a 40km (25-mile) front.

MAY 14

SOUTHERN USSR, *LAND WAR*
The Kharkov Offensive is already running out of steam, with the Twenty-Eighth and Thirty-Eighth Armies grinding to a halt. Indeed, counterattacks by the 3rd and 23rd Panzer Divisions against the junction of the two armies push back the Soviet frontline. South of Kharkov the Sixth Army and Group Bobkin are having more success, pushing on towards Krasnograd. In the Crimea the Soviet Forty-Fourth and Fifty-First Armies have been annihilated. The German 170th Infantry Division enters Kerch.

MAY 15

FINLAND, *LAND WAR*
The German XXXVI Corps and Finnish III Corps attack the Soviet Twenty-Sixth Army at Kastenga. However, the attacks are beaten off.

SOUTHERN USSR, *LAND WAR*
North of Kharkov the German 3rd and 23rd Panzer Divisions continue their attacks, forcing the Soviet Twenty-Eighth and Thirty-Eighth Armies on to the defensive. However, Soviet success to the south of the city means Timoshenko can think about committing his mobile units to exploit the advance. If Krasnograd falls, the German Sixth and Seventeenth Armies will be endangered. In the Crimea the German Eleventh Army mops up after its victory. The Soviet Crimean Front has lost 162,282 dead or captured, 14,284 wounded and 1100 artillery pieces, 260 tanks and 3800 vehicles either destroyed or captured. In addition, the Soviets have lost more than 300 aircraft shot down.

GERMANY, *STRATEGY*
The High Command determines to counterattack the Southwestern Front and destroy it, thus increasing the chances of success for its own offensive in the area.

MAY 17

SOUTHERN USSR, *LAND WAR*
Under German pressure the Soviet Twenty-First, Twenty-Eighth and Thirty-Eighth Armies north of Kharkov are falling back. To the south of the city the German Group Kleist (III Panzer, XXXXIV and LII Corps) begins its counterattack between Barvenkovo and Slavyansk, hitting the Soviet Ninth Army head on. By the evening the Germans have captured Barvenkovo and created a 14.4km (9-mile) hole between the Ninth and Fifty-Seventh Armies and pushed 32km (20 miles) into the Soviet rear. To the west, meanwhile, Red Army units continue to attack, the 21st and 23rd Tank Corps advancing through the Soviet Sixth Army's positions.

KEY WEAPONS

T-34

The T-34 was one of the greatest tanks of World War II and certainly one of the most influential. One of the most innovative designs was its sloped armour, which not only saved weight compared with rolled plate, but was also more difficult for anti-tank rounds to penetrate. In addition, its Christie-type suspension, combined with a diesel powerplant, gave it an excellent power-to-weight ratio and good cross-country mobility.

It did have its drawbacks, such as no turret floor to revolve with the turret, which meant crewmen had to walk around on the top of ammunition boxes as the turret turned. This became difficult in battle when the turret floor was littered with empty shell cases. In addition, its 76.2mm main gun was outclassed by the 75mm models mounted on the Panzer IV and Panther tanks in the German Army in mid-1943. Indeed, by Kursk, 88 percent of T-34s hit by German guns were penetrated, compared with 46 percent in 1942. Nevertheless, the T-34 was an all-round excellent armoured fighting vehicle and could be produced in thousands. By Kursk, the T-34/76C had appeared, which had a commander's cupola. In an effort to make the T-34 more potent, its armour protection was increased and it was armed with an 85mm gun. The new vehicle was designated the T-34/85 and it entered service in February 1944 – the first units to receive it being 2nd, 6th, 10th and 11th Guards Tank Corps. In total, 49,000 T-34s were built during World War II.

Weight: 30,900kg (67,980lb)
Crew: 4
Speed: 55kmh (34.3mph)
Range: 250km (156 miles)
Dimensions: length: 6.1m (20ft); width: 3m (9.84ft); height: 2.4m (7.87ft)
Armament: 1 x 76mm cannon, 2 x 7.62mm machine guns
Ammunition: 100 x 76mm, 3150 x 7.62mm
Armour: front (maximum): 52mm (2in); side (maximum): 52mm (2in)

▲ ***A German soldier, photographs of his family pinned to a tree, awaits the enemy during the Soviet Kharkov Offensive. Note the stick grenades on the lip of his trench – essential for close-quarter fighting.***

MAY 19

SOUTHERN USSR, *LAND WAR*
The Soviet Twenty-Eighth and Thirty-Eighth Armies try yet again to resume their attacks but are stopped in their tracks by German artillery. As the German XXXXIV Corps approaches Izyum, Red Army units inside the Barvenkovo salient are in danger of being encircled, particularly the Fifty-Seventh Army. In response the Soviets attempt to form defensive positions, the 21st and 23rd Tanks Corps having been ordered east. To the north, the Soviet Sixth Army continues its attacks, although with few gains. Timoshenko asks Stalin for permission for the Southwestern Front to go on to the defensive, but it is too late. Hitler orders Kleist to drive for Balakleya to complete the encirclement of all Soviet forces in the pocket.

▲ ***Some of the prisoners taken by the Germans after the failure of the Kharkov Offensive. Once again the Germans had displayed a mastery of mobile warfare.***

MAY 22

SOUTHERN USSR, *LAND WAR*
German forces seal the Barvenkovo Pocket by the day's end. Timoshenko orders the Thirty-Eighth Army to the north to attack to link up with the trapped units, but this formation is unable to move in time. He also orders the trapped Sixth and Fifty-Seventh Armies to break out.

MAY 23

FINLAND, *LAND WAR*
Finnish attacks in the Kastenga area come to an end; the Soviet Twenty-Sixth Army has beaten off all attacks and inflicted heavy losses on the Finns.

SOUTHERN USSR, *LAND WAR*
The Germans widen their corridor between Barvenkovo and Balakleya in the face of feeble attempts by the Soviet Ninth and Thirty-Eighth Armies to re-establish contact with the pocket.

MAY 26

BRITAIN, *DIPLOMACY*
The USSR and Britain sign a 20-year Mutual Assistance Agreement in London. In June, Molotov, Soviet foreign minister, will say of the agreement: "The treaty consolidates the friendly relations which have been established between the Soviet Union and Great Britain and their mutual military assistance in the struggle against Hitlerite Germany. It transforms these relations into a stable alliance. The treaty also defines the general line of our joint action with Great Britain in the post-war period." Stalin will actually renege on any agreements reached with Britain regarding the map of post-war Europe.

MAY 29

SOUTHERN USSR, *LAND WAR*
The fighting in the Barvenkovo Pocket comes to an end. It is another major disaster for the Red Army, with 170,958 killed or taken prisoner, 106,232 wounded and 1250 tanks and 2000 artillery pieces either destroyed or

▲ ***German panzergrenadiers during the Kharkov battles. The Wehrmacht had shown its superior tactics by turning a potential defeat into a stunning victory.***

captured. For its part the German Sixth Army has suffered 20,000 casualties.

UNITED STATES, *DIPLOMACY*
Molotov, Soviet foreign minister, is at the White House. President Roosevelt promises him that the Western Allies will open a second front in 1942. Molotov rejects a suggestion by Roosevelt that the USSR agrees a treaty with Germany on the prisoners of war issue. Soviet troops in German hands do not have any international protection as the USSR has not signed the Geneva Convention of 1929, which specifies humane treatment for prisoners of war. This official posture stems from the Soviet concept of battlefield behaviour. The Red Army field manual states that a loyal soldier is either fighting or is dead; surrender is considered to be treason. The wartime edition of the standard Soviet encyclopedia states that "the penalty for premeditated surrender into captivity not necessitated by combat conditions is death by shooting".

MAY 30

NORTHERN USSR, *LAND WAR*
A German counterattack along the River Volkhov cuts off the Soviet Second Shock Army, which is desperately short of food and ammunition. The efforts by the Fifty-Second and Fifty-Ninth Armies to reach the Second Shock Army come to nothing.

USSR, *ARMED FORCES*
The Central Staff of the USSR Partisan Movement is set up in Moscow to direct partisan operations behind German lines.

▲ ***Red Army troops during the Kharkov Offensive. The soldier in the foreground is armed with a 7.62mm Degtaryev machine gun, the standard section support weapon.***

▼ ***A Fieseler Fi 156 Storch observation aircraft flies over a Wehrmacht column after the reduction of the Barvenkovo Pocket. The ground was very dry at this time – it was 90 degrees in the shade.***

▶ *A hauptmann (captain), an Iron Cross pinned to his breast, of the German Eleventh Army during the assault on Sevastopol. On his left hip is a holster that contains his 9mm P38 handgun.*

JUNE 2

SOUTHERN USSR, *LAND WAR*

Manstein's Eleventh Army commences the air and artillery bombardment of the heavily defended port fortress of Sevastopol. This is no easy task as some of the fortress's defences date back to the days before the Crimean War, and have been reinforced with modern, concrete strongpoints. It also has numerous defence lines belted around the city, heavily entrenched in favourable mountainous terrain. Finally, there are heavy coastal artillery batteries on the shores. Most of the troops available to the Eleventh Army will be used for this operation. The German forces are supplemented by the Romanian VII Corps (10th and 19th Infantry Divisions), 4th Mountain Division and 8th Cavalry Brigade. The bombardment involves 1300 artillery pieces and Luftwaffe attacks.

JUNE 4

GERMANY, *DIPLOMACY*

Hitler visits Marshal Mannerheim in Finland to offer congratulations on the Finn's 75th birthday, and to strengthen the mutual relationships between Germany and Finland. The two men meet near the quiet Finnish border town of Imatra. The meeting is not a success: at one point Hitler demands that Finnish Jews be deported; Mannerheim answers, "over my dead body".

JUNE 5

USSR, *PARTISAN WAR*

The Germans launch Operation Birdsong between Roslavl and Bryansk with 5000 troops. Their target is 2500 partisans that are operating in the area. Over the next four weeks 1198 partisans will be killed for the loss of 58 dead. But the partisan attacks continue. One German officer states: "The partisans continued their old tactic of evading, withdrawing into the forests, or moving in larger groups into the areas south and southwest of the Roslavl–Bryansk highway and into the Kletnya area."

▶ *German forces on the eve of Operation Blue. Because of manpower shortages, German infantry divisions now comprised seven battalions instead of nine, with the strength of companies fixed at 80 men, not 180.*

JUNE 7

SOUTHERN USSR, *LAND WAR*
Following artillery and aerial bombardments, the Germans assault Sevastopol. The main thrust of the attack is launched from the north/northeast by LIV Corps (22nd, 24th, 50th and 132nd Infantry Divisions). The attack in the south is carried out by XXX Corps (72nd and 170th Infantry Divisions and 28th Light Division). In the centre the Romanians pin down the enemy and cover the German flanks. Soviet fire is accurate and deadly, resulting in many casualties.

JUNE 10

NORTHERN USSR, *LAND WAR*
The Soviet Fifty-Second Army, trying to punch a way through to the encircled Second Shock Army, is forced to retreat by the Luftwaffe.

CENTRAL USSR, *LAND WAR*
The Second Panzer Army holds an attack by the Soviet Western Front.

SOUTHERN USSR, *LAND WAR*
The German Sixth Army launches Operation Wilhelm, aimed at destroying the Soviet Twenty-Eighth Army near Volchansk to facilitate the smooth running of the forthcoming German offensive into the Caucasus.

JUNE 11

GERMANY, *ARMED FORCES*
The court martial of 26-year-old army captain Michael Kitzelmann ends in Orel. Kitzelmann, who holds an Iron Cross Second Class for bravery, has spoken out against atrocities being committed on the Eastern Front. He told his follow officers: "If these criminals should win I would have no wish to live any longer." A devout Catholic, he had written in a letter: "At home they banish the crucifixes from the schools, while here they tell us we're fighting

KEY PERSONALITIES

EWALD VON KLEIST

Born in 1885, Kleist saw service in World War I with the hussars. A corps commander during the invasion of Poland in 1939, he led a panzer group during the fall of France in May–June 1940. Although initially inexperienced in the proper use of armoured forces, he learnt quickly and had able subordinates such as Guderian and Zeitzler. Thus, by the spring of 1941 he was equipped to command mobile forces, and his First Panzer Group achieved rapid success in the Balkans campaign. During Barbarossa, his panzer group was attached to Army Group South, taking part in the great Uman and Kiev encirclements, before being ordered north to close the southern part of the Vyazma encirclement. On October 6, 1941, his panzer group became the First Panzer Army; it had taken Rostov by November, but was then forced to withdraw from the city and spend the winter of 1941–42 on the defensive.

During Operation Blue, Kleist and his army advanced into the Caucasus, but long supply lines and Red Army counterattacks forced him to retire once more at the end of 1942. By this time he was commander of Army Group A and had been promoted to field marshal. His army group by this time consisted of the Seventeenth Army, which was ordered to hold the Crimea at all costs. As commander of Army Group A he could not halt the Red Army during the spring of 1944, and was relieved of his command. After the war he was first arrested by the Yugoslavs as a war criminal and sentenced to 15 years in prison in 1948, before being handed over to the Soviets in 1949. He died in a Russian prison in November 1954.

▼ ***A German infantry section about to move forward during the assault on Sevastopol. The port was a tough nut to crack, as remarked upon by Manstein, the Eleventh Army's commander: "the task facing us at Sevastopol involved not only taking a fortress but also fighting an army."***

against godless communism." Before his execution he forgave the sergeant who had denounced him. His farewell letter stated: "God has granted me the grace of a holy death. I go ahead of you to our heavenly homeland. Divine Redeemer, grant me a merciful judgement when I come to you. Praised be Jesus Christ!" Kitzelmann is shot later in the day.

JUNE 15

SOUTHERN USSR, *LAND WAR*
The German Sixth Army completes the defeat of the Twenty-Eighth Army and pushes it back over the River Donets.

JUNE 17

NORTHERN USSR, *LAND WAR*
The Soviet 29th Tank Brigade creates a small corridor through to the trapped Second Shock Army. The troops of the latter make a dash for freedom, but are massacred by German fire.

SOUTHERN USSR, *LAND WAR*
In the Crimea, at Sevastopol, LIV Corps captures Fort Siberia after intense fighting; XXX Corps' 72nd Infantry Division takes the North Nose, Chapel Mount and Ruin Hill strongpoints; and the 170th Infantry Division storms Kamary. The supply efforts of the Soviet Black Sea Fleet to land troops and ammunition are proving inadequate.

▲ ***The Red Army occupants of a bunker on the outskirts of Sevastopol surrender on June 28. The final German assault against the inner fortress area began the next day.***

JUNE 19

SOUTHERN USSR, *GERMAN STRATEGY*
Plans for the German offensive into the Caucasus, codenamed Blue, are captured by the Soviets when an aircraft carrying a staff officer of the 23rd Panzer Division, Major Reichel, is forced down. Reichel has in his possession a complete set of plans for the part XXXX Panzer Corps will play in Operation Blue. The plans are forwarded to the Stavka in Moscow, but Stalin comes to the conclusion that they are phoney and a German ploy: the Nazis want the Soviets to find them in order to throw them off the trail of the impending Moscow attack. This is truly a stroke of luck for Hitler.

JUNE 22

SOUTHERN USSR, *LAND WAR*
The German Sixth and First Panzer Armies commence a limited offensive to destroy the Soviet Ninth and Thirty-Eighth Armies in the Kupyansk area.

GERMANY, *ARMED FORCES*
Army Group South is now ready to launch Operation Blue. Its order of battle is as follows: Sixth Army (330,000 troops and 300 tanks and assault guns); Second Army (95,000 troops); Seventeenth Army (150,000 troops and 180 tanks and assault guns); First Panzer Army (220,000 troops and 480 tanks and assault guns); and Fourth Panzer Army (200,000 troops

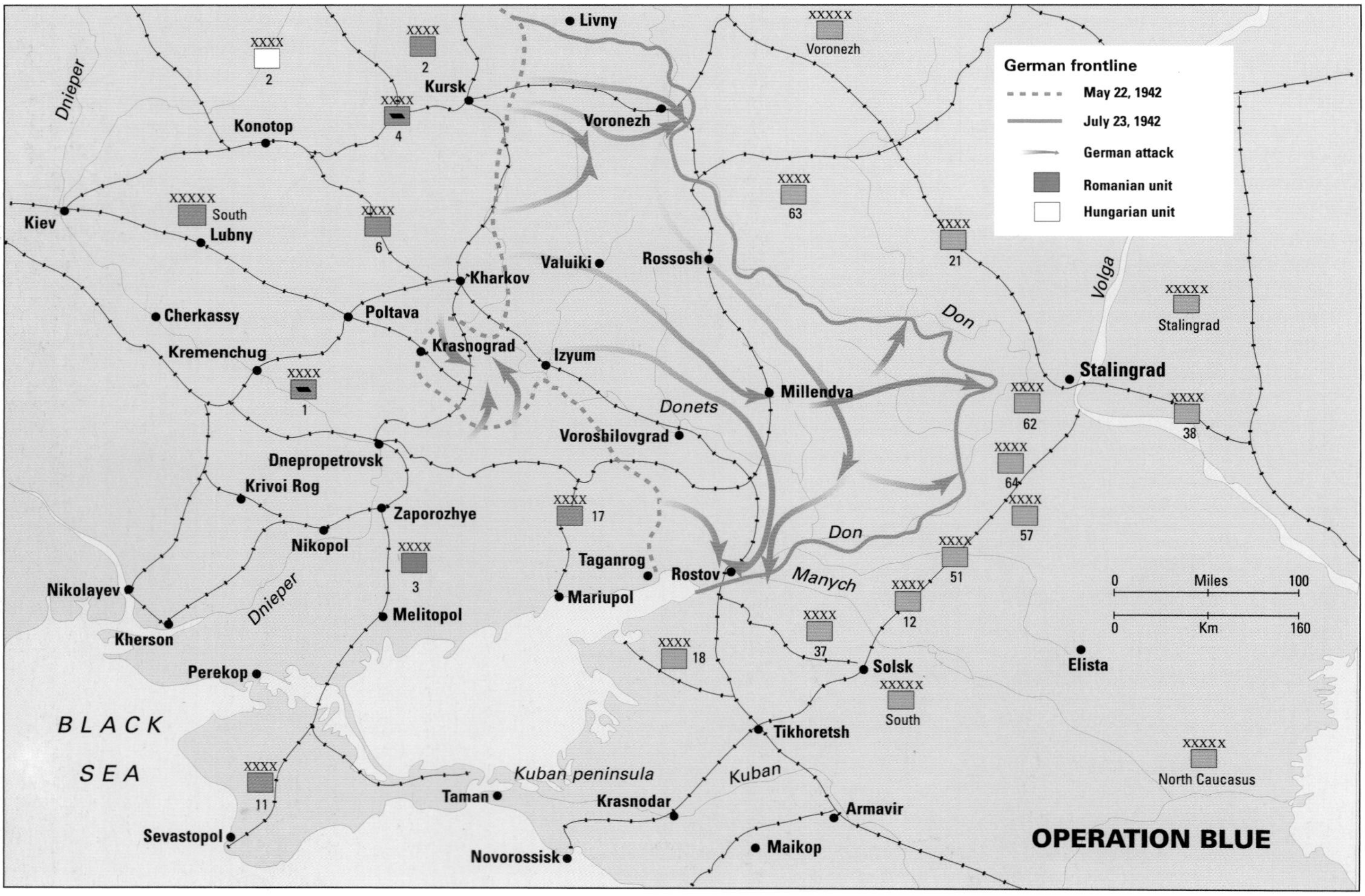

OPERATION BLUE

German frontline
May 22, 1942
July 23, 1942
German attack
Romanian unit
Hungarian unit

▶ *Troops of the German Eleventh Army attacking at Sevastopol. Fortunately for the Germans, the Red Army withdrew from the port rather than fight to the last man.*

and 480 tanks). The Hungarian Second and Italian Eighth Armies, at present in transit, will also support the offensive. Luftwaffe support totals 2690 aircraft.

JUNE 25

NORTHERN USSR, *LAND WAR*
The Soviet Second Shock Army is annihilated by the Germans. Its commander, General Vlassov, has fallen into German hands. The disaster on the Volkhov has cost the Red Army 54,774 killed and missing and 39,977 wounded.

JUNE 26

SOUTHERN USSR, *LAND WAR*
The Sixth Army completes its operations against the Soviet Ninth and Thirty-Eighth Armies, who have suffered more than 40,000 troops captured. At Sevastopol the German Eleventh Army continues to grind its way into the city. The last Soviet supply ships leave the port loaded with wounded troops – there will be more. The Stavka has written off the garrison.

JUNE 27

USSR, *ARMED FORCES*
On the eve of Operation Blue, Soviet forces facing Army Group South are as follows: Bryansk Front (169,000 troops), Southwestern Front (610,000 troops) and Southern Front (522,500 troops). These fronts have a combined tank total of 3470, including 2300 T-34s and KVs.

JUNE 28

SOUTHERN USSR, *LAND WAR*
Operation Blue opens as the Fourth Panzer Army, supported by the Second Army, smashes into the junction of the Soviet Thirteenth and Fortieth Armies. By the evening XXXX Panzer Corps has reached the headquarters of the Fortieth Army, which becomes disorganized. In the Crimea the German 50th Infantry Division takes Inkerman.

GERMANY, *ATROCITIES*
OKW chief Keitel sends a telegraph to his commanders in the East: "Fleeing prisoners of war are to be shot without preliminary warning to stop. All resistance of POWs, even passive, must be entirely eliminated immediately by the use of arms."

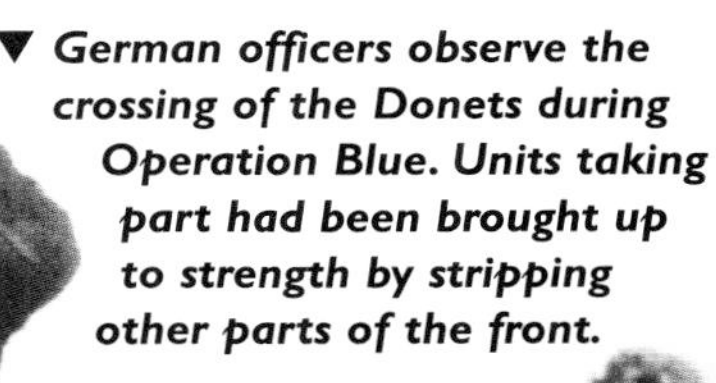

▼ *German officers observe the crossing of the Donets during Operation Blue. Units taking part had been brought up to strength by stripping other parts of the front.*

JULY 2

SOUTHERN USSR, *LAND WAR*
The Red Army retreats before the German advance, with the Fourth, Seventeenth, Twenty-Fourth and Fortieth Armies pulling back towards Voronezh. This means that the Fourth Panzer and Sixth Armies, as they link up at Stary Oskol, fail to trap any Red Army units.

JULY 4

ARCTIC, *SEA WAR*
The Allied convoy PQ-17 (35 merchant ships plus escort) is attacked by U-boats and aircraft, prompting the issuing of the order for the convoy to scatter. The convoy had left Iceland on June 27. Heavy ice floes were encountered by June 30, and a German aircraft sighted the ships the next day. From July 1 to July 10 a large part of the convoy was wiped out. On July 2 the Germans made several attacks.

On July 4 there are attacks in which two American ships, the *Christopher Newport* and the *William Hooper*, are sunk by torpedoes. About an hour and a half before midnight, the convoy receives orders to disperse. The British Admiralty receives intelligence that German capital ships, including *Tirpitz* and *Prinz Eugen*, have left Trondheim to intercept the convoy. This proves to be untrue. However, the convoy's orders leave the slow and heavily loaded merchant ships virtually defenceless.

Only 11 of the 35 merchantmen who left Iceland finally made it to the Soviet Union, either Archangel or Murmansk. Fourteen of the ships sunk were American. More than two-thirds of the convoy had gone to the bottom, along with 210 combat planes, 430 Sherman tanks, 3350 vehicles and nearly 105,000 tonnes (100,000 tons) of other cargo. More than 120 seamen were killed and countless others were crippled and maimed. To compound the disaster, the suspicious Soviets refused to believe that 24 ships from one convoy had been sunk. They openly accused their Western allies of lying about the disaster.

SOUTHERN USSR, *LAND WAR*
In response to XXXXVIII Panzer Corps crossing the River Don west of Voronezh, the Stavka commits the Fifth Tank Army to seal the gap between the Bryansk and Southwestern Fronts. Unfortunately, its 600 tanks are committed piecemeal, thus reducing their effectiveness. Luftwaffe attacks degrade their fighting capability further. In the Crimea Sevastopol has fallen to the Eleventh Army. The Red Army has lost 156,880 killed and missing and 43,601 wounded around the port since October 1941. Manstein takes 90,000 prisoners, together with 460 artillery pieces, 760 mortars and 155 anti-tank guns.

GERMANY, *ARMED FORCES*
Army Group South is reorganized, being divided into Army Groups A and B. Army Group B (Second, Fourth Panzer and Sixth Armies and the Hungarian Second Army) is ordered to destroy Soviet forces between the upper Donets and middle Don and secure a crossing of the Don near Voronezh. The Fourth Panzer and Sixth Armies will then race east to Stalingrad, from whence they will sweep south to support Army Group A in the Caucasus. The army group is supported by VIII Air Corps. Army Group A (First Panzer, Seventeenth and Eleventh Armies) is to destroy enemy forces on the River Mius and then drive into the Caucasus. The army group is supported by IV Air Corps.

JULY 5

CENTRAL USSR, *LAND WAR*
The Western Front again attacks the Second Panzer Army to tie it down.

SOUTHERN USSR, *LAND WAR*
The Fourth Panzer Army enters Voronezh; the Second Army is covering its left flank.

USSR, ARMED FORCES
Stalin creates the Voronezh Front made up of the Third, Sixth and Fortieth Armies.

JULY 7

SOUTHERN USSR, *LAND WAR*
Voronezh is cleared of defenders as the German Fourth Panzer and Sixth Armies link up at Vayluki. However, the haul of prisoners is low – the Southwestern Front is trading space for time.

▶ A destroyer of the Soviet Black Sea Fleet lies crippled in Sevastopol harbour after being hit by Luftwaffe bombs. The Germans enjoyed overwhelming air power during the battle for the city.

◀ *A cargo ship of convoy PQ17 sinks after being torpedoed. The British decision to scatter the convoy, following reports that Kriegsmarine capital ships were approaching, doomed the merchantmen.*

JULY 10

SOUTHERN USSR, *LAND WAR*
Having run out of fuel, the Fourth Panzer Army is on the move again along the Don after receiving fresh supplies. Together with the Sixth Army it is mopping up on the river's west bank. Meanwhile, the German First Panzer and Seventeenth Armies are advancing towards the River Don and Rostov against little resistance.

JULY 11

SOUTHERN USSR, *LAND WAR*
Hitler orders the First and Fourth Panzer Armies to converge at Kamensk and Millerovo prior to a thrust into the Caucasus; the Sixth Army alone will advance on Stalingrad. Hitler believes that the Red Army has been defeated west of the Don and will not now secure the Volga before an attack south.

Hitler also issues Directive No 43 on the conduct of the war in the Crimea: "After clearing the Kerch Peninsula and capturing Sevastopol, the first task of the Eleventh Army will be ... to make all preparations for the main body of the army to cross the Kerch strait by the middle of August at the latest. The aim of this operation will be to thrust forward on either side of the western foothills of the Caucasus in a southeasterly and easterly direction. The operation will be known by the codename Blücher."

JULY 12

SOUTHERN USSR, *LAND WAR*
The Stavka creates the new Stalingrad Front (led by Timoshenko) to combat a German advance to the Volga. It includes the Sixty-Second, Sixty-Third and Sixty-Fourth Armies – 540,000 troops. The Southwestern Front retains the Twenty-First, Twenty-Eighth, Thirty-Eighth and Fifty-Seventh Armies, although the Twenty-Eighth and Thirty-Eighth will soon be taken out of the line and converted into the First and Fourth Tank Armies.

JULY 13

SOUTHERN USSR, *LAND WAR*
The Fourth Panzer Army and XXXX Panzer Corps link up at Boguchar, trapping just 14,000 prisoners. Hitler thinks this signals the end of Red Army resistance. All supplies are thus directed to the two panzer armies, leaving the Sixth Army stranded in the Don Elbow, thus allowing the Soviets to build up their strength at Stalingrad.

JULY 18

GERMANY, *STRATEGY*
Having dismissed Bock on the 15th for supposed lack of vigour in pursuing objectives, Hitler again changes priorities. Army Group B will now resume the advance on Stalingrad.

JULY 19

SOUTHERN USSR, *LAND WAR*
The Sixth Army is reinforced to enable it to fulfil Hitler's wishes. Again, Hitler changes his mind: the First and Fourth Panzer Armies will now advance on a broad front into the Caucasus.

USSR, *ATROCITIES*
Heinrich Himmler, SS chief, orders the start of Operation Reinhard. Its objectives are: to kill Polish Jews; to exploit the skilled or manual labour of some Polish Jews before killing them; to secure the personal property of the Jews (clothing, currency, jewellery); and to identify and secure immovable assets such as factories, apartments and land. The camps used for the extermination will be Belzec (opened March 1942), Sobibor (opened May 1942) and Treblinka (opened July 1942). In total 1.7 million Jews will be killed during Reinhard, plus an unknown number of Poles, gypsies and Soviet prisoners of war.

JULY 20

NORTHERN USSR, *LAND WAR*
Heavy fighting rages south of Leningrad as the Soviet Forty-Second Army tries to wear down the Eighteenth Army.

SOUTHERN USSR, *LAND WAR*
Re-supplied, the German Sixth Army attacks the Soviet Sixty-Second and Sixty-Fourth Armies (combined strength 160,000 troops), inflicting heavy losses.

JULY 23

SOUTHERN USSR, *LAND WAR*
The Sixth Army's attacks are causing the Soviet Sixty-Second and Sixty-Fourth Armies to break apart. At Rostov the 13th Panzer and 5th SS *Wiking* Divisions tighten their grip around the city. Buoyed by these successes, Hitler issues Directive No 45. It states: "The next task of Army Group A is to encircle enemy forces which have escaped across the Don in

▶ *A Soviet position explodes during the siege of Sevastopol. During the battle the Red Army turned the English Cemetery, containing the graves of soldiers killed in the Crimean War, into a strongpoint.*

the area south and southeast of Rostov, and to destroy them. Two armoured formations of Army Group A (including 24th Panzer Division) will come under command of Army Group B for further operations southeastwards.

"After the destruction of enemy forces south of the Don, the most important task of Army Group A will be to occupy the entire eastern coastline of the Black Sea, thereby eliminating the Black Sea ports and the enemy Black Sea Fleet. For this purpose the formations of Eleventh Army already designated (Romanian Mountain Corps) will be brought across the Kerch Straits as soon as the advance of the main body of Army Group A becomes effective, and will then push southeast along the Black Sea coast road.

"At the same time a force composed chiefly of fast-moving formations will give flank cover in the east and capture the Grozny area. Detachments will block the military road between Osetia and Grozny, if possible at the top of the passes. Thereafter the Baku area will be occupied by a thrust along the Caspian coast. These operations by Army Group A will be known by the cover name Edelweiss.

"The task of Army Group B is, as previously laid down, to develop the Don defences and, by a thrust forward to Stalingrad, to smash the enemy forces concentrated there, to occupy the town, and to block the land communications between the Don and the Volga, as well as the Don itself. Closely connected with this, fast-moving forces will advance along the Volga with the task of thrusting through to Astrakhan and blocking the main course of the Volga in the same way. These operations by Army Group B will be known by the cover name Heron."

▲ ***German forces in the rubble of Rostov. It took the Germans 50 hours of fierce fighting to clear the city, and the battle against NKVD machine-gunners on the Taganrog road was particularly brutal.***

JULY 24

SOUTHERN USSR, *LAND WAR*

Rostov falls to the Germans. Since the beginning of Operation Blue the Red Army has suffered the following losses: Bryansk Front, 37,000 killed and missing and 65,000 wounded; Voronezh Front, 43,000 killed and missing and 32,000 wounded; and Southern Front, 128,000 killed and missing and 65,000 wounded.

JULY 25

SOUTHERN USSR, *LAND WAR*

As German land and air attacks wear down the Soviet Sixty-Fourth Army, Army Group A begins its offensive from the River Don. The First Panzer Army pushes back the Soviet Twelfth and Thirty-Seventh Armies.

JULY 28

SOUTHERN USSR, *LAND WAR*

The German Sixth Army runs out of fuel and grinds to a halt, allowing the Soviet Sixty-Second and Sixty-Fourth Armies to fall back east. In the Caucasus the Southern Front is in a complete shambles (it has lost 15,000 killed and wounded in three days), prompting the Stavka to disband it and allocate its units to the North Caucasus Front. The latter has two main formations: Don Group (Twelfth, Thirty-Seventh and Fifty-First Armies) is to halt the First Panzer Army; and Coastal Group (Eighteenth, Forty-Seventh and Fifty-Sixth Armies and XVII

▼ ***German infantry on the way to the River Don. A German recorded in his diary: "On this steppe ... there were no forests to give protection from aircraft, and, above all, no water for the men and horses."***

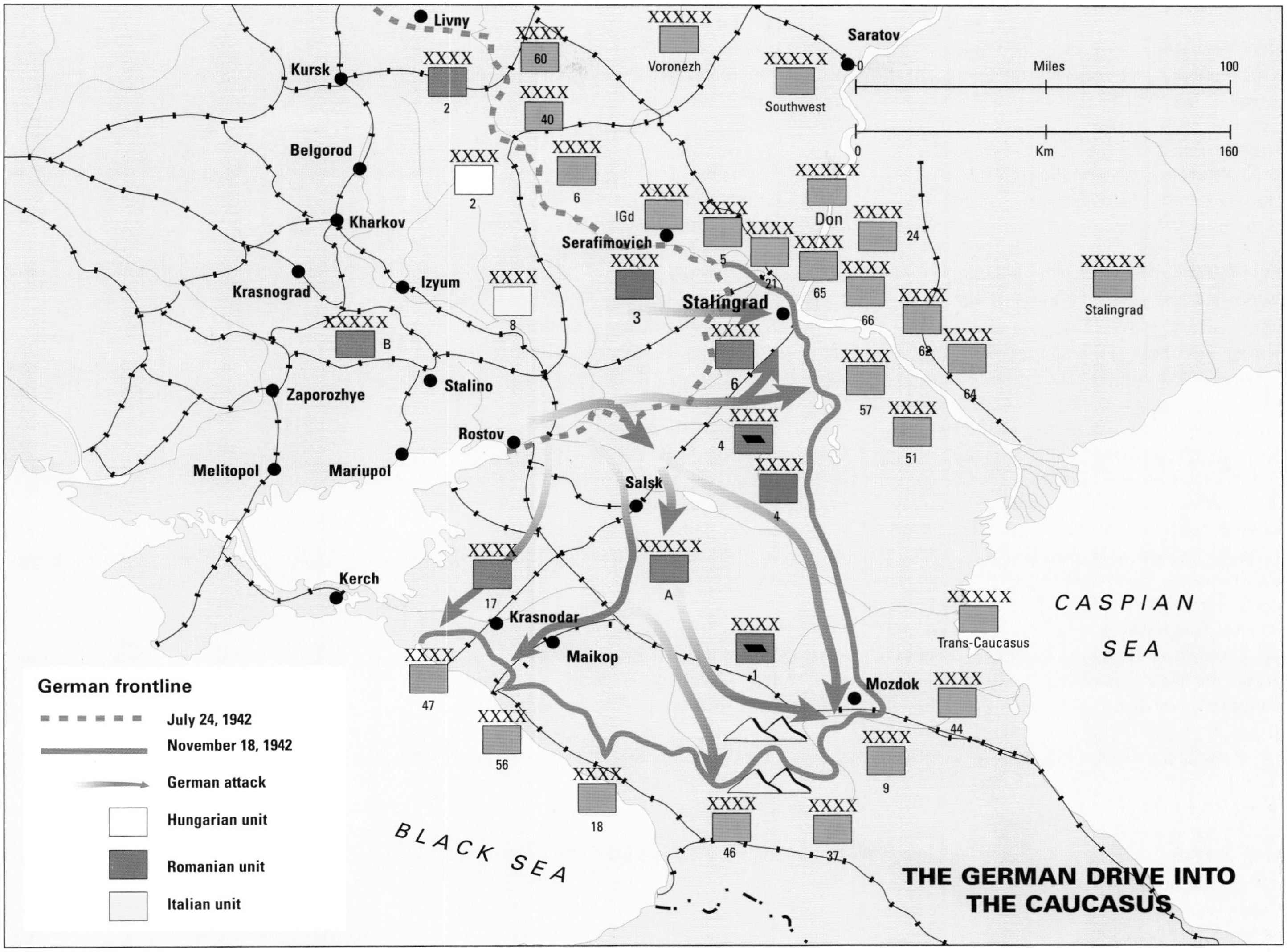

THE GERMAN DRIVE INTO THE CAUCASUS

German frontline
July 24, 1942
November 18, 1942
German attack
Hungarian unit
Romanian unit
Italian unit

Cossack Cavalry Corps) is to stop the German Seventeenth Army and protect the Kuban and approaches to Krasnodar.

USSR, *STRATEGY*

Stalin issues Order No 227. In this he alludes to his concern about German gains: "The territory of the Soviet Union is not a wilderness, but people - workers, peasants, intelligentsia, our fathers and mothers, wives, brothers, children. Territory of USSR that has been captured by the enemy and which the enemy is longing to capture is bread and other resources for the army and the civilians, iron and fuel for the industries, factories and plants that supply the military with hardware and ammunition; this is also railroads. With the loss of Ukraine, Belorussia, the Baltics, Donets basin and other areas we have lost vast territories; that means that we have lost many people, bread, metals, factories and plants. We no longer have superiority over the enemy in human resources and in bread supply. Continuation of retreat means the destruction of our Motherland.

"The conclusion is that it is time to stop the retreat. Not a single step back! This should be our slogan from now on."

JULY 30

CENTRAL USSR, *LAND WAR*

The Kalinin Front (Twenty-Ninth, Thirtieth and Third Air Armies) and Western Front (Twentieth, Thirty-First and First Air Armies) launch the Rzhev-Sychevka Offensive.

SOUTHERN USSR, *LAND WAR*

The Stalingrad Front launches a counter-attack with the First and Fourth Tank Armies, resulting in a tank battle with XIV Panzer Corps. The Luftwaffe pummels the two Soviet armoured units. Meanwhile, the Soviet Sixty-Second and Sixty-Fourth Armies continue to suffer heavy losses.

▶ ***Destroyed Red Army vehicles west of Stalingrad. The diversion of the Fourth Panzer Army from the city to the lower Don meant the Germans lost the chance of taking Stalingrad without a fight in July.***

JULY 31

SOUTHERN USSR, *LAND WAR*

The Soviet First and Fourth Tank Armies are stopped in their tracks; both have suffered massive losses. The Fourth Panzer Army fractures the Soviet Fifty-First Army and throws it back to Kotelnikovo. During July the Germans have lost 38,000 killed on the Eastern Front, insignificant compared to Red Army losses.

AUGUST 3

SOUTHERN USSR, *LAND WAR*
The right flank of the Soviet Sixty-Second Army is broken by the German Sixth Army, which reaches the River Don. As the Fourth Panzer Army continues to push back the Soviet Fifty-First Army, in the Caucasus the Don and Coastal Groups are forced apart by the Germans.

AUGUST 5

SOUTHERN USSR, *LAND WAR*
The Fourth Panzer Army attacks the Soviet Fifty-Seventh and Sixty-Fourth Armies southwest of Stalingrad, but becomes bogged down in enemy defences and is then stopped by a counterattack. However, farther north the German Sixth Army ploughs into the Soviet Sixty-Fourth Army. To the south the First Panzer Army crosses the River Kuban as the Red Army retreats before it. In an effort to catch and destroy the Soviet units, Army Group A is divided: Group Ruoff (Seventeenth Army) will destroy the Coastal Group and secure the Black Sea coast; Group Kleist (First Panzer Army) will capture Baku and the oil fields.

AUGUST 6

NORTHERN USSR, *LAND WAR*
The Soviet Eleventh Army attacks the Demyansk salient, aimed at isolating the German units therein.
CENTRAL USSR, *LAND WAR*
Heavy armoured engagements rage around Rzhev as the Soviets commit the 8th Tank Corps and 2nd Guards Cavalry Corps as reinforcements for the Twentieth and Thirty-First Armies.
SOUTHERN USSR, *LAND WAR*
The First Panzer Army crosses the Kuban after having taken Armavir. Group Kleist continues its southern advance, the Soviet Twelfth and Eighteenth Armies retreating before it.

AUGUST 9

SOUTHERN USSR, *LAND WAR*
The Soviet Sixty-Second Army and parts of the First Tank Army are encircled by

▼ Troops of the First Panzer Army on the open steppe southeast of Rostov. Führer Directive No 45 gave the army the task of advancing to Baku – 1120km (700 miles).

▲ ***German infantry attacking a Soviet position east of Rostov. The hot weather meant that the infantry were very quickly caked with a layer of dust.***

◀ ***The German Sixth Army on the way to Stalingrad. The steppe between the Don and Volga, bone dry in August, was good tank country.***

the 16th and 24th Panzer Divisions. Kleist's panzers enter Maikop. The Germans had planned to start pumping oil right away but they find the oil fields burning – sabotaged by the retreating Red Army.

AUGUST 11

SOUTHERN USSR, *LAND WAR*

The units of the Soviet Sixty-Second Army in the Don bend are destroyed, some 35,000 troops being killed or captured. The German Sixth Army rolls into Kalach as Red Army units fall back towards Stalingrad.

AUGUST 12

USSR, *DIPLOMACY*

As the fighting rages around Stalingrad and in the Caucasus, the First Moscow Conference begins. It is attended by British Prime Minister Winston Churchill and US Ambassador W Averell Harriman, representing President Roosevelt. The main purpose is to discuss a common war strategy. Churchill, with the support of Ambassador Harriman, informs Stalin that it will be impossible for the British and Americans to open a second front in Europe in 1942.

NORTHERN USSR, *LAND WAR*

Heavy rain halts Red Army attacks against the neck of the Demyansk salient.

SOUTHERN USSR, *LAND WAR*

The German Seventeenth Army captures Slavyansk as the Coastal Group fights desperately to prevent the Germans from capturing the Black Sea coast.

GERMANY, *ARMED FORCES*

The Eleventh Army is broken up, the headquarters being ordered to the Leningrad area, four divisions remaining in the Crimea and the rest scattered along the Eastern Front.

AUGUST 15

SOUTHERN USSR, *LAND WAR*

A new offensive by the German Sixth Army shatters the Soviet First Guards and Fourth Tank Army in the Don Elbow and also hits the flank of the Sixty-Second Army at Perepolnyi. Red Army units continue to stream back across the Don. The city of Stalingrad is becoming the focus of the campaign as each side reinforces its armies in the battle for the city. On the Soviet side the Stalingrad

Front has the First Guards, Fourth Tank, Twenty-First, Twenty-Fourth, Sixty-Third and Sixty-Sixth Armies – 414,000 troops, 200 tanks and 200 artillery pieces. The Southeastern Front has the Fifty-First, Fifty-Seventh, Sixty-Second and Sixty-Fourth Armies – 160,000 troops, 70 tanks and 1400 artillery pieces. On the German side the Sixth Army under General Friedrich Paulus numbers 430,000 troops, 440 tanks and 5300 artillery pieces, and General Hermann "Papa" Hoth's Fourth Panzer Army musters 158,000 troops and 2100 artillery pieces.

▲ ***Ju 87 Stukas on their way to bomb Stalingrad, August 23. The air raid terrorized the city's inhabitants: at the hospital the staff abandoned their patients and fled.***

AUGUST 16

CENTRAL USSR, *LAND WAR*
In the fighting around Rzhev the German Ninth Army has thus far suffered 20,000 casualties holding off attacks by the Soviet Twentieth, Twenty-Ninth, Thirtieth and Thirty-First Armies.

SOUTHERN USSR, *LAND WAR*
The German conquest of the Kuban is complete. Army Group A starts to regroup for the next phase of the campaign. The First Panzer Army will advance southeast towards Grozny and Baku in an effort to trap enemy forces against the Turkish border. The Seventeenth Army will advance down the Black Sea coast to the Turkish border.

▶ ***On the fringes of the Reich: a German machine-gunner in the Caucasus Mountains. Army Group A was stretched very thin in the Caucasus, as well as being at the end of a very long and vulnerable supply chain.***

AUGUST 19

NORTHERN USSR, *LAND WAR*
The Soviet Neva Group and Thirteenth Air Army of the Leningrad Front, plus the Volkhov Front's Second Shock, Eighth and Fourteenth Air Armies, launch the Sinyavino Offensive and capture small bridgeheads on the left bank of the Neva.

AUGUST 20

SOUTHERN USSR, *LAND WAR*
A Soviet attack against the Italian Eighth Army, which provides flank protection to the German Sixth Army, causes the Italians some discomfort but does not halt the Sixth's assault. To the south, the Fourth Panzer Army unleashes the 14th and 24th Panzer Divisions and 29th Panzergrenadier Division against the southwestern approaches to Stalingrad. The panzers are temporarily halted by minefields and Red Army resistance. Stalingrad, "the city of Stalin", will act as a magnet for German forces because, for Hitler, it will assume a massive psychological significance – he

will become obsessed by it. Similarly, for Stalin the city will also become an obsession. It has been named after him as a result of his defence of the city during the Russian Civil War. He insists that it should be held at all costs. On a more practical level, he knows that if the Germans take the city Moscow will be vulnerable to an attack from the south.

AUGUST 23

SOUTHERN USSR, *LAND WAR*
XIV Panzer Corps crosses the River Don at Vertyachi and races east. By early evening the 16th Panzer Division has reached the River Volga and secured Spartakovka to the north of Stalingrad. Fierce Red Army resistance slows the advance of the rest of the corps, which does not reach the 16th Panzer. A platoon of the 1st Gebirgsjäger Division hoists the swastika on the summit of Mount Elbrus, the highest peak in the Caucasus.

SOUTHERN USSR, *AIR WAR*
The Luftwaffe launches a massive air raid against Stalingrad. In total 600 bombers conduct 4000 sorties over two days. Oil storage tanks along the River Volga burst into flame and fires break out in the city. The population numbers 600,000, and up to 40,000 are killed in the raids.

AUGUST 27

NORTHERN USSR, *LAND WAR*
The Soviet Volkhov Front begins an offensive designed to relieve Leningrad, the Second Shock Army hitting the German Eighteenth Army hard near Gaitolovo. Fortunately for the Germans, units of the Eleventh Army arrive on the scene to prevent the siege of the city being lifted.

SOUTHERN USSR, *LAND WAR*
The Red Army continues to put up fierce resistance on the approaches to Stalingrad, so much so that the 16th Panzer Division is in danger of being destroyed. The Sixth Army continues to grind its way forward, but the Stavka is concentrating the First Guards, Twenty-Fourth and Sixty-Sixth Armies to threaten XIV Panzer Corps.

AUGUST 28

SOUTHERN USSR, *LAND WAR*
Red Army pressure against XIV Panzer Corps prevents it from advancing into Stalingrad itself. The 3rd Panzergrenadier Division links up with the beleaguered 16th Panzer Division, which has successfully fought off assaults by the Soviet Sixty-Sixth Army (which is now in a state of exhaustion).

ARMED FORCES

PRISONERS OF WAR

It is often stated that the failure of the USSR to sign the Geneva Convention of 1929, which required that belligerents treat prisoners of war humanely, furnish information about them, and permit official visits to prison camps by representatives of neutral states, gave the Nazis licence to mistreat Soviet prisoners of war (POWs) during World War II. However, even if the Soviets had signed the convention, the Germans would not have treated Russian POWs any less brutally. Hitler's war in the East was one of ideological destruction, a conflict in which "sub-human" Slav prisoners could expect little mercy.

The Germans captured 5.7 million Red Army soldiers between June 1941 and the end of the war. Of these, 3.3 million died in captivity; almost 2 million were dead by February 1942. This high death rate was due to inhumane treatment, inadequate accommodation, the manner of their transportation, hunger and the murder of specific groups of prisoners (Jews and Communist Party members). By August 1941, on average only one-fifth of Soviet prisoners in a transport arrived at their destination alive, a consequence of inadequate nourishment. Prisoners were often forced to march for hundreds of kilometres to reach prison camps, which were often just empty fields with barbed wire fences and no buildings (prisoners had to exist in holes or mud huts that they built themselves). The death rate increased with the onset of winter: between October and December 1941, 46 percent of Soviet prisoners held in occupied Poland and in the Ukraine died.

Hundreds of thousands of prisoners died during the long marches to the camps, exhausted prisoners being shot on the spot. Others froze to death in the winter while being transported in open railway wagons: in December 1941, 25–70 percent of prisoners died during transportation to the camps. Even if prisoners survived the transportation, lack of nutrition and the Russian winter, the SS was constantly trawling the camps looking for Jews and communists, who were either shot on the spot or sent to concentration camps. Finally, the survivors were packed off to factories or farms to work as slave labourers to feed the German war effort, often being worked to death.

The Soviets captured 3,155,000 Wehrmacht personnel in the war. Of these, 1,185,000 died in captivity. German prisoners were forced to work in the camps of the Gulag, many until the 1950s. The Soviets did not embark on a conscious policy to work their captives to death, but they did keep them in conditions that were very similar to those in which Soviet POWs had existed during the war: inadequate rations, poor shelter, transportation in sub-zero conditions and brutal guards. As such, thousands died of malnutrition, exhaustion, disease and ill treatment.

AUGUST 30

SOUTHERN USSR, *LAND WAR*
The German LI and VIII Corps secure the Don-Volga land bridge as XXXXVIII Panzer Corps advances to within 48km (30 miles) of Stalingrad. The Soviet Sixty-Second and Sixty-Fourth Armies retreat into the city. In the Caucasus, meanwhile, the First Panzer Army approaches Grozny and crosses the Terek at Ishcherskaya. As at Stalingrad, the Red Army is battling fiercely and giving ground grudgingly.

AUGUST 31

SOUTHERN USSR, *LAND WAR*
The Soviet First Guards Army attacks XIV Panzer Corps north of Stalingrad, while to the south XXXXVIII Panzer Corps advances close to Pitomnik in the rear of the Sixty-Second and Sixty-Fourth Armies. In the Caucasus, the Soviets are unable to prevent the First Panzer Army from strengthening its bridgeheads on the Terek. Red Army losses in the region have been severe, North Caucasus Front losing 35,000 killed and missing since the end of July, and the Trans-Caucasus Front suffering 7300 killed and missing in the same period. However, Army Group A is experiencing fuel shortages, which are hampering panzer operations.

▲ ***German troops order Soviet prisoners to the rear. Operation Blue failed to trap large enemy formations, which meant the German haul of prisoners was low.***

September 3

▶ ***General Paulus directing his artillery at Stalingrad. The Sixth Army's commander was not in the best of health, suffering from recurrent dysentery and stress.***

September 3

SOUTHERN USSR, *LAND WAR*
In an attempt to take the pressure off the Sixty-Second and Sixty-Fourth Armies, the Soviet First Guards Army, located north of Stalingrad, attacks XIV Panzer Corps. The operation is a shambles, with the Soviets suffering greatly at the hands of German artillery. The attack is called off. The Fourth Panzer and Sixth Armies continue to push the two aforementioned Soviet armies back into the city, but they have missed an opportunity to encircle them. In the Caucasus, both the Seventeenth and First Panzer Armies continue their advance, but both are having their strength reduced and are at the end of very long supply lines.

SOUTHERN USSR, *AIR WAR*
Air Fleet 4 continues to pound Stalingrad, but is merely turning the city into an environment that is aiding the defence and making panzer operations very difficult in the rubble.

September 4

NORTHERN USSR, *LAND WAR*
The arrival of the German Eleventh Army on the Volkhov is paying dividends. Manstein deploys XXVI Corps on the northern wing and XXX Corps in the south to contain the Soviet threat.

SOUTHERN USSR, *LAND WAR*
Yet another futile Soviet attack by the First Guards, Twenty-Fourth and Sixty-Sixth Armies against XIV Panzer Corps suffers at the hands of German artillery and comes to nothing. Overhead, the Luftwaffe continues its round-the-clock attacks against the city.

September 7

SOUTHERN USSR, *LAND WAR*
The German LI Corps of the Sixth Army attempts to reach Stalingrad city centre, specifically the Mamayev Kurgan hill, whose heights hold a commanding position over the whole city, the Volga and the area across the river. Both sides realize that he who holds the hill holds the city. As such, it will be the centre of

▶ ***Halftracks of XIV Panzer Corps on the approaches to Stalingrad. The vehicle on the right is an SdKfz 251/10 mounting a Pak 35/36 anti-tank gun.***

KEY WEAPONS

YAK-9

The Yak-9 was the mainstay of the Soviet Air Force in the middle and later years of World War II, and was produced in greater numbers than any other Soviet fighter. By the middle of 1944, for example, there were more Yak-9s in service than all other Soviet fighters combined. First flying in June 1942, it was powered by a liquid-cooled "V" engine, the VK-105PF, which generated 1260 horsepower. Armament comprised one 20mm cannon firing through the centre of the propeller boss, and two 12.7mm machine guns firing through the engine cowling. The Yak-9 could also carry up to six rockets or two 100kg (220lb) bombs.

The Yak-9T was a tank-busting, ground-attack version that entered service in early 1943. It was usually armed with a 32mm or 37mm cannon and had wing racks for anti-personnel bomblets in special containers. The long-range DD version escorted US bombers shuttling to the USSR. The excellent fighter could from the beginning out-fly the German Messerschmitt Bf 109, and later variants could out-perform the Focke-Wulf 190.

Type: single-seat fighter
Powerplant: 1 x 1260hp Klimov VK-105PF
Wingspan: 10m (32.8ft)
Length: 8.54m (28ft)
Height: 2.44m (8ft)
Maximum speed: 600kmh (375mph)
Service ceiling: 10,500m (34,500ft)
Maximum range: 890km (550 miles)
Armament: 1 x 20mm cannon, 2 x 12.7mm machine gun, 2 x 100kg (220lb) bombs

fierce battles during the coming weeks. In the Caucasus the Soviet Forty-Seventh Army tries to throw the German Seventeenth Army out of Novorossisk.

SEPTEMBER 9

SOUTHERN USSR, *LAND WAR*

The German LI Corps approaches Mamayev Kurgan in Stalingrad, as the Soviet Sixty-Second Army is hit in the centre by LI Corps, in the north by XIV Panzer Corps and in the south by XXXXVIII Panzer Corps. The Fourth Panzer Army is also closing on the city from the south, grinding into the Sixty-Fourth Army as it does so.

GERMANY, *ARMED FORCES*

Hitler relieves Field Marshal Wilhelm List from command of Army Group A for not achieving more (an indication of the Führer's continuing frustration with his senior army commanders, and his failure to understand military logistics), deciding that he will take personal command of the formation.

SEPTEMBER 11

SOUTHERN USSR, *LAND WAR*

The German Sixth and Fourth Panzer Armies continue to push their way into Stalingrad. In the north they secure a stretch of the Volga river bank, allowing them to range their artillery on Soviet river traffic. In the Caucasus, the fight for Novorossisk goes on.

◀ German panzergrenadiers near Stalingrad. The lack of Soviet aircraft in the skies at this time meant German vehicles could move unimpeded outside the city.

SEPTEMBER 12

SOUTHERN USSR, *LAND WAR*

General Vasily Chuikov assumes command of the Sixty-Second Army. The German Sixth and Fourth Panzer Armies have a combined total of 590,000 troops, 10,000 artillery pieces and 100 tanks. Facing them are the Stalingrad Front (First Guards, Twenty-Fourth, Twenty-First, Sixty-Sixth and Fourth Tank Armies) and Southeastern Front (Sixty-Second, Sixty-Fourth, Fifty-Seventh, Fifty-First Armies), with a combined total of 590,000 troops, 7000 artillery pieces and 600 tanks.

SEPTEMBER 13

SOUTHERN USSR, *LAND WAR*

A massive German assault begins at Stalingrad. The 71st, 76th and 295th Infantry Divisions attack from Gumrak against the centre of the Sixty-Second Army. Farther south, the 94th Infantry, 29th Panzergrenadier and 14th and 24th Panzer Divisions smash through the Yelshanka and Dar Gova suburbs and reach the Volga. The fighting rages throughout the night. Stalin orders the 13th Guards Rifle Division to cross the Volga into the city to reinforce the Sixty-Second Army.

SEPTEMBER 14

SOUTHERN USSR, *LAND WAR*

The German assaults, backed up by massive artillery fire and Luftwaffe aircraft, continue. XXXXVIII Panzer Corps takes the Tsaritsyn quarter while, south of Mamayev Kurgan, the 76th Infantry Division makes steady gains, taking the railway station (it changes hands four times during the day). Mamayev Kurgan falls to the 295th Infantry Division, cutting the Sixty-Second Army in two. During the night the 13th Guards Rifle Division crosses the river and establishes a small bridgehead in the face of fierce resistance.

SOUTHERN USSR, *AIR WAR*

The Luftwaffe drops mines in the River Volga at Stalingrad.

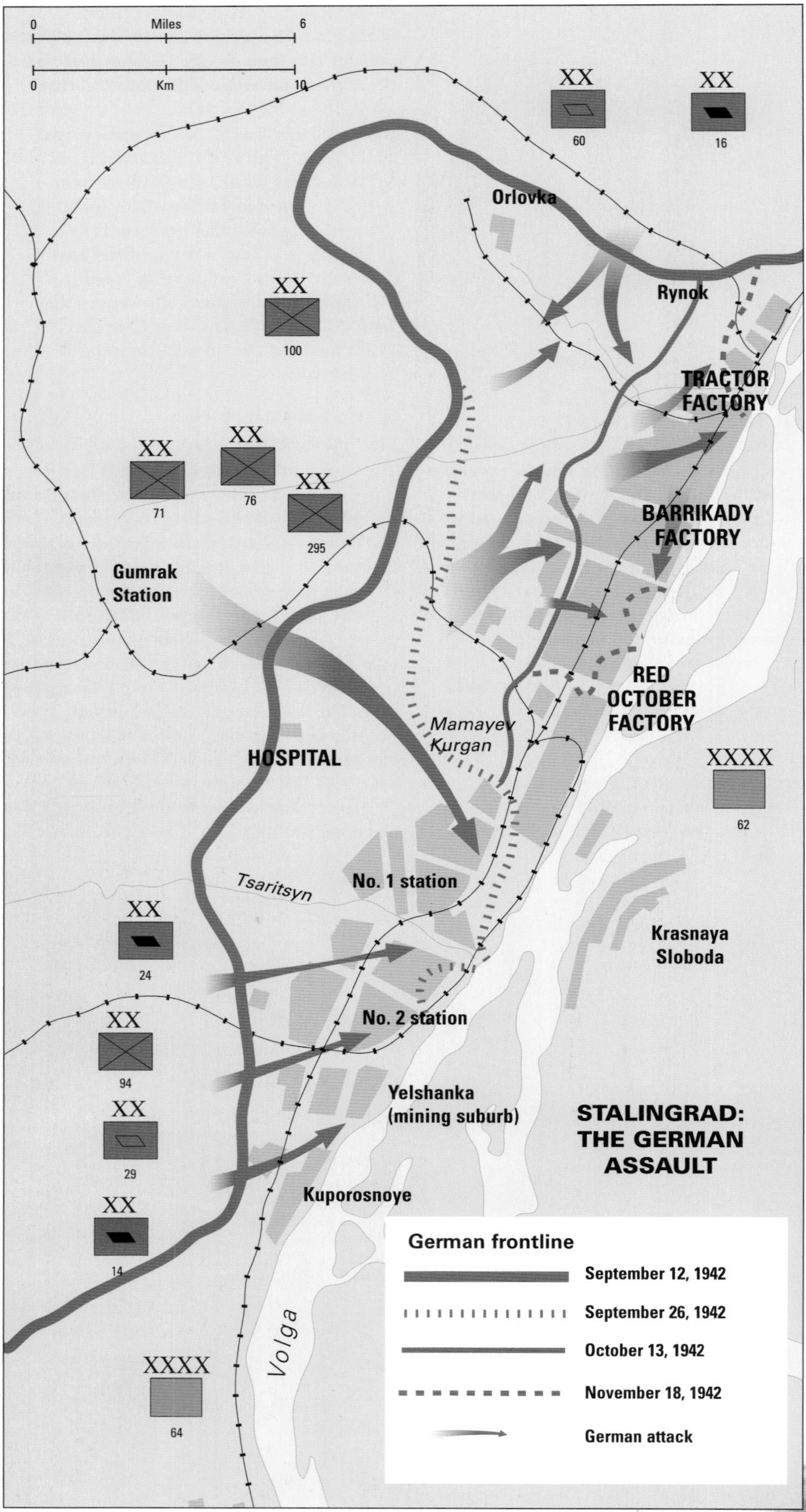

SEPTEMBER 15

SOUTHERN USSR, *LAND WAR*

The railway station becomes the focus of the fighting at Stalingrad, while the 13th Guards Division attacks the Mamayev Kurgan. To the south the German 94th Infantry, 14th and 24th Panzer Divisions increase their efforts to prise apart the Soviet Sixty-Second and Sixty-Fourth Armies at Kuporosnoye.

SEPTEMBER 16

SOUTHERN USSR, *LAND WAR*

The Soviet 13th Guards Division retakes the railway station and Mamayev Kurgan, the latter with the help of the 112th Rifle Division. It then doggedly defends the hill in the face of massive German firepower.

SEPTEMBER 18

SOUTHERN USSR, *LAND WAR*

An attack by the Soviet First Guards Army north of Stalingrad is halted by German artillery and Luftwaffe attacks. A counterattack then throws the First Guards back to its start lines. The 92nd Rifle Brigade wards off all German efforts to dislodge it from the grain elevator. Similarly, LI Corps tries to retake Mamayev Kurgan, to no avail. The bombing and shelling results in a permanent pall of smoke hanging over the city.

SEPTEMBER 20

SOUTHERN USSR, *LAND WAR*

The Soviet First Guards, Twenty-Fourth and Sixty-Sixth Armies launch assaults to break through to the beleaguered Sixty-Second Army, but all fail. Under ferocious artillery and Luftwaffe assaults, followed by infantry and panzers, the 13th Guards Division is forced out of the railway station into the nail factory.

▲ ***Germans on the western edge of Stalingrad. The fighting was much harder than expected, an ill omen for the future.***

◀ ***German troops near the tractor factory in Stalingrad. At the end of September the Germans squeezed the Orlovka salient, forcing the Soviets back towards the tractor and Barrikady factories.***

SEPTEMBER 21

NORTHERN USSR, *LAND WAR*
The German Eleventh Army counter-attacks at Gaitolovo and soon has the enemy surrounded in a pocket, which is then hammered by constant artillery bombardments and aerial attacks.

SOUTHERN USSR, *LAND WAR*
The German Sixth Army fends off attacks by the First Guards, Twenty-Fourth and Sixty-Sixth Armies. In Stalingrad the Soviets are forced out of the nail factory. XXXXVIII Panzer Corps clears the bed of the Tsaritsyn stream and thus isolates the 92nd and 42nd Rifle Brigades on the southern flank of the Sixty-Second Army. Fighting continues around Mamayev Kurgan and the grain elevator.

SEPTEMBER 23

SOUTHERN USSR, *LAND WAR*
The Soviet 284th Rifle Division crosses the Volga at Stalingrad and, together with the 95th Rifle Division, drives the Germans back from the southern slopes of Mamayev Kurgan to the railway station. Farther south, the 42nd and 92nd Rifle Brigades are worn down by German fire and are amalgamated. In the Caucasus, Group Ruoff begins Operation Attica designed to destroy Soviet defences in the Caucasus Mountains. Employing two corps of the Seventeenth Army, they strike the Eighteenth and Fifty-Sixth Armies but make little headway.

SEPTEMBER 24

SOUTHERN USSR, *LAND WAR*
The German Sixth Army regroups for a fresh attack at Stalingrad. Paulus will direct his attacks against the factory district and Orlovka salient on the Sixth Army's left flank. Fresh attacks will be made against Mamayev Kurgan and the Red October factory.

GERMANY, *ARMED FORCES*
Halder is dismissed as Chief of the General Staff and replaced by Kurt Zeitzler. Hitler states: "I dismissed General Halder because he could not understand the spirit of my plans."

SEPTEMBER 27

SOUTHERN USSR, *LAND WAR*
Chuikov launches a spoiling attack inside Stalingrad with the Sixty-Second Army and 36th Guards Rifle Division of the Sixty-Fourth Army, which is stopped by Luftwaffe attacks. The Germans then assault the Mamayev Kurgan and the Red October factory, taking the summit of the hill. The Germans reach the Volga on an 8km (5 mile) front in the south. The Soviet 193rd Rifle Division crosses the river and deploys in the Red October coke house. In the Caucasus, the German 13th Panzer, 370th Infantry and 5th SS *Wiking* Divisions storm Elchetvo.

SEPTEMBER 28

USSR, *ARMED FORCES*
The Stavka reorganizes its Stalingrad formations. The Southeastern Front becomes the Stalingrad Front, and the old Stalingrad Front becomes the Don Front under General Konstantin Rokossovsky.

SEPTEMBER 29

SOUTHERN USSR, *LAND WAR*
The Orlovka salient is attacked by the German 16th Panzer, 60th Panzer-grenadier and 389th and 100th Infantry Divisions, forcing the defending units back into Orlovka itself. In Stalingrad, fighting continues on the Mamayev Kurgan and at the Red October factory.

SEPTEMBER 30

SOUTHERN USSR, *LAND WAR*
More Red Army units are fed into Stalingrad: the reformed 42nd Rifle Brigade, the 92nd Rifle Brigade to relieve the 23rd Tank Corps and the 4000-strong 39th Guards Division to support the 193rd Rifle Division west of the Red October factory. The Stavka also plans to send the Third and Fifth Tank and the Forty-Third Armies from the reserve to Stalingrad.

▼ ***Stalingrad under attack on September 28, when heavy Luftwaffe attacks against the Volga ferries resulted in substantial Soviet losses. On the west bank of the river, the Germans attacked the Red October and Silikat factories.***

OCTOBER 1

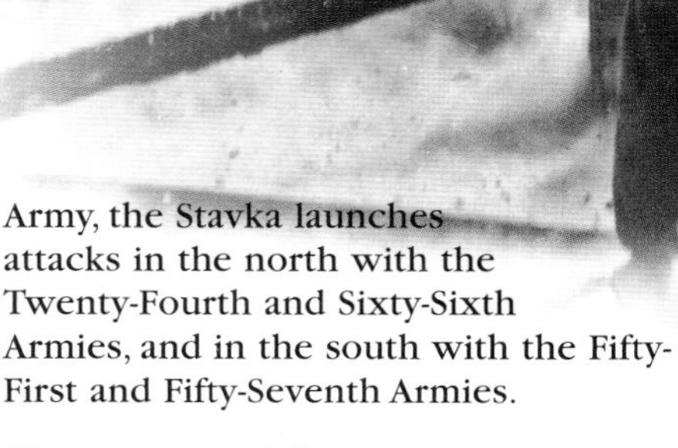

OCTOBER 1

SOUTHERN USSR, *LAND WAR*
German attacks in the Orlovka sector continue. In the factory district the Germans pound the 193rd Rifle Division in front of the Red October factory, and also strike the 284th Rifle and 13th Guards Divisions. However, the latter units defeat all German efforts to break through to the Volga. But the Soviets are hard pressed, prompting Chuikov to deploy the 39th Guards Division to the Red October workshops. The Sixth Army has suffered 40,000 casualties since September 13; the Soviet Sixty-Second Army, 78,000.

OCTOBER 2

NORTHERN USSR, *LAND WAR*
What is left of the Soviet Second Shock Army in the Gaitolovo Pocket is wiped out, with 24,000 troops captured and killed, plus 300 artillery pieces, 500 mortars and 240 tanks lost.

SOUTHERN USSR, *LAND WAR*
The Soviet 13th Guards Division defeats an assault by the 295th Division as German forces penetrate into the Barrikady, tractor and Red October installations at Stalingrad. An attack in the south by the Sixty-Fourth Army is defeated. During the night the Soviet 308th Rifle and 37th Guards Divisions cross the Volga to reinforce the Sixty-Second Army.

▼ A German soldier takes aim in Stalingrad. In mid-October the Germans launched a fresh offensive in the city involving 90,000 troops and 300 tanks.

OCTOBER 5

SOUTHERN USSR, *LAND WAR*
The Soviets unleash a 300-gun barrage against German units in the factory area of Stalingrad, inflicting heavy casualties. But the Soviets are forced out of the Silikat factory and the 42nd and 92nd Rifle Brigades and 6th Guards Tank Brigade are isolated.

OCTOBER 7

SOUTHERN USSR, *LAND WAR*
The Germans finally clear the Orlovka sector at Stalingrad, as the 37th Guards Division struggles to hold the tractor factory against intensive attacks. German units also battle the 193rd Rifle Division in the city's sports stadium.

OCTOBER 9

SOUTHERN USSR, *LAND WAR*
The fighting temporarily halts in Stalingrad as the Germans are exhausted.

USSR, *ARMED FORCES*
The Red Army ends its system of dual leadership by abolishing the position of communist political commissar in favour of a single military commander in each unit. Party representatives will continue to serve in the army, but will no longer direct military operations.

OCTOBER 14

SOUTHERN USSR, *LAND WAR*
The German offensive in Stalingrad resumes, with the 94th and 389th Infantry, 100th Jäger and 14th and 24th Panzer Divisions attacking the factory districts. By the afternoon the Germans have surrounded the 112th and 37th Guards Divisions and annihilated the right flank of the 308th Rifle Division. During the night the Germans reach the tractor factory and break through to the Volga. The 37th Guards Division has been all but destroyed. Chuikov ferries the 138th Rifle Division across the river during the night. In the Caucasus, Group Ruoff again fails to breach Red Army defences to reach the Black Sea.

OCTOBER 15

SOUTHERN USSR, *LAND WAR*
German firepower halts all daytime traffic across the Volga as the Germans isolate enemy forces in the tractor factory. In an effort to relieve the Sixty-Second Army, the Stavka launches attacks in the north with the Twenty-Fourth and Sixty-Sixth Armies, and in the south with the Fifty-First and Fifty-Seventh Armies.

OCTOBER 18

SOUTHERN USSR, *LAND WAR*
The Germans have taken the tractor factory and wiped out the 37th Guards Division. They break through the 84th Tank Brigade and attack the Barrikady factory, fighting every inch of the way.

OCTOBER 21

SOUTHERN USSR, *LAND WAR*
The German 79th Infantry Division is repulsed from the Red October and Barrikady factories. The Germans make minor gains in the Red October area.

OCTOBER 22

SOUTHERN USSR, *LAND WAR*
The first snows fall at Stalingrad. The Soviet Sixty-Fourth Army launches an attack from the Beketovka salient designed to link up with the Sixty-Second. It is stopped by intensive German artillery fire, which inflicts heavy casualties.

USSR, *ARMED FORCES*
Plans for the Soviet counteroffensive around Stalingrad, codenamed Uranus, are gathering pace. The Southwestern Front under General Nikolay Vatutin is activated, comprising the Fifth Tank, Twenty-First and Sixty-Third Armies and the Second and Seventeenth Air Armies. The Don Front comprises the Twenty-Fourth, Sixty-Fifth and Sixty-Sixth Armies. The Stavka also has the Second Guards Army that it

◀ ***German artillery at Stalingrad, with the grain elevator in the background. Despite their massive firepower, the Germans had to reduce enemy pockets one by one.***

intends to use against the Romanian Fourth Army.

OCTOBER 25

SOUTHERN USSR, *LAND WAR*
As the Germans continue to blast their way into the Red October and Barrikady factory complexes, the Soviet Sixty-Fourth Army launches a fresh attack towards Stalingrad, meeting fierce German resistance. In the Caucasus, an assault by III Panzer Corps towards Nalchik forces the Soviet Thirty-Seventh Army to retreat.

USSR, *STRATEGY*
For Operation Uranus the Stavka will deploy the Southwestern Front (340,000 troops), Don Front (292,000 troops) and Stalingrad Front (383,000 troops).

OCTOBER 27

SOUTHERN USSR, *LAND WAR*
The Germans can now fire on Red Army landing areas on the west bank of the Volga, causing heavy casualties among Soviet units before they even enter the battle. However, the Sixth Army is all but exhausted, having used up its reserves.

OCTOBER 28

SOUTHERN USSR, *LAND WAR*
XIV Panzer and LI Corps can make no impression upon the Red October and Barrikady factories at Stalingrad.

OCTOBER 30

USSR, *STRATEGY*
The Stavka finalizes its Uranus plans. The Southwestern Front will attack the Chir and Kalach lines while the Stalingrad Front will strike for Sovetski and Kalach. The battered Sixty-Second Army will pin the Sixth Army in Stalingrad and the Sixty-Fourth Army will attack from the Beketovka salient.

OCTOBER 31

GERMANY, *ATROCITIES*
In a secret memorandum, Keitel confirms Hitler's orders for the use of Soviet prisoners in German industry: "The lack of workers is becoming an increasingly dangerous hindrance for the future German war and armaments industry. The expected relief through discharges from the armed forces is uncertain as to the extent and date; however, its possible extent will by no means correspond to expectations and requirements in view of the great demand.

"The Führer has now ordered that the working power of the Russian prisoners of war should be utilized to a large extent by large-scale assignment for the requirements of the war industry. The prerequisite for production is adequate nourishment."

KEY WEAPONS

TIGER

Following encounters with Soviet T-34 and KV-1 tanks in 1941, German tank designers were instructed to produce a heavy tank that would restore mastery of the battlefield to the Germans. The result was the Panzer VI Ausf E – the Tiger I – which entered service in August 1942. It was armed with the powerful 88mm gun (originally developed from the 88mm Flak 36 L/56 gun), which meant it could knock out any Allied tank then in service. Its thick (but not shot-deflecting) armour made it virtually indestructible (the US Sherman, armed with a 76mm gun, and Russian T-34/85, armed with an 85mm gun, only stood a chance against a Tiger at close range, and only with a shot against its side or rear).

The Tiger had a five-man crew: commander, gunner, loader, radio operator and driver. The tank's suspension was composed of driving sprocket, rear idler and inter-leaved road wheels (36 in total). This arrangement gave a very smooth ride cross-country, but in cold weather caused mud, ice and rocks to jam the track mechanism and immobilize the tank. To overcome this problem, the running gear needed constant attention.

In the right hands the Tiger could be very effective: on July 7, 1943, at Kursk, a single Tiger commanded by *SS-Oberscharführer* Franz Staudegger of the 1st SS Panzer Division *Leibstandarte*, engaged 50 T-34s. Staudegger used up his entire ammunition after destroying some 22 enemy tanks, while the rest retreated. For his achievement Staudegger was awarded the Knight's Cross.

Weight: 57,000kg (125,400lb)
Crew: 5
Engine: 1 x Maybach HL 230 P45
Speed: 45.4kmph (28mph)
Range: 125km (78 miles)
Length: 8.45m (27.7ft)
Width: 3.7m (12ft)
Height: 2.93m (9.61ft)
Armament: 1 x 88mm cannon, 2 x 7.92mm machine gun
Ammunition: 92 x 88mm, 5700 x 7.92mm
Armour: front (maximum): 110mm (4.33in); side (maximum) 80mm (3.14in)

NOVEMBER 2

SOUTHERN USSR, *LAND WAR*
In the Caucasus, the 3rd Panzer Division nears Ordzhonikidze, the most south-easterly point reached by the Wehrmacht in World War II. The first snows begin to fall in this sector.

NOVEMBER 4

USSR, *STRATEGY*
The Stavka prepares Operation Saturn, the destruction of the Italian Eighth Army by the Southwestern and Voronezh Fronts, leading to the Red Army reaching the River Dnieper and cutting off Army Groups A and B. It will be spearheaded by the First Guards and Sixth Armies.

NOVEMBER 11

SOUTHERN USSR, *LAND WAR*
The German Sixth Army commences its final offensive at Stalingrad, preceded by artillery and air strikes. It succeeds in taking most of the Red October factory and isolating the Soviet 138th Division south of the Barrikady factory. By the evening, the Sixty-Second Army occupies three small pockets along the Volga: in the north 1000 troops at Rynok and Spartakovka; in the centre 500 troops near the Barrikady factory; and in the south 45,000 troops and 20 tanks.

NOVEMBER 17

SOUTHERN USSR, *LAND WAR*
In Stalingrad, the German assaults are annihilating the Sixty-Second Army. The group at Rynok and Spartakovka has been reduced to 300 troops at the hands of the 16th Panzer Division. Another problem now besets the Soviets: ice on the Volga.

▲ Paulus observes the Sixth Army's final assault at Stalingrad. It was a series of hammer blows designed to crush the Soviet Sixty-Second Army.

Ice on the river stopped boat traffic three days ago, as the river was impassable. Efforts to air-drop supplies to the Sixty-Second Army have come to nothing, because the Red Army has such a slender strip of land and most of the material falls into German hands. Luftwaffe reconnaissance has detected Soviet build-ups to the northwest of the city, which worry Paulus.

NOVEMBER 18

SOUTHERN USSR, *LAND WAR*
The eve of Operation Uranus. The Stavka has amassed the following forces for the offensive: Southwestern Front (First Guards, Twenty-First and Fifth Tank Armies, 3rd Guards Cavalry and 4th Tanks Corps, and Seventeenth and Second Air Armies) – 398,000 troops, 6500 artillery pieces, 150 Katyushas, 730 tanks and 530 aircraft; Don Front (Twenty-Fourth, Sixty-Fifth and Sixty-Sixth Armies and Sixteenth Air Army) – 307,000 troops, 5300 artillery pieces, 150 Katyushas, 180 tanks and 260 aircraft; and Stalingrad Front (Fifty-First, Fifty-Seventh, Sixty-Second and Sixty-Fourth Armies, 4th and 13th Mechanized Corps, 4th Cavalry Corps and Eighth Air Army) – 429,000 troops, 5800 artillery pieces, 145 Katyushas and 650 tanks. Facing the Don and Southwestern Fronts is the Romanian Third Army (100,000 troops), while the Romanian Fourth Army (70,000 troops) faces the Soviet Fifty-First and Fifty-Seventh Armies. These are extremely weak formations to have as flank protection for the Fourth Panzer and Sixth Armies at Stalingrad.

NOVEMBER 19

SOUTHERN USSR, *LAND WAR*
Operation Uranus begins as the Southwestern and Don Fronts attack the Romanian Third Army. The Romanians defend stoutly and at first the Soviet Fifth Tank, Twenty-First and Sixty-Fifth Armies make slow progress. However, an assault by the 1st and 26th Tank Corps of the Fifth Tank Army eventually rips a hole in the Romanian front, through which the Soviets pour. By the end of the day the Romanians have suffered a staggering 55,000 casualties. The German XXXXVIII Panzer Corps is ordered to restore the situation, but attacks by the Romanian 1st Armoured Division north of Zhirkovski and 22nd Panzer Division from Peschany are costly failures. Paulus, ordered to restore his northern flank, decides to employ his three panzer divisions.

NOVEMBER 20

SOUTHERN USSR, *LAND WAR*
The Romanian 1st Armoured Division is destroyed by the Soviet Fifth Tank Army, which also mauls the 22nd Panzer Division as it falls back to the Chir. At Stalingrad a fuel shortage delays the advance of XIV Panzer Corps. To the south, the Romanian Fourth Army is hit by the Soviet Fifty-First, Fifty-Seventh and Sixty-Fourth Armies. As they retreat, only the German 29th Panzergrenadier and 297th Infantry Divisions hold up the attack.

GERMANY, ARMED FORCES
Hitler creates Army Group Don, led by Field Marshal Manstein, which is ordered to safeguard positions on the Chir and Don and restore the Sixth Army's flanks.

NOVEMBER 21

SOUTHERN USSR, *LAND WAR*
The German flanks behind Stalingrad are collapsing. The Fifth Tank Army brushes aside the 24th Panzer Division near the Don bridges.

▼ "I know about the difficulties of the battle for Stalingrad and about the loss of troops ... however, the difficulties are even greater for the Russians." Hitler to Paulus, November 17, 1942.

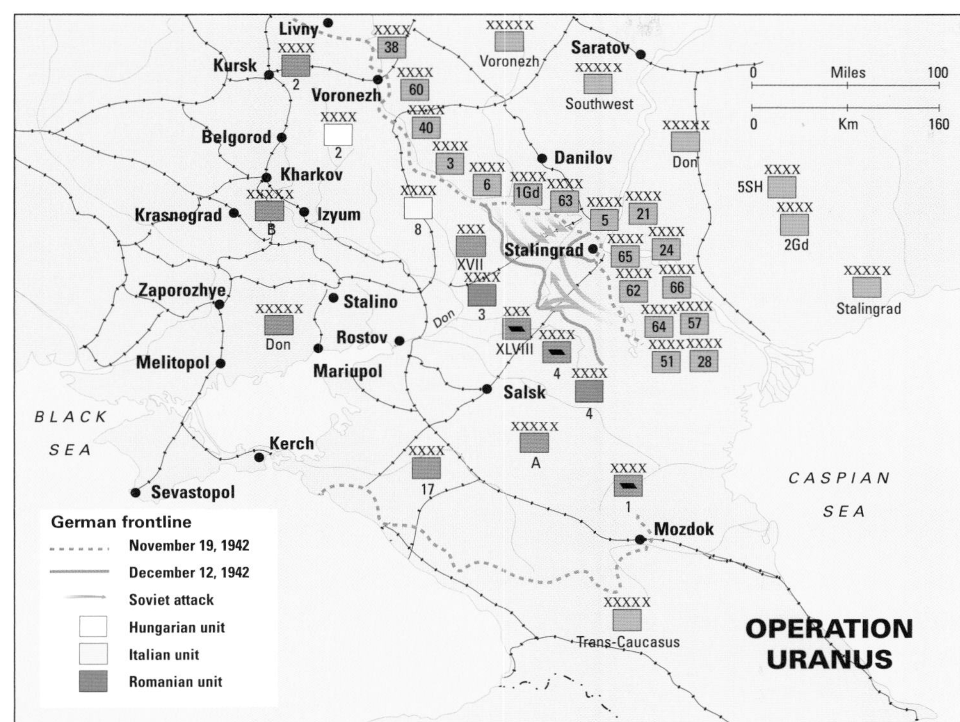

NOVEMBER 23

SOUTHERN USSR, *LAND WAR*

Some 27,000 Romanian soldiers surrender, signalling the end of their Third Army, which has lost 90,000 casualties since the start of Uranus. Red Army units link up at Kalach, thus trapping the German Sixth, part of the Fourth Panzer and what is left of the Romanian Fourth Armies – 256,000 German troops, 11,000 Romanians, 100 tanks, 1800 artillery pieces, 10,000 motor vehicles and 23,000 horses.

General Paulus put his forces into a giant hedgehog defensive posture as part of the grandly titled "Fortress Stalingrad". However, he has serious problems. First, establishing an effective defensive perimeter at Stalingrad is difficult due to a desperate shortage of infantry and the lack of prepared positions. Second, to the south and west lay almost completely treeless, shelter-free steppes. Third, a lack of fuel, which prevents the rapid deployment of his three panzer and three panzergrenadier divisions as mobile reserves. Fourth, a general shortage of artillery ammunition also weakens the German defence.

NOVEMBER 24

CENTRAL USSR, *LAND WAR*

The eve of Operation Mars, Zhukov's plan to destroy enemy forces along the Moscow axis in the Rzhev salient (the German Ninth Army). This will be no easy task, as General Model's Ninth Army has built strong defences around the salient and fortified all cities and towns along the salient's edges, especially the key cities of Rzhev, Belyi and Sychevka.

SOUTHERN USSR, *AIR WAR*

Luftwaffe chief Hermann Göring assures Hitler that his aircraft can supply the Stalingrad Pocket. Zeitzler does not believe this boast. Wolfram von Richthofen, commander of the 4th Air Fleet, believes it will be impossible to supply the Sixth Army – he has just 298 transport aircraft for the task of landing 355 tonnes (350 tons) of supplies a day (he needs at least 500 transports).

NOVEMBER 25

CENTRAL USSR, *LAND WAR*

Operation Mars begins as the Soviet Twentieth, Thirty-First, Thirty-Ninth, Twenty-Second, Forty-First and Third Shock Armies smash into German positions. The Soviets make gains at Molodi Tud, Belyi and Velikiye Luki.

SOUTHERN USSR, *LAND WAR*

The Soviets have consolidated an inner ring around the German pocket at Stalingrad, consisting of the Twenty-First, Twenty-Fourth, Fifty-Seventh, Sixty-Second, Sixty-Fourth, Sixty-Fifth and Sixty-Sixth Armies – 490,000 troops.

NOVEMBER 27

CENTRAL USSR, *LAND WAR*

The Soviet 6th Tank Corps halts due to supply difficulties as the Twenty-Second and Thirty-Ninth Armies try to bludgeon their way forward. The result is heavy German and Soviet losses. Fierce battles continue around Belyi and Velikiye Luki.

NOVEMBER 30

CENTRAL USSR, *LAND WAR*

The Soviet 6th Tank Corps is destroyed near Osuga. At Belyi, the 1st and 20th Panzer Divisions force back the Forty-First Army.

SOUTHERN USSR, *LAND WAR*

Group Hollidt engages the Soviet Fifth Tank Army on the River Chir.

▶ ***Troops of XXXV Corps, Italian Eighth Army, which held a sector of the River Don north-west of Stalingrad.***

DECEMBER 3

SOUTHERN USSR, *LAND WAR*
The Soviet Fifth Tank Army has established a bridgehead on the Chir at Nizhne Kalinovski, and the Fifty-First Army assaults the railway at Kotelnikovo, the launch pad of the German Stalingrad relief operation. Units of LVII Panzer Corps (6th Panzer Division) detrain and counterattack, throwing the Soviets back.

DECEMBER 7

CENTRAL USSR, *LAND WAR*
The Soviet Forty-First Army near Belyi is being encircled, the 19th Panzer Division having cut off the 1st Mechanized and 6th Rifle Corps.

SOUTHERN USSR, *LAND WAR*
The 11th Panzer Division halts the advance of the Soviet Fifth Tank Army near Surovikino. Meanwhile, the Soviet Fifth Shock Army moves up to the Chir Front.

DECEMBER 9

CENTRAL USSR, *LAND WAR*
The Soviet 1st Mechanized and 6th Rifle Corps are surrounded at Belyi.

SOUTHERN USSR, *LAND WAR*
On the Chir the 11th Panzer Division destroys an enemy bridgehead at Oblivskoye. The Soviet Fifth Tank Army has sustained heavy casualties. Red Army probes against the Stalingrad Pocket have revealed a larger number of trapped Axis troops than was estimated. This forces the Stavka to amend its Operation Saturn, the objective of which is now the destruction of the Italian Eighth Army and isolation of Group Hollidt. Its codename is Little Saturn.

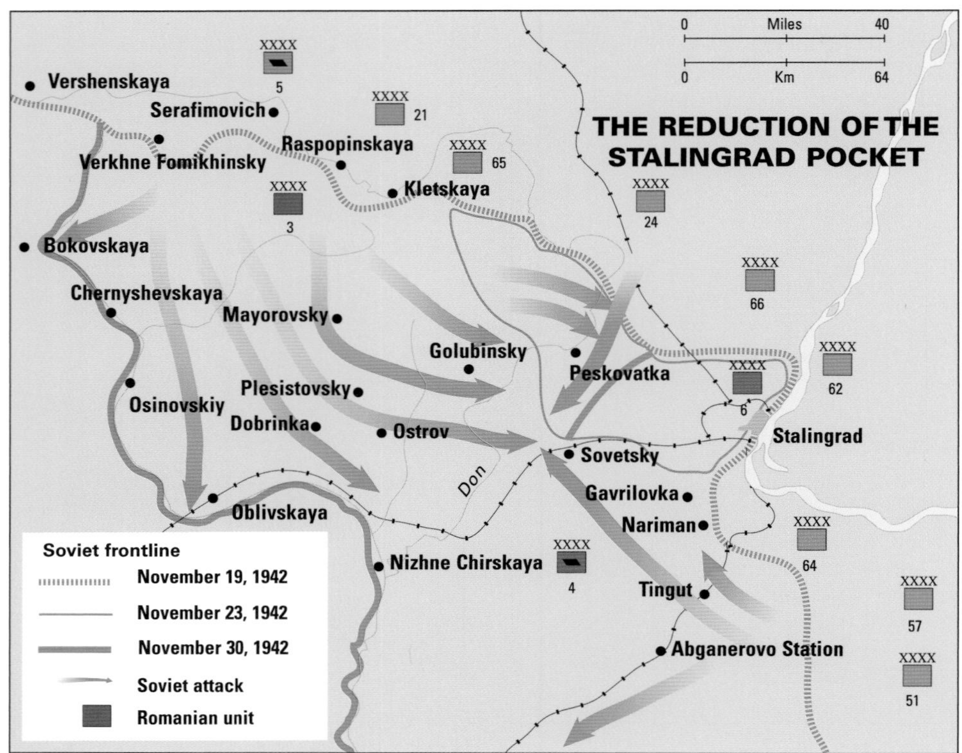

DECEMBER 12

SOUTHERN USSR, *LAND WAR*
The 11th Panzer Division continues its fire-fighting role along the Chir, destroying a Soviet bridgehead at Lissinski and containing another at Nizhne Kalinovski. Meanwhile, Manstein's attempt to relieve the Sixth Army, codenamed Winter Storm, gets under way. LVII Panzer Corps (23rd Panzer Division, 6th Panzer Division and the Romanian VI and VII Corps) – 30,000 troops and 190 tanks and 40 self-propelled guns – smashes through the Soviet Fifty-First Army at Kotelnikovo. The weather results in an advance of only 19km (12 miles), and Eremenko deploys the Soviet 13th Tank Corps and 4th Mechanized Corps to reinforce the Fifty-First Army.

DECEMBER 14

CENTRAL USSR, *LAND WAR*
The Soviet Third Shock Army continues to make gains around Velikiye Luki.

SOUTHERN USSR, *LAND WAR*
On the Chir the Soviet Fifth Shock and Fifth Tank Armies continue to pin down XXXXVIII Panzer Corps. The advance of LVII Panzer Corps is slowing as the Soviet 4th Mechanized and 13th Tank Corps enter the fray.

SOUTHERN USSR, *AIR WAR*
The Luftwaffe has delivered only 152 tonnes (150 tons) of supplies thus far to the trapped Sixth Army.

DECEMBER 16

SOUTHERN USSR, *LAND WAR*
The Stavka launches Operation Little Saturn, involving 425,000 Red Army troops and 5000 artillery pieces. The Soviet First Guards and Sixth Armies attack the Italian Eighth Army (216,000 troops) but make only limited gains, their units encountering minefields and effective resistance from the Axis reserve (27th Panzer Division). The Soviet Third Guards Army makes good initial progress but is then forced back by the 22nd Panzer Division. Meanwhile, the Soviet Fifty-First Army gives ground grudgingly to the painfully slow-moving LVII Panzer Corps.

GERMANY, *STRATEGY*
Hitler issues an order on how to deal with partisans on the Eastern Front: "If

▼ Ju 87 dive-bombers in the Caucasus, December 18, 1942. The Luftwaffe had 495 aircraft in the Caucasus in mid-October. This had fallen to 240 by January 1943 due to the demands of the Don sector.

the repression of bandits in the East, as well as in the Balkans, is not pursued by the most brutal means, the forces at our disposal will, before long, be insufficient to exterminate this plague. The troops, therefore, have the right and the duty to use any means, even against women and children, provided they are conducive to success. Scruples of any sort are a crime against the German people and against the German soldiers."

DECEMBER 19

SOUTHERN USSR, *LAND WAR*
Little Saturn continues to make progress, with the Italian Eighth Army on the verge of collapse: 15,000 Italians are surrounded at Vertyakhovski. The Romanian I Corps on Hollidt's left flank has collapsed, endangering the rear of the Chir line and Army Group Don. The 11th Panzer Division continues to fend off Soviet attacks, knocking out large numbers of Red Army tanks at Nizhne Kalinovski. Hoth's 6th Panzer Division reaches the River Myshkova, 48km (30 miles) from the Sixth Army. Manstein signals the codeword Thunderclap, ordering Paulus to break out and link up with his force. Hitler, however, orders Paulus to stand firm.

The 15th Panzer Regiment, 11th Panzer Division, attacks a force of Soviet tanks of the Fifth Tank Army in the rear 8km (5 miles) south of Oblivskaya, south of the Chir. In the engagement the Germans destroy 65 Red Army tanks.

Soviet tank tactics are still poor, the formation going into battle without coordination, and without the cooperation of numerous infantry divisions.

▲ The Italian Eighth Army on the retreat from the Don. Lacking tanks and anti-tanks guns and having hardly any motor transport, the Italians suffered greatly from incessant Soviet attacks.

DECEMBER 20

SOUTHERN USSR, *LAND WAR*
As Manstein tries to get Hitler to agree to a breakout, Group Hoth is attacked on the Myshkova by the Second Guards Army. The 17th Panzer Division (which was transferred to the relief force because Hoth had lost the 11th Panzer Division) is down to just eight tanks.

DECEMBER 24

SOUTHERN USSR, *LAND WAR*
The German line on the Chir is falling apart, the Soviet 25th Tanks Corps and 1st Guards Mechanized Corps surrounding Morozovsk and the 24th Tanks Corps capturing Tatsinskaya and its airfield (a Luftwaffe base for relief flights to Stalingrad). Some 56 Luftwaffe aircraft are destroyed attempting to take off from the airfield. The 6th Panzer Division completes its switch to Group Hollidt, leaving LVII Panzer Corps with only the weak 17th and 23rd Panzer Divisions – 28 tanks and 20,000 troops. Facing them are the Fifty-First and Second Guards Armies – 149,000 troops and 635 tanks. The latter now counterattack, forcing the Germans back, a situation made worse by the annihilation of the Romanian VI and VII Corps on the flanks. Operation Winter Storm is over.

DECEMBER 29

SOUTHERN USSR, *LAND WAR*
The 2nd Guards Tank Corps breaks out of Tatsinskaya, being pursued by the 6th and 11th Panzer Divisions. Over the next 24 hours the two panzer divisions will inflict heavy losses on the forces of the Third Guards Army.

DECEMBER 31

SOUTHERN USSR, *LAND WAR*
The Soviet Fifth Shock Army recaptures Tomorsin as the Germans recreate XXIX Corps around Morozovsk. Operations Uranus and Little Saturn have compelled Hitler to order an evacuation from the Caucasus, with XXXX Panzer Corps withdrawing from the Terek.

The Red Army has achieved much since November 19. However, it has paid a high price in blood for its successes: Southwestern Front, 64,600 killed and missing; Stalingrad Front, 43,000 killed and missing; Northern and Black Sea Groups, 132,000 killed and missing.

There has also been operational shortcomings, especially with regard to coordinating infantry and armoured units: as the tank corps advanced, the infantry fell behind and were unable to catch up once German forces moved in. Such was the fate of the 24th Tank Corps at Tatsinskaya, for example. In addition, poor coordination between the tanks corps allowed the Germans to engage them in a piecemeal fashion and inflict heavy casualties.

▼ Soviet troops advance on the Don Front in late 1942. Their somewhat bulky appearance is due to the layers of clothing worn under their camouflage smocks, including padded trousers.

The defeat at Stalingrad was a catastrophe for the Germans on the Eastern Front, and marked a decisive turning point in the Soviet Union's Great Patriotic War, signalling that Germany would no longer be able to win a military victory on the Eastern Front. And the defeat at Kursk in July, followed by numerous Soviet offensives, indicated that Germany would lose the war on the Eastern Front, and indeed would lose World War II. Only one question remained: how long would the war last?

JANUARY 1

CENTRAL USSR, *LAND WAR*
With the Germans besieged in the citadel at Velikiye Luki, officers of the Soviet Third Shock Army demand their surrender, an offer that is rejected.

USSR, *ARMED FORCES*
At Stalingrad the Stalingrad Front (Eremenko) is moved to the outer ring, leaving the Don Front (Rokossovsky) to surround the pocket.

JANUARY 2

SOUTHERN USSR, *LAND WAR*
Another airfield falls to the Soviets as the Third Guards Army recaptures the one at Morozovsk, further reducing the number of Luftwaffe relief flights to Stalingrad. Farther south, the First Panzer Army falls back from the Terek.

JANUARY 4

CENTRAL USSR, *LAND WAR*
The German LIX Corps and Group Wohler attempt to relieve Velikiye Luki, resulting in fierce fighting with the Third Shock Army.

JANUARY 8

SOUTHERN USSR, *LAND WAR*
Rokossovsky offers surrender terms to Paulus at Stalingrad. His terms are generous on paper: "We guarantee the safety of all officers and men who cease to resist, and their return after the

◀ ***Axis allies in retreat: frozen troops of the Italian Eighth Army on their way west. By mid-January the army had ceased to exist.***

◀ *Men of the Soviet Volkhov and Leningrad Fronts meet near Workers' Settlement No 5 on January 18, 1943, thus creating a narrow corridor to Leningrad.*

end of the war to Germany or to any other country to which these prisoners of war may wish to go. All personnel who surrender may retain their military uniforms, badges of rank, decorations, personal belongings and valuables and, in the case of high-ranking officers, their swords. All officers, noncommissioned officers and men who surrender will receive normal rations." Hitler forbids any surrender. Those Germans who did surrender after the fall of the city would find their captors in a less generous mood.

JANUARY 10

SOUTHERN USSR, *LAND WAR*

The Don Front (281,000 troops, 257 tanks and 10,000 artillery pieces) commences Operation Ring, the destruction of the German Sixth Army at Stalingrad. Facing this force are the freezing 191,000 troops of the Sixth Army, with 7700 artillery pieces and 60 fuel-starved tanks. The Twenty-First, Twenty-Fourth, Fifty-Seventh and Sixty-Fifth Armies, supported by the Sixteenth Air Army, launch a series of blistering attacks.

JANUARY 11

SOUTHERN USSR, *LAND WAR*

The Sixth Army at Stalingrad is being torn apart, although Paulus is reminded by OKH that surrender is out of the question. To the west the Soviet Second Guards and Fifty-First Armies are approaching Rostov and, in the Caucasus, the German Army Group A continues its withdrawal.

JANUARY 12

NORTHERN USSR, *LAND WAR*

The Red Army launches Operation Iskra, designed to push the German Eighteenth Army out of the Schlusselburg-Mga salient and thus reopen a supply line to the besieged city of Leningrad. The Sixty-Seventh Army (130,000 troops) attacks from south of the city, and the Second Shock Army (114,000 troops) assaults from the Volkhov. In between lie German troops in well-entrenched positions.

SOUTHERN USSR, *LAND WAR*

The Don Front's attack at Stalingrad has incurred 26,000 casualties, but Paulus has lost 60,000 troops and massive stocks of weapons. In the Caucasus, attacks by the Soviet Eighteenth and Forty-Sixth Armies encounter heavy resistance.

▼ *German wounded being evacuated from Stalingrad. Inside the aircraft the men were laid on straw. Nearly 850 aircraft were used in the German airlift.*

JANUARY 13

NORTHERN USSR, *LAND WAR*

As the Second and Sixty-Seventh Armies continue to attack on the Neva and Volkhov, the Soviet Eighth Army joins the assault. The result is that the German XXVI and XXVIII Corps suffer heavy losses.

SOUTHERN USSR, *LAND WAR*

The offensive by the Soviet Fortieth Army against the Hungarian Second Army – part of a larger Red Army offensive involving the Voronezh, Bryansk and Southwestern Fronts along a 480km (300-mile) front – begins. The Hungarian 7th Division is soon destroyed.

JANUARY 15

CENTRAL USSR, *LAND WAR*

The Soviet Third Shock Army captures Velikiye Luki. It is a great success for Operation Mars, although bought at a heavy price: 31,600 Red Army troops killed and missing and 72,300 wounded. The Germans have lost 17,000 troops in and around the town.

SOUTHERN USSR, *LAND WAR*

Trapped Axis troops in Chertkovo attempt to break out. At Stalingrad, Pitomnik airfield, one of only two remaining

January 16

German air bases in the pocket, comes under Red Army artillery fire.

January 16

SOUTHERN USSR, *LAND WAR*
The Hungarian Second Army falls apart, allowing Soviet units to drive west. At Stalingrad the Red Army captures Pitomnik airfield; only Gumrak air base remains.

January 18

NORTHERN USSR, *LAND WAR*
Schlusselburg is recaptured by the Soviet Second Shock and Sixty-Seventh Armies. With a narrow corridor created through German lines south of Lake Ladoga, Leningrad can now be supplied.

SOUTHERN USSR, *LAND WAR*
As the Soviet Third Tank and Fortieth Armies link up at Alexievka, three Hungarian corps and the Italian Alpine Corps are encircled. Gumrak airfield is now under Red Army attack.

USSR, *ARMED FORCES*
Notwithstanding the failure of Mars, Zhukov is promoted to Marshal of the Soviet Union and Deputy Supreme Commander of the Soviet Armed Forces. Considering the losses incurred during what was his brainchild, his promotion is perhaps somewhat surprising. Mars cost the Red Army nearly 500,000 troops killed, wounded or captured (German casualties were around 40,000). The Twentieth Army lost 58,524 troops out of its original strength of more than 114,000. The 1st Mechanized Corps lost 8100 of its 12,000 troops and all of its 220 tanks, and the accompanying 6th Stalin Rifle Corps lost more than 20,000 of its 30,000 men. At lower levels the cost was even higher. Red Army tank losses during the operation amounted to 1700.

January 19

SOUTHERN USSR, *LAND WAR*
What is left of the Hungarian Second Army surrenders at Ostrogozh (50,000 men) as the Soviet Voronezh Front develops its assaults against Army Group B. The 7th Cavalry Corps races into Vayluki and annihilates the Italian garrison. At Stalingrad, Gumrak airfield is now being pounded by Red Army artillery.

January 20

YUGOSLAVIA, *PARTISAN WAR*
In response to increasing partisan activity, the Germans launch Operation Weiss headed by General Lueters, Commander of German Troops in Croatia. Cooperating with Italian forces, its objective is the annihilation of partisan units west and northwest of Sarajevo. German units include the 7th SS Mountain, 369th and 717th Infantry Divisions, and a regiment of the 187th Infantry Division. The Italian contingent is V Corps of the Second Army. In the first attack the Axis troops inflict 8500 casualties on the partisans and capture a further 2010. German losses are 335 dead and 101 missing. Weiss will conclude on February 18, 1943.

▲ ***A 105mm le FH18 howitzer of the German Eighteenth Army in action near Leningrad at the end of January 1943.***

January 23

SOUTHERN USSR, *LAND WAR*
At Stalingrad Gumrak falls to the Soviet Twenty-First Army. The

THE SOVIET SINYAVINO OFFENSIVE

Soviet Frontlines
12 January 1943
14–16 January 1943
19 January 1943

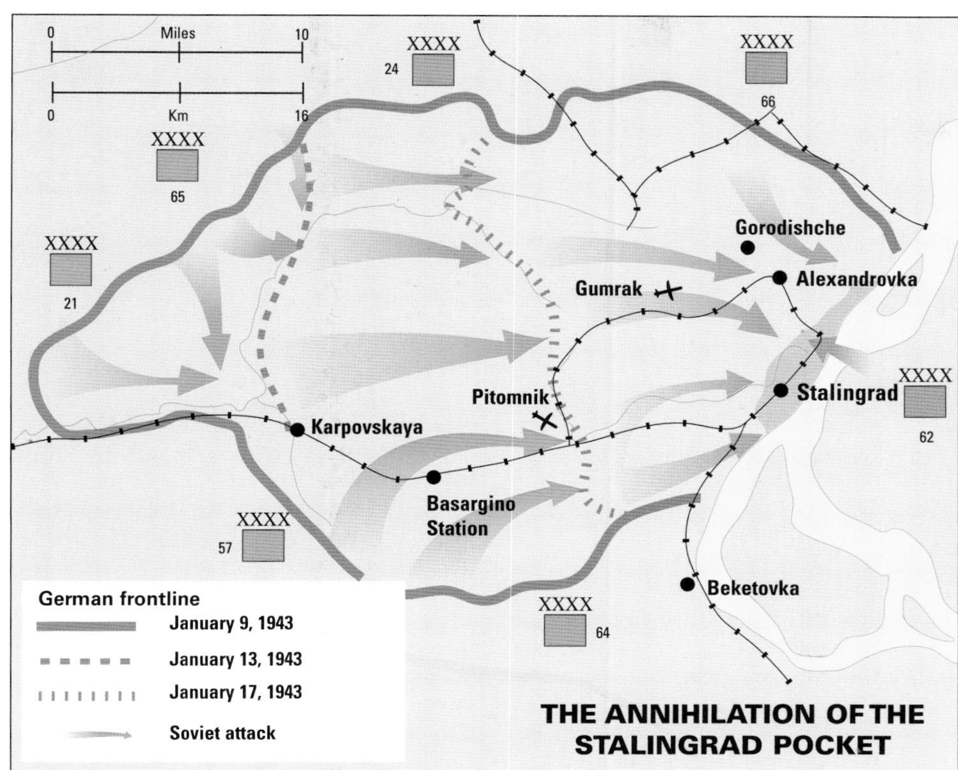

▲ *A sick Field Marshal Paulus meets Soviet commanders at Stalingrad to negotiate the surrender of the Sixth Army.*

Soviet bridgehead on the River Manych, which was established by the Soviet Southern Front's Second Guards Army, is destroyed by two German divisions.

JANUARY 24

SOUTHERN USSR, *LAND WAR*
The Soviet offensive continues to score successes, with the Sixtieth Army recapturing Voronezh and the Fortieth Army cracking open the southern flank of the German Second Army. In the Kuban the Stavka orders that the German Seventeenth Army is to be surrounded by the Southern Front; the Forty-Fourth and Fifty-Eighth Armies will assault Bataisk; and the Ninth and Thirty-Seventh Armies will cooperate with the Black Sea Group. Hitler orders Paulus at Stalingrad to fight to the end: "Surrender is forbidden. Sixth Army will hold their positions to the last man and the last round and by their heroic endurance will make an unforgettable contribution towards the establishment of a defensive front and the salvation of the Western world."

◀ *Yugoslav partisans retreat with their wounded following the German Operation Weiss near Sarajevo.*

JANUARY 26

SOUTHERN USSR, *LAND WAR*
In the Stalingrad Pocket the survivors of the German 297th Infantry Division surrender to the 38th Guards Rifle Division, the Sixty-Fifth Army links up with the Sixty-Second Army between Mamayev Kurgan and the Red October factory, and the Twenty-First and Sixty-Fourth Armies link up with the Sixty-Second Army. What is left of the Sixth Army is now trapped in two small pockets.

JANUARY 29

NORTHERN USSR, *LAND WAR*
The fighting calms down around Leningrad. The Soviet armies have suffered substantial losses: Sixty-Seventh Army, 12,000 killed and missing and 28,700 wounded; Second Shock Army, 19,000 killed and 46,000 wounded; and Eighth Army, 2500 killed and 5800 wounded.

SOUTHERN USSR, *LAND WAR*
The Soviet Southwestern Front commences its operation to outflank the German Army Group Don as enemy units retreat towards Izyum.

JANUARY 30

SOUTHERN USSR, *LAND WAR*
Hitler promotes Paulus to field marshal, a cynical move to prompt the commander at Stalingrad to commit suicide rather than surrender (no German field marshal has yet surrendered to the enemy).

In a radio broadcast Hermann Göring proclaims to the nation: "A thousand years hence Germans will speak of this battle with reverence and awe, and that in spite of everything Germany's ultimate victory was decided there. In years to come it will be said of the heroic battle on the Volga: when you come to Germany, say you have seen us lying at Stalingrad, as our honour and our leaders ordained that we should, for the greater glory of Germany!"

JANUARY 31

SOUTHERN USSR, *LAND WAR*
Paulus surrenders at Stalingrad. Now only XI Corps in the northern pocket in the city continues to hold out. Hitler is disgusted, stating: "Here is a man who can look on while fifty or sixty thousand are dying and defending themselves with courage to the end – how can he give himself up to the Bolsheviks?"

South of Izyum, at Slavyansk, the 3rd and 7th Panzer Divisions move into the frontline in an effort to halt the Red Army's advance.

▲ *A StuG III SdKfz 142 Ausf C of the Fourth Panzer Army in early February. At this time Army Group Don was outnumbered eight to one by Soviet forces.*

FEBRUARY 1

SOUTHERN USSR, *LAND WAR*
At Stalingrad the German XI Corps suffers 4000 killed and wounded during fighting in the tractor factory. To the west of the city, the Don Front advances to engage enemy forces in the Ukraine, as the Voronezh Front commences offensives towards Kursk and Kharkov. The Southwestern Front's First Guards and Sixth Armies attack across the River Donets.

FEBRUARY 2

SOUTHERN USSR, *LAND WAR*
The remnants of the German XI Corps surrender at Stalingrad, bringing this titanic struggle to an end. During the Stalingrad battles the Sixth Army has suffered 150,000 dead and another 90,000 taken prisoner, including 24 generals and 2000 officers (only 6000 will return home in the 1950s). The Luftwaffe has lost approximately 488 aircraft and 1000 air crews during the Stalingrad airlift. Don Front's losses are 46,000 killed and missing and 123,000 wounded. To the west the Voronezh Front's Third Tank, Fortieth and Sixtieth Armies force back German forces around Kupyansk. And the Southwestern Front unleashes its First Guards, Third Guards, Fifth Tank and Sixth Armies, supported by the Seventeenth Air Army's 300 aircraft, against Army Group Don. The Third Guards Army crosses the Donets near Voroshilovgrad. Farther south, the German Seventeenth Army (350,000 troops) is now isolated in the Kuban.

▼ *German prisoners captured at Stalingrad are paraded through Moscow. In 1955 there were still 2000 German survivors of Stalingrad in Soviet prisons.*

FEBRUARY 4

USSR, *ARMED FORCES*
Stalin orders the creation of a communist-led Polish Army to be a counterweight to the Western Allied-sponsored Polish Army that is being formed in Iran. Both units are being staffed by Poles who were former prisoners of the Soviets. Because of the lack of Polish cadres left in the USSR, many of the commanders and specialists in Stalin's Polish Army will be Russian. The first unit to see combat will be the 1st Tadeusz Kosciuszko Infantry Division, commanded by General Berling.

SOUTHERN USSR, *LAND WAR*
The Soviet Third Tank Army reaches the Donets but is then halted by the newly arrived SS *Leibstandarte* Division. At Slavyansk, XXXX Panzer Corps fights to hold its position. In the Caucasus, the Seventeenth Army contains Soviet amphibious landings at Novorossisk and Ozerreyka Bay. Since January 1, the Southern Front has lost 54,000 killed and missing and 47,000 wounded, the Trans-Caucasian Front 12,000 killed and missing and 30,000 wounded, and the North Caucasus Front 3000 killed and missing and 7000 wounded.

FEBRUARY 6

SOUTHERN USSR, *LAND WAR*
As the Soviet Third Tank Army continues to be contained on the Donets by the Waffen-SS, XXXX Panzer Corps retreats across the river, allowing the First Guards Army to recapture Lisichansk. The panzer corps continues to defend Slavyansk.

FEBRUARY 8

SOUTHERN USSR, *LAND WAR*
The Soviet steamroller continues, with the Sixtieth Army recapturing Kursk and the Third Tank Army advancing south of Kharkov. The SS *Leibstandarte* Division continues to display its fighting prowess, slowing the Sixth Army considerably.

FEBRUARY 10

SOUTHERN USSR, *LAND WAR*
The Soviet Fortieth and Sixty-Ninth Armies begin their assault on Kharkov, with some units of the Fortieth moving towards Oboyan, Grayvoron and Bogodukhov. The SS *Leibstandarte* Division finally has to yield before the Donets and falls back, allowing the Third Tank Army to recapture Chuguyev and Merefa. Farther south, XXXXVIII Panzer Corps fights a rearguard action as it falls back to Stalino. In the Caucasus the North Caucasus Front's Krasnodar Offensive Operation, involving 390,000 troops, is threatening the southern flank of the Seventeenth Army.

FEBRUARY 12

CENTRAL USSR, *LAND WAR*
The Bryansk Front assists the offensive in the Ukraine by committing its Thirteenth and Forty-Eighth Armies against the Second Panzer Army in front of Orel.

SOUTHERN USSR, *LAND WAR*
As the Soviet Fortieth Army advances north of Kharkov, around the city the Third Tank Army is engaged in bitter battles with the SS *Leibstandarte* Division. Vatutin is determined to push his First Guards, Third Guards, Fifth Tank and Sixth Armies further into the Ukraine to seize Stalino and Zaporozhye. In the Kuban the German Seventeenth Army is pushed out of Krasnodar.

▲ ***Field Marshal Erich von Manstein (left), who was tasked with saving Army Group South from being overwhelmed.***

DECISIVE MOMENT

THE RED ORCHESTRA

The Red Orchestra was established in 1939 by Leopold Trepper, an agent in the Soviet military intelligence service. It collected intelligence from agents in Nazi-occupied Europe and neutral Switzerland. It comprised three main sections: the network in France, Belgium and Holland; a network in Berlin (which included Harro Schulze-Boysen, an intelligence officer assigned to the German Air Ministry, and Arvid von Harnack, who worked in the Ministry of Economics); and the "Lucy Spy Ring" that operated from Switzerland. The latter included some high-ranking German individuals: Lieutenant-General Fritz Theile, Wehrmacht communications branch; and Rudolf von Gersdorff, who became Army Group Centre's intelligence officer on the Eastern Front.

With such sources the Soviets were privy to high-level intelligence concerning Wehrmacht operations on the Eastern Front. Thus, Stalin had prior knowledge of the launch date of Operation Barbarossa, including that supplied by Richard Sorge, an agent working for the Red Orchestra in Japan. He obtained accurate intelligence about the German invasion as early as December 1940, as well as the fact that the Japanese would not attack the Soviets in the Far East, plus information on the German attack on Moscow in late 1941, as well as the Stalingrad Offensive in 1942. Much of this valuable information was squandered by Stalin, who distrusted spies. Furthermore, his distrust of the information provided to him was increased by the fact that a multitude of warnings concerning a German invasion had been sent to him for months, and no invasion had taken place. Indeed, so irritable did he become that, by May 1941, reports from Soviet spies concerning German invasion plans were being filed in the "folder of dubious and misleading reports". On one report from a German source at Luftwaffe headquarters, Stalin wrote in the margin: "Maybe we should tell this 'source' to go f*** himself. He's not a source but a liar."

Following the German invasion in June 1941, the Red Orchestra continued to send intelligence to Moscow, with the Lucy Ring alerting the Soviets to the German offensive at Kursk in 1943. By this time, however, the Gestapo was tracking down the ring's agents, the first arrests having been made in the spring of 1942. Over the next 18 months, 600 people were arrested, including Schulze-Boysen and Harnack. After often brutal interrogations, the Germans were able to destroy most of the spy network in France, Holland and Germany, with 58 members of the Red Orchestra being executed and dozens of others being imprisoned. Trepper himself escaped arrest and remained in hiding in Paris until its liberation in 1944.

FEBRUARY 14

SOUTHERN USSR, *LAND WAR*
With the Soviet Third Tank and Fortieth Armies south and southwest of Kharkov, the German *Grossdeutschland*, SS *Das Reich*, SS *Leibstandarte*, 168th and 320th Infantry Divisions are in danger of being encircled. The Fourth Panzer Army redeploys to the Dnepropetrovsk area as the Soviet Third Guards Army takes Voroshilovgrad and the Second Guards and Twenty-Eighth Armies retake Rostov.

FEBRUARY 15

NORTHERN USSR, *LAND WAR*
The German II and X Corps withdraw from the Demyansk salient, laying mines and booby traps as they do so. At the same time the Soviet Eleventh, Thirty-Fourth and Fifty-Third Armies of the Northwestern Front, supported by the Kalinin Front's First Shock Army, attack but cannot effect a breakthrough.

▲ ***A German supply column of Army Group South. The captured sleds are being pulled by hardy Russian panje horses.***

SOUTHERN USSR, *LAND WAR*
Paul Hausser, commander of the SS corps, ignores Hitler's orders and authorizes a withdrawal from Kharkov.

FEBRUARY 16

SOUTHERN USSR, *LAND WAR*
The Soviet Sixty-Ninth Army's 15th Tank Corps and 160th Rifle Division, Fortieth

▲ ***Goebbels addresses a hand-picked audience at the Sports Palace. His two-hour speech ended with the words: "Now people, arise – and storm burst forth."***

Army's 160th and 183rd Rifle Divisions, 5th Tank Corps and units of the Third Tank Army have taken possession of the centre of Kharkov.

FEBRUARY 18

SOUTHERN USSR, *LAND WAR*
Red Army units are nearing attritional exhaustion as the offensive in the Ukraine continues. The Soviet Third Tank Army (110 tanks) recaptures Merefa and advances towards Valki. The First Guards Army stops a counterattack by XXXX Panzer Corps, and recaptures Pavlograd and Novomoskovsk.

GERMANY, *STRATEGY*
Propaganda Minister Goebbels delivers a speech in Berlin's Sports Palace in front of a carefully selected audience, which is broadcast to the nation. He rails against the "storm from the Steppes" which relegates "all former dangers facing the West to the shadows". Behind the onrushing Soviet divisions, Goebbels foresees "the Jewish liquidation commandos" whom international Jewry are using to plunge the world into chaos. To thunderous applause he announces the implementation of total war: "Do you want total war? Do you want it, if necessary, more total and more radical than we could even imagine today?" Afterwards Goebbels writes in his diary: "This hour of idiocy! If I had said to the people, jump out the fourth floor of Columbushaus, they would have done that too."

THE SOVIET ADVANCE TO ROSTOV

Soviet frontline
December 13, 1942
January 18, 1943
February 18, 1943
Soviet attack

◀ ***Troops of I SS Panzer Corps in southern Russia. By February 19 the SS corps had assembled east of Poltava, prior to taking part in Manstein's counterattack.***

FEBRUARY 19

SOUTHERN USSR, *LAND WAR*
The tank spearhead of the Soviet Sixth Army advances to only 48km (30 miles) from Manstein's HQ at Zaporozhye, which Hitler is visiting, but then runs out of fuel and is knocked out by a German counterattack. The Führer flies back to Germany, giving his field marshal a free hand to launch his counteroffensive. Knowing that the Soviets are at the end of their supply lines, he has waited for the right moment to strike. Army Detachment Hollidt is on the Mius, the First Panzer Army (III, XXX and XXXX Panzer Corps) is south of Krasnoarmieskoye, the Fourth Panzer Army (XXXXVIII Panzer and LVII Corps) is at Zaporozhye, and the SS Panzer

Corps (*Leibstandarte*, *Das Reich* and *Totenkopf* Divisions) is near Krasnograd. Manstein unleashes his attack, with the SS Corps shattering the flank of the Sixth Army at Zmiyev, and XXXX Panzer Corps also hits the Soviet Sixth Army.

FEBRUARY 20

SOUTHERN USSR, *LAND WAR*

The SS Corps links up with XXXXVIII Panzer Corps south of Krasnograd as XXXX Panzer Corps smashes into Group Popov on the Mius line.

FEBRUARY 21

SOUTHERN USSR, *LAND WAR*

Despite the German offensive, the Soviets are still pushing west: the Third Tank Army enters Lyubotin, and the Sixth Army reaches Sinelnikovo. But Manstein's forces are also making gains, with the Fourth Panzer Army advancing on Pavlograd, XXX Corps attacking Krasnoarmieskoye, the First Panzer Army advancing towards Izyum, and the SS Panzer Corps and Corps *Raus* advancing from the north. Suddenly, Soviet forces south of Kharkov are in danger of being encircled. The Luftwaffe flies 1145 sorties in support of Manstein's forces.

FEBRUARY 23

SOUTHERN USSR, *LAND WAR*

Although the Soviet Sixth Army is still advancing west, the SS Panzer Corps is nearing Pavlograd and XXXXVIII Panzer Corps is moving on Barvenkovo. To the north, XXXX Panzer Corps continues to pummel Group Popov.

FEBRUARY 25

CENTRAL USSR, *LAND WAR*

As Army Group Centre pulls out of the Rzhev salient, the Soviet Central Front joins the Bryansk Front, attacking enemy forces in the salient, with the Second Tank and Sixty-Fifth Armies' assault supported by the 2nd Guards Cavalry Corps. The offensive is also designed to prevent Army Group Centre lending support to Army Group South.

SOUTHERN USSR, *LAND WAR*

Although the Soviet Third Tank Army takes Valki and Novaya Vodolaga, the SS Panzer Corps is striking from Pavlograd, inflicting heavy losses on retreating Soviet units. XXXX and XXXXVIII Panzer Corps are also making gains.

▼ T-34 tanks of the Voronezh Front in late February. By this stage of the Soviet offensive fuel shortages were becoming acute: the 25th Tank Corps was stuck fast on February 24 due to no fuel.

FEBRUARY 26

NORTHERN USSR, *LAND WAR*

The German Demyansk salient comes under pressure on the Lovat as the First Shock Army launches a series of attacks.

CENTRAL USSR, *LAND WAR*

The German Second Army holds off an attack by the Central Front's Second Tank and Sixty-Firth Armies before Bryansk.

SOUTHERN USSR, *LAND WAR*

The Soviets defend Lozovaya against the SS Panzer Corps as XXXX Panzer Corps battles its way into Barvenkovo.

FEBRUARY 28

NORTHERN USSR, *LAND WAR*

The last German units leave the Demyansk salient; it has cost the Soviet Northwestern Front 10,016 killed and 23,647 wounded to establish a line on the Lovat.

SOUTHERN USSR, *LAND WAR*

The Soviet Fortieth Army is across the River Psel but is unable to take Sumy due to enemy resistance. As XXXXVIII Panzer Corps reaches the Donets west of Izyum, the Soviets retreat from Barvenkovo to Izyum to avoid being cut off.

MARCH 1

SOUTHERN USSR, *LAND WAR*
Manstein's offensive has thus far inflicted losses on the Soviets of 23,000 killed and 9000 captured, plus 65 tanks and 350 artillery pieces destroyed or captured. The offensive continues, forcing the Fortieth Army to assume defensive positions on the Psel and the SS Panzer Corps stopping the Third Tank Army's offensive.

MARCH 3

CENTRAL USSR, *LAND WAR*
The Germans are pulling out of the Rzhev salient, where they have no fewer than 30 divisions. As they do so Rzhev itself falls to the Kalinin Front.
SOUTHERN USSR, *LAND WAR*
The SS Panzer Corps destroys the Soviet Third Tank Army and III Panzer Corps captures Slavyansk. Since January, Red Army units have lost 1000 tanks, 2100 artillery pieces and 300 aircraft.

MARCH 5

SOUTHERN USSR, *LAND WAR*
The Fourth Panzer Army attacks what is left of the Third Tank Army near Krasnograd as the SS Panzer Corps approaches Kharkov from the southwest.

MARCH 7

CENTRAL USSR, *LAND WAR*
The Central Front's Second Tank Army recaptures Sevsk on the southern flank of Army Group Centre. There is fierce fighting south of Orel as the Soviet Sixty-Fifth and Seventieth Armies continue their advance. The German Second Army fends off probes by the Thirty-Eighth and Sixtieth Armies at Lgov.
SOUTHERN USSR, *LAND WAR*
As the German threat to Kharkov increases, the élite *Grossdeutschland* Division attacks the Soviet Sixty-Ninth Army from Chudovo as XXXXVIII Panzer Corps assaults Taranovka and the SS Panzer Corps rolls into Valki.

▼ ***Well-padded Waffen-SS grenadiers on the outskirts of Kharkov during Manstein's counterattack. The machine gun on the right is an MG42.***

MARCH 9

SOUTHERN USSR, *LAND WAR*
The *Grossdeutschland* Division mauls the Soviet Sixty-Ninth Army at Bogodukhov as the SS Panzer Corps prevents the Fortieth Army helping the hard-pressed Sixty-Ninth. The SS corps also takes Lyubotin, and XXXXVIII Panzer Corps has reached Zmiyev. Kharkov is now in danger of being surrounded.

▲ ***A Panzer III and troops of the SS* Leibstandarte *Division in Kharkov. It took the division three days of hand-to-hand fighting to capture the city's Red Square.***

MARCH 11

SOUTHERN USSR, *LAND WAR*
The *Grossdeutschland* Division captures Bogodukhov; the SS Panzer Corps fights its way into Kharkov. The Stavka orders the First Tank and Twenty-First Armies to the north of Belgorod and the Sixty-Fourth Army from the reserve in an effort to save the situation at Kharkov.

MARCH 13

SOUTHERN USSR, *LAND WAR*
As the *Grossdeutschland* Division prises apart the Soviet Fortieth and Sixty-Ninth Armies, the SS *Totenkopf* Division severs the enemy's lines of communication east out of Kharkov. The depleted Third Tank Army is now cut off in the city.
POLAND, *ATROCITIES*
The Germans begin the liquidation of the Krakow Ghetto. The ghetto is divided into

two parts: Ghetto A for workers and Ghetto B for non-workers. Ghetto A is liquidated today, with all its workers being sent to Plaszow concentration camp. The action is led by *SS-Untersturmführer* Amon Göth, the new commandant of Plaszow. The SS will liquidate Ghetto B tomorrow, many people being killed in courtyards or in the streets. Since its creation the ghetto has held 20,000 Jews.

MARCH 16

NORTHERN USSR, *LAND WAR*
The Soviet Third Shock Army recaptures Cholm after a prolonged battle.

SOUTHERN USSR, *LAND WAR*
The SS Panzer and XXXXVIII Panzer Corps link up and drive east of Kharkov. The SS *Totenkopf* Division takes Chuguyev and pursues Red Army units back to the River Donets. Fighting will end in Kharkov on March 20 as German forces complete mopping-up operations.

MARCH 18

SOUTHERN USSR, *LAND WAR*
The SS Corps and *Grossdeutschland* Division eject the Soviet Sixty-Ninth Army from Belgorod. This is the last significant action in the southern sector of the front as the spring thaw has halted operations.

MARCH 23

CENTRAL USSR, *LAND WAR*
The Soviet Rzhev-Vyazma Operation, conducted by the Kalinin and Western Fronts, comes to an end. Red Army losses are 38,862 killed or missing and 99,715 wounded. Total Red Army losses this year on the Eastern Front amount to 726,714 killed and missing and 1,425,692 wounded.

▲ *A machine gunner of the SS Panzer Corps during the Kharkov battles. The SS corps suffered 11,500 casualties during three days of street fighting in the city.*

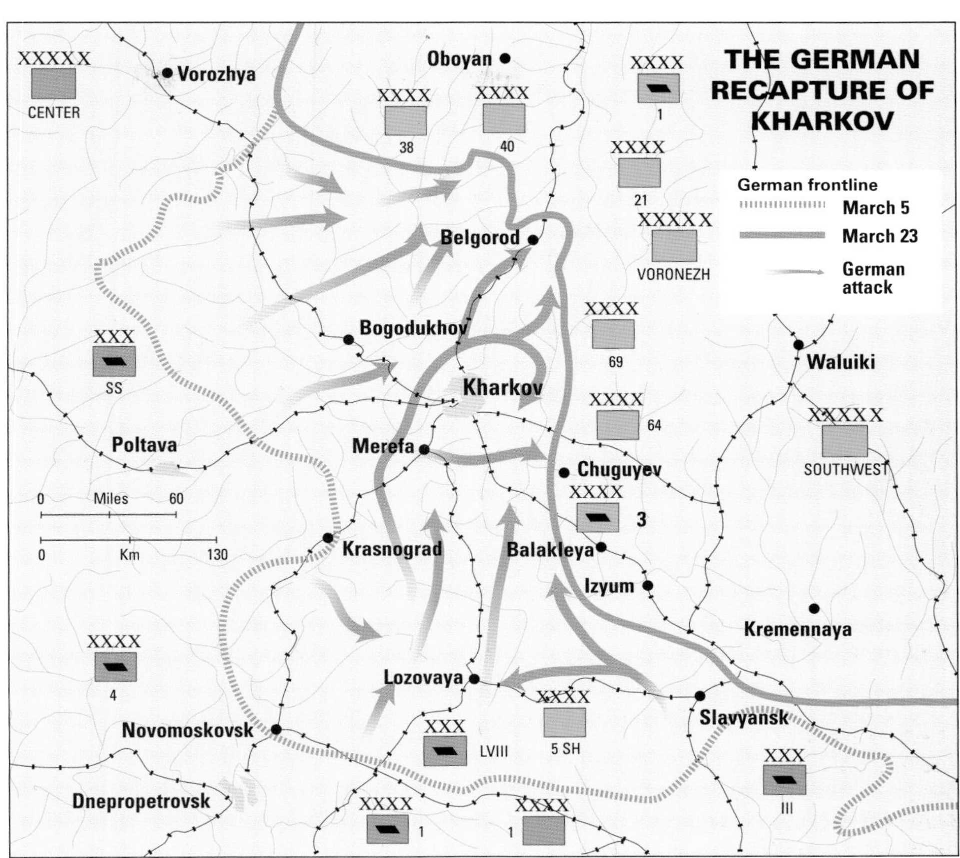

KEY PERSONALITIES

ERICH VON MANSTEIN

One of the greatest generals of World War II was born in 1887 in Berlin. He fought and was wounded in World War I, and commanded the 18th Division in Silesia after the war. He first came to prominence in early 1940, when his plan for an armoured attack through the Ardennes caught Hitler's attention. The Führer liked the plan, which he adopted and launched with great success. However, Manstein had upset the General Staff and so he was "banished" to Silesia to help form the new XXXVIII Corps.

He was given command of LXI Panzer Corps for the invasion of the USSR in 1941 as part of Army Group North, and then appointed head of the Eleventh Army in September 1941 and ordered to conquer the Crimea. The subsequent campaign in the Crimea was one of the epics of the war on the Eastern Front. Sevastopol fell in July 1942, and Manstein was made a field marshal in the same month. He was then ordered north again, and successfully destroyed a Red Army penetration south of Leningrad in September 1942. At the end of 1942 Manstein was ordered south again, this time to rescue the Sixth Army trapped in Stalingrad. His relief force got to within 56km (35 miles) of the German lines, before it was driven back by the Soviets. In early 1943, the Red Army steamroller smashed into the Ukraine, and it appeared that the whole of the German front in southern Russia was about to collapse. However, Manstein delivered a devastating counterattack against the Red Army that recaptured Kharkov, killed 23,000 enemy soldiers and stabilized the front. It was one of the greatest examples of the expert use of mobile tactics on the Eastern Front. His ideas about an elastic defence were, however, at odds with those of Hitler. Manstein was sent into retirement in April 1944. After the war he wrote his autobiography, *Lost Victories*, one of the best accounts of command during World War II. Manstein died in Germany in 1973 at the age of 85.

April 8

POLAND, *ATROCITIES*

Exterminations at Chelmno concentration camp cease. The camp was built for the extermination of the Jews from the Warthegau (the provinces of Poznan, almost the whole of Lodz province, and a part of the province of Warsaw). Since December 8, 1941, around 1000 people a day have been gassed at the camp. Victims were herded into the back of a large lorry and, when one batch had been forced into the back, the door was shut and the engine started, poisoning with its exhaust fumes those who were locked inside. Besides the 300,000 Jews from the Warthegau, about 5000 gypsies and 1000 Poles and Russian prisoners of war have been murdered at Chelmno, although the latter were usually taken straight to the nearby woods and shot. The camp will be reopened by the Nazis in 1944 for further gassings of victims.

▲ ***German StuG III SdKfz 142 Ausf G assault guns in the Ukraine in April. The arrival of the muddy season brought military operations to a halt on the Eastern Front.***

April 9

USSR, *STRATEGY*

Following the end of Manstein's attack in the south, the Red Army now holds a huge salient in the central sector of the front that bulges into German-held territory: the Kursk salient. It quickly becomes obvious to Zhukov that this salient will be a prime target for the Wehrmacht during the coming summer. He reports to Stalin: "I consider that it would be pointless for our forces to go over to the offensive in the near future in order to pre-empt the enemy. It would be better for us to wear out the enemy on our defences, to smash his tanks and then, by introducing fresh reserves and going over to a general offensive, to beat the main enemy force once and for all." Stalin agreed, and on April 12 the Stavka gave the order that the Kursk salient would be defended in great depth. This was in fact the first part of a three-part strategy for the conduct of the war in the second half of 1943. First, the Red Army would conduct a deliberate defence of the Kursk salient to wear down enemy forces in a so-called battle of attrition. Second, once the Germans were exhausted the Red Army would launch a series of offensives in the Kursk region. Finally, these offensives would be expanded to the flanks with the aim of reaching the River Dnieper and, if possible, advance into Belorussia and the Ukraine.

▲ ***The remains of Polish officers, part of a mass grave discovered by the Germans in Katyn Wood, near Smolensk. The Poles had been murdered by the NKVD in 1940.***

April 12

GERMANY, *STRATEGY*

Hitler issues Operational Order No 6 for the destruction of enemy forces in the Kursk salient. Codenamed Operation Citadel, it will begin on May 3. Hitler realizes that 1943 is his last chance to avoid defeat in the East, a position made more urgent by the impending defeat of Axis forces in North Africa, U-boat losses in the Atlantic and the threat of an Allied invasion of Western Europe. Thus, Germany's ultimate fate depends on a favourable outcome on the Eastern Front in 1943. The Führer believes that if the Soviets can be exhausted, they will be more receptive to a negotiated separate peace.

April 13

USSR, *ATROCITIES*

Radio Berlin announces the discovery of a mass grave (at the Russian forest village of Katyn) of 4500 Polish officers who have been murdered, it claims, by the Soviet NKVD. The Soviet Government responds two days later, counter-charging that the Germans have killed the Poles. On April 23, 1943, Churchill will assure Soviet Ambassador Maisky in London: "We shall certainly oppose vigorously any investigation by the International Red Cross or any other body in any territory under German authority. Such investigation would be a fraud and its conclusions reached by terrorism." (The Russians will in November 1989 admit responsibility for the Katyn shootings.)

April 15

USSR, *ARMED FORCES*

Lieutenant Yakov Stalin, the son of the Soviet dictator who has been a German prisoner since July 1941, dies in Sachsenhausen camp after running into the electric fence surrounding the camp, apparently so overcome by shame at the news of his father's massacre of Polish officers at Katyn. The Germans had wanted to exchange him for General Paulus, but Stalin would not hear of it.

April 19

POLAND, *ARMED FORCES*

The Warsaw uprising begins. Organized by the ZOB (*Zydowska Organizacja Bojowa* – Jewish Fighting Organization), which is led by 23-year-old Mordecai Anielewicz, it is sparked by German troops and police entering the ghetto to deport its surviving inhabitants. Around 750 fighters with few weapons and no military training fight the heavily armed

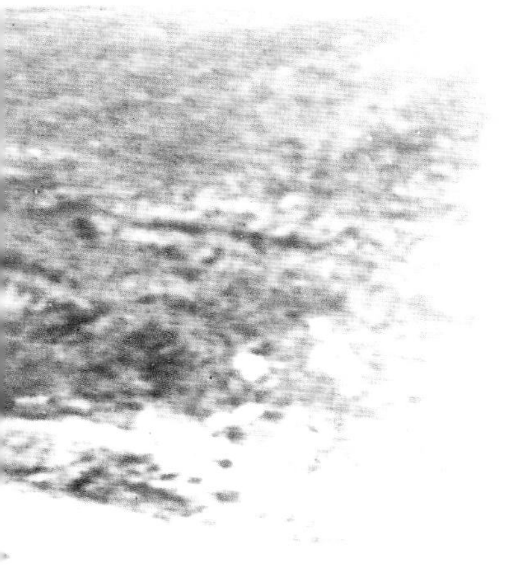

Germans. The ghetto fighters were able to hold out for nearly a month, but by May 16, 1943, the Germans had crushed the revolt. Of the more than 56,000 Jews captured, about 7000 were shot, and the remainder were deported to concentration camps.

APRIL 26

USSR, *DIPLOMACY*

Moscow breaks off relations with the Polish government-in-exile in London and recognizes the Union of Polish Patriots as the official representatives of the Polish people. This organization comprises Polish communists resident in the USSR and under the control of Moscow.

▼ A Red Army motorcycle patrol in the Kursk salient. The delay of Operation Citadel allowed the Soviets time to build strong defence lines in the salient.

ARMED FORCES

WAFFEN-SS PANZER DIVISIONS

There were more than 40 Waffen-SS divisions by the end of World War II. The best were the panzer divisions that, during the course of the war, had a decisive impact on numerous occasions on the Eastern Front. Following the grim winter of 1941–42 in the East, during which the German assault on Moscow had petered out and the Red Army had launched a massive counterattack all along the line, the SS divisions in Russia (*Leibstandarte*, *Das Reich*, *Wiking*, *Totenkopf* and *Polizei*) had obeyed their Führer's order to stand fast and not yield an inch of ground. They had suffered terribly in doing so, but their steadfastness was a turning point in the history of the Waffen-SS.

Hitler was delighted with the performance of his SS legions during that fateful winter, pointing to their tenacity in the face of adversity as an indication of what soldiers could achieve if they were imbued with "National Socialist will". In contrast, he was particularly scathing about the performance of many army units and their commanders, who always seemed to want to withdraw to save themselves. Henceforth Hitler would look to his Waffen-SS divisions to deliver results on the Eastern Front. But, to achieve what he wanted, they needed to be rebuilt and expanded. The Führer had began to dream of SS corps and even SS armies, formations that would deliver victory over the Bolsheviks. The *Leibstandarte*, *Das Reich*, *Wiking* and *Totenkopf* were already motorized when they entered Russia in June 1941, but they would now be recreated as panzergrenadier divisions. In the summer and autumn of 1942, the *Leibstandarte*, *Das Reich* and *Totenkopf* Divisions were withdrawn from the Eastern Front and moved to France for reorganizing as Waffen-SS panzergrenadier divisions. *Wiking* remained in the southern sector of the Eastern Front and was reinforced steadily with so-called "foreign volunteers" from occupied countries, but it was never as powerful as the three original SS panzergrenadier divisions.

The Waffen-SS panzergrenadier divisions were equipped so lavishly with tanks and armoured vehicles that, in reality, they were far more powerful than army line panzer divisions. The strike power of the Waffen-SS divisions lay in their panzer regiments, which boasted two battalions of tanks. In 1942 a tank battalion had three companies – one of heavy Panzer IVs and two with lighter Panzer IIIs, each having a complement of 22 tanks. The *Leibstandarte*'s companies, however, all had Panzer IVs in frontline roles, with Panzer IIIs reduced to command tasks. For added punch, each Waffen-SS panzer regiment also had a company of the heavy Tiger I tanks attached in 1942.

To give an idea of the tank inventories of the SS panzer divisions, in February 1943 the *Leibstandarte* Division had the following panzers in its order of battle: 12 Panzer IIs, 10 Panzer IIIs, 52 Panzer IVs, 9 Tiger Is and 9 command tanks. Five months later, just before the Battle of Kursk, the division could field 4 Panzer IIs, 13 Panzer IIIs, 67 Panzer IVs, 13 Tiger Is and 9 command tanks.

At the heart of the Waffen-SS divisions were their two panzergrenadier regiments (although due to shortages only one was equipped with armoured halftracks; the other used trucks to transport its troops). These units were able to trace their lineage back to the original SS regiments, and they made great play of their Nazi heritage. They generally had honorific titles as well as numerical designations. For example, *Das Reich* had the *Deutschland* and *Der Führer* Regiments, *Totenkopf* had the *Thule* (later *Totenkopf*) and *Theodor Eicke* Regiments, and *Wiking* had the *Germania*, *Nordland* and *Westland* Regiments. The *Leibstandarte* was, however, unique in that all its sub-units included numerical designations and the title *Leibstandarte SS Adolf Hitler*, abbreviated to LSSAH.

By 1944, the élite Waffen-SS divisions were fully fledged panzer divisions, with an authorized order of battle as follows: one panzer regiment (two battalions); two panzergrenadier regiments; artillery regiment (one battalion of 12 150mm howitzers, one battalion of eight towed 150mm howitzers and four field guns, and one battalion of eight self-propelled 105mm howitzers and four self-propelled 150mm howitzers); armoured reconnaissance battalion; assault gun battalion (around 40 StuG IIIs); anti-tank battalion (28 75mm assault guns or tank destroyers and 12 towed anti-tank guns); anti-aircraft battalion (12 88mm guns and nine 37mm guns); engineer battalion; armoured signals brigade; and divisional services. Authorized strength was 19,500 troops.

SS Chief Himmler tried to ensure his panzer divisions were always up to strength. Thus, in June 1944, despite high losses the previous year on the Eastern Front, the *Leibstandarte* had 103 Panzer IVs, 72 Panthers and 45 StuG IIIs, and *Das Reich* had 50 Panzer IVs, 26 Panthers and 41 StuG IIIs.

KEY PERSONALITIES

IVAN KONEV

Konev was the main Soviet rival to Zhukov. Born in 1897, Konev finished school at 12 and was later conscripted into the Imperial Russian Army. He later fought with the Red Army during the Russian Civil War and became a commissar in the Far East. In the 1920s he attended the Frunze Military Academy and was a corps commander by 1937. Konev commanded the Second Independent Red Banner Far Eastern Army in 1938, but Zhukov arrived a few months later to steal his glory by defeating the Japanese at Khalkhin Gol, fuelling their mutual hostility.

As the Germans approached Moscow in 1941 Konev was commander of the Nineteenth Army, and in the subsequent battles around Vyazma and Bryansk his forces lost heavily. Stalin rather unfairly blamed him for the disaster and demoted him, but then he pushed the Germans back more than 160km (100 miles) from the gates of Moscow at the end of 1941. He had done well, but it was only when he became commander of the Steppe Front in 1943 that his true talents emerged. He found himself in command of large armoured forces for the first time, and during early 1944 let them loose against German forces in the Ukraine. The enemy could not stop him, and by the beginning of 1945 he had reached Breslau in Poland.

Initially, Stalin gave the honour of taking Berlin to Zhukov, but when he got bogged down Konev was allowed to divert some of his armoured forces to link up with Zhukov's troops and isolate the city. After the war, his rivalry with Zhukov continued, and Konev seemingly won when he was made Commander-in-Chief of Warsaw Pact Forces in 1956. However, he was retired in 1960 on the orders of Khrushchev, who now viewed him as a threat. Konev died in 1973.

▲ ***Panzer IIIs prior to taking part in Operation Citadel. They have been fitted with schürzen (armoured skirts) to their hulls and turrets for anti-tank protection.***

MAY 2

SOUTHERN USSR, *LAND WAR*

The German Seventeenth Army is being put under severe pressure in the Kuban.

MAY 4

GERMANY, *STRATEGY*

Hitler decides to delay Operation Citadel to June 13 so that more Tiger and the new Panther tanks can take part in the coming offensive.

MAY 15

USSR, *DIPLOMACY*

In a gesture designed to reassure his Western Allies that the USSR is no longer trying to foment world revolution, Stalin dissolves the Comintern. The latter, founded in 1919 by Lenin and the Bolsheviks, is dedicated "by all available means, including armed force, for the overthrow of the international bourgeoisie and for the creation of an international Soviet republic as a transition stage to the complete abolition of the State". The Americans in particular were keen for this organization to be disbanded.

MAY 16

POLAND, *PARTISAN WAR*

Organized resistance in the Warsaw Ghetto comes to an end. SS-Brigadeführer Jörgen Stroop, the SS commander during the rising, writes the following missive about the revolt in the battle diary: "The resistance offered by the Jews and bandits could be broken only by the energetic, tireless deployment of storm patrols night and day. On April 23, 1943, the Reichsführer-SS, through the Higher SS and Police Führer for the East, in Kracow, issued the order that the Warsaw ghetto be combed out with maximum severity and ruthless determination. I therefore decided to carry out the total destruction of the Jewish quarter by burning down all residential blocks, including the blocks attached to the armament factories. One by one the factories were systematically cleared and then destroyed by fire. Almost always the Jews then emerged from their hiding places and bunkers. Not rarely, the Jews stayed in the burning houses until the heat and fear of being burned to death

▶ ***Panther tanks on their way to the Kursk sector. These are Ausf D variants, the first production model, many of which broke down in battle.***

caused them to jump from the upper floors after they had thrown mattresses and other upholstered objects from the burning houses to the street. With broken bones they would then try to crawl across the street into buildings which were not yet, or only partially, in flames. Often, too, Jews changed their hiding places during the night, by shifting into the ruins of buildings already burned out and taking refuge there until they were found by one of the shock troop units. Only as a result of the unceasing and untiring efforts of all forces did we succeed in capturing altogether 56,065 Jews."

MAY 24

SOUTHERN USSR, *LAND WAR*
With the German Seventeenth Army in the Kuban fending off every assault, the Stavka brings the Krasnodar Offensive to an end. It has cost the North Caucasus Front 66,814 killed and 173,902 wounded.

JUNE 1

CENTRAL USSR, *AIR WAR*
The Red Air Force attacks German rear communications and airfields at Smolensk, Orel and Bryansk.

JUNE 2

CENTRAL USSR, *LAND WAR*
The Red Air Force bombs Kiev and Roslavl, while the Luftwaffe bombs the city of Kursk.

JUNE 4

The Luftwaffe bombs the massive Soviet tank factory at Gorki.

JUNE 8

CENTRAL USSR, *AIR WAR*
As the build-up in and around the Kursk salient continues, the Soviet First, Second and Fifteenth Air Armies begin a series of raids against German airfields around the salient, destroying some 220 aircraft on the ground.

JUNE 13

GERMANY, *STRATEGY*
The start date for Citadel passes. Hitler is still waiting for his Panther tanks.

JUNE 21

USSR, *ATROCITIES*
SS Chief Himmler orders: "All Jews who may still be found in ghettos in the Ostland must be confined in concentration camps. All non-essential inhabitants of the Jewish ghettos are to be referred to the East. The reorganization in concentration camps is to be completed by August 1, 1943." "Referred to the East" means extermination, although those Jews who can work will be kept alive to serve the German economy. Further to Himmler's orders, a number of ghettos were liquidated: Bialystok in August; Vilna and Minsk in September; and Riga in November. Inexplicably, two ghettos in Lithuania-Kovno (Kaunas) and Shavli (Siauliai) were left intact until mid-1944.

STRATEGY & TACTICS

SOVIET DEFENCES AT KURSK

The ordinary Red Army soldier was a master of defence, and it was a measure of Zhukov's brilliance that he realized that he could make use of the Red Army's greatest strength at Kursk. His tactics were simple: build intricate defence lines in depth, and let the Germans waste themselves in futile efforts trying to breach them.

Zhukov knew that his men would pay a heavy price in blood for their defence, but no matter. So he ordered the defences to be constructed. And his men, experts as they were in field defences, went on a frenzied bout of digging. They dug trenches, anti-tank ditches, laid minefields, built wire obstacles, mortar pits, artillery positions and other entanglements. They fortified villages and drafted in 300,000 civilians, mainly women and children, to aid construction of the defence lines.

At Kursk, therefore, for the first time in the war, a battle would be fought on the Russians' terms, and the Germans would pay dearly. The attacking heavy German tanks would be stopped by 85mm anti-aircraft guns (used in the ground role), with 122mm and 152mm howitzers providing heavy fire support. The length of the Red Army frontline in the Kursk salient was 450km (300 miles) with a depth of 190km (110 miles). Into this area were deployed 20,000 artillery pieces and mortars, 6000 anti-tank guns and hundreds of Katyusha rocket launchers. In the ground were up to 2700 anti-personnel and 2400 anti-tank mines, every 1.6km (1 miles). Above all, it was the tenacity of the ordinary Russian soldier that was the key to success at Kursk. He dug in to his position and remained there. He was ordered to remain at his post, and he did, often until he was killed by the enemy.

▲ ***Waffen-SS troops and halftracks on the eve of Operation Citadel. The SS panzer divisions were among the best-equipped units in the German order of battle.***

JULY 4

CENTRAL USSR, *LAND WAR*

The Germans are finally ready to launch Operation Citadel. Their order of battle is as follows: on the northern shoulder of the salient stands the Ninth Army, under the command of Colonel-General Model (335,000 men, 590 tanks and 424 assault guns), made up of 21 German and 3 Hungarian divisions. The Hungarian divisions are used for anti-partisan and security duties and therefore will not be part of the offensive force. Of the 21 German divisions, six – the 2nd, 4th, 9th, 12th, 18th and 20th – are panzer formations, with the 10th Panzergrenadier Division and 14 infantry divisions completing the line-up.

XLVII Corps: the 2nd, 9th and 20th Panzer Divisions, 6th Infantry Division and 21st Panzer Brigade. The armoured divisions of this corps are equipped with Panzer IIIs and IVs, plus StuG IIIs. However, the 21st Brigade has three Tiger companies in the 505th Panzer Detachment with 45 Tigers and 15 Panzer IIIs, and the 909th Assault Gun Detachment has a total of 36 vehicles.

XLVI Corps: the 4th and 12th Panzer Divisions, as well as the 10th Panzergrenadier Division, with a total of 184 tanks (held in reserve).

XLI Corps: the 18th Panzer Division, as well as the 86th and 292nd Infantry Divisions. It also comprises the 653rd and 654th Heavy Tank Destroyer detachments, recently formed and equipped with the entire production run, to date, of Porsche Ferdinand tank destroyers and a small number of Panzer IVs. Additional firepower is provided by the StuG IIIs of the 177th and 244th Assault Gun Brigades, and by the 66 Brummbar assault guns of the 216th Panzer Battalion.

XX Corps: four infantry divisions.

XXIII Corps: three and one-third infantry divisions.

On the southern shoulder of the salient is the Fourth Panzer Army, commanded by Colonel-General Hermann Hoth; and Army Detachment Kempf, commanded by General Walter Kempf. The strength of Manstein's command is nearly 350,000 men, 1269 tanks and 245 assault guns, excluding reserves.

LII Corps, on the left, consists of three infantry divisions, which will assume a mainly defensive posture.

XXXXVIII Panzer Corps, in the centre, comprises the 3rd and 11th Panzer Divisions, the 167th Infantry Division, and the *Grossdeutschland* Panzergrenadier Division, which includes the 200 Panthers of the 10th Panzer Brigade – in all, 535 tanks and 66 assault guns.

II SS Panzer Corps, to the south, is made up of the three SS Panzer Divisions – *Leibstandarte*, *Das Reich* and *Totenkopf* – with a total of 390 tanks and 104 assault guns, including 42 of Army Group South's 102 Tigers.

Army Detachment Kempf is tasked with guarding the right flank of the Fourth Panzer Army, and consists of three army corps.

III Panzer Corps: the 6th, 7th, and 19th Panzer Divisions with 299 tanks; 228th Assault Gun Detachment with 25 StuG IIIs; and the 168th Infantry Division. The cutting edge of III Panzer Corps is the 503rd Panzer Detachment with 45 Tigers.

XI Corps (Corps Rauss): the 106th and 320th Infantry Divisions and the 905th and 393rd assault gun detachments with 25 StuG IIIs each.

XLII Corps: the 39th, 161st and 282nd Infantry Divisions plus the Nashorn-equipped 560th Heavy Panzer Destroyer

▼ ***A battery of German 105mm le FH 18 howitzers at Kursk. In the early hours of July 5, Red Army guns shelled all known German artillery positions.***

Detachment with 40 tank destroyers, and Heavy Tank Destroyer Detachment C with approximately 40 assault guns.

In support is XXIV Panzer Corps, which includes the 17th Panzer Division and the 5th SS Panzer Division *Wiking*, a total of 112 tanks.

The Wehrmacht has amassed an impressive force, but its Red Army opponent is equally strong. To the north of Army Group Centre is the Western Front: Fiftieth Army, Eleventh Guards Army and the First Air Army, a total of 211,458 troops, 4285 guns and mortars, 144 rocket launchers, 745 tanks and self-propelled guns and 1300 aircraft.

Opposite Army Group Centre is the Bryansk Front: Third Army, Sixty-First Army, Sixty-Third Army and the Fifteenth Air Army: 433,616 troops, 7642 guns and mortars, 160 rocket launchers, 794 tanks and self-propelled guns and 1000 aircraft.

In the Kursk salient is Rokossovsky's Central Front: Forty-Eighth Army, Thirteenth Army, Seventieth Army, Sixty-Fifth Army, Sixtieth Army, Second Tank Army and the Sixteenth Air Army, a total of 711,575 troops, 11,076 guns and mortars, 246 rocket launchers, 1785 tanks and self-propelled guns and 1000 aircraft.

Also in the salient is the Voronezh Front: Thirty-Eighth Army, Fortieth Army, First Tank Army, Sixth Guards Army, Seventh Guards Army, Sixty-Ninth Army and the Second Air Army, a total of 625,591 troops, 8718 guns and mortars, 272 rocket launchers, 1704 tanks and self-propelled guns and 900 aircraft.

In reserve is the Steppe Military District: Fifth Guards Tank Army, Fifth Guards Army, Fourth Guards Tank Army, Twenty-Seventh Army, Forty-Seventh Army, Fifty-Third Army and the Fifth Air Army, a total of 573,195 troops, 8510 guns and mortars, 1639 tanks and self-propelled guns.

To the south, opposite Army Group South, stands the Southwestern Front: Fifty-Seventh Army and the Seventeenth Air Army, a total of 65,000 troops and 80 tanks. Inside the salient are in-depth and complex defences: up to 2400 anti-tank and 2700 anti-personnel mines were laid per mile in the Sixth Guards Army sector, amounting to 69,688; and 64,340 mines in its first line of defence alone. In the second and subsequent defence belts the density of mines falls off sharply, but the basic principle of channelling the advancing tanks has not been ignored. On the Voronezh Front alone 60,000 mines of all types have been laid. The length of the frontline is close to 450km (300 miles) and the depth is almost 190km (110 miles), dividing roughly into eight lines. Across the "neck" of the salient, the line to be held by Steppe Military District, lies another defensive belt with yet another running along the River Don to the north and south of Voronezh.

▲ *Erich von Manstein (right) observes enemy positions at Kursk. The commander of Army Group South disagreed with Hitler's continual postponement of Citadel.*

▶ *German Tiger tanks at Kursk. During the battle, one Tiger unit, Heavy Tank Battalion 503 (45 Tigers), destroyed 72 Soviet tanks in nine days of combat.*

STRATEGY & TACTICS

PANZERKEIL

The Germans at Kursk were faced with deep Soviet defences and no way to go around them. They therefore devised a new tactical formation to break through. The *Panzerkeil*, or armoured wedge, can be likened to a tin opener that had to rip open the Soviet pak-fronts. They were led by Tiger I heavy tanks and Ferdinand tank destroyers, which were heavily armoured and largely immune to enemy anti-tank rounds that hit them head on. The lighter Panthers, Panzer IVs and Panzer IIIs followed on behind, with about 100m (328ft) between each tank. To aid the advance, there was constant radio contact between each *Panzerkeil* and Luftwaffe ground-attack aircraft and supporting ground artillery.

During the battle, Red Army tanks and anti-tank guns had to be knocked out by the panzers and Luftwaffe aircraft, while enemy trenches and pillboxes had to cleared by German infantry using small arms and hand grenades. Often, the *Panzerkeils* were held up by minefields, through which a route had to be cleared by engineers. As a result, the advance was often agonizingly slow and bloody, as each metre of ground had to be fought over. Soon after the battle started, some panzer divisions were suffering daily tank losses of 10 percent. This rate of attrition was just what the Stavka had wanted.

JULY 5

CENTRAL USSR, *AIR WAR*

In support of Citadel, the Luftwaffe flies 4462 sorties against the Kursk salient.

CENTRAL USSR, *LAND WAR*

Following exchanges between German and Soviet artillery, the Battle of Kursk begins at 05:30 hours when XXIII Corps on the right flank of the Ninth Army attacks at the junction of the Soviet Thirteenth and Forty-Eighth Armies. Anti-personnel mines take a high toll on the men of the 78th, 216th and 38th Infantry Divisions. They advance no more than 1.5km (1.2 miles) towards their objective, the town of Maloarkhangelsk. The 20th Panzer Division has more success: by 09:00 hours it has reached the village of Bobrik and driven into the defensive positions of the Soviet 15th Rifle Division to a depth of some 5km (3 miles). By the evening the Ninth Army has advanced 8km (6 miles) but has sustained 20 percent losses in its panzer units – 200 out of the 300 tanks and assault guns committed, and nearly 20,000 casualties.

In the south, XXXXVIII Panzer Corps and II SS Panzer Corps make their attacks up two converging roads leading north through Pokrovka and Oboyan towards Kursk itself. By nightfall XXXXVIII Panzer Corps has fallen short of its objectives. Hausser's II SS Panzer Corps, having negotiated the minefields, launches its 390 tanks and 104 assault guns along the main road towards Bykovka. The SS corps is supported by VIII Air Corps and the entire Nebelwerfer brigade. By the end of the first day Hausser's men have advanced almost 20km (16 miles), broken into the second Soviet defensive belt and sliced the 52nd Rifle Division in two.

▶ ***Infantry of the SS Das Reich Division at Kursk. On the first day the SS men were drenched by rain.***

The southernmost German force to attack is Army Detachment Kempf. Army Detachment Kempf attacks across the Northern Donets River before breaking out from its bridgehead at Mikhailovka near Belgorod. Facing it is the Seventh Guards Army, which suffers heavy losses but holds up the German advance.

JULY 6

CENTRAL USSR, *LAND WAR*

In the northern sector of the Kursk salient both sides focus their efforts on the ridges stretching between Ponyri and the heavily defended villages of Olkhovatka and Samodurovka. The Soviet 16th Tank and 17th Guards Rifle Corps attack but are thrown back. The Russian withdrawals are followed closely by tanks of XLVII Panzer Corps advancing to the second defensive belt held by 17th Guards Rifle Corps' 70th and 75th Guards Rifle Divisions. To the east of the line XLI Panzer Corps again tries to split the Thirteenth and Forty-Eighth Armies, but fails to do so. In the early evening the Soviets launch a counterattack, the 150 tanks of the 19th Tank Corps hitting the tip of the German 20th and 2nd Panzer Divisions in the Bobrik-Samodurovka sector. The tanks are stopped by German firepower, but once again both sides suffer heavy losses. The German Ninth Army has again failed to make a breakthrough.

In the south the German attack is aimed at Oboyan, launched by the 3rd Panzer, 11th Panzer and *Grossdeutschland* Divisions following a 90-minute period of artillery preparation. The Luftwaffe flies some 200 ground-attack missions in support. However, despite eight separate attacks by XXXXVIII Panzer Corps, the Germans cannot break through. II SS Panzer Corps defeats the T-34 tanks of V Guards Tank Corps south of Iakovlevo, but cannot dislodge the 3rd Mechanized Corps' 1st Guards Tank Brigade and 51st Guards Rifle Division from Pokrovka and Bol'shie Maiachki on its left flank. Army Detachment Kempf attacks out of its bridgehead over the River Northern Donets with the tanks of the 7th and 19th Panzer Divisions leading the way, joined later in

KEY WEAPONS

PANTHER

The appearance of the Soviet T-34 tank on the Eastern Front in 1941 was a nasty surprise for the Germans. In response, December 1941 saw both Daimler-Benz and MAN instructed to begin designing a new, powerful medium tank. MAN eventually won the contract with its design. The result was the Panzer V Panther, which incorporated many features of the T-34, but was larger and heavier. Features included wide tracks for better traction and improved cross-country performance, a powerful engine, a powerful main gun and sloping armour for extra protection.

In December 1942, the Panther Ausf D entered production, the first models leaving the factory on January 11, 1943. The Panther was armed with a newer version of the 75mm KwK 42 L/70 gun, which was mounted in a hydraulically powered turret. Its weak spot was its side armour, which was only between 40mm (1.57in) and 50mm (1.96in) thick, depending on the variant.

The Panther made its combat debut at the Battle of Kursk. Because of technical problems, especially with the transmission and suspension, many Panthers broke down before and during the battle. Nevertheless, the Panther's problems were ironed out and it went on to become one of the best tanks of the war. Its effectiveness may be judged by an encounter between seven Panthers of the SS *Das Reich* Division and 70 T-34s near Kolomak on September 12, 1943. During the 20-minute battle, the Panthers knocked out 28 T-34s for no losses of their own.

Highly mobile, able to knock out any Allied tank in service and hard to knock out itself, the Panther was probably the finest tank of World War II. A total of 6000 Panthers were produced between 1943 and 1945.

Weight: 43,000kg (94,600lb)
Crew: 5
Engine: 1 x Maybach HL 230 P 30
Speed: 46kmh (28.75mph)
Range: 200km (125 miles)
Length: 8.86m (29ft)
Width: 3.4m (11.1ft)
Height: 2.98m (9.77ft)
Armament: 1 x 75mm cannon, 2 x 7.92mm machine gun
Ammunition: 79 rounds (75mm), 5100 rounds (7.92mm)
Armour: front (maximum): 100mm (3.93in); side (maximum): 45mm (1.77in)

the afternoon by the 6th Panzer Division. The 19th Panzer Division takes Belovskoe but is halted by the last reserves of the 81st Guards Rifle Division near Iastrebovo. The lead elements of XXXXVIII Panzer Corps link up with those of II SS Panzer Corps near Iakovlevo, establishing a clear threat to Oboyan. In response, the Stavka orders the 2nd and 5th Tank Corps from the reserves to reinforce the Voronezh Front. The front's plans for dealing with the German threat are as follows: 31st Tank Corps will advance towards the right flank of II SS Panzer Corps, 2nd Tank Corps and 5th Tank Corps will threaten the SS left flank, while 6th Tank Corps and 3rd Mechanized Corps will halt XXXXVIII Panzer Corps' progress on the Oboyan road.

JULY 7

CENTRAL USSR, *LAND WAR*

The Ninth Army's efforts today centre on the village of Ponyri, which controls the road and rail links with Kursk from the north. Supported by tanks of the 18th Panzer Division, the troops of the 292nd Infantry Division launch attacks on the lines held by the 307th Rifle Division in the village. After fierce fighting, by the end of the day the Germans have captured half the village. Another attack by the 2nd Panzer Division, with the Tigers of the 505th Panzer Detachment and the 20th Panzer Division, on the right against the Soviet lines between Samodurovka and Olkhovatka fails.

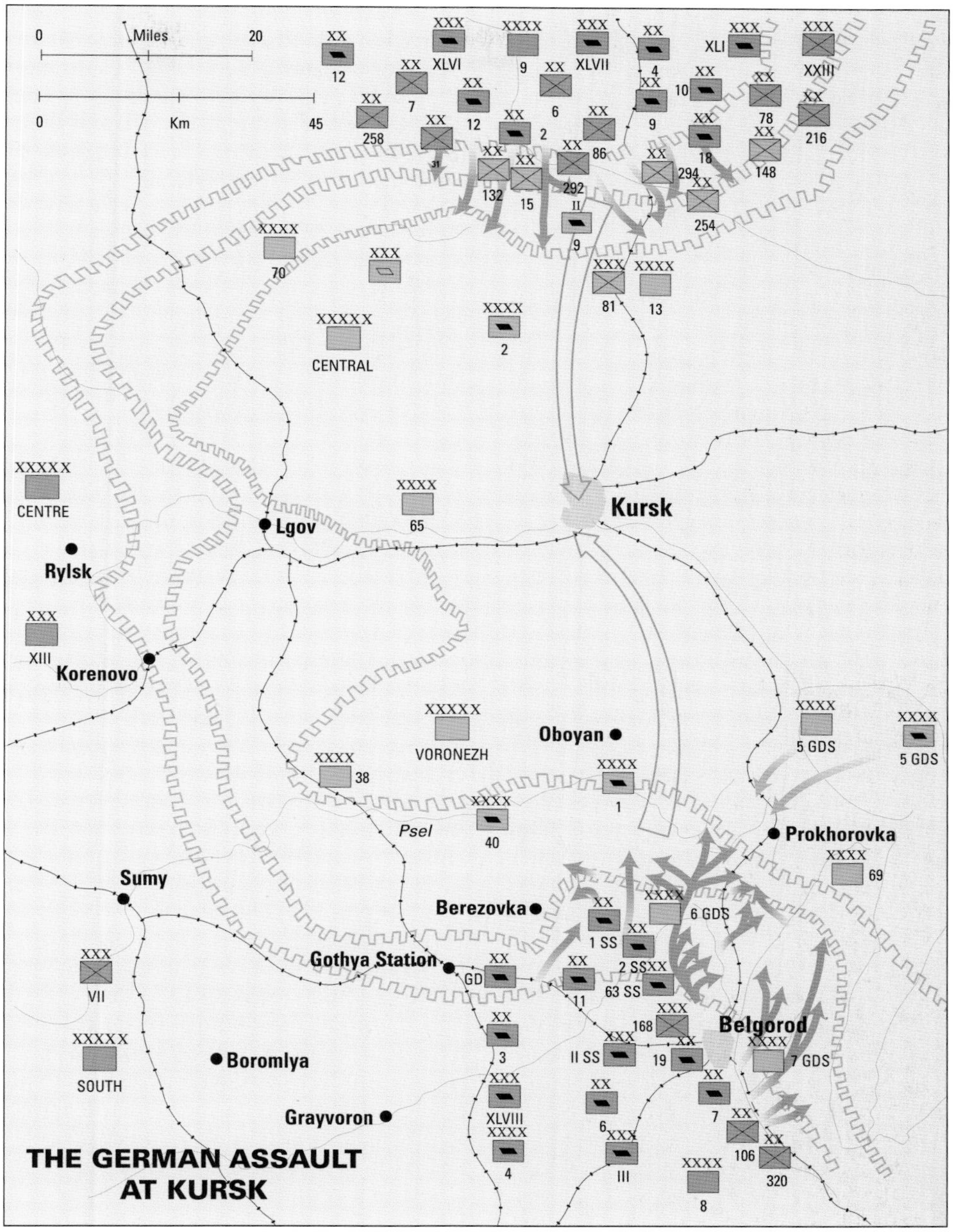

THE GERMAN ASSAULT AT KURSK

In the south, the day begins with a series of German attacks along the whole of the Fourth Panzer Army's front. As dawn breaks in the east, so XXXXVIII Panzer Corps rolls forward. The Germans attack Dubrova and Syrtsevo and clear Soviet defenders from the west bank of the River Pena. Meanwhile, the *Leibstandarte*'s 1st SS Panzer Regiment and *Das Reich*'s 2nd SS Panzer Regiment of II SS Panzer Corps advance up the Prokhorovka road, driving parts of the 5th Guards Tank Corps ahead of them, through and past Teterevino.

Army Detachment Kempf's 7th Panzer Division, the 45 Tigers of the 503rd Heavy Panzer Detachment and the 6th Panzer Division advance towards the vital road junction of Miasoedovo. In the evening, the Soviets commit two

◀ ***SS troops hitch a lift on a Panzer III at Kursk. One of the SS panzer divisions, the Totenkopf, lost half its tanks and vehicles during three days of fighting at Kursk.***

KEY PERSONALITIES

NIKOLAY VATUTIN

This stocky peasant general was born in the Belgorod region in 1901. He joined the Red Army in 1920 and the Communist Party a year later. He rose steadily through the ranks until he was deputy chief of the general staff on the Stavka in 1941. He was a great planner, and distinguished himself during the Soviet winter counteroffensive in late 1941 as chief of staff of Konev's Kalinin Front. In 1942 he took a leading part in the operation to trap the German Sixth Army in Stalingrad as commander of the Southwest Front, and then advanced into the Donets basin in early 1943. In mid-March 1943, he became commander of the Voronezh Front, leading it at the Battle of Kursk. After the battle he led his front into the Ukraine, but was ambushed by a group of Ukrainian nationalist partisans and wounded in the hip on February 29, 1944. He died of his wounds on April 15, 1944, at Kiev and is buried there.

▼ A Red Army 45mm Model 1937 anti-tank gun at Kursk. Though its effectiveness diminished as German tank armour became thicker, its ability to fire both anti-tank and high-explosive ammunition meant it stayed in service throughout the war.

divisions of the 35th Guards Rifle Corps to support the collapsing defences, which are east of Belgorod. On the left flank of III Panzer Corps, the 19th Panzer Division takes Blizhniaia Igumenka in the rear of the 81th Guards Rifle Division, but fails to cross the River Northern Donets.

JULY 8

CENTRAL USSR, *LAND WAR*
On the northern flank of the Kursk salient, the Soviet 307th Rifle Division counterattacks at Ponyri. The Soviet 51st and 103rd Tank Brigades simultaneously strike at the 1st May State Farm, which they take after three hours of fighting. Meanwhile, II SS Panzer Corps destroys 121 Soviet tanks and links up with XXXXVIII Panzer Corps at Sukho-Solotino. However, Hausser is forced to use *Das Reich* as the right flank guard. In Kempf's sector, the 6th Panzer Division advances 8km (4.9 miles) and captures the next key road junction at Melikhovo, east of the River Lipovyi Donets. However, both the 7th and 19th Panzer Divisions have failed to keep up. Although III Panzer Corps is clear through the first Soviet defensive belt east of the River Northern Donets, it cannot break through the line of the River Lipovyi Donets and into the rear of the Russians, east of Belgorod.

JULY 9

CENTRAL USSR, *LAND WAR*
On the northern flank of the Kursk salient, the German 508th Grenadier Regiment, supported by six Ferdinands, attacks Hill 253.3 and takes it. However, it cannot advance any further. The offensive in this sector of the front is effectively stalled. In the south, XXXXVIII Panzer Corps advances towards Novoselovka, which is defended by the 3rd Mechanized Corps and the 67th Guards Rifle Division. Verkhopen'e is taken during the morning. The Germans advance to Point 244.8, but such is the ferocity of Red Army resistance that the strength of the corps is severely sapped. II SS Panzer Corps has more success, reaching the River Psel and capturing the village of Krasni Oktiabr. The fall of Krasni Oktiabr signifies the breaching of the last defensive barrier

in front of Kursk. The River Psel is bridged and the Germans now have the opportunity to wheel northwards into the Soviet rear. The *Leibstandarte*, having linked up with the 11th Panzer Division, crosses the River Solotinka but is then held on the outskirts of Kochetovka by the Soviet 10th Tank Corps. The 6th Panzer Division regroups near Melikhovo as the 7th Panzer and 19th Panzer Divisions hold their ground east of the Northern Donets.

JULY 10

CENTRAL USSR, *LAND WAR*
German success at Kursk now hinges on the Fourth Panzer Army. The *Totenkopf* crosses the Psel and captures the northern slopes of Hill 226.6. The *Leibstandarte* advances up the Prokhorovka road and captures the Komsomolets State Farm and becomes engaged in vicious fighting for Hill 241.6. The hill is taken shortly after nightfall. After a gruelling battle of attrition, *Das Reich* gains only a foothold in the small village of Ivanovskii Vyselok. II SS Panzer Corps has made slow progress, but enough for Hitler to order that Operation Citadel be continued. On the Soviet side, the Fifth Guards Army arrives at Prokhorovka during

◀ ***Panzer III Ausf Ms at Kursk. This variant entered production in October 1942 and a total of 250 were produced. Over 400 Panzer IIIs fought at the Battle of Kursk.***

the night and the Fifth Guards Tank Army moves into assembly areas in the Fifth Guards Army's rear.

JULY 11

CENTRAL USSR, *LAND WAR*

In the north of the Kursk salient, Model commits the 10th Panzergrenadier Division, which launches a series of desperate attacks at Ponyri. Although the Germans now hold most of the town, it is impossible to move forward as their losses have been too great. To the west, the Soviet 17th Guards Rifle Corps takes the full force of the German attack, especially around Hill 257. But again the Germans fail to break through. II SS Panzer Corps continues its advance, the *Leibstandarte*'s panzers advancing along both sides of the Prokhorovka road supported by the Luftwaffe. Driving the elements of the already depleted Soviet 2nd Tank Corps before it, the *Leibstandarte* Division is subjected to flank attacks and artillery fire. The SS division takes Hill 252.2 and pushes on to capture the Oktiabr'skii State Farm. The *Leibstandarte* has driven a wedge into the Russian lines in front of Prokhorovka, and 2nd Tank Corps' defences are in disarray. However, its losses have been heavy and it now has only 60 tanks, 10 assault guns and 20 self-propelled tank destroyers in working order.

JULY 12

CENTRAL USSR, *LAND WAR*

To stop the Germans breaking through to Kursk in the south, Vatutin has been ordered to attack with the First Tank, Sixth Guards, Fifth Guards Tank and Fifth Guards Armies against the most immediate German threat: Hausser's II SS Panzer Corps and Knobelsdorff's XXXXVIII Panzer Corps. In addition, Seventh Guards Army's 40th Rifle Corps is ordered to strike the right flank of Army Detachment Kempf east of Razumnoe to prevent III Panzer Corps from making progress in its drive to link up with Hausser's men. The 500 tanks and assault guns of the Fifth Guards Tank Army attack at 08:30 hours, driving back the panzers of the *Leibstandarte* towards Oktiabr'skii. By the end of the day the *Leibstandarte* will have destroyed 192 Soviet tanks and 19 anti-tank guns for the loss of only 30 tanks. At 08:30 hours, 120 tanks of the 2nd Guards Tank Corps went into the attack, preventing *Das Reich* from supporting the *Leibstandarte*'s assault on Prokhorovka and from defending the *Leibstandarte*'s right flank. South of the River Psel, with 121 tanks and assault guns, the *Totenkopf* has, by midday, captured Hill 226, greatly weakening Rotmistrov's right flank. But it is unable to advance farther than Polezhaev.

As the tank battles rage around Prokhorovka, the German situation to the west is deteriorating. With XXXXVIII Panzer Corps poised to cross the River Psel and push on to Oboyan, yet another

KEY WEAPONS

MG42

Nicknamed "Hitler's Buzz Saw", the MG42 machine gun was designed to replace the MG34, although in reality it never did. The MG42 would be mass produced and more rugged in the field than the high-maintenance MG34. The result of these efforts created perhaps the world's best machine gun, which had a unique delayed blow-back system of firing. Here, an additional restraint or brake is placed on the bolt or other breech closure in order to delay or slow down the opening, although not actually locking the breech. Robust, reliable and possessing an incredible rate of fire, this weapon was the pride of the German infantry. Its rate of fire was 1500 rounds per minute, or 25 rounds per second! This meant Red Army infantry attacks could be broken up with short bursts.

Fire rates as high as this caused barrels to overheat, but the designers had thought of this and had devised a quick-change facility. This meant a trained gunner could change a barrel in less than seven seconds. A total of 414,964 MG42s were built during the war.

Calibre: 7.92mm
Magazine capacity: 250-round belt feed
Length: 1220mm (48in)
Weight: 11.5kg (25.3lb) on bipod
Muzzle velocity: 710mps (2329fps)

of Vatutin's spoiling attacks erupts against the Fourth Panzer Army. Some 100 tanks of the 22nd Guards Rifle Corps break through the German 332nd Infantry Division's positions, the 5th Guards Tank Corps (70 tanks) reaches Rakovo, and the 10th Tank Corps has driven the 3rd Panzer Division back towards Verkhopen'e and Berezovka. The 3rd Panzer Division (fewer than 50 tanks) needs assistance if the western flank of the entire southern pincer is not to collapse. Thus, the *Grossdeutschland* is redeployed to counter the threat. This isolates the 11th Panzer Division (50 tanks), which is attacked in the afternoon but to no effect.

The Soviet Operation Kutuzov begins against the German Orel salient, conducted by the Bryansk Front (170,000 troops and more than 350 tanks and self-propelled guns), attacking the nose and southern flank of the salient, with the left wing of the Western Front (211,458 troops, 4285 guns and mortars and 745 tanks and self-propelled guns) attacking along the northern flank of the salient. The Third Guards Tank Army, with 731 tanks and self-propelled guns, is held in reserve. Facing these forces is the Second Panzer Army (XXXV, LIII and LV Corps) – 160,000 troops and 350 tanks and assault guns. The offensive opens at 03:30 hours, Soviet artillery battering the German lines until just after 06:00 hours. By the afternoon, the Eleventh Guards Army has pushed into the German lines, only to be held up by the 5th Panzer Division. Nevertheless, by nightfall the Soviets have forged 10km (7 miles) into the German lines.

▲ ***Tiger tanks of the SS* Das Reich*'s Heavy Panzer Company at Kursk. The company had 14 Tigers at Kursk, with the division fielding 104 tanks and 33 assault guns.***

USSR, *DIPLOMACY*

The Soviets establish the National Committee for a Free Germany at the Krasnogorsk prisoner of war camp outside of Moscow. It consists of 38 members, 25 being soldiers and officers, including Field Marshal Paulus, and the remainder communist émigrés from Germany. The committee claims that the only hope for German survival is to remove Hitler and replace him with a new government with which the Allies might enter into peace negotiations.

JULY 13

GERMANY, *STRATEGY*

Worried about a possible Allied invasion in the south of Europe (the Allies had landed in Sicily on July 10), Hitler informs the commanders of Army Group Centre and South: "I must prevent that. And so I need divisions for Italy and the Balkans. And since they can't be taken from any other place, apart from the transfer of the 1st Panzer Division from France to the Peloponnese, they will have to be released from the Kursk Front. Therefore I am forced to stop Citadel."

◀ ***A T-34 burns on the Kursk battlefield. The Red Army lost 1614 tanks and self-propelled guns out of a total of 5035 tanks and self-propelled guns.***

JULY 14

CENTRAL USSR, *LAND WAR*

German forces in the south of the Kursk salient continue limited offensives. The *Grossdeutschland* and 3rd Panzer Divisions counterattack the Soviet 5th Guards and 10th Tank Corps, which have been reinforced by the 6th Tank Corps. The German units drive the Soviets back. In addition, III Panzer Corps and the *Das Reich* Division wipe out an enemy pocket between the River Lipovyi-Donets and River Northern Donets.

JULY 17

SOUTHERN USSR, *LAND WAR*

The Soviet Southern and Southwestern Fronts begin their Donets-Mius Operation

near Izyum, forcing Manstein to redeploy II SS Panzer Corps to the area, and later XXIV Panzer Corps.

JULY 19

CENTRAL USSR, *LAND WAR*

The Soviet Third Guards Tank Army joins the offensive east of Orel, joining the Third and Sixty-Third Armies in the attack on the city, as the Eleventh and Eleventh Guards Armies move on Bryansk.

JULY 22

NORTHERN USSR, *LAND WAR*

In an effort to secure the precarious link with Leningrad, the Soviet Sixty-Seventh Army on the Neva and the Eighth Army on the west bank of the Volkhov (combined total of 253,000 troops) launch the Mga Offensive Operation.

CENTRAL USSR, *LAND WAR*

Hitler has given the commander of the Ninth Army, Model, permission to conduct a mobile defence in the Orel salient. The general is thus fortifying the River Desna at the base of the salient.

JULY 26

GERMANY, *STRATEGY*

Mussolini has been arrested by the Italians in Italy. Hitler announces that II SS Panzer Corps will leave for Italy immediately, and that several other divisions will follow on after. To release these troops, the Orel salient is to be evacuated as quickly as possible (Operation Autumn Journey will be authorized on July 28). Supported by the recently arrived *Grossdeutschland* Division, the Germans begin to pull back to the Hagen Line (at the base of the salient). Despite partisan raids, the Germans manage to evacuate trains full of the wounded and fresh supplies. There is little threat from the Soviets at this point. The plethora of Soviet units involved in Operation Kutuzov has led to confusion in the command and control system, and the reorganization of their forces gives the Germans time to pull back.

▲ The last moments of a T-34 at Kursk, as seen through the sight of a panzer. Seconds after this photograph was taken, the T-34 had its turret blown off.

KEY WEAPONS

JU 87G-1

The G-1 was the tank-busting version of the Junkers Ju 87 Stuka dive-bomber. It was created from converted D-5 model aircraft by attaching two 37mm Flak 18 cannon in under-wing pods. This aircraft was very successful in the hands of experienced pilots who could survive daylight operations with the poor flight performance of the Stuka. For example, at the Battle of Kursk in July 1943, Hans-Ulrich Rudel, piloting a G variant Stuka, destroyed 12 T-34s single-handedly.

The G-1 had reduced speed and range due to the armour plating installed to protect the pilot and rear gunner when flying anti-tank missions. The one saving grace for pilots on anti-tank missions was that they usually approached their targets from the rear, in order to hit the thinner engine housing. Thus, they were actually flying towards their own lines in battle, which increased their chances of making it back to friendly territory if hit. By mid-1943 the Germans had lost air superiority over the Eastern Front, and flying a Stuka was a risky business indeed.

Type: anti-tank aircraft
Powerplant: 1 x 1300hp Junkers Jumo 211J
Wingspan: 13.8m (45.27ft)
Length: 11m (36ft)
Height: 3.77m (12.36ft)
Maximum speed: 344kmh (215mph)
Service ceiling: 7500m (24,606ft)
Maximum range: 1000km (625 miles)
Armament: 2 x 37mm, 2 x 7.92mm

◀ *A Red Army 152mm gun-howitzer firing during Operation Rumyantsev. Each Soviet howitzer regiment was equipped with 24 152mm howitzers.*

AUGUST 1

SOUTHERN USSR, *AIR WAR*
The top-scoring Soviet female pilot, Junior Lieutenant Lydia Litvak of the 73rd Guards Fighter Air Regiment, is shot down and killed in the Ukraine. Her awards are as follows: Order of the Red Star; Order of the Red Banner; medal "For the Defence of Stalingrad"; Order of the Patriotic War, 1st degree; and Hero of the Soviet Union (the latter awarded posthumously in 1990).

GERMANY, *ARMED FORCES*
The 1st Cossack Cavalry Division is formally established in the army's order of battle. It comprises two brigades, each one made up of three sabre squadrons and an artillery battalion.

AUGUST 3

SOUTHERN USSR, *LAND WAR*
The Soviet Operation Rumyantsev begins. Its objectives are the destruction of both the Fourth Panzer Army and Sixth Army by reaching the Black Sea coast behind them. The Voronezh and Steppe Fronts have more than 980,000 troops, 2439 tanks and self-propelled guns, 12,627 guns and mortars and nearly 1300 aircraft, against 300,000 men, 250 tanks and assault guns, 3000 guns and mortars, and fewer than 1000 aircraft. The offensive begins at 05:00 hours, and by early afternoon the German lines have been penetrated sufficiently for Vatutin to commit four tank brigades to exploit the breach, which they do to a depth of 25km (16 miles). By the end of the day the Soviets have driven a 10km (6-mile) wedge between the Fourth Army and Army Detachment Kempf. The Steppe Front is not so successful. Manstein brings the SS panzer divisions *Das Reich* and *Totenkopf* back from the River Mius and, along with the battered 3rd Panzer Division, they are placed under III Panzer Corps. This force is given instructions to halt the Soviet armour northwest of Kharkov. Army Detachment Kempf is reinforced by the 5th SS Panzer Division *Wiking*.

AUGUST 5

CENTRAL USSR, *LAND WAR*
The Soviet Third and Sixty-Third Armies recapture Orel.

SOUTHERN USSR, *LAND WAR*
The Soviet Fifth Guards and Sixth Armies batter enemy forces around Tomarovka as the Twenty-Seventh and Fortieth Armies advance to the west of the town. Towards evening, the units of XXXXVIII Panzer Corps begin a fighting withdrawal from the town to save themselves. The Soviet First Tank and Twenty-Seventh Armies approach Bogodukhov as the Fifty-Third Army severs the Belgorod–Kharkov road. Inside the city, the Seventh Guards and Sixty-Ninth Armies eject the German defenders and establish bridgeheads over the Donets.

AUGUST 7

CENTRAL USSR, *LAND WAR*
The Soviet Western Front (Fifth, Tenth Guards and Thirty-Third Armies and Sixty-Eighth Army) opens its offensive to recapture Smolensk. The front strength is 824,000 troops. It will be joined by the 428,000 troops of the Kalinin Front, which will assault the German Fourth and Third Panzer Armies north of the city.

KEY WEAPONS

SU-76

The SU-76 *Samokhodnaya Ustanovka* (self-propelled mounting) was a Soviet self-propelled gun. In June 1941, when the Germans invaded Russia, there were no self-propelled guns in the Red Army. Therefore, in October 1942, the Soviet Defence Ministry decided to produce its own self-propelled gun. The basis of the vehicle was the T-70 tank chassis, which was widened and given another suspension unit.

The engine, fuel tanks and driving positions were all changed and moved to the right front of the vehicle. Some SU-76s had rear doors and others open backs; some had the radiators on the track covers and others in the engine compartment. The SU-76 was deployed in self-propelled gun regiments in mechanized and armoured corps. By April 1943, there were self-propelled gun regiments that had four or five batteries containing five SU-76s each. In 1944, several rifle and guards rifle divisions received their own SU-76 units. By June 1945, 14,292 SU-76s had been built, 60 percent of the total number of all Soviet self-propelled guns produced during the war.

The main gun fired high-explosive, armour-piercing high-explosive, hyper-velocity armour-piercing and high-explosive anti-tank rounds. The SU-76 was not popular with crews because it was unreliable. Indeed, it was nicknamed *suka* (bitch).

Weight: 10,800kg (23,760lb)
Crew: 4
Engine: 2 x GAZ-203 gasoline
Speed: 45kmh (28mph)
Range (road): 320km (200 miles)
Length: 4.9m (16ft)
Width: 2.7m (8.85ft)
Height: 2.2m (7.2ft)
Armament: 1 x 76.2mm cannon
Ammunition: 60 rounds
Armour: front (maximum): 30mm (1.1in); side: 15mm (0.59in)

SOUTHERN USSR, *LAND WAR*
The Soviet Fifth Guards and Sixth Armies eject the German LII Corps from Borisovka, the Wehrmacht losing 5000 killed and captured during the retreat. The Soviet First Tank Army recaptures Bogodukhov, but is then engaged in

▼ ***German troops retreating in the Ukraine in mid-August, the strain of combat etched on their faces, during the Red Army's drive to the Dnieper.***

◀ ***Red Army soldiers captured during a German counterattack near Kharkov. By August, 1943 the Red Army had six million troops in the field.***

heavy armoured combat to the east by elements of III Panzer Corps.

AUGUST 9

SOUTHERN USSR, *LAND WAR*
German resistance is stiffening as III Panzer Corps battles the First Tank Army near Merefa, LII Corps counterattacks at Grayvoron and the Fifth Guards Tank Army is slowed by III Panzer Corps near Olshany.

AUGUST 12

SOUTHERN USSR, *LAND WAR*
The Soviet First Tank Army recaptures Vysokopolye. The Soviet Fifty-Seventh Army takes Chuguyev as units of the Steppe Front reach Kharkov's outskirts.

AUGUST 13

NORTHERN USSR, *LAND WAR*
The Mga Offensive continues but is achieving little save a high butcher's bill.
CENTRAL USSR, *LAND WAR*
The Kalinin Front joins the attack against Smolensk, its Thirty-Ninth and Forty-Third Armies advancing towards Dukhovshina.
SOUTHERN USSR, *LAND WAR*
The Steppe Front is tightening its grip on Kharkov. The Soviet Southwestern Front begins its Donbas Offensive against the First Panzer Army (which has been weakened by the deployment of panzer units to the north to counter other Soviet offensives). The front has 565,000 troops.

AUGUST 15

SOUTHERN USSR, *LAND WAR*
The Soviet Southern Front (446,000 troops) opens an offensive along the River Mius against the German Sixth Army, with the Fifth Shock Army striking XVII Corps. In Kharkov the German defenders are resisting the sledgehammer blows of the Steppe Front, the Soviets losing 20 tanks destroyed in the streets of the city.
USSR, *ATROCITIES*
The Bialystok Ghetto is cleared by Wehrmacht, SS troops and Ukrainian auxiliary forces backed up by artillery. As 30,000 exhausted Jews head towards the evacuation point, the Jewish underground in the ghetto launches an uprising. For the next five days fierce battles rage in the ghetto. A detachment of German soldiers and police, backed by armoured vehicles and tanks, is brought into the ghetto, and the main bunker of the underground is surrounded on August 19. Deportations from the ghetto begin on August 18 and go on for three days, in the course of which all the inhabitants of the ghetto

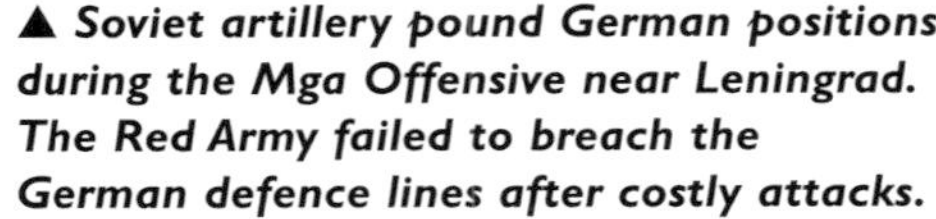

▲ ***Soviet artillery pound German positions during the Mga Offensive near Leningrad. The Red Army failed to breach the German defence lines after costly attacks.***

save 2000 are sent to Majdanek and Treblinka. The remaining 2000 are murdered three weeks later.

AUGUST 18

CENTRAL USSR, *LAND WAR*
Having cleared the Orel salient, the Red Army takes stock of its losses. They are, as usual, high: the Bryansk Front has lost 39,000 killed and 123,000 wounded, and the Central Front 47,700 killed and 117,000 wounded. The two fronts have also lost a combined total of 2586 tanks, 892 artillery pieces and 1014 aircraft.

SOUTHERN USSR, *LAND WAR*
The Southern Front's offensive is making gains, with the German XVII and XXIX Corps (Sixth Army) coming under severe pressure and the Fifth Shock Army moving south towards Taganrog.

USSR, *ATROCITIES*
As the Red Army pushes west, the Germans are trying to erase all traces of their killings. A special unit, Sonderkommando 1005, made up of prisoners, begins to exhume and cremate the corpses at Babi Yar (those who slacken are shot at once). The prisoners haul the bodies to a cremation pyre composed of wooden logs, doused in gasoline, on a base of railroad ties. The bones that cannot be incinerated are crushed by tombstones from a local Jewish cemetery. The ashes are then sifted for any gold or silver they might contain.

AUGUST 21

GERMANY, *ARMED FORCES*
Army Group South reports on the current strength of its divisions. It is a telling indication of how German divisions have been worn down by their participation in the Battle of Kursk and battling subsequent Soviet offensives. The Sixth Army has 10 infantry divisions, whose fighting power is equivalent to 3.5 divisions. Its one panzer division has the fighting power equivalent to half a panzer division. The First Panzer Army possesses eight infantry and three panzer and panzergrenadier divisions, which have the fighting power equivalent to 5.5 and 1.25 divisions respectively. The Eighth Army has an impressive 12 infantry and 5 panzer divisions, but these only have the fighting power equivalent to 5.75 and 2.3 divisions respectively, while the Fourth Panzer Army has eight infantry and five panzer divisions, which have a fighting power equivalent to three and two divisions respectively.

AUGUST 22

NORTHERN USSR, *LAND WAR*
The Stavka ends the Mga Offensive, which has proved a costly failure with the Red Army losing 20,890 killed and missing and 59,047 wounded.

SOUTHERN USSR, *LAND WAR*
With the fighting in Kharkov still raging, Manstein decides to abandon the city (contrary to Hitler's orders). Army Group South is being bled white by the Red Army's offensives.

KEY WEAPONS

PE-2

The Petlyakov Pe-2 was one of the most important aircraft in the USSR's inventory, fighting from the beginning of Barbarossa until the surrender of Germany in 1945. It entered service in August 1940 as a multi-role dive- and attack-bomber, having a crew of three and being armed with four 7.62mm machine guns: two fixed firing ahead above the nose; one aimed from the upper rear position; and one from a retracting ventral mount. Because of its speed and manoeuvrability, German fighter pilots found the Pe-2 difficult to catch and shoot down. From August 1941, the even-faster reconnaissance Pe-2 version began to appear over the Eastern Front (these aircraft lacked dive brakes and were fitted with additional fuel tankage in the bomb bay and had three cameras in the rear fuselage). In total, 11,400 Pe-2s of all variants were produced.

Type: attack-bomber
Powerplant: 2 x 1100hp Klimov M-105R
Wingspan: 17.2m (56.4ft)
Length: 12.66m (41.5ft)
Height: 3.5m (11.48ft)
Maximum speed: 540kmh (337mph)
Service ceiling: 8800m (28,871ft)
Maximum range: 1200km (750 miles)
Armament: 4 x 7.62mm machine gun, 1000kg (2200lb) bomb load

◀ *Some of Rotmistrov's T-34s approach Kharkov. On August 20, 200 T-34s assaulted German defences outside the city – 150 were knocked out by the day's end.*

August 23

SOUTHERN USSR, *LAND WAR*
German forces withdraw from Kharkov as III Panzer Corps counterattacks at Bogodukhov against the First Tank and Sixth Guards Armies. As the German Sixth Army withdraws from its Mius positions the Fifth Shock Army encircles the German XXIX Corps at Taganrog. The Red Army has suffered great losses during its battles for the eastern Ukraine: Voronezh Front 48,300 killed and missing and 108,000 wounded, and Steppe Front 23,000 killed and missing and 75,000 wounded. Combined equipment losses are 1864 tanks, 423 artillery pieces and 153 aircraft.

August 26

CENTRAL USSR, *LAND WAR*
Yet another Red Army offensive begins as the Central Front (579,600 troops) attacks the German Second Army, intent on recapturing Poltava and reaching the Dnieper. The main axis of the Soviet attack is towards Sevsk, which is heavily defended by the Germans. Nevertheless, the Soviet Sixtieth Army manages to punch its way through the Second Army's lines. The Germans have no reserves, and so suddenly the Soviets are threatening to split Army Groups Centre and South.

August 27

CENTRAL USSR, *LAND WAR*
As Sevsk is captured by the Soviet Sixty-Fifth Army, the Germans are offered a reprieve when the Second Tank Army suffers heavily at the hands of entrenched anti-tank guns.

SOUTHERN USSR, *LAND WAR*
As the Voronezh Front advances to the west of Kharkov, the Soviet Fifth Shock and Fifty-First Armies smash through the lines of the German IV and XVII Corps.

August 28

CENTRAL USSR, *LAND WAR*
The Central Front continues to split the German Second Army, expanding the gap between Army Groups Centre and South. The Western Front joins in the offensive against German defences at Smolensk, commencing with a strike against Yelnya.

August 30

CENTRAL USSR, *LAND WAR*
Yelnya falls to the Soviet Fifth and Tenth Guards Armies, with the Fourth Army's IX Corps being pushed back west.

SOUTHERN USSR, *LAND WAR*
Tagonrog is captured by the Southern Front's Forty-Fourth Army.

August 31

CENTRAL USSR, *LAND WAR*
The Soviet Sixtieth Army has now penetrated 80km (50 miles) into the German rear.

SOUTHERN USSR, *LAND WAR*
The German First Panzer and Sixth Armies prepare to fall back to the Dnieper, Manstein having finally convinced Hitler of the need for a mobile defence. However, this will only buy time for the Wehrmacht in the Ukraine; it will not stave off defeat. August has been a disastrous month for the Germans in the East, the army having lost a total of 218,000 troops (133,000 from Army Group South). There are only 2555 armoured vehicles along the whole front, of which a third are operational. Facing them are 6200 Red Army tanks alone. Army Groups Centre and South can muster 1.4 million troops, but the Soviet Central, Voronezh, Steppe, Southwestern and Southern Fronts can muster 2,630,000 troops and 2400 tanks.

▶ *A German halftrack and towed anti-tank gun pulling back in the face of the Soviet Western Front's offensive against Smolensk.*

▲ ***German Ju 87s being directed to their target by a halftrack ground-to-air communications vehicle.***

SEPTEMBER 2

CENTRAL USSR, *LAND WAR*
The Soviet Thirty-Eighth Army captures Sumy.

SOUTHERN USSR, *LAND WAR*
The Soviet Third Guards Army captures Lisichansk; and the Fifty-First Army Kommunarsk.

SEPTEMBER 5

USSR, *ATROCITIES*
As the German Army retreats, evidence of its atrocities are being uncovered. A report by a committee in Kharkov issued today reveals the fate of the city's Jewish population: "The Commission opened up two pits near the village of Rogan in the valley of Drobitzki, one of them 100 metres long and 18–20 metres wide, and the second 60 metres long and 20 metres wide. According to the findings of the Expert Medical Commission, upwards of 15,000 bodies were buried in these pits (attached: the report of the Medico-Legal Commission). Five hundred bodies were removed from the pits, of which 215 were submitted to medico-legal examination. They included the bodies of 83 men, 117 women and 60 children and infants. It was established that the cause of death of almost all these persons whose bodies had been examined was a wound and hole in the back of the skull caused by the passage of a bullet. This indicated that the shooting was carried out from behind the person to be killed and from a short distance away."

SEPTEMBER 8

SOUTHERN USSR, *LAND WAR*
The Soviet Fifth Shock Army occupies Stalino as the Third Guards Army takes possession of Krasnoarmyansk.

SEPTEMBER 10

SOUTHERN USSR, *LAND WAR*
The Soviet juggernaut shows no sign of halting as Mariupol is occupied by the Twenty-Eighth and Forty-Fourth Armies and Barvenkovo by the First Guards Army. In the Kuban, the Soviet North Caucasus Front hurls 250,000 troops against the beleaguered Seventeenth Army. As fighting rages in Novorossisk, the Germans being to evacuate their forces west into the Crimea.

SEPTEMBER 14

CENTRAL USSR, *LAND WAR*
As the German Ninth Army pulls back from Bryansk, fighting erupts in and around the city. The Kalinin Front joins the offensive against Smolensk.

SEPTEMBER 16

CENTRAL USSR, *LAND WAR*
The Soviets grind their way forward, the Thirty-First Army capturing Yartsevo, the

▼ ***Red Army cavalry in the Ukraine. Soviet cavalry divisions in the last two years of the war numbered 6000 men each, and a cavalry corps numbered 21,000 troops.***

Tenth Army crossing the Desna and the Sixtieth Army taking Novgorod Seversky.

SOUTHERN USSR, *LAND WAR*
Romny is captured by the Voronezh Front, and in the Kuban Novorossisk is taken by the Eighteenth Army.

SEPTEMBER 22

SOUTHERN USSR, *LAND WAR*
The Soviet Central Front reaches the River Dnieper, and the Third Guards Army crosses the waterway at Veliki Bukrin. The cost of reaching the river line has been high: the Southwestern Front has lost 40,000 killed and missing and 117,000 wounded, the Southern Front losing 26,000 killed and missing and 90,000 wounded. Elsewhere, the First Panzer Army is hit hard in the Dnepropetrovsk bridgehead and the German Seventeenth Army continues with its skilful withdrawal from the Kuban.

SEPTEMBER 24

CENTRAL USSR, *LAND WAR*
With the Soviet Thirty-First Army to the north of the city and the Fifth and Sixty-Eighth Armies to the east and south, Smolensk is virtually surrounded. The Germans are thus forced to abandon the city, which is occupied by the three Soviet armies the next day.

SOUTHERN USSR, *LAND WAR*
The Bukrin bridgehead is consolidated by the Soviet Third Guards Tank, Twenty-Seventh and Fortieth Armies.

SEPTEMBER 26

SOUTHERN USSR, *LAND WAR*
The Soviets continue to pierce the Dnieper line, the Thirty-Eighth Army crossing north of Kiev at Lyutezh and the Sixth Army at Dnepropetrovsk. The Fourth Panzer Army's XIII Corps attacks at Lyutezh to eradicate the bridgehead but fails. The German Sixth Army comes under heavy attack from the Fifth Shock, Second Guards, Twenty-Eighth and Forty-Fourth Armies of the Southern Front.

SEPTEMBER 27

SOUTHERN USSR, *GROUND WAR*
The Soviet bridgehead at Bukrin comes under heavy attack from XXXXVIII Panzer Corps but the German assault fails to destroy it.

SEPTEMBER 30

SOUTHERN USSR, *LAND WAR*
The Germans have retreated behind the Dnieper, and the Red Army has again achieved great successes, liberating many towns and inflicting losses of 230,000 on the Germans. However, the Red Army's tactics have left a lot to be desired, often relying on mass to achieve results. The cost has again been high: in five days the Voronezh, Steppe and Central Fronts have suffered a staggering combined total of 102,500 killed and missing.

Army Group South has completed the evacuation of 200,000 wounded soldiers west over the River Dnieper.

ARMED FORCES

SOVIET ARTILLERY DIVISIONS

On October 31, 1942, the Stavka ordered the raising of 26 Red Army artillery divisions. The original divisional organization was three howitzer regiments (each with 20 122mm howitzers), two gun regiments (each with 18 122mm or 152 gun-howitzers), three tank-destroyer artillery regiments (each with 24 76mm guns) and an observation battalion. As with infantry and armoured formations, the artillery underwent numerous reorganizations. In April 1943, for example, five artillery corps headquarters were created to control the groupings of artillery divisions and, at the same time, a new divisional format was established: the breakthrough artillery division.

The new division comprised: an observation battalion; a light brigade (three regiments, each one with 24 76mm guns); a howitzer brigade (three regiments, each one with 28 122mm howitzers); a gun brigade (two regiments, each one with 18 152mm gun-howitzers); and a mortar brigade (three regiments, each one with 36 120mm mortars). In addition, two heavy howitzer brigades (one of four battalions, each one with eight 152mm howitzers; and one of four battalions, each one equipped with six 203mm howitzers) were attached to divisional headquarters. Each division numbered 11,000 troops and was equipped with 1100 trucks and 175 tractors.

▼ ***Romanian troops in southern Russia. Hitler's Axis ally eventually committed 700,000 troops to the Eastern Front. Often poorly trained and ill-equipped, they suffered heavy casualties, losing 173,000 men alone at Stalingrad.***

OCTOBER 5

SOUTHERN USSR, *LAND WAR*
The Soviet Eighth Guards Army of the Steppe Front forces its way across the Dnieper, south of Dnepropetrovsk, in the face of desperate resistance.

OCTOBER 6

CENTRAL USSR, *LAND WAR*
The Soviet Third and Fourth Shock Armies capture Nevel at the junction of Army Groups North and Centre, cutting communications between the two.

SOUTHERN USSR, *LAND WAR*
The German XIII and LIX Corps try to wipe out the Lyutezh bridgehead during a series of attacks, but to no avail.

OCTOBER 9

SOUTHERN USSR, *LAND WAR*
The North Caucasus Front has liberated the north Caucasus, losing 13,900 killed and missing and 50,000 wounded. The German Seventeenth Army is now in the Crimea. But it is threatened from the north when the Soviet Southern Front attacks the Sixth Army. If it succeeds the Soviets will pour through Melitopol and cut off the Seventeenth Army.

OCTOBER 10

CENTRAL USSR, *LAND WAR*
The Soviet Central Front assaults enemy forces at Gomel.

SOUTHERN USSR, *LAND WAR*
The Soviet Southwestern Front assaults the Zaporozhye bridgehead with the Third Guards, Eighth Guards and Twelfth Armies. The German XXXX Panzer and XVII Corps try to stem the tide.

GERMANY, *ARMED FORCES*
The Spanish Blue Division, which has fought on the Eastern Front since 1941, is recalled by the Spanish Government. General Franco began negotiations with Hitler to withdraw his fighting men from the conflict in the spring of this year due to increased Allied pressure, as well as his own realization that Germany will lose the war on the Eastern Front. However, 3000 Spaniards will choose to remain on the Eastern Front to carry on fighting.

▲ ***German troops scan the sky for enemy aircraft. The Luftwaffe lost 1030 aircraft in July and August, and was on the defensive.***

▼ ***Men of the German Seventeenth Army in the Crimea. Hitler forbade any retreat from the Crimea, thus dooming the army.***

OCTOBER 14

SOUTHERN USSR, *LAND WAR*
The Soviet Third and Eighth Guards and Twelfth Armies capture Zaporozhye, forcing the Germans to abandon their bridgehead. The Sixth Army continues to hold off the Soviets at Melitopol.

USSR, *ATROCITIES*
The inmates of Sobibor extermination camp revolt. Several Ukrainian guards and 11 SS men are killed and some 300 prisoners manage to escape, most of whom are killed by their pursuers. Those who had refused to join the revolt are all murdered. After the uprising the Germans abandon the idea of turning Sobibor into a concentration camp and close it down.

OCTOBER 15

SOUTHERN USSR, *LAND WAR*
The Voronezh Front continues to attack from the Bukrin bridgehead, but the Third Guards Tank, Twenty-Seventh and Fortieth Armies are held by XXXXVIII Panzer Corps. The Soviet Fifth Guards Army has more success at Kremenchug, which batters LVII Panzer Corps with the aid of the Fifth Air Army, allowing its armour to break into the First Panzer Army's rear.

▲ German troops retreating west. In October, 37 Soviet armies were attacking on the Eastern Front.

OCTOBER 17

CENTRAL USSR, *LAND WAR*
The Soviet Forty-Third Army creates a breach between the German IX and LIII Corps near Vitebsk as units of the Central Front cross the Dnieper at Loyev.

SOUTHERN USSR, *LAND WAR*
The Red Army is failing to enlarge its Bukrin bridgehead. There is some success in the south, however, as the Steppe and Southwestern Fronts force the German Eighth and First Panzer Armies back towards Krivoi Rog.

OCTOBER 18

USSR, *DIPLOMACY*
A conference of the Allied powers takes place in Moscow, attended by Cordell Hull representing US President Roosevelt, British Foreign Secretary Anthony Eden and Soviet Foreign Minister Molotov. The governments of the US, USSR, China and Britain make a number of declarations, including the early establishment of an international organization to maintain peace and security (the United Nations). Regarding German atrocities, the conference resolves: "Those responsible ... will be sent back to the countries in which their abominable deeds were done in order that they may be judged and punished according to the laws of these liberated countries." Britain and the US assure the USSR that a second front will be created by the following spring.

OCTOBER 20

USSR, *ARMED FORCES*
In recognition of the Red Army's advances, the Stavka renames a number of fronts. The Voronezh Front becomes the 1st Ukrainian Front, the Steppe Front the 2nd Ukrainian, the Southwestern Front the 3rd Ukrainian, and the Southern Front the 4th Ukrainian. The Central Front is renamed Belorussian Front, the Kalinin Front becomes the Baltic Front and the Baltic Front is retitled 2nd Baltic.

OCTOBER 23

SOUTHERN USSR, *LAND WAR*
The German Sixth Army retreats from Melitopol to the Dnieper, thus leaving the Seventeenth Army isolated in the Crimea.

OCTOBER 25

SOUTHERN USSR, *LAND WAR*
The Fifth Guards Tank Army attacks Krivoi Rog but is frustrated by heavy rains. The Eighth Guards and Forty-Sixth Armies (3rd Ukrainian Front) capture Dnepropetrovsk after defeating XXX Corps.

OCTOBER 27

SOUTHERN USSR, *LAND WAR*
The Soviet Fifth Guards Tank Army is temporarily worsted by a counterattack by XXXX Panzer Corps at Krivoi Rog.

OCTOBER 30

SOUTHERN USSR, *LAND WAR*
The Soviets have reached Perekop and thus cut the land route out of the Crimea.

ARMED FORCES

PANZERGRENADIER DIVISIONS

Panzergrenadier divisions were integral to Blitzkrieg warfare, with motorized infantry accompanying and supporting the fast-moving panzer divisions. The infantry travelled in halftrack armoured personnel carriers to and on to the battlefield. However, there were never enough halftracks, so each division also used trucks to transport its men. In addition, earlier motorized divisions also had large numbers of motorcycle-mounted troops, although they disappeared as the war went on because motorcycles were vulnerable to small-arms fire.

Panzergrenadier divisions had a tank element, which could be quite sizeable. At the Battle of Kursk, for example, the élite *Grossdeutschland* Division had 45 Panzer IVs, 46 Panthers, 13 Tiger Is and 35 assault guns. By the middle of the war, the panzergrenadiers that travelled in halftracks preceded the panzers on to the battlefield, to search out and destroy enemy anti-tank gun positions and enemy infantry tank-destruction parties lying in wait for the panzers.

On paper each division numbered 13,900 troops, divided between two motorized infantry regiments; one armoured battalion; one artillery regiment (with 12 105mm howitzers, 16 150mm howitzers and eight self-propelled 105mm howitzers); one anti-tank battalion (28 75mm assault guns or tank destroyers and 12 towed 75mm anti-tank guns); an armoured reconnaissance battalion; an anti-aircraft battalion; engineer battalion; signals battalion; and support services.

NOVEMBER 1

NOVEMBER 1

SOUTHERN USSR, *LAND WAR*
The Fourth Panzer Army at Kiev is attacked by the Soviet Thirty-Eighth Army. The Stavka will not expand the Bukrin bridgehead, but orders the Twenty-Seventh and Fortieth Armies to launch assaults from there in order to mask their build-up in the Lyutezh bridgehead. XXXX Panzer Corps continues to fight at Krivoi Rog.

In the Crimea, the Soviet Fifty-First Army attacks at Perekop and Armyansk as the Fifty-Sixth Army crosses the Kerch strait. The German Seventeenth Army contains these assaults with difficulty.

NOVEMBER 3

SOUTHERN USSR, *LAND WAR*
The Soviet offensive to liberate Kiev begins as the Thirty-Eighth and Sixtieth Armies attack from the Lyutezh bridgehead, supported by the Second Air Army (the 1st Ukrainian Front has committed 671,000 troops to the offensive). The Fourth Panzer Army suffers heavy casualties during the attack.

USSR, *ATROCITIES*
Following the rebellion at Sobibor, and to prevent further revolts, SS Chief Heinrich Himmler orders Jakob Sporrenberg, senior commander of the SS and the police in the Lublin district, to liquidate the Jewish forced labour camps. The operation is codenamed Harvest Festival. During the next two days the SS will murder the prisoners at Trawniki, Poniatowa and Majdanek camps, a total of 43,000 victims.

NOVEMBER 5

SOUTHERN USSR, *LAND WAR*
The Soviet Thirty-Eighth Army fights its way into Kiev, while to the southwest of the city the Sixtieth Army cuts into the rear of the Fourth Panzer Army. The German XIII and LIX Corps are forced back to Korosten and Zhitomir.

NOVEMBER 6

SOUTHERN USSR, *LAND WAR*
Kiev falls to the Thirty-Eighth Army. In response, Manstein redeploys XXXXVIII Panzer Corps from Bukrin to Belaya Tserkov, from where it can attack the rapidly forming Soviet salient.

NOVEMBER 8

CENTRAL USSR, *LAND WAR*
The Soviet Third and Fourth Shock Armies attack the positions of the Third Panzer Army around Nevel, smashing into IX and LIII Corps.

SOUTHERN USSR, *LAND WAR*
As the 1st Ukrainian Front drives west, the Fourth Panzer Army is reinforced by XXIV and XXXXVIII Panzer Corps.

NOVEMBER 10

CENTRAL USSR, *LAND WAR*
The Belorussian Front commences the Gomel-Rechitsa Offensive south of Loyev, striking Army Group Centre's flank.

NOVEMBER 12

SOUTHERN USSR, *LAND WAR*
The 1st Ukrainian Front captures Zhitomir while the 2nd Ukrainian Front's Fifty-Second Army crosses the Dnieper at Cherkassy and drives back the Eighth Army's XI Corps.

NOVEMBER 15

SOUTHERN USSR, *LAND WAR*
As the 1st Ukrainian Front continues its advance west, Manstein counterattacks from the southern base of the Soviet salient. His aim is to retake Kiev as his forces head for Zhitomir. The 2nd Ukrainian Front, which is aiming to destroy the German First Panzer and Eighth Armies, is battering LII Corps around Krivoi Rog. The Germans counterattack with XXXX and LVII Panzer Corps.

NOVEMBER 17

CENTRAL USSR, *LAND WAR*
The Eleventh and Forty-Eighth Armies (Belorussian Front) have almost surrounded Gomel despite the efforts of the German Ninth Army.

SOUTHERN USSR, *LAND WAR*
Manstein's counterattack is in full swing, with XXXXVIII Panzer Corps capturing Zhitomir in the rear of the 1st Ukrainian Front. On the northern shoulder of the salient, the front's Thirteenth Army captures Ovruch as it advances west.

NOVEMBER 18

SOUTHERN USSR, *LAND WAR*
In response to Manstein's counterattack, the 1st Ukrainian Front falls back from

▼ *A German 150mm Nebelwerfer 41 rocket launcher. Each Nebelwerfer regiment had 324 rocket launchers.*

DECISIVE MOMENT

WHY DID THE GERMANS KEEP ON FIGHTING?

The question of why German troops continued to fight the Red Army when it was obvious that Germany would lose the war on the Eastern Front is an interesting one. The reasons why they did so were provided by a senior German officer who fought on the Eastern Front, General von Mellenthin: "In 1943, the flower of the German Army had fallen in the Battle of Kursk, where our troops attacked with a desperate determination to conquer or die. They had gone into battle with a spirit no less determined than that of the storm troops of 1918, and it might be thought that a weakening of morale would follow our withdrawal from the ill-fated salient of Kursk. Actually, nothing of the sort occurred; our ranks had been woefully thinned, but the fierce resolve of the fighting troops remained unshaken. This is not the place for a detailed discussion of this question, but it is obvious that the character of our adversary had much to do with this unyielding spirit of the troops. The Churchill-Roosevelt demand for 'Unconditional Surrender' gave us no hope from the West, while the men fighting on the Russian Front were well aware of the horrible fate which would befall eastern Germany if the Red hordes broke into our country." Of course, a German general is going to extoll the virtues of his troops, but Mellenthin probably summarizes accurately the view of the Wehrmacht's rank and file between 1943 and 1945.

▲ *The Red Army drives west. In November Manstein told OKH that Army Group South was "completely at the enemy's mercy".*

Zhitomir, having lost 3000 killed and 150 tanks and 320 artillery pieces destroyed.

NOVEMBER 22

CENTRAL USSR, *LAND WAR*
The Soviet Belorussian Front opens a fresh offensive against the German Ninth Army at Propaisk.

NOVEMBER 25

CENTRAL USSR, *LAND WAR*
As Propaisk falls to the Belorussian Front, the Western Front launches an attack against the Fourth Army.

SOUTHERN USSR, *LAND WAR*
In the face of superior numbers Manstein's counterattack grinds to a halt short of Kiev.

▼ *One of the 6000 artillery pieces and mortars of the 1st Ukrainian Front west of Kiev in late November.*

NOVEMBER 28

IRAN, *DIPLOMACY*
The start of the Tehran Conference attended by Stalin, Roosevelt and Churchill. The "Big Three" reach agreement on military matters:
(1) The Partisans in Yugoslavia should be supported by supplies and equipment to the greatest possible extent, and also by commando operations.
(2) Agreed that, from the military point of view, it was most desirable that Turkey should come into the war on the side of the Allies before the end of the year.
(3) Took note of Marshal Stalin's statement that if Turkey found herself at war with Germany, and as a result Bulgaria declared war on Turkey or attacked her, the Soviets would immediately be at war with Bulgaria. The Conference further took note that this fact could be explicitly stated in the forthcoming negotiations to bring Turkey into the war.
(4) Took note that Operation Overlord [the Allied invasion of France] would be launched during May 1944, in conjunction with an operation against Southern France. The latter operation would be undertaken in as great a strength as availability of landing craft permitted. The Conference further took note of Marshal Stalin's statement that the Soviet forces would launch an offensive at about the same time with the object of preventing the German forces from transferring from the Eastern to the Western Front.
(5) Agreed that the military staffs of the Three Powers should henceforward keep in close touch with each other in regard to the impending operations in Europe. In particular it was agreed that a cover plan to mystify and mislead the enemy as regards these operations should be concerted between the staffs concerned."
Stalin reiterates that the USSR will retain the frontiers laid down by the Nazi-Soviet Non-aggression Treaty of 1939 and the Russo-Finnish Treaty of 1940. He also states his hostility towards the Polish government-in-exile in London.

NOVEMBER 30

SOUTHERN USSR, *LAND WAR*
XXXXVIII Panzer Corps launches a fresh attack in the Zhitomir area, and the German LIX Corps recaptures Korosten from the Soviet Sixtieth Army.

DECEMBER 6

DECEMBER 6

SOUTHERN USSR, *LAND WAR*
XXXXVIII Panzer Corps resumes its attack, aiming to destroy enemy forces around Meleni. On the flanks the German XIII and LIX Corps are also heavily engaged.

DECEMBER 8

SOUTHERN USSR, *LAND WAR*
XXXXVIII Panzer Corps reaches the River Teterev but is being slowed by enemy resistance. The corps has nevertheless inflicted substantial losses on the Soviet Thirteenth and Sixtieth Armies.

DECEMBER 10

SOUTHERN USSR, *LAND WAR*
The Soviet Fifth Guards Tank and Fifth Guards Armies destroy German resistance at Znamenka. In addition, the Soviet Fourth Guards and Fifty-Second Armies link up at Cherkassy.

DECEMBER 12

USSR, *DIPLOMACY*
Dr Benes, the Czech government-in-exile president in London, signs the Czech-Soviet Friendship Treaty in Moscow. Benes believes that under Moscow's protection the Slavs will be safe from German aggression (something the Western Allies have hitherto been unable or unwilling to guarantee). In addition, under this "new Slavism" Benes hopes to transform Czechoslovakia into a homogeneous Slav national state (which will mean expelling Czechoslovakia's non-Slav nationalities). This can only be carried out with the full support of the USSR.

▲ *German troops in Zhitomir after its recapture in November. It became Soviet again at the end of December.*

DECEMBER 14

NORTHERN USSR, *LAND WAR*
The Third Panzer Army is attacked by the Soviet 1st Baltic Front at Nevel but holds its positions.

DECEMBER 16

SOUTHERN USSR, *LAND WAR*
As XXXXVIII Panzer and LIX Corps strike enemy forces around Meleni, it becomes apparent that there are more Red Army units in the salient than the Germans originally believed. The 1st, 7th and SS *Leibstandarte* Divisions of XXXXVIII Panzer Corps try to contain Soviet forces in the Meleni Pocket. However, inside the pocket are no less that three armoured and four rifle enemy corps.

DECEMBER 21

CENTRAL USSR, *LAND WAR*
The Soviet Forty-Eighth and Sixty-Fifth Armies maul the German XXXXI Panzer and LV Corps at Zhlobin.
SOUTHERN USSR, *LAND WAR*
As XXXXVIII Panzer Corps continues its actions at Meleni, the German Sixtieth Army relinquishes its hold on the Kherson bridgehead, the 4th Ukrainian Front nearing the mouth of the Dnieper. The Ukrainian offensive has been costly since the end of September: 2nd Ukrainian Front, 77,400 killed and missing; 3rd Ukrainian Front, 34,000 killed and missing; and 4th Ukrainian Front, 61,000 killed and missing. Combined front totals for wounded are a staggering 580,000.

◀ *A Red Army soldiers glances at a dead German during the Soviet liberation of the Ukraine in late 1943.*

DECEMBER 23

SOUTHERN USSR, *LAND WAR*
XXXXVIII Panzer Corps halts its attacks around Meleni in the face of superior enemy forces.

DECEMBER 24

SOUTHERN USSR, *LAND WAR*
The Stavka launches its next offensive in the Ukraine against Army Group South. All four Ukrainian fronts are earmarked to take part, a combined total of 2,365,000 troops, 2000 tanks, 29,000 artillery pieces and 2360 aircraft. Against this force Army Group South can muster 1,760,000 troops, 2200 tanks and assault guns (but only 50 percent are operational), 16,000 artillery pieces and

1400 aircraft (only 30 percent are operational). The 1st Ukrainian Front attacks after a heavy preliminary artillery and aerial barrage, the First Guards and Eighteenth Armies hitting XIII Corps in front of Zhitomir; the Thirteenth and Sixtieth Armies assaulting LIX Corps to the north; and the Twenty-Seventh, Thirty-Eighth and Fortieth Armies striking VII and XXIV Panzer Corps in the south. The German line quickly collapses, and soon the First Tank and Third Guards Tank Armies are advancing towards Vinnitsa and Zhitomir, respectively.

DECEMBER 27

SOUTHERN USSR, *LAND WAR*
Having failed to stop the Soviet Third Guards Tank Army, XXXXVIII Panzer Corps is directed to the Berdichev sector to stem the Soviet tide. The corps by now has just 150 tanks.

DECEMBER 28

SOUTHERN USSR, *LAND WAR*
As XXXXVIII Panzer Corps fails to halt the First Tank Army at Kazatin, Manstein begins to pull back the First Panzer Army to lend support to the threatened Fourth Panzer Army.

DECEMBER 29

SOUTHERN USSR, *LAND WAR*
The Soviet Sixtieth Army captures Korosten and the Third Guards Army has cut off Zhitomir, trapping units of XIII Corps in the town.

The SS *Leibstandarte* Division, operating in the Kazatin sector, is attacked by a force of 140 Red Army tanks. In the subsequent battle 68 Red Army tanks are destroyed.

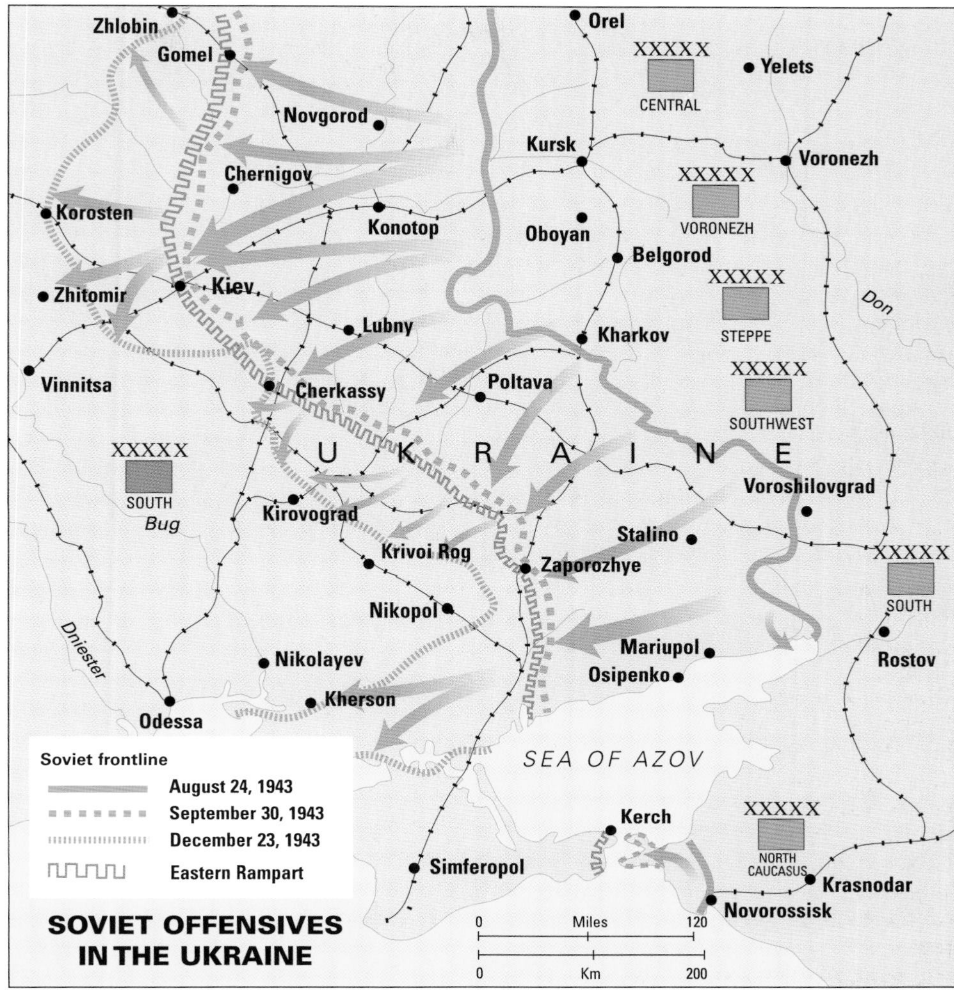

DECEMBER 31

USSR, *AIR WAR*
Luftwaffe strength on the Eastern Front stands at 1683 combat aircraft, whereas Red Army Military Aviation (VVS) can deploy 8818 combat aircraft, with a further 313 held in reserve.

CENTRAL USSR, *LAND WAR*
The Third Panzer Army at Nevel is again attacked and the Western Front forces the German VI Corps back between Orsha and Vitebsk.

SOUTHERN USSR, *LAND WAR*
Enemy numbers, firepower and mobility are taking their toll on Army Group South: Zhitomir falls to the Third Guards Tank and Eighteenth Armies, VII and XXIV Panzer Corps are in full retreat to Vinnitsa, and XXXXVIII Panzer Corps is falling back to Berdichev. XXXXVIII Panzer Corps destroys 67 Red Army tanks in defensive fighting at Berdichev. The Germans capture a substantial number of enemy prisoners, some of whom are boys aged between 13 and 16. At this time the panzer corps has around 100–150 tanks in working order – equivalent to a full-strength panzer division.

CENTRAL USSR, *PARTISAN WAR*
There are an estimated 360,000 armed Soviet partisans operating in Belorussia.

▼ The "Big Three" (from right to left), Churchill, Roosevelt and Stalin, at the Tehran Conference.

▲ *Soviet artillery of the 2nd Ukrainian Front shells German units trapped in the Cherkassy Pocket.*

At the beginning of 1944, the Stavka was faced with a highly favourable state of affairs. Its strategy for the first four months of the year involved clearing German forces from the Ukraine, lifting the siege of Leningrad and creating the conditions for an offensive against the German Army Group Centre. For the Germans, 1944 was one large catastrophe, compounded by the Allied landings in France in June. By the end of the year, the Red Army was nearing the borders of Germany itself.

▼ *Red Army forces near Leningrad. The Leningrad and Volkhov Fronts amassed 677,000 troops, 1200 tanks, 14,300 artillery pieces and 720 aircraft for the offensive to free the city.*

JANUARY 3

SOUTHERN USSR, *LAND WAR*
The Soviet First Tank Army is nearing Uman and the Third Guard Tank Army is approaching Vinnitsa. The 3rd Ukrainian Front is assaulting Kirovograd with its Fifth Guards, Seventh Guards and Fifty-Third Armies, tying down XXXX Panzer and LII Corps in the process.

JANUARY 5

SOUTHERN USSR, *LAND WAR*
The Soviet Third Guards Tank and Eighteenth Armies capture Berdichev. The 2nd Ukrainian Front opens its offensive against the German Eighth Army. The Fourth Guards, Fifty-Second and Fifty-Third Armies attack in the Kirovograd sector, with the Fifth and Seventh Guards assaulting farther south. The under-strength Eighth Army is made up of LII, XXXXVII Panzer and XI Corps.

JANUARY 8

SOUTHERN USSR, *LAND WAR*
The reserve unit of the 2nd Ukrainian Front, the Fifth Guards Tank Army, captures Kirovograd.

JANUARY 10

CENTRAL USSR, *LAND WAR*
The Belorussian Front's Sixty-First and Seventieth Armies launch a minor offensive against the German Second Army.

SOUTHERN USSR, *LAND WAR*
The 3rd Ukrainian Front commences its offensive against the German Sixth Army in the Dnieper Elbow.

◀ *Army Group South troops and StuG IIIs. By January 1944, the army group had lost 405,409 men (dead, wounded or missing) in six months.*

JANUARY 11

SOUTHERN USSR, *LAND WAR*
The 4th Ukrainian Front begins its offensive in the Dnieper Elbow, the Third Guards and Fifth Shock Armies hitting the German IV and XVII Corps.

JANUARY 12

NORTHERN USSR, *LAND WAR*
The 1st Baltic Front's Third Shock and Tenth Guards Armies attack the German Sixteenth Army near Novosokolinikov.
SOUTHERN USSR, *LAND WAR*
The Soviet Thirteenth Army captures Sarny and the Sixtieth Army nears Shepetovka. There is fierce fighting around Nikopol as the Soviet Third Guards and Sixth Armies try to advance west.

JANUARY 14

NORTHERN USSR, *LAND WAR*
The offensive by the Soviet Leningrad and Volkhov Fronts to free Leningrad begins. The Second Shock Army launches an assault from the Oranienbaum bridgehead which mauls III SS Panzer Corps.

JANUARY 15

NORTHERN USSR, *LAND WAR*
The Soviet Forty-Second and Sixty-Seventh Armies join the offensive around Leningrad, against the German LIV and XXVI Corps. The Soviet Eighth Army advances towards Mga, the Fifty-Fourth Army towards Lyuban and the Fifty-Ninth Army towards Novgorod.

JANUARY 17

NORTHERN USSR, *LAND WAR*
The Leningrad Offensive is mauling the Sixteenth and Eighteenth Armies. Thus the army group commander, Küchler, commits his reserve of three infantry divisions against the Eighth Army at Mga.

JANUARY 19

NORTHERN USSR, *LAND WAR*
The Soviet Second Shock and Forty-Second Armies link up at Ropsha, signalling the end of the Leningrad siege. The Forty-Second Army also captures Krasnoye Selo, and the Fifty-Ninth Army surrounds Novgorod.

JANUARY 21

NORTHERN USSR, *LAND WAR*
Novgorod was captured by the Fifty-Ninth Army yesterday, and today the Eighth Army takes Mga.

JANUARY 24

NORTHERN USSR, *LAND WAR*
The Soviet Second Shock Army cuts the railway line to Narva and the Forty-Second Army captures Pushkin and Pashovsk.
SOUTHERN USSR, *LAND WAR*
The Soviet Korsun-Cherkassy Offensive begins against the German Cherkassy salient (held by XXXXII Corps). The corps is assaulted by 1st Ukrainian Front's Twenty-Seventh Army, while the 2nd Ukrainian Front's Fourth Guards, Fifty-Second and Fifty-Third Armies attack the German XI Corps.

JANUARY 26

NORTHERN USSR, *LAND WAR*
The Soviet Eighth and Fifty-Fourth Armies push back the German Eighteenth Army to Tosno and Lyuban.
SOUTHERN USSR, *LAND WAR*
The Soviet Sixth Tank, Twenty-Seventh and Fortieth Armies advance to link up with the Fifth Guards Tank Army as the latter heads for Shpola.

JANUARY 28

NORTHERN USSR, *LAND WAR*
The Soviet Fifty-Fourth Army captures Lyuban. Küchler orders a retreat to the River Luga to save his army group.
SOUTHERN USSR, *LAND WAR*
The link-up of the 1st and 2nd Ukrainian Fronts at Zvenigorodka signals the encirclement of the German XI and XXXXII Corps in the Cherkassy Pocket – 56,000 troops. The Stavka orders the 2nd Ukrainian Front's Fourth Guards, Twenty-Seventh and Fifty-Second Armies to reduce the pocket. Meanwhile, Manstein orders III and XXXXVII Panzer Corps to make plans for a relief operation.

JANUARY 29

NORTHERN USSR, *LAND WAR*
Having sanctioned the withdrawal of the Eighteenth Army yesterday, Hitler replaces Küchler with General Walther Model. The Soviet Fifty-Fourth Army, meanwhile, takes Chudovo as the 1st Baltic Front captures Novosokolinikov.
SOUTHERN USSR, *LAND WAR*
The German XIII and LIX Corps are forced back as the Soviet Thirteenth and Sixtieth Armies cross the River Styr.

JANUARY 30

SOUTHERN USSR, *LAND WAR*
The German Sixth Army is attacked by the 3rd and 4th Ukrainian Fronts. The 3rd Ukrainian Front's Sixth, Eighth, Thirty-Seventh and Forty-Sixth Armies assault from Krivoi Rog; and the Third Guards, Fifth Shock and Twenty-Eighth Armies (all 4th Ukrainian Front) attack the Nikopol bridgehead. The Soviets have 257,000 troops and 1400 tanks, the Germans 47,000 troops and 250 tanks.

▲ *Georg von Küchler was sacked as head of Army Group North for ordering the withdrawal of the Eighteenth Army.*

FEBRUARY 1

NORTHERN USSR, *LAND WAR*
As the Soviet Second Shock Army captures Kingisepp, the Fifty-Ninth Army drives into the right flank of the retreating Eighteenth Army despite an ineffective counterattack mounted by the German I Corps.

SOUTHERN USSR, *LAND WAR*
The fate of the Cherkassy Pocket hinges on a relief attempt by XXXXVII Panzer Corps. But the panzers are currently stuck in thick mud due to a thaw.

FEBRUARY 3

NORTHERN USSR, *LAND WAR*
III SS Panzer Corps manages to hold the River Narva line against attacks by the Second Shock Army. German counterattacks also manage to halt the Soviet Fifty-Ninth Army.

SOUTHERN USSR, *LAND WAR*
As German units inside the Cherkassy Pocket group towards the southwest, III Panzer Corps launches a relief operation. The 2nd Ukrainian Front is intensifying its efforts to prevent any such relief, however.

FEBRUARY 5

SOUTHERN USSR, *LAND WAR*
German units are under threat at Krivoi Rog and Nikopol as the Soviet Thirteenth and Sixtieth Armies capture Rovno and Lutsk and the Forty-Sixth Army takes Apostolovo. Hollidt thus asks for permission to withdraw the Sixth Army.

FEBRUARY 6

SOUTHERN USSR, *LAND WAR*
III Panzer Corps' relief attempt is abandoned due to mud, lack of fuel and enemy resistance, factors that are also hindering XXXXVII Panzer Corps.

▼ ***A German 75mm Pak 40 anti-tank gun in the Ukraine. The Pak 40 was the army's standard anti-tank gun.***

FEBRUARY 7

SOUTHERN USSR, *LAND WAR*
The Soviet Third Guards and Sixth Army capture Nikopol as the Eighth Guards and Forty-Sixth Armies drive into the rear of the German Sixth Army.

FEBRUARY 11

SOUTHERN USSR, *LAND WAR*
Reinforced by the 1st SS Panzer Division *Leibstandarte*, III Panzer Corps attempts yet again to fight its way through to the Cherkassy Pocket. However, although it is making progress, the Soviet Second Tank Army is deploying to block its way.

FEBRUARY 12

NORTHERN USSR, *LAND WAR*
The German-held city of Luga is being assaulted by the Soviet Fifty-Fourth, Fifty-Ninth and Sixty-Seventh Armies.

SOUTHERN USSR, *LAND WAR*
As III Panzer Corps approaches the Cherkassy Pocket, there are fierce armoured clashes with the Soviet Fifth Guards and Sixth Tank Armies. The German tanks are fought to a standstill, and inside the pocket an attack by the 5th SS Panzer Division *Wiking* at Shanderovka fails.

FEBRUARY 13

NORTHERN USSR, *LAND WAR*
Soviet forces complete the capture of Luga, Polna and Lyady. The Stavka disbands the Volkhov Front, which has lost 12,000 killed and 38,000 wounded, and incorporates its units into the Leningrad Front.

SOUTHERN USSR, *LAND WAR*
Inside the Cherkassy Pocket the *Wiking* Division captures Shanderovka, but outside the pocket III Panzer Corps is held up at Lysyanka. The commander of the forces inside the pocket, Stemmerman, continues to group his units for the breakout attempt.

FEBRUARY 15

NORTHERN USSR, *LAND WAR*
Army Group North is authorized to fall back from the Luga to the borders of the Baltic states.

SOUTHERN USSR, *LAND WAR*
With the fall of Chilki to the German 72nd Infantry Division, the forces inside the rapidly shrinking Cherkassy Pocket have a springboard for a breakout attempt. Stemmerman thus moves his forces to their jump-off positions. Outside the pocket, III Panzer Corps can make no impression on the outer Soviet perimeter.

FEBRUARY 16

SOUTHERN USSR, *LAND WAR*
The Cherkassy breakout begins – desperate German soldiers forcing their way towards III Panzer Corps.

FEBRUARY 17

SOUTHERN USSR, *LAND WAR*
Stemmerman is killed, but his troops begin to link up with III Panzer Corps. The 2nd Ukrainian Front intensifies its efforts to annihilate the pocket. The German 57th and 88th Infantry Divisions stage a desperate rearguard action.

FEBRUARY 18

NORTHERN USSR, *LAND WAR*
Staraya Russa is captured by the Soviet First Shock Army.

SOUTHERN USSR, *LAND WAR*
Some 30,000 German soldiers have escaped from

▲ ***With its 88mm Pak 43/1 L/71 gun, the Nashorn was a potent tank hunter. This one, near Cherkassy, belongs to III Panzer Corps.***

the Cherkassy Pocket, although they have left almost all their equipment behind. Now III Panzer Corps has to disengage and withdraw west.

FEBRUARY 22

NORTHERN USSR, *LAND WAR*
The Soviet First Shock and Fifty-Fourth Armies capture Dno.

SOUTHERN USSR, *LAND WAR*
The Red Army captures Krivoi Rog.

FEBRUARY 23

USSR, ATROCITIES
The NKVD begins the mass deportation of Chechens and Ingush from their homelands following Stalin's accusation that they have aided the Germans (who is encouraged in his paranoia by NKVD chief Lavrenti Beria). Some 362,000 Chechens and 134,000 Ingush old men, women and children are rounded up and packed on to 180 train convoys in the space of just over a week. Some 20,000 NKVD troops are used, most families being given 5–10 minutes to pack up their belongings and food for the trip (no food is supplied). Tens of thousands die during journeys which last up to two months (bodies are often left in overcrowded cattle wagons for weeks). In sub-zero temperatures, the survivors are dumped in Siberia or on the Kazak steppes. Around half of all those deported will die.

▼ ***A German bunker of the Eighteenth Army. As it pulled back from Leningrad, the army was incessantly shelled and bombed.***

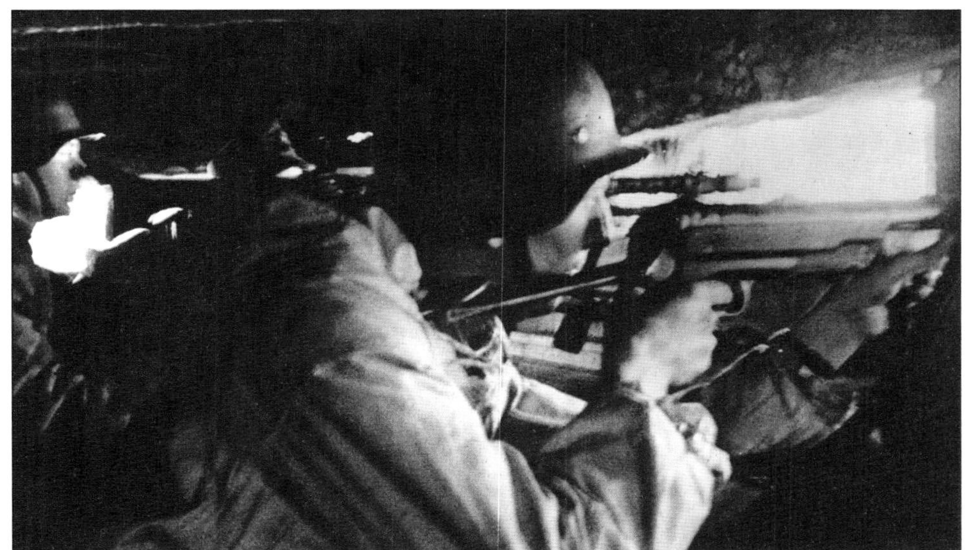

KEY PERSONALITIES

WALTHER MODEL

Model, born in 1891, fought in the German Army in World War I and won the Iron Cross (both classes), ending the war a lieutenant. During the inter-war years he became a believer in mechanized warfare, and after Hitler came to power in 1933 he made a favourable impression on the Führer and the Nazi hierarchy.

Model fought in Poland, France and during the German advance into Russia in 1941 (becoming a panzer corps commander in October 1941). By January 1942, he was given command in the Rzhev salient, where the Ninth Army was in a desperate state, suffering from partisan attacks in its rear and threatened on three sides by the Red Army. He pulled his command together by deploying a panzer corps around Rzhev and, despite stormy meetings with Hitler, held the salient for almost a year. When he was ordered to withdraw in early 1943, he authorized the systematic destruction of towns and their populations, an act that got him branded a war criminal by the Soviets. He commanded the Ninth Army at the Battle of Kursk, despite telling Hitler beforehand that he thought the offensive would fail.

After Kursk, he conducted a magnificent fighting withdrawal in the Ukraine, earning the nickname the "lion of the defence" as his Ninth Army retreated with Army Group Centre. Hitler decided that he had saved the Eastern Front from collapse (which he had indeed helped to do), and promptly sent him to France in mid-August as Commander-in-Chief West to stave off the British and Americans. In early 1945, Model and his Army Group B were encircled in the Ruhr Pocket. After declaring "a field marshal does not become a prisoner", he walked into woods near Duisberg and shot himself on April 21, 1945. His body was never found.

▲ *A Soviet flamethrower operator in the Ukraine. Red Army flamethrowers were designed like infantry rifles.*

MARCH 4

SOUTHERN USSR, *LAND WAR*
The Soviet 1st Ukrainian Front opens its Proskurov-Chernovits offensive against the German First Panzer and Fourth Armies. Within hours the Soviet First Guards and Sixtieth Armies have broken through the enemy, the German LIX Corps suffering particularly at the hands of the Soviet troops.

MARCH 5

SOUTHERN USSR, *LAND WAR*
The Soviet 2nd Ukrainian Front opens the Uman-Botoshany Offensive, the Fifth Guards Army hitting the right flank of the German Eighth Army, quickly followed by the Second Tank and Fifth Guards Tank Armies. Soon the German First Panzer and Eighth Armies are reeling. Meanwhile, the Third Guards Tank and Fourth Tank Armies pass through the First Guards and Sixtieth Armies to lance into the German rear. The German LIX Corps is shattered in the process.

MARCH 6

SOUTHERN USSR, *LAND WAR*
The 1st Ukrainian Front has created a 48km (30-mile) gap between the German First Panzer and Fourth Armies, as has the 2nd Ukrainian Front against the First Panzer and Eighth Armies. The 3rd Ukrainian Front's Bereznegovatoe-Snigirovka offensive begins, the Eighth Guards and Forty-Sixth Armies attacking the junction of the German Eighth and Sixth Armies.

MARCH 8

SOUTHERN USSR, *LAND WAR*
The German Eighth Army is in retreat, being pursued by the Soviet Fifth and Seventh Guards Armies. Hitler decides that the answer to the Soviet steamroller is to declare towns and cities to be fortified places, which means condemning their garrisons to destruction.

FINLAND, *DIPLOMACY*
Following secret meetings, the Finns reject the offer of a Soviet armistice on account of the harshness of Moscow's terms.

MARCH 10

SOUTHERN USSR, *LAND WAR*
The Soviet First Guards Army is involved in fierce fighting at Tarnopol, which is now besieged as the First Panzer Army retreats. Uman is captured by the Soviet Second Tank Army as the 3rd Ukrainian Front heads for the River Bug.

MARCH 11

SOUTHERN USSR, *LAND WAR*
XXXXVIII Panzer Corps counterattacks the 1st Ukrainian Front at Cherny

Ostrov, which only temporarily halts the Soviets. The 2nd Ukrainian's Second Tank Army crosses the Bug at Dzhulinka and the Sixth Tank Army at Grayvoron.

MARCH 14

SOUTHERN USSR, *LAND WAR*
The Soviet Eighth and Twenty-Eighth Armies link up and trap 14,000 German troops of XXIX Corps (Sixth Army) at Nikolayev; 4000 surrender later in the day.

MARCH 19

SOUTHERN USSR, *LAND WAR*
The Soviet Forty-Seventh Army (2nd Belorussian Front) captures Kovel, the Second Tank Army takes Soroki and the Sixth Tank Army reaches the River Dniester. The First Panzer Army is being encircled between Mogilev Podolsky and Tarnopol.

GERMANY, *DIPLOMACY*
German forces occupy Hungary under an operation codenamed Margaret. Ever since the Hungarian Army suffered huge losses

▼ *Under German artillery fire, Red Army sappers of the 2nd Belorussian Front cut barbed-wire defences to allow the infantry to attack.*

▲ ***T-34 tanks of the Soviet Second Tank Army near the Dniester in mid-March. On the turret of the nearest tank can be seen a metal hand rail that allowed troops to ride on the outside of the tank.***

around Stalingrad in early 1943, Hungary has been a lukewarm member of the Axis. Indeed, from April 1943 Premier Miklos Kallay has committed only a small number of poorly armed troops to the Axis war effort. Hitler has received reports proving that Hungary has been clandestinely dealing with the enemy and, in mid-March, Himmler learnt from agents in Budapest that Kallay was advocating the sabotage of German military trains running through Hungary to Manstein's and Kleist's army groups on the Eastern Front. In view of all these things, and fearing that Hungary might conclude a separate peace, Hitler has ordered the occupation of Hungary and will force its government to increase its contribution to the war effort. Kallay flees to Turkey. Dome Sztojay, a pro-Nazi, becomes the new prime minister. His government will jail political leaders, dissolve the unions and resume the deportation of Hungarian Jews to the death camps.

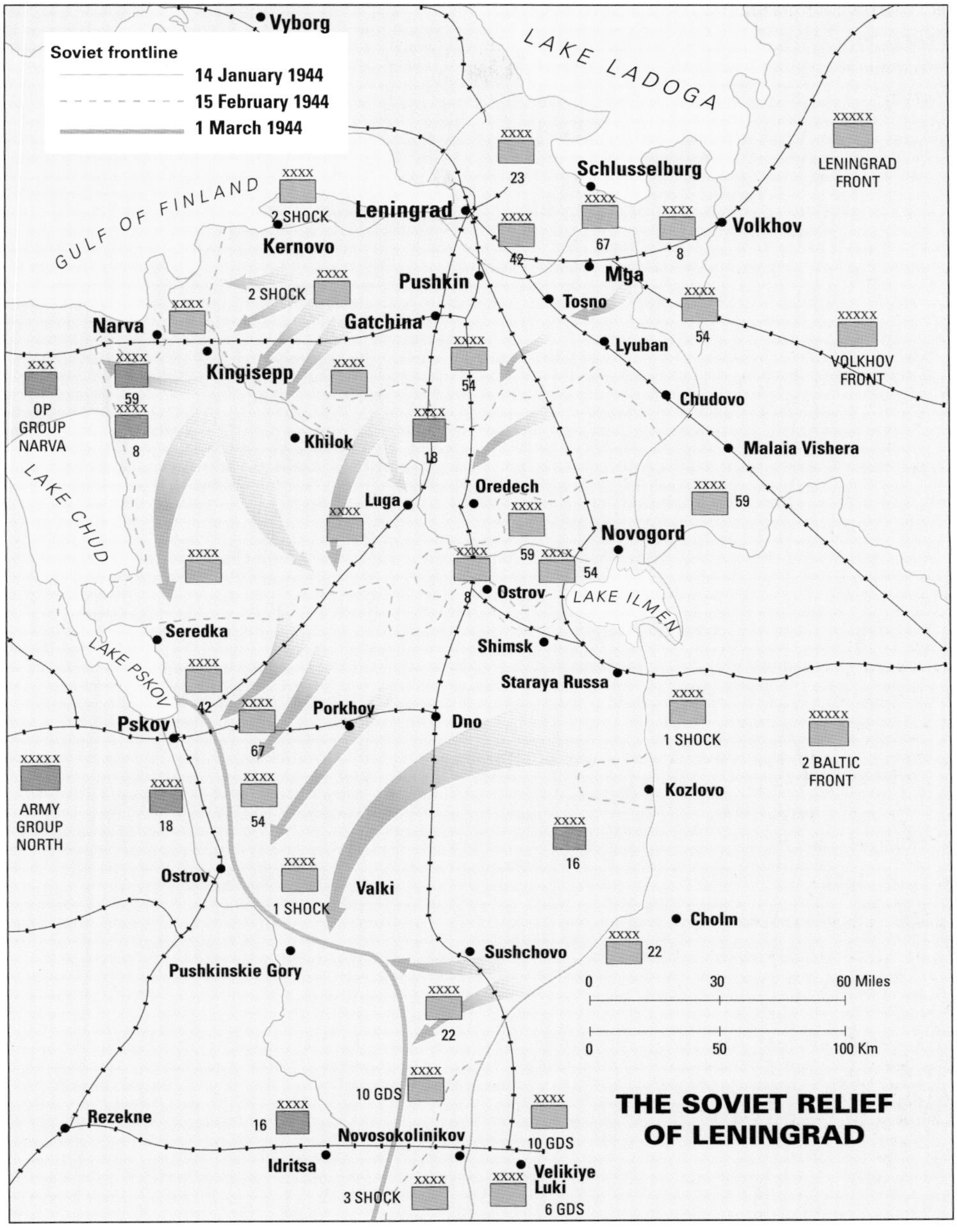

MARCH 20

SOUTHERN USSR, *LAND WAR*

The Soviet First and Fourth Tank Armies capture Vinnitsa. German forces cannot establish a frontline as the Soviet Sixth Tank Army takes Mogilev Podolsky. The Fifth Guards Tank Army approaches the Dniester and the 3rd Ukrainian Front mauls the German Sixth Army on the Bug.

MARCH 24

SOUTHERN USSR, *LAND WAR*

The Soviet First Tank Army reaches the River Dniester at Zaleschik, effectively cutting off the escape route west of the First Panzer Army. The Soviet army then pushes across the river as the Fortieth Army (2nd Ukrainian Front) reaches the River Prut near Lipkany. At Tarnopol the Soviet First Guards Army tightens its grip on the besieged garrison.

MARCH 26

SOUTHERN USSR, *LAND WAR*

The First Tank Army consolidates on the Dniester as the Twenty-Seventh and Fortieth Armies of the 2nd Ukrainian Front cross the Prut and advance into Romania.

MARCH 27

SOUTHERN USSR, *LAND WAR*

The capture of Kamenets Podolsk by the Soviet Fourth Tank Army means the First Panzer Army is now encircled.

THE SOVIET RELIEF OF LENINGRAD

Soviet frontline
14 January 1944
15 February 1944
1 March 1944

MARCH 28

SOUTHERN USSR, *LAND WAR*

The Soviet Sixth Tank Army reaches Khotin and severs the First Army's line of retreat to the Prut. The First Guards Army breaks into Tarnopol.

MARCH 30

GERMANY, *ARMED FORCES*

Hitler, increasingly irritated by the continual retreats in the Ukraine, relieves both Manstein and Kleist of their commands. Model is assigned to command Army Group North Ukraine (formerly Army Group South), and Ferdinand Schörner is assigned to command Army Group South Ukraine (formerly Army Group A). Georg Lindemann replaces Model in command of Army Group North.

April 2

▶ ***Troops and tanks of the Fourth Panzer Army retreating in the Ukraine. Despite its recapture of Kovel, the army was pushed out of the Ukraine by the end of April.***

April 2

SOUTHERN USSR, *LAND WAR*
The Soviet Fourth Tank Army crosses the Prut near Chernovtsy as the German Sixth Army encounters heavy weather, which slows its escape across the Dniester.

April 4

SOUTHERN USSR, *LAND WAR*
LIX Corps (Fourth Panzer Army) recaptures Kovel. In the Kamenets Pocket, the First Panzer Army strikes west to link up with the relief attack of I and II SS Panzer Corps. The Soviet First Guards and Thirty-Eighth Armies stand in their way.

April 7

SOUTHERN USSR, *LAND WAR*
The First Panzer Army links up with the two SS corps at Buchach.

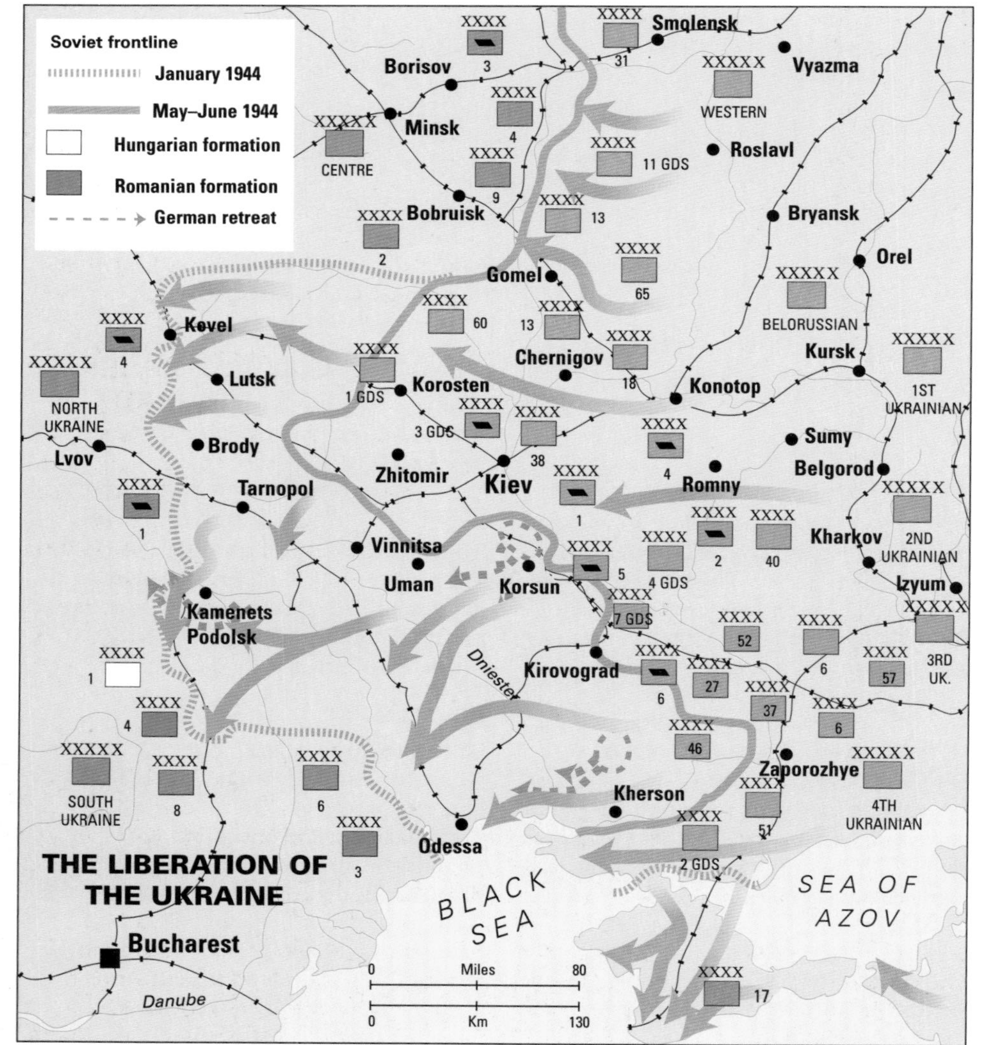

April 8

SOUTHERN USSR, *LAND WAR*
The Soviet Crimean Offensive opens, the 4th Ukrainian Front (278,000 troops, 6000 artillery pieces and 500 tanks) attacking the German 11th, 50th and 336th Infantry Divisions and the Romanian 10th Infantry Division of the Seventeenth Army (235,000 troops and 70 assault guns). Fighting still rages at Tarnopol as the 2nd Ukrainian Front captures Botosani, Dorohoi and Siret in Romania.

April 9

SOUTHERN USSR, *LAND WAR*
The German Seventeenth Army holds its positions against the 4th Ukrainian Front as the Independent Coastal Army attacks from Kerch, assaulting V Corps. But there is no breakthrough. The Soviet Fifth Shock, Sixth and Eighth Guards Armies begin their assault on Odessa and capture most of the city by the day's end.

April 10

SOUTHERN USSR, *LAND WAR*
The Red Army captures Odessa, and in the Crimea the German XXXXIX Mountain Corps begins to yield before the Second Guards Army. The Soviet Fifty-First Army smashes its way through the Romanian 10th Division, and the German V Corps is also forced to withdraw. The Soviet front commander, General Fyodor Tolbukhin, unleashes his armour against the infantry of the Seventeenth Army.

April 13

SOUTHERN USSR, *LAND WAR*
As the Soviet First Guards Army continues to pummel the remnants of the German garrison of Tarnopol in the Crimea, the Seventeenth Army is facing defeat. The Fifty-First Army has reached the outskirts of Simferopol, Feodosia falls to the Independent Coastal Army and the Second Guards Army takes Evatoria.

▶ ***B-24 Liberators of the US Fifteenth Air Force bombing the oil refineries at Ploesti. Such raids had a devastating effect on Germany's fuel production.***

APRIL 15

SOUTHERN USSR, *LAND WAR*
A relief operation mounted by XXXXVIII Panzer Corps towards Tarnopol is costing the corps many tanks and much fuel. In the town, the garrison of 1300 plus 700 wounded are preparing to break out.

APRIL 16

SOUTHERN USSR, *LAND WAR*
The breakout at Tarnopol begins, but the result is slaughter as the troops of the Soviet First Guards Army hunt down the fleeing soldiers. Only 50 reach the safety of XXXXVIII Panzer Corps.

APRIL 17

SOUTHERN USSR, *LAND WAR*
Soviet troops are now probing the defences of Sevastopol as 124,000 Axis troops dig in around the port.

Since December 24, 1943, the 1st Ukrainian Front has lost 124,000 killed and 332,000 wounded; the 2nd Ukrainian, 66,000 killed and 200,000 wounded; the 3rd Ukrainian, 55,000 killed and 214,000 wounded; and the 4th Ukrainian, 22,000 killed and 84,000 wounded.

APRIL 27

SOUTHERN USSR, *LAND WAR*
The Independent Coastal Army probes the southern perimeter of Sevastopol.

▲ ***A Soviet female sniper at Sevastopol. Women in the Red Army fought as snipers and mortar crews, though more served as medics and in anti-aircraft units.***

MAY 5

SOUTHERN USSR, *LAND WAR*
The 4th Ukrainian Front (470,000 troops, 6000 artillery pieces and 600 tanks) assaults Sevastopol. Evacuations have reduced the garrison to 65,000 men. The Second Guards Army attacks XXXXIX Mountain Corps to the north of the city but makes little initial progress.

MAY 7

SOUTHERN USSR, *LAND WAR*
At Sevastopol, XXXXIX Mountain Corps is almost spent. The Soviet Fifty-First Army attacks V Corps on the Sapun Heights and breaks into the Inkerman Valley.

MAY 8

SOUTHERN USSR, *LAND WAR*
As the Soviet Fifty-First Army captures most of Sevastopol, the German defenders retreat to the Khersonnes Peninsula. The city falls the next day.

MAY 12

SOUTHERN USSR, *LAND WAR*
Having been under sustained attack for two days, the German defence collapses on the Khersonnes Peninsula. The German Seventeenth Army has ceased to exist, having lost 80,000 troops in the Crimea. It has managed to evacuate 130,000 troops from the area. The 4th Ukrainian Front has lost 13,000 killed and 50,000 wounded; the Independent Coastal Army, 4000 killed and 16,000 wounded.

MAY 31

ROMANIA, *AIR WAR*
The US Fifteenth Air Force (480 Boeing B-17 Flying Fortresses and Consolidated B-24 Liberators) bombs oil refineries and communications targets in the Ploesti area; 15 bombers are lost during the sortie.

USSR, *STRATEGY*
The Stavka issues its orders for the coming offensive against Army Group Centre in Belorussia, codenamed Bagration. The Red Army has cleared the Ukraine and lifted the siege of Leningrad, and its advance in the north and south has created a large German salient that bulges into the east. Occupied by Army Group Centre, it resembles the Kursk salient of a year previously, although with one difference: it contains weakened German forces that have no reserves upon which to draw.

On the Eastern Front, the Germans have 1.5 million troops, mostly in under-strength and ill-equipped divisions. In addition, the advance of the Red Army to the borders of Germany's Axis allies, Hungary and Romania, has weakened the resolve of these two countries to such an extent that German troops now occupy Hungary to prevent its defection. On the opposite side, the Red Army fields 52 armies staffed with 5.5 million men for its offensive. The Stavka is also determined to defeat Finland, and thus the Leningrad and Karelian Fronts have been reinforced. Their combined strength is 450,000 troops, 10,000 artillery pieces, 800 tanks and 1000 Katyushas, supported by 530 aircraft.

▶ ***Red Army troops manhandle a 76mm gun during the Soviet offensive from Kerch against the German V Corps. These troops are probably members of the Independent Coastal Army.***

▲ *Some of the 1738 artillery pieces deployed by the Soviet 2nd Belorussian Front on the eve of Operation Bagration. The front also had 974 anti-tank guns.*

JUNE 6

ROMANIA, *AIR WAR*

As part of the ongoing Operation Frantic, 104 B-17 bombers and 42 P-51 Mustang fighters (having flown to the USSR from Italy on June 2) of the US Fifteenth Air Force attack the airfield at Galati and then return to Soviet bases.

JUNE 10

FINLAND, *LAND WAR*

The Soviet Karelian Offensive begins. Following an artillery bombardment, the Twenty-First Army attacks and forces the Finns back across the Sestra. The Twenty-Third Army launches probing attacks, supported by the Thirteenth Air Army.

JUNE 11

FINLAND, *LAND WAR*

The Soviet Twenty-Third Army begins its offensive, piercing the first Finnish line.

JUNE 13

FINLAND, *LAND WAR*

The Soviet Twenty-Third Army captures Terijiko and Yalkena.

JUNE 15

FINLAND, *LAND WAR*

The Finns have retreated to their last defence line before Viipuri, which the Soviet Twenty-First and Twenty-Third Armies are preparing to assault.

JUNE 19

USSR, *PARTISAN WAR*

In preparation for Operation Bagration, the 350,000 partisans operating behind Army Group Centre attack German railway lines. In total, the partisans lay 15,000 demolition charges on the railway lines running through the area and blow up 10,500 lengths of track during the night. Their main effort is directed against the supply lines for the Third Panzer Army, the unit that will be the focus of the initial Soviet attack. The partisan attacks result in the blocking of all double-track lines for 24 hours, and the disruption in the operation of single-track lines for 48 hours.

JUNE 20

FINLAND, *LAND WAR*

As the Finnish Southeastern Army falls apart, the Soviets roll into Viipuri. The Finns are forced to take units from the Army of Karelia to shore up the front, thus allowing the Red Army to begin its next offensive in Finland, against the Army of Karelia.

JUNE 21

FINLAND, *LAND WAR*

The Soviet Karelian Front begins its offensive on the Svir River, the Seventh and Thirty-Second Armies leading the assault. The Soviets immediately lance 16km (10 miles) into the Finnish positions.

USSR, *STRATEGY*

The Red Army is ready to launch Operation Bagration: 2.5 million troops, 5200 tanks, 31,000 artillery pieces, 2300 Katyushas, 70,000 motor vehicles and 5300 aircraft will be involved in the attack. On the northern flank is the 1st Baltic Front (Fourth, Shock, Sixth and Forty-Third Armies – 359,000 troops and 582 tanks and self-propelled guns, supported by 1094 aircraft of the Third Air Army); to the south stands the 3rd Belorussian Front (Fifth, Fifth Guards Tank, Eleventh Guards, Thirty-First and Thirty-Ninth Armies – 579,000 troops and 1500 tanks and self-propelled guns, supported by 1991 aircraft of the First Air Army); in the centre is the 2nd Belorussian Front (Thirty-Third, Forty-Ninth and Fiftieth Armies – 319,000 troops and 251 tanks and self-propelled guns, supported by 593 aircraft of the Fourth Air Army); to its south is the 1st Belorussian Front (Third, Twenty-Eighth, Forty-Eighth, Sixty-First and

▶ *Red Army sappers clear German mines and obstacles prior to the launch of Bagration. All Soviet fronts enjoyed the support of engineer-sapper brigades.*

Sixty-Fifth Armies – front total of 1,071,000 troops and 896 tanks and self-propelled guns, supported by 2033 aircraft of the Sixteenth Air Army).

The 1st Baltic and 3rd Belorussian Fronts will annihilate the flanks of the Third Panzer Army. The 3rd Belorussian Front will strike towards Minsk, the 1st Belorussian Front will encircle the German Ninth Army at Bobruisk and then link up with the 3rd Belorussian at Minsk. Both fronts will then advance to the Russo-Polish border. As they do so the 2nd Belorussian Front will engage and hold the German Fourth Army. The 1st Baltic and 3rd Belorussian Fronts are under the command of Marshal Zhukov, the 1st and 2nd Belorussian Fronts under Marshal Vasilevsky.

German Army Group Centre totals 580,000 troops: Third Panzer Army in the north (VI, IX and LIII Corps, plus two reserve divisions – 160,000 troops); Fourth Army (XII, XXVII and XXXIX Corps plus one reserve division – 165,000 troops); Ninth Army (XXXV, XXXXI and LV Corps plus one reserve division – 170,000 men); and Second Army (VIII, XX and XXIII Corps – 85,000 troops). The army group has 9500 artillery pieces and 900 tanks, the 6th Air Fleet deploying 775 aircraft.

ARMED FORCES

WOMEN IN FRONTLINE ROLES

Hundreds of thousands of Soviet women served in uniform during World War II. Women had been granted full civil, legal and electoral equality in January 1918 by the new Bolshevik regime, and during the civil war 74,000 women fought on the side of the Reds, suffering casualties of 1800. When the Germans invaded the USSR in June 1941, thousands of women volunteered for service (later the Soviets drafted unmarried women). More than 70 percent of the 800,000 Soviet women who served in the Red Army fought at the front, with 100,000 being decorated for their bravery. In addition, Komsomol, the Communist youth organization, mobilized 500,000 women and girls for military service. Women initially trained in all-female groups but, after training, were posted to regular army units and fought alongside men. About 30 percent of servicewomen received additional instruction in mortars, light and heavy machine guns or automatic rifles. In common with many women in uniform, Ludmilla Pavlichenko was trained as a sniper. She is credited with killing 309 Germans. Lance-Corporal Maria Ivanova Morozova also served as a sniper with the 62nd Rifle Battalion and won 11 combat decorations.

About 1000 women aviators were trained as fighter and military transport pilots, 30 of them being awarded for their heroism in combat. Three aviation regiments, the 586th Women's Fighter Regiment, the 587th Women's Bomber Regiment and the 588th Women's Night Bomber Regiment (the so-called "Night Witches", later elevated to the 46th Guards Bomber Aviation Regiment) were staffed by women pilots, engineers and mechanics.

The Germans were initially slow to mobilize women, partly due to Nazi ideology, which viewed the main role of women as being at home bearing children. Indeed, initially Nazi leaders proclaimed that the USSR's use of women soldiers demonstrated the Soviets were a weak enemy who would easily be defeated. A lengthening war and huge losses changed this view, and by 1944 there were 500,000 German women in uniform serving as support troops (100,000 in Luftwaffe anti-aircraft batteries). At the end of the war, Hitler even approved the raising of all-female Volkssturm battalions. In addition, young girls of the *Bund Deutscher Madel* reportedly fought in the Battle of Berlin in April 1945.

JUNE 22

CENTRAL USSR, *LAND WAR*
Operation Bagration begins. Preceded by massive air and artillery strikes, the 1st Baltic and 3rd Belorussian Fronts attack. Soon the German VI and IX Corps are in retreat as the front is ripped apart at Vitebsk and Obol. By the end of the day the Third Panzer Army's flanks have been largely destroyed.

SOUTHERN USSR, *AIR WAR*
The Luftwaffe launches a surprise air raid against the US air base at Poltava. The Eighth Air Force loses 43 B-17 and 15 P-51 aircraft, with ammunition and fuel dumps also being destroyed. This incident will further sour US-Soviet relations, the Soviets refusing to allow US night fighters to defend the bomber bases, insisting that air defence is their responsibility. Having little faith in the Soviet capacity to do so, the Americans will abandon plans permanently to station three heavy bomber groups on Soviet airfields. Indeed, logistical problems and growing Soviet intransigence will force the cancellation of so-called shuttle bombing later this year.

▲ ***The night sky is lit up by flares and anti-aircraft fire as German aircraft bomb the US shuttle air base at Poltava.***

FINLAND, *DIPLOMACY*
In view of the ongoing Soviet offensive, the Finnish Government reopens contacts with Moscow regarding bringing hostilities to an end.

JUNE 23

CENTRAL USSR, *LAND WAR*
The Soviet Sixth Guards and Forty-Third Armies smash through German lines and head for the Dvina, cutting the road west out of Vitebsk. The German VI Corps is severely mauled, and near Orsha the Soviet Fifth, Eleventh Guards and Thirty-First Armies pummel XXVII Corps. The Stavka moves the Fifth Guards Tank Army from the reserves ready to exploit the situation. The 2nd Belorussian Front's Thirty-Third, Forty-Ninth and Fiftieth Armies attack the German Fourth Army as they aim for Orsha and Mogilev. Soon, the German XXXIX Corps is under pressure.

▲ ***Using the shell of a knocked-out Red Army T-34, German infantry keep a watch on no-man's land to their front.***

FINLAND, *LAND WAR*
The Soviet Seventh Army pursues Finnish forces to the Svir.

June 24

▶ ***A German Panther counterattacks Soviet forces during Bagration. By the end of June Army Group Centre had lost a total of 130,000 killed, 60,000 captured and 900 tanks and assault guns destroyed.***

June 24

CENTRAL USSR, *LAND WAR*

The Soviet Sixth Guards and Forty-Third Armies cross the River Dvina, brushing aside a counterattack by the German IX Corps. The German VI Corps is largely annihilated by the Soviet Thirty-Ninth Army, and LIII Corps is now isolated in Vitebsk. The Thirty-Ninth and Forty-Third Armies then link up on the road to Mogilev. The Soviet Eleventh Guards Army batters the German XXVII Corps. The 1st Belorussian Front opens its offensive with the Third and Eighth Armies, which quickly overwhelm XXXV Corps. Soon the junction of the Fourth and Ninth Armies is being prised apart by the Soviet Third Army, prompting a counterattack by the 20th Panzer Division. To the south XXXXI Corps is forced to retreat. Hitler orders the 5th Panzer Division from the Ukraine to reinforce Army Group Centre – a single division to stop Bagration!

June 25

CENTRAL USSR, *LAND WAR*

Bagration continues apace, with the Fourth Shock and Sixth Guards Armies advancing on the northern flank. Soviet troops fight their way into Vitebsk as the German LIII Corps attempts to retreat. The German VI Corps is attacked by aircraft from the Soviet Third Air Army, XXVII Corps collapses, and XXXIX Corps is overcome by the Soviet Forty-Ninth and Fiftieth Armies. The 1st Belorussian's Third and Forty-Eighth Armies outflank XXXV Corps, and the Twenty-Eighth and Sixty-Fifth Armies advance from the south. The counterattack by the 20th Panzer Division in support of XXXV Corps fails.

June 26

CENTRAL USSR, *LAND WAR*

Amid scenes of carnage, the Soviet Thirty-Ninth Army captures Vitebsk, wiping out most of LIII Corps. As the German Fourth Army falls back in tatters to the Dnieper, the Fifth Guards Tank Army is committed to battle, advancing to Tolochin and capturing the town. Orsha falls to the Eleventh Guards and Thirty-First Armies as the Forty-Ninth Army crosses the Dnieper. Hitler agrees to the withdrawal of the Fourth Army to the Berezina, which is taking place anyway. In the south the Ninth Army falls apart, with XXXV Corps encircled at Bobruisk. Hitler dismisses the army commander, Hans Jordan, and then refuses to allow the army group commander, Busch, to pull back his forces.

June 27

FINLAND, *LAND WAR*

The Soviet Seventh Army captures Petrozavodsk as the Finns continue to fall back east of Lake Ladoga.

CENTRAL USSR, *LAND WAR*

The last remnants of the German LIII Corps – 35,000 troops – are wiped out. As XII, XXVII and XXXIX Corps of the German Fourth Army withdraw, a tank battle erupts between the 5th Panzer Division and Fifth Guards Tank Army near Borisov. Meanwhile, a breakout attempt

▼ ***Red Army infantry attack during Operation Bagration as Soviet artillery shells explode on German positions in the background.***

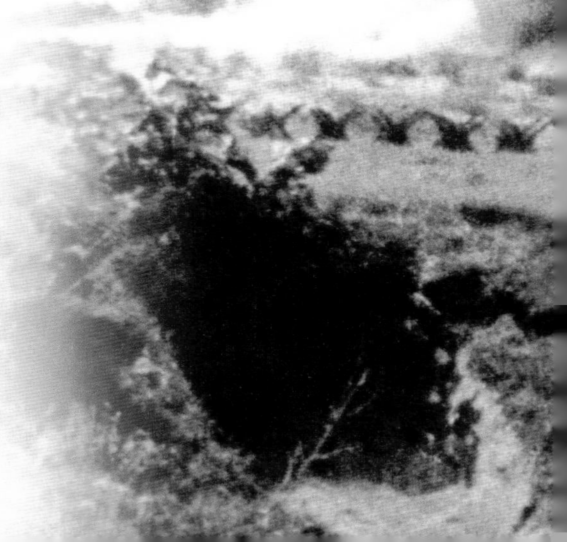

SOVIET PARTISANS

The rapid advance of German armies into the USSR in the mid-1941 resulted in thousands of Red Army soldiers being cut off behind German lines in the Ukraine, Belorussia and the Baltic states. Many took refuge in the forests of the western USSR and in the Pripet Marshes, thus forming the nucleus of a partisan movement. The first partisan activities were spontaneous and uncoordinated, without any assistance from Moscow (both Stalin and his secret police chief, Beria, were suspicious of armed bands outside their sphere of control). However, recognizing that partisan detachments could be useful, Stalin in late 1941 began to send cadres behind German lines to coordinate resistance. The first coordinated partisan attacks took place during the winter of 1941–42, and in May 1942 the Soviets established the Central Partisan Staff to direct the operations of an estimated 142,000 partisans operating behind German lines. Prior to the Battle of Kursk in July 1943, the Central Partisan Staff ordered that all partisan activity be directed against German communications in the central sector. This resulted in 2500 partisan attacks against German railroads in June and July 1943. Such large-scale partisan activity meant the Germans had to deploy substantial forces in their rear areas. In 1942, 25 special security divisions, 30 regiments and more than 100 police battalions were involved in anti-partisan duties.

There is little doubt that the Germans aided partisan recruitment. Treating the locals as sub-humans, random reprisals in response to partisan attacks, and laying waste whole areas to deny partisans supplies did little to endear the Germans to the populace. By 1943, for example, typical anti-partisan sweeps involved 10,000 troops. Although Soviet claims that partisans killed 300,000 Germans during the first two years of the war are exaggerated, it is certainly true that the partisan movement made a significant contribution to the Soviet war effort.

by Ninth Army's XXXV Corps from Bobruisk is shattered by the Soviet Third Army and Sixteenth Air Army. The Ninth Army itself is being torn apart.

JUNE 28

CENTRAL USSR, *LAND WAR*

The German Third Panzer Army has virtually ceased to exist. Soviet forces are driving west: the 1st Baltic Front's Forty-Third Army takes Lepel, 2nd Belorussian's Forty-Ninth and Fiftieth Armies capture Mogilev, and the Fifth Guards Tank Army is across the Berezina. Fierce fighting rages around Bobruisk where 70,000 troops of the German XXXV and XXXXI Corps are trying to escape west.

GERMANY, *ARMED FORCES*

As Bagration unfolds, Hitler replaces Lindermann, commander of Army Group North, with Field Marshal Freissner. Busch is sacked and replaced by Model, who cedes operational command of Army Group North Ukraine to General Harpe.

JUNE 29

CENTRAL USSR, *LAND WAR*

The German Fourth Army falls back across the River Drut but the troops of XXXV Corps fail to break out of Bobruisk. XXXXI Corps is also under severe pressure near the town.

JUNE 30

CENTRAL USSR, *LAND WAR*

The Soviet Eleventh Guards and Fifth Guards Tank Armies link up at Borisov to cut off the German Fourth Army east of the Berezina. At Bobruisk, 20,000 Germans manage to escape.

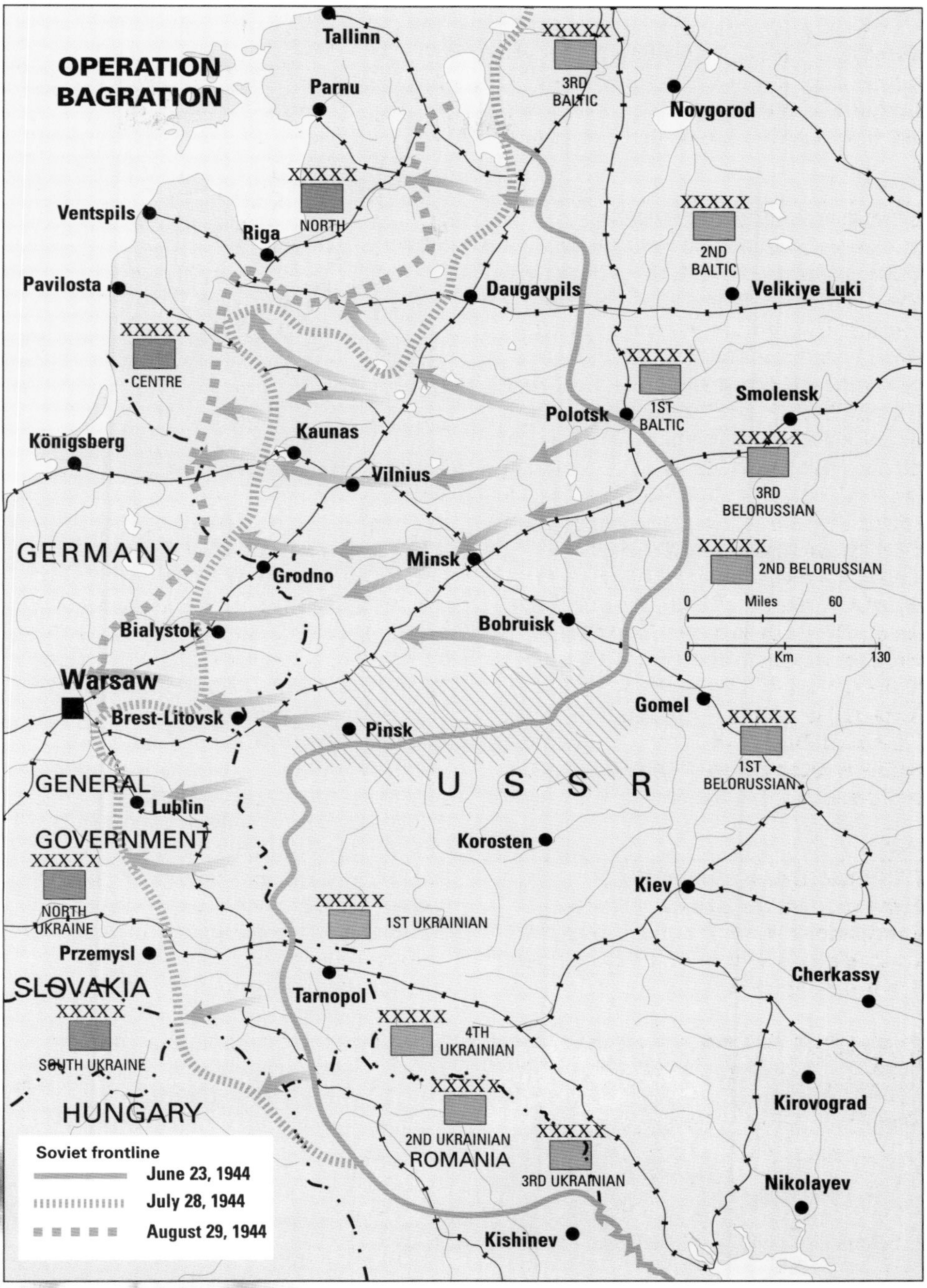

▲ *German infantry retreat during Bagration. Some Soviet reports spoke of German officers and men being drunk during counterattacks.*

JULY 1

CENTRAL USSR, *LAND WAR*
German units continue to retreat over the Berezina, XXVII Corps near Zhukovets and XII and XXXIX Corps at Berezino.

JULY 2

CENTRAL USSR, *LAND WAR*
The Soviet 1st and 3rd Belorussian Fronts are approaching Minsk, the Fifth Guards Tank and Thirty-First Armies reaching the outskirts despite the efforts of the 5th Panzer Division. The Soviet Third Army is also approaching the city from the south. Hitler agrees to the evacuation of the city, but the German Fourth Army is cut off far to the east.

JULY 3

CENTRAL USSR, *LAND WAR*
As the Soviets capture Minsk and the Third Army links up with the forces of the 3rd Belorussian Front, the fate of 100,000 troops of the German Fourth Army is sealed.

JULY 4

NORTHERN USSR, *LAND WAR*
The 1st Baltic Front's Fourth Shock Army captures Polotsk, thus endangering the flank of the German Sixteenth Army.
CENTRAL USSR, *LAND WAR*
XII, XXVII and XXXIX Corps of the Fourth Army attempt to fight their way west from the Minsk area, but they suffer heavy casualties doing so.

▼ Red Army infantry and artillery during Bagration. To support ground units, Soviet aviation formations were flying up to 600 sorties per day throughout July.

JULY 6

CENTRAL USSR, *LAND WAR*
The Soviet Forty-Seventh Army captures the city of Kovel.

JULY 8

CENTRAL USSR, *LAND WAR*
The German Fourth Army has been annihilated, with 60,000 troops being killed attempting to flee and a further 40,000 being captured. The 1st and 3rd Belorussian Fronts continue to push west.
USSR, *ATROCITIES*
Because the Soviets are approaching Kovno, the Germans begin to move Jews in the ghetto to concentration camps in Germany. Many Jews take refuge in underground hideouts that they have prepared, only to be flushed out with dogs, smoke grenades and grenades. Around 2000 Jews die of asphyxiation as the ghetto is razed to the ground; a further 4000 Jews are transported west.

JULY 10

FINLAND, *LAND WAR*
The Red Army reaches the Suvilahti and Lormada rivers.
LATVIA, *LAND WAR*
The German Sixteenth Army is assaulted by the Third Shock and Tenth Guards Armies, while to the south the Second Guards and Fourth Shock Armies advance to link up with the Sixth Guards Army at Daugavpils. Hitler forbids any retreat of Army Group North to the Dvina.

JULY 12

NORTHERN USSR, *LAND WAR*
The Third Shock, Fourth and Tenth Guards Armies, 2nd Baltic Front, create a 80km (50 mile) gap in the Sixteenth Army's front.
LITHUANIA, *LAND WAR*
The Soviet Fifth Army enters Vilnius.

JULY 13

CENTRAL USSR, *LAND WAR*
Vilnius falls to the Soviet Fifth Army, and the Eleventh Guards Army crosses the River Niemen.
SOUTHERN USSR, *LAND WAR*
Konev's 1st Ukrainian Front (First Guards, First Guards Tank, Third Guards, Third Guards Tank, Fourth Tank, Fifth Guards, Thirteenth, Eighteenth, Thirty-Eighth and Sixtieth Armies – 840,000 troops, 14,000 artillery pieces, 1600 tanks plus 2800 aircraft of the Second and Eighth Air Armies) begins the Lvov-Sandomir Offensive against Army Group North Ukraine (Hungarian First, First Panzer and Fourth Panzer Armies – 500,000 troops, 900 tanks, 6000 artillery pieces and 700 aircraft). The army group also has the left flank of the 1st Belorussian Front on its flank: Polish First, Second Tank, Eighth Guards, Forty-Seventh, Sixty-Ninth and Seventieth

◄ *German Hummel self-propelled heavy howitzers west of Minsk. Armed with a 150mm gun, they were deployed with the artillery detachments of panzer divisions.*

Armies. The Soviet Thirty-Eighth and Sixtieth Armies spearhead the offensive near Brody, the Thirteenth Army at Radekhov. The Thirty-Eighth Army breaks though the German line near Zolochev. Counterattacks by XXXXVI and XXXXVIII Panzer Corps are met by the First Guards and Third Guards Armies.

JULY 14

CENTRAL USSR, *LAND WAR*
The Soviets capture Pinsk, and the Thirty-First Army crosses the Niemen at Grodno and nears the border of East Prussia.

SOUTHERN USSR, *LAND WAR*
Konev's offensive gathers pace, the Red Air Force having achieved air superiority. The 1st Belorussian Front attacks the northern flank of the Fourth Panzer Army as the Third Guards and Thirteenth Armies continue to assault the junction of the panzer armies, destroying the German XIII Corps. The only bright spot for the Germans is the slowing of the Thirty-Eighth and Sixtieth Armies' advance to Lvov.

▼ *The remains of a German artillery battery following a clash with units of the 2nd Belorussian Front near Minsk.*

JULY 15

FINLAND, *LAND WAR*
The Finns manage to halt the Soviet advance on the Karelian Isthmus.

NORTHERN USSR, *LAND WAR*
The Soviet Tenth Guards Army captures the town of Opochka.

SOUTHERN USSR, *LAND WAR*
The Soviet Third Guards Tank and Fourth Tank Armies are committed to the offensive, both being counterattacked by XXXXVI and XXXXVIII Panzer Corps, respectively. The latter corps loses many panzers to enemy ground-attack aircraft.

JULY 17

NORTHERN USSR, *LAND WAR*
The 3rd Baltic Front commences operations against Army Group North, with the First Shock Army capturing Sebezh and the Twenty-Second Army winning Osveya.

CENTRAL USSR, *LAND WAR*
The 1st Belorussian Front attacks the northern flank and centre of the Fourth Panzer Army.

SOUTHERN USSR, *LAND WAR*
The Soviet First Guards Tank Army crosses the River Bug near Sokal. The Soviet Fourth Tank and Thirty-Eighth Armies are held up by German resistance before Lvov.

JULY 18

POLAND, *LAND WAR*
The Soviet Thirty-First Army crosses the East Prussian border but is then halted by fierce German resistance.

SOUTHERN USSR, *LAND WAR*
The 1st Belorussian Front opens the Lublin-Brest Offensive against the Fourth Panzer Army. The Polish First and Eighth Guards Armies pierce the German line north of Kovel. To the south the First Guards Army nears Stanislav, and the Fourth Tank Army captures Olshantsa. The Soviet Thirteenth and Thirty-Eighth Armies link up and surround 65,000 troops of XIII Corps near Brody.

JULY 20

NORTHERN USSR, *LAND WAR*
The Soviet First Shock Army pierces the front of the Eighteenth Army near Ostrov as the Third Panzer Army buckles under assaults from the Second Guards and Fifty-First Armies.

SOUTHERN USSR, *LAND WAR*
The Fourth Panzer Army is crumbling, the Soviet Eighth Guards Army having reached the River Bug. A relief attack by XXXXVIII Panzer Corps towards the Brody Pocket fails.

GERMANY, *ARMED FORCES*
A group of German officers, led by Claus Schenk von Stauffenberg, attempts to assassinate Adolf Hitler, but fails. Widespread reprisals against real and suspected plotters follow.

JULY 21

FINLAND, *LAND WAR*
The Soviet Thirty-Second Army is now at the Finnish border, having inflicted heavy losses on the Finns.

NORTHERN USSR, *LAND WAR*
The Soviet First Shock Army captures Ostrov.

POLAND, *LAND WAR*
The Soviet Second Tank Army is approaching the River Vistula.

SOUTHERN USSR, *LAND WAR*
Efforts by XIII Corps to break out of the Brody Pocket fail. The Germans move three divisions to Lvov to cover the northern approach to the city.

GERMANY, ARMED FORCES
Zeitzler, advocate of retreat during Bagration, is replaced as Chief of the General Staff by Heinz Guderian.

POLAND, *POLITICS*
The Soviets form the *Polski Komitet Wyzwolenia Narodowego* (PKWN – Polish Committee of National Liberation) from the NKVD-controlled Union of Polish Patriots. It will later be known as the Lublin Committee and will become the official legal authority, according to the Soviets, in liberated territory.

In January 1945, the Lublin Committee became a provisional government recognized by the Soviet Union. The Lublin Committee was opposed to the Polish Home Army, the military arm of the Polish government-in-exile in London.

Today the PKWN is flown into the town of Helm, and tomorrow it will issue its pro-Soviet political manifesto.

JULY 22

NORTHERN USSR, *LAND WAR*
The Soviet Forty-Second Army captures most of Pskov, and the Fifty-First Army takes Panevesus as Army Group North falls back.

POLAND, *LAND WAR*
The Soviet Second Tank Army captures Chelm.

SOUTHERN USSR, *LAND WAR*
The Brody Pocket is annihilated: 35,000 German troops are killed and 17,000 captured. Only 12,000 troops escape.

JULY 23

NORTHERN USSR, *LAND WAR*
Pskov falls to the Red Army.

POLAND, *LAND WAR*
The Soviet Sixty-Fifth Army approaches Brest-Litovsk. The Eighth Guards and Second Tank Armies enter Lublin to engage in fierce fighting with the defending Fourth Panzer Army. The Soviets liberate the Majdanek concentration camp. The Soviet First Guards Tank Army crosses the River San near Yaroslav.

▲ ***An SU-152 heavy assault gun of the Soviet 2nd Baltic Front in northern Russia in July 1944. The SU-152 was armed with the ML-20 152mm gun-howitzer.***

JULY 24

NORTHERN USSR, *LAND WAR*
As III SS Panzer Corps consolidates its position in Narva, the Soviet Narva Operational Group launches strong attacks against the German positions.

POLAND, *LAND WAR*
The Soviets capture Lublin as the First Panzer Army pulls out of Lvov. The Soviet Third Guards Tank Army takes Yavorov.

JULY 25

NORTHERN USSR, *LAND WAR*
The Soviet Narva Operational Group assaults III SS Panzer Corps around Narva as the Second Shock Army launches a support attack, which forces the Germans out of the town towards the so-called Tannenberg Line. The forces of the 2nd Baltic Front are nearing Daugavpils.

POLAND, *LAND WAR*
The 1st Belorussian Front is tightening its grip on Brest-Litovsk, although the Germans are mounting counterattacks. The Soviet Second Tank Army is now on the Vistula near Deblin, followed by the Polish First Army.

JULY 27

LATVIA, *LAND WAR*
The Soviet Fourth Shock Army takes Daugavpils, and the Tenth Guards Army captures Rezekne.

LITHUANIA, *LAND WAR*
Attempts by the Third Panzer Army to hold Siauliai fail as the town is taken by the Soviet Fifty-First Army.

POLAND, *LAND WAR*
The Soviet Twenty-Eighth, Sixty-Fifth and Seventieth Armies attack and encircle the German Second Army in Brest-Litovsk. As the Polish First Army joins the Second Tank Army to consolidate the bridgehead on the Vistula, the Sixty-Ninth Army reaches the river at Pulawy. Meanwhile, Lvov is abandoned by the Germans.

JULY 29

LITHUANIA, *LAND WAR*
The advance of the Soviet Fifty-First Army from Siauliai threatens to cut off the German Sixteenth and Eighteenth Armies

▶ ***Red Army troops, possibly of the First Guards Tank Army, on the outskirts of Lvov. The First Guards Tank Army had severed German communications with the city on 23 July.***

in Latvia and Estonia. Third Panzer Army thus moves north to secure a land corridor to the west. The Soviet Fifth Army captures Vilnius and then moves west towards Kaunas.

POLAND, *LAND WAR*
A German counterattack at Wolomin by XXXIX Panzer Corps against the Second Tank Army is launched. Meanwhile, the Soviet Third Guards Tank Army establishes a bridgehead over the Vistula at Sandomierz.

JULY 30

LATVIA, *LAND WAR*
The Soviet Fifty-First Army strikes for the Gulf of Riga to cut off the Sixteenth and Eighteenth Armies, assisted by the Second Guards Army, which is holding the Third Panzer Army.

LITHUANIA, *LAND WAR*
The Soviet Fifth Army battles its way into Kaunas.

POLAND, *LAND WAR*
The First Guards Tank and Thirteenth Armies cross the Vistula at Baranow.

JULY 31

FINLAND, *LAND WAR*
The Soviet Karelian and Leningrad Fronts advance to the Finnish border.

LATVIA, *LAND WAR*
The Soviet Fifty-First Army reaches the Baltic west of the city of Riga, thus cutting off the German Sixteenth and Eighteenth Armies.

LITHUANIA, *LAND WAR*
The Soviet Fifth Army captures Kaunas, inflicting losses of more than 40,000 dead on the defending German IX Corps.

POLAND, *LAND WAR*
The Soviet Forty-Seventh Army takes Siedlce. The Soviet Second Tank Army enters the Praga suburb of Warsaw but is then counterattacked by XXXIX and IV SS Panzer Corps (*Totenkopf* and *Wiking* Panzer Divisions), forcing it to retire.

USSR, *ARMED FORCES*
The stunning victories achieved by the Red Army thus far during Operation Bagration have, as usual, been bought at a heavy price in casualties: 1st Baltic Front, 41,000 killed and 125,000 wounded; 1st Belorussian Front, 65,000 killed and 215,000 wounded; 2nd Belorussian Front, 26,000 killed and 90,000 wounded; and 3rd Belorussian Front, 45,000 killed and 155,000 wounded.

▲ ***T-34/85s of the Soviet 1st Baltic Front in Lithuania. The T-34/85, with its 85mm gun, was the response to the German Panther. It entered service in the spring of 1944.***

AUGUST 1

FINLAND, *POLITICS*
President Ryti resigns, his place being taken by Marshal Mannerheim. The Finns hope this will facilitate negotiations with the Soviets.

WARSAW, *PARTISAN WAR*
The Home Army in Warsaw rises against the Germans. Led by General Tadeusz Komorowski, there are 38,000 insurgents in the city. The Home Army is under the command of the government-in-exile in London. As such, it can expect little aid from the Soviets.

AUGUST 2

POLAND, *PARTISAN WAR*
The Home Army fails to capture Okacie airfield. Erich von dem Bach-Zelewski is appointed commander of the German units ordered to crush the revolt.

POLAND, *LAND WAR*
The battle at Wolomin continues, with the Germans feeding in the 4th Panzer Division. The Soviet Sixty-Ninth Army crosses the Vistula at Pulawy.

AUGUST 4

LATVIA, *LAND WAR*
The trapped German Sixteenth Army launches an ineffectual counterattack against the Fifty-First Army at Jelgava.

POLAND, *PARTISAN WAR*
The Home Army now controls the Mokotow, Czerniakow, Powisle, Old Town and Zoliborz districts of Warsaw.

POLAND, *LAND WAR*
The Soviet Fifth Guards Army reinforces the Sandomierz bridgehead.

AUGUST 5

LATVIA, *LAND WAR*
The Soviet Fourth Shock Army is advancing along the River Dvina towards Riga, but is being slowed by the German Eighteenth Army.

POLAND, *PARTISAN WAR*
The Home Army in Warsaw has suffered 15,000 casualties as it tries to hold out against heavy German land and aerial assaults. It controls three-fifths of the city, but the Germans have split the Polish-occupied area into two.

POLAND, *LAND WAR*
The Germans launch a counterattack against the Eighth Guards Army at the Magnuszew bridgehead, to little effect.

▼ ***German troops pulling a Goliath remote-controlled tracked demolition charge during the Warsaw Uprising. Originally designed for clearing minefields, it carried a 75kg (165lb) demolition charge.***

AUGUST 7

POLAND, *ATROCITIES*
The Germans liquidate the Lodz Ghetto; deportations to Auschwitz concentration camp begin. Trapped Jews try to hide in the hope of surviving until the Red Army can liberate the town. However, the Germans comb the ghetto and will eventually transport 74,000 Jews from the ghetto to the gas chambers at Auschwitz.

AUGUST 10

LATVIA, *LAND WAR*
The Soviet First Shock and Sixty-Seventh Armies join the advance towards Riga.

POLAND, *LAND WAR*
The Third and Forty-Eighth Armies cross the River Narew near Bialystok.

AUGUST 14

LATVIA, *LAND WAR*
The German Third Panzer Army launches a relief assault towards Riga, pushing back the Soviet Fifty-First Army.

POLAND, *LAND WAR*
The Soviet Second Tank Army attacks to the south of Warsaw and the Forty-Seventh Army to the north, but both are held by German armoured forces, especially IV SS Panzer Corps.

AUGUST 17

LATVIA, *LAND WAR*
The Third Panzer Army continues to advance towards Riga, being supported by the Sixteenth Army attacking south of Jelgava. As a result, the Soviet Second Guards and Fifty-First Armies are thrown on to the defensive.

EAST PRUSSIA, *LAND WAR*
The Soviet Thirty-Third Army has established a bridgehead over the River Sesupe.

AUGUST 18

LITHUANIA, *LAND WAR*
The Soviet Fifth Guards Tank Army moves to the north of the Second Guards Army to shield Siauliai, and also fends off attacks by XXXIX and XXXX Panzer Corps.

AUGUST 19

LATVIA, *LAND WAR*
The Soviet Third Shock Army is halted just beyond the River Oger

▲ ***Insurgents in Warsaw examine a PIAT anti-tank weapon delivered during an RAF supply drop. The refusal of Stalin to allow the RAF to land on Soviet soil hamstrung Allied efforts to aid the Home Army.***

by an assault by three divisions of the German Eighteenth Army to the north.

POLAND, *PARTISAN WAR*
The Home Army in Warsaw launches counterattacks from Zoliborz, but all fail.

ROMANIA, *LAND WAR*
The Soviet 2nd and 3rd Ukrainian Fronts launch probing attacks around Jassy and Tiraspol in preparation for the Jassy-Kishinev Offensive. This will be Stavka's attempt to destroy German and Romanian forces in Romania, capture the Ploesti oil fields and then cross into Bulgaria, and threaten the rear of German forces in Greece and Yugoslavia. For this mission the two fronts have been substantially reinforced. The 2nd Ukrainian Front comprises the Fourth Guards, Sixth Tank, Seventh, Twenty-Seventh, Fortieth, Fifty-Second and Fifty-Third Armies – 771,000 troops, 11,000 artillery pieces, 1300 tanks and 900 aircraft. The 3rd Ukrainian Front deploys the Fifth Shock, Thirty-Seventh, Forty-Sixth and Fifty-Seventh Armies – 523,000 troops, 8000 artillery pieces, 600 tanks and 1000 aircraft.

Facing this massive force is Army Group South Ukraine. This group comprises the Eighth Army (Romanian I, VII and LVII Corps and German XVII Corps) – 43,000 German and 112,000 Romanian troops; Romanian Fourth Army (Romanian IV and VI Corps and German IV Corps) – 43,000 German and 88,000 Romanian troops; Sixth Army (VII, XXX, XXXXIV and LII Corps) – 212,000 German and 25,000 Romanian troops; and Romanian Third Army (Romanian II and III and German XXIX Corps, with the 13th Panzer Division in reserve) – 14,000 German and 75,000 Romanian troops. The Luftwaffe has 318 aircraft to support the army group, which deploys a total of 400 tanks and assault guns.

AUGUST 20

POLAND, *PARTISAN WAR*
The Home Army in Warsaw attacks from Zoliborz and the Old Town, but incurs heavy losses while doing so.

ROMANIA, *LAND WAR*
The Soviet Jassy-Kishinev Offensive begins. The 2nd Ukrainian Front launches a devastating assault on the Romanian Fourth Army, the IV and VI Corps being shattered. The Soviet Fifty-Second Army crashes into the junction between the German IV and Romanian IV Corps at Jassy, while the Twenty-Seventh Army pummels the Romanian VI Corps. Soon the Romanians are fleeing and the Soviet Fifty-Third Army is inside Jassy.

The 3rd Ukrainian Front enjoys similar success. XXX and XXIX Corps are attacked by the Soviet Thirty-Seventh, Forty-Sixth and Fifty-Seventh Armies and,

KEY PERSONALITIES

KONSTANTIN ROKOSSOVSKY

Rokossovsky (1896–1968) joined the Russian Army in 1914 and then the Red Army in 1918. During the 1920s, he and Zhukov became close friends, a relationship that continued throughout World War II. During Stalin's purges, Rokossovsky was arrested in August 1937 for being a "counter-revolutionary", beaten severely and imprisoned under harsh conditions. Released in March 1940 on the orders of the Chief of the General Staff, Shaposhnikov, he was then given command of V Cavalry Corps.

During Barbarossa, he was in the Smolensk region, and in August 1941 he was the commander of the Sixteenth Army. He was badly wounded in March 1942 but returned to duty to command the Bryansk Front until September, when he took over the Don Front. His conduct during the Stalingrad operations earned him promotion to colonel-general, and in February 1943 he took over the Central Front, fighting at Kursk.

After the Battle of Kursk he led his front, renamed 1st Belorussian, into Poland and inflicted a crushing defeat on the Germans. However, he failed to help the Polish Home Army in August 1944 when it rose up in Warsaw against the Germans, despite being just to the west of the city. Undoubtedly on the orders of Stalin, Rokossovsky just watched as the insurgents were crushed by the Germans. He finished the war as head of the 2nd Belorussian Front, his command fighting in East Prussia and Pomerania.

In a bitter twist of irony for the Poles, Rokossovsky was made commander of the army of post-war Poland, a country in which he was widely loathed. He died in 1968.

following heavy fighting, are put to flight. The Soviet Fifth Shock Army attacks LII Corps at Kishinev as an assault by the 13th Panzer Division fails.

AUGUST 21

ROMANIA, *LAND WAR*

The Soviet Fifty-Second Army captures Jassy as the commander of the 2nd Ukrainian Front, Marshal Rodion Malinovsky, unleashes his Sixth Tank Army against retreating Axis forces. As the German Eighth Army is attacked, its Romanian units flee, while to the south the Sixth Army is facing annihilation (for the second time in its career): the Forty-Sixth and Forty-Seventh Armies are hammering XXX Corps and the 13th Panzer Division has lost all its tanks. The army group commander, Freissner, orders a general withdrawal to the River Prut.

AUGUST 22

ROMANIA, *LAND WAR*

The Romanian units of Army Group South Ukraine have effectively ceased to exist as the Red Army runs riot: the Sixth Tank Army is advancing from the north, the Fourth Guards and Fifty-Second Armies have captured Kastuleni and Ungeny, and the Forty-Sixth Army has brushed aside XXIX Corps to drive deep into the German rear.

ROMANIA, *POLITICS*

In response to impending military disaster, the Romanians depose Antonescu and place him under arrest. Orders are issued to Romanian units to stop fighting, surrender to the Russians or disband and go home (in fact, many Romanians have deserted *en masse* to the Red Army).

AUGUST 23

ROMANIA, *LAND WAR*

The Soviet Fifty-Second Army has severed the German line of retreat by cutting the road to Husi, VII Corps has been destroyed by the Fourth Guards Army, IV Corps is mauled on the River Barludi, and to compound the army group's difficulties XXX, XXXXIX and LII Corps have collapsed.

AUGUST 24

ESTONIA, *LAND WAR*

The German Eighteenth Army is pushed back into Tartu, while Group Narva is still fending off the Second Shock, Eighth and Fifty-Ninth Armies.

ROMANIA, *LAND WAR*

The link-up between the Soviet Thirty-Seventh and Fifty-Second Armies between Husi and Leovo signals the encirclement of the German Sixth Army. Kishinev falls to the Fifth Shock Army as the Fourth Guards, Fifth Shock, Thirty-Seventh and Fifty-Seventh Armies begin the reduction of the German pocket. Meanwhile, the Sixth Tank, Twenty-Seventh, Forty-Sixth and Fifty-Second Armies continue to power west. Group Meith (formally IV Corps) attempts to escape encirclement at Husi. Bucharest rises against German authority, prompting Hitler to order the 5th Flak Division (which had been defending the Ploesti oil fields) to suppress the revolt. When it comes under heavy fire and calls in Luftwaffe support, the revolt spreads rapidly to other parts of the country.

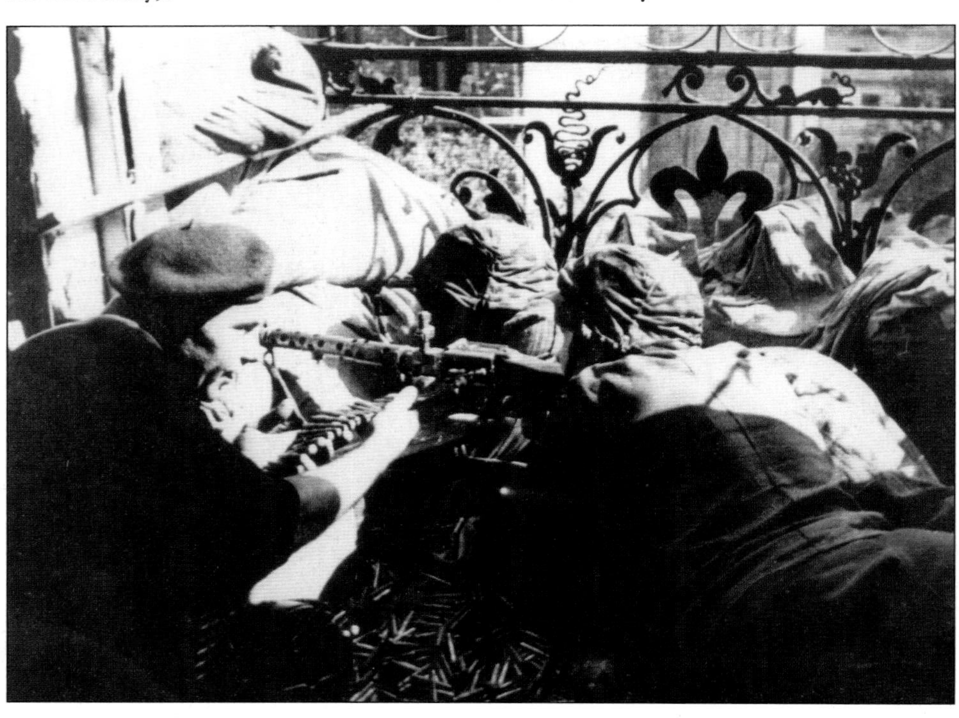

▶ ***Home Army fighters in Warsaw. By the end of August the Germans had retaken the Old Town, finding only wounded. These were doused with petrol and burnt.***

▲ ***Soviet artillery pounds the positions of IV SS Panzer Corps east of Wolomin. The weight of the Soviet attack pushed the corps back west towards Warsaw.***

AUGUST 25

FINLAND, *DIPLOMACY*
The Finnish Government agrees armistice terms with Moscow, conditional on German forces leaving Finnish territory by September 15.

ESTONIA, *LAND WAR*
Tartu falls to the Soviet Sixty-Seventh Army.

POLAND, *LAND WAR*
Heavy fighting continues around Warsaw as the Soviet Forty-Seventh Army attacks IV SS Panzer Corps.

ROMANIA, *LAND WAR*
German forces in the Leovo Pocket fail to break out, as does Group Meith at Husi.

ROMANIA, *POLITICS*
Following a Luftwaffe air raid, the Romanian Government declares war on Germany and orders all German troops to be disarmed and imprisoned. This threatens 315,000 German troops in Greece, Yugoslavia and in the Aegean.

AUGUST 29

ROMANIA, *LAND WAR*
Group Meith is destroyed, signalling the annihilation of the German Sixth Army – more than 250,000 troops. The Soviet Fifty-Seventh Army captures Constanta, and the Forty-Sixth Army takes Buzau. The losses for the 2nd Ukrainian Front thus far are 7000 killed and 32,000 wounded; for the 3rd Ukrainian Front, 5800 killed and 21,000 wounded.

SLOVAKIA, *PARTISAN WAR*
Since the summer Slovak partisans of the Czechoslovak Army in Slovakia (18,000 in number) have been engaged in guerrilla activity against German targets, mainly in the central mountains. In response, the Germans move 48,000 troops into Slovakia, prompting the outbreak of the Slovak national uprising.

HUNGARY, *POLITICS*
Admiral Horthy removes the pro-Nazi Szotaj government and replaces it with the pro-Soviet Lakatos regime.

AUGUST 30

POLAND, *PARTISAN WAR*
The Home Army in Warsaw is forced out of the Old Town, using the sewers to escape to the city centre and Zoliborz.

ROMANIA, *LAND WAR*
The Ploesti oil fields fall to the Soviets.

AUGUST 31

ROMANIA, *LAND WAR*
The Soviet Fifty-Third Army captures Bucharest, the Romanian capital.

▼ ***The tanks of General Krauchenk's Soviet IV Guards Corps, 2nd Ukrainian Front, enter Bucharest on August 31.***

SEPTEMBER 2

FINLAND, *DIPLOMACY*
Helsinki breaks off diplomatic relations with Germany and demands the exit of its forces from the country by September 15.

SEPTEMBER 4

POLAND, *LAND WAR*
The Soviet Sixty-Fifth and Seventieth Armies approach the Narew near Pultusk.

ROMANIA, *LAND WAR*
The Soviets capture Brasov and Senaia as the Fifty-Third Army advances to the River Danube at Turnu Severin.

SEPTEMBER 5

HUNGARY, *LAND WAR*
The Hungarian Second Army assaults and pushes back the Romanian Fourth Army (now fighting alongside the Red Army) near Sibiu. However, the Soviet Sixth Tank Army is ordered to Sibiu to lend support.

USSR, *DIPLOMACY*
The USSR declares war on Bulgaria, which surrenders at once.

SEPTEMBER 6

FINLAND, *LAND WAR*
The German Twentieth Mountain Army, commanded by Colonel-General Lothar Rendulic, begins to withdraw to a new defensive line across northern Finland from Lyngen through Ivalo to Petsamo. This operation is codenamed Birke.

POLAND, *PARTISAN WAR*
The Germans have now cleared Home Army forces from the banks of the Vistula.

HUNGARY, *LAND WAR*
LVII Panzer Corps is deployed to reinforce the new German Sixth Army in Hungary as the Eighth Army is assaulted by the Soviet Seventh Guards and Fortieth Armies. The Hungarian Second Army has been halted south of Cluj.

SEPTEMBER 8

POLAND, *PARTISAN WAR*
The Home Army is facing a desperate situation. Low on food and ammunition, the Poles have begun surrender talks, which so far have come to nothing.

POLAND, *LAND WAR*
The Soviet Thirty-Eighth Army and the 4th Ukrainian Front (combined total of 363,000 troops) begin operations to break through the Dukla Pass. The defending First Panzer Army resists stubbornly.

BULGARIA, *LAND WAR*
The Soviet Thirty-Seventh and Fifty-Seventh Armies occupy Bulgaria, which undergoes a pro-Soviet coup and promptly declares war on Germany.

SEPTEMBER 10

POLAND, *LAND WAR*
The Soviet Forty-Seventh Army is fighting in the Warsaw suburb of Praga. The First Panzer Army is holding off the Soviet Thirty-Eighth Army near Krosno.

SEPTEMBER 14

LATVIA, *LAND WAR*
The Soviet Baltic Offensive begins, against the German Sixteenth and Eighteenth Armies between Riga and Narva. The formations involved are the Leningrad Front (Second Shock, Eighth and Fifty-Ninth Armies) – 195,000 troops; 1st Baltic Front (Second Guards, Fourth Shock, Sixth Guards, Thirty-Ninth, Forty-Third and Fifty-First Armies) – 621,000 troops; 2nd Baltic Front (Third Shock, Tenth Guards and Twenty-Second Armies) – 339,000 troops; and 3rd Baltic Front (First Shock, Forty-Second, Fifty-Fourth and Sixty-Seventh Armies) – 345,000 troops. The Germans can muster 400,000 troops. The offensive begins with the Forty-Third Army advancing towards Jelgava, the Soviets running into strong defences.

KEY PERSONALITIES

GEORGI ZHUKOV

The greatest Red Army general of World War II was born in 1896 into an impoverished peasant family near Moscow. He was going to be a craftsman, but the outbreak of World War I changed his life forever. Drafted in 1915 into the Imperial Russian Army, by 1918 he was serving in the Red Army cavalry and a year later joined the Communist Party. What marked him out was his thirst for knowledge. During the next 20 years he devoured a large amount of written work on the military art. By 1938 he was in command of the élite 4th Cavalry Division, having narrowly escaped the Great Purges, being charged only with "political shortsightedness" – he avoided arrest. When he was transferred to Mongolia he gained his first victory, over the Japanese at Khalkhin Gol in August 1939.

By May 1940 he was a general of the army and in charge of the Kiev Military District. When the Germans invaded the Soviet Union in June 1941, Zhukov advocated abandoning Kiev, an idea that prompted an outburst from Stalin. Zhukov offered to resign but Stalin, probably recognizing his general was right, refused the offer, replying: "Don't be so hot-headed." Kiev fell anyway and Zhukov was given command of the reserve forces to the east of Moscow. He was briefly sent to Leningrad in September 1941 to shore up the city's defences, but was recalled in early October when the Germans were nearing Moscow. When the German Moscow offensive stalled at the end of November 1941, Zhukov launched a counteroffensive along the whole front, which not only saved Moscow but also gave the Germans their first strategic defeat of the war.

In August 1942, Zhukov became deputy supreme commander-in-chief of the Red Army, second only to Stalin. He masterminded the operation that destroyed the German Sixth Army at Stalingrad (Operation Uranus) and then planned and executed the Red Army defence at Kursk in July 1943 (by which time he was a Marshal of the Soviet Union). His greatest operation was probably Operation Bagration in June 1944, which destroyed the German Army Group Centre. Although Stalin was jealous of Zhukov's popularity and military victories, he agreed to allow him the honour of taking Berlin in 1945. This he did, albeit with terrible losses. After the war he was effectively exiled by Stalin, rehabilitated after Stalin's death but then retired in 1957. He was reinstated as a national war hero by Leonid Brezhnev in 1965 and died in 1974.

▼ Soviet infantry in Poland. The rather elongated weapon on the left is a 14.5mm PTRD anti-tank rifle. Despite being largely obsolete by 1943, the cumbersome PTRD remained in Red Army service until 1945.

POLAND, *PARTISAN WAR*
Although the Soviet Forty-Seventh Army has cleared Praga, the 25th Panzer Division is pummelling the Home Army in Zoliborz and Czernaikow.

SEPTEMBER 15

LATVIA, *LAND WAR*
The Germans put up stout resistance against the Soviet First Shock Army near Valk and the Third Shock, Tenth Guards and Twenty-Second Armies near Madona.

FINLAND, *LAND WAR*
The German Twentieth Mountain Army launches an abortive attack against the port of Suursaari, prompting the Finnish Government to demand its immediate withdrawal from the country.

SEPTEMBER 16

LATVIA, *LAND WAR*
The German Third Panzer Army launches a counterattack with 400 tanks against the Fifth Guards and Fifty-First Armies, aimed at linking up with the Sixteenth and Eighteenth Armies. The Sixteenth also counterattacks against the Soviet Twenty-Second Army at Dobele.

HUNGARY, *LAND WAR*
In an effort to slow the 2nd Ukrainian Front, Freissner launches the Hungarian Second and German Eighth Armies against the Romanian Fourth and Soviet Seventh Guards and Fortieth Armies east of Cluj.

SEPTEMBER 19

ESTONIA, *LAND WAR*
The Soviet Second Shock and Eighth Armies link up northwest of Lake Peipus.

LATVIA, *LAND WAR*
The First Shock Army captures Valk.

HUNGARY, *LAND WAR*
Freissner's attack is making gains against the 2nd Ukrainian Front.

SEPTEMBER 21

POLAND, *PARTISAN WAR*
The last air drop by Western aircraft to the Home Army in Warsaw takes place.

KEY WEAPONS

IL-2

In 1938, the Soviet Ilyushin design bureau began work on a heavily armoured, low-level attack aircraft called *shturmovik* in Russian. Designated Il-2, it entered production in 1940. Its armament consisted of two wing-mounted armour-piercing cannon, two machine guns, eight rockets and a bomb load of 400kg (880lb). It had protective armour up to 12mm (0.47in) thick around the engine and a two-man cockpit, although the rear fuselage was made of plywood.

The aircraft's easy handling, powerful armament and ability to resist ground fire made it a devastating ground-attack aircraft, especially with the tenacity of desperate pilots; the Germans called it the "Black Death". However, its low speed made it vulnerable to German fighters and losses were extremely high, even after a rear gun was added for self-defence. The Luftwaffe even formed specially trained fighter units to target Il-2s, and several of Germany's highest-ranking aces gained most of their kills against Il-2s, with Il-2 losses to the enemy running into the thousands (14,200 were claimed downed in 1943 and 1944 alone). The Il-2 made an important contribution to the war on the Eastern Front, with a total of 36,000 being built.

Type: single-seat or two-seat attack aircraft
Powerplant: 1 x 1750hp AM-38F
Wingspan: 14.6m (47.9ft)
Length: 12m (39.3ft)
Height: 3.4m (11.1ft)
Maximum speed: 370kmh (231mph)
Service ceiling: 6500m (21,325ft)
Maximum range: 600km (375 miles)
Armament: 2 x 20mm cannon, 2 x 7.62mm machine gun, 8 x 82mm rockets, 4 x 100kg (220lb) bombs

SEPTEMBER 22

ESTONIA, *LAND WAR*
The Soviet Eighth and Fifty-Ninth Armies capture Tallinn as the Third Panzer Army, having lost 140 tanks, abandons its attack. The Soviet Fourth Shock and Forty-Third Armies then attack and push the German Sixteenth Army back to Riga.

SEPTEMBER 23

ESTONIA, *LAND WAR*
The Second Shock Army captures Parnu.

POLAND, *LAND WAR*
The Polish First Army is halted north of Magnuszew, having suffered heavy losses. The Home Army in Warsaw has abandoned Mokotow.

USSR, *STRATEGY*
The Stavka suspends the Baltic Offensive due to poor gains, and plans to concentrate on the destruction of the Third Panzer Army rather than the Sixteenth Army.

SEPTEMBER 24

POLAND, *PARTISAN WAR*
Inside Warsaw, the 19th Panzer Division forces the Home Army back from Mokotow.

HUNGARY, *LAND WAR*
Army Group South Ukraine's attack near Cluj peters out.

GERMANY, *ARMED FORCES*
Army Group North Ukraine is renamed Army Group A, while Army Group South Ukraine becomes Army Group South.

SEPTEMBER 26

POLAND, *PARTISAN WAR*
Following a vicious three-day battle, 2000 members of the Home Army surrender in Mokotow, with 600 others escaping through the sewers.

SEPTEMBER 28

HUNGARY, *LAND WAR*
The Soviet Belgrade Offensive begins. The Fifty-Seventh Army attacks from Vidin, but Army Group F resists strongly.

SEPTEMBER 29

POLAND, *PARTISAN WAR*
German forces destroy a Home Army unit at the Skierniewice-Zyrandow railway, the Poles losing 2400 out of 2500 insurgents.

HUNGARY, *LAND WAR*
The German Sixth Army and Hungarian Second Army resume their attack at Cluj. To the south, the Fifty-Seventh Army plus the 4th Mechanized Corps (combined total 200,000 troops) continue the advance to Belgrade, reinforced by the Forty-Sixth Army (93,500 troops) deployed to the north.

OCTOBER 1

FINLAND, *LAND WAR*
The Finnish Army makes an assault landing against the German garrison at Tornio in the Gulf of Bothnia.

HUNGARY, *DIPLOMACY*
A Hungarian delegation arrives in Moscow to sign a secret armistice with the Soviets.

OCTOBER 2

POLAND, *PARTISAN WAR*
The remnants of the Polish Home Army surrender in Warsaw. The army has lost 15,000 dead, plus 200,000 civilians killed. The Germans have lost 10,000 killed, 7000 missing and 9000 wounded.

OCTOBER 3

GERMANY, *STRATEGY*
Hitler approves OKW's plan for the Twentieth Mountain Army in Norway to withdraw to the Lyngen position: Operation Nordlicht. The units involved are XIX, XXVI and XVIII Mountain Corps.

OCTOBER 5

LITHUANIA, *LAND WAR*
The Soviet Memel Offensive against the Third Panzer Army begins. The forces involved are the 1st Baltic Front (Second Guards, Third Shock, Fourth Shock, Fifth Guards, Fifth Guards Tank, Sixth Guards, Forty-Third and Fifty-First Armies); 2nd Baltic Front (Tenth Guard and Twenty-Second Armies); 3rd Baltic Front (First Shock, Second Shock, Fifty-Fourth, Sixty-First and Sixty-Seventh Armies); and the 3rd Belorussian Front's Thirty-Ninth Army.

Massive Red Army artillery barrages strike the Third Panzer Army between Siauliai and Raseiniai, and then the Second Guards, Sixth Guards and Forty-Third Armies attack. The Germans are pulling the Eighteenth Army out of Latvia as fast as they can.

▼ ***German panzergreandiers in Hungary. At the beginning of October there were 31 German divisions in Hungary, with a total of 293 tanks and assault guns.***

OCTOBER 6

LITHUANIA, *LAND WAR*
The Third Panzer Army is reeling as the Soviet Fourth Shock, Fifth Guards Tank, Sixth Guards, Thirty-Ninth, Forty-Third and Fifty-First Armies join the offensive and the weather allows the Soviet First Air Army to fly ground-support missions. Hitler forbids the abandonment of Riga.

HUNGARY, *LAND WAR*
The Soviet Debrecen Offensive opens. The 2nd Ukrainian Front (Group Pliev, the Seventh Guards, Sixth Guards Tank, Twenty-Seventh, Fortieth, Forty-Sixth and Fifty-Third Armies) attacks between Oradea and Arad, smashing the Hungarian Third Army. In the northeast of the country, the Soviet First Guards and Eighteenth Armies (4th Ukrainian Front) engage the First Panzer and Hungarian First Armies. Pancevo falls to the Soviet Forty-Sixth Army.

▲ ***Troops of the German Army Group F on the retreat north. The Soviet advances into Romania and Hungary threatened the army group with encirclement.***

OCTOBER 7

FINLAND, *LAND WAR*
The Soviet Fourteenth Army (96,806 men), Karelian Front, commences the Petsamo-Kirkenes Offensive against the German XIX Mountain Corps (56,000 troops) aimed at clearing the Germans from the Murmansk sector. Soviet preparations have been thorough, and Lieutenant-General Shcherbakov's Fourteenth Army has substantial support for the operation. This includes a total of 2100 mortars and artillery pieces plus 120 multiple rocket launchers. Air support consists of 747 bombers, ground-attack aircraft, fighters and reconnaissance types (German aircraft in this sector number 160). In the absence of suitable roads, many of the supplies needed to sustain the offensive will be transported by animals. To this end the Fourteenth Army has 141 horses and over 500 reindeer. In addition, dogs are on hand to detect wounded soldiers left on the battlefield, who will be removed on sleds, litters and flat-bottomed boats to field stations.

The offensive commences at 08:00 hours with an artillery barrage, the Soviets firing over 100,000 rounds in 150 minutes. Then the infantry of the 99th and 131st Rifle Corps attack. The 131st Rifle Corps breaks through German positions to establish a bridgehead on the west bank of the River Titovka, but the 99th

Rifle Corps struggles to advance in the face of determined opposition.

LITHUANIA, *LAND WAR*
The Soviet Fifth Guards Tank Army is on the outskirts of Memel, with the Forty-Third following close behind.

OCTOBER 8

FINLAND, *LAND WAR*
As the Soviet Fourteenth Army continues to make headway, General Rendulic orders the 6th Mountain Division of XIX Mountain Corps to withdraw to positions along the River Titovka. The 2nd Mountain Division is also to pull back to positions east of Luostari. Recognizing the peril German units face, front commander Meretskov orders the Fourteenth Army to capture Luostari by late on October 9.

HUNGARY, *LAND WAR*
Group Pliev has lanced 112km (70 miles) into German territory, and the Forty-Sixth Army is across the River Tisza near Szeged. The Soviet Sixth Tank Army has been held up by the German Sixth Army at Oradea.

YUGOSLAVIA, *LAND WAR*
The Soviet Fifty-Seventh Army captures Velika Plana as the Bulgarian First Army and Tito's XIII Corps attack units of Army Group E at Nis.

OCTOBER 9

FINLAND, *LAND WAR*
Units of the Soviet 99th Rifle Corps begin to cross the River Titovka on log rafts and at fording sites, though German pockets are still fighting on the east bank of the river. The absence of roads is seriously affecting the Soviet advance by delaying ammunition re-supply and the movement of artillery units. This is seriously depleting artillery support for the infantry. Overhead, the weather permits the Soviets to fly over 1000 air support sorties. The Germans respond with 200 air sorties.

USSR, *DIPLOMACY*
The Second Moscow Conference opens. Attended by Churchill, Stalin, Harriman and their advisors, it will concern the USSR's entry into the war against Japan; post-war division of the Balkans; and the future of Poland. The main focus of the conference is Soviet influence in a post-war Eastern Europe. Stalin debates with Churchill the influence that Britain and the USSR should have in the Balkans. Churchill writes details on a piece of paper that divides Romania, Greece, Yugoslavia, Hungary and Bulgaria between the Western Allies and the USSR. Recognizing the realities of the situation in Eastern Europe, Churchill gives Stalin 90 percent of Romania, 10 percent of Greece, 50 percent of Yugoslavia, 50 percent of Hungary and 75 percent of Bulgaria (subsequent debates between the British and Russian foreign secretaries altered the percentages of Bulgaria and Hungary to suit the Russians). Churchill's main interest is Greece, and, with Stalin's approval, he authorizes British soldiers to be dispatched there. But Churchill's proposal of a meeting between the leader of the Polish government in London and the Soviets to determine a Polish-Soviet frontier comes to nothing.

OCTOBER 10

FINLAND, *LAND WAR*
The position of the German XIX Mountain Corps is perilous: it faces an

DECISIVE MOMENT

DESERTION OF GERMANY'S AXIS ALLIES

While Germany was enjoying military success on the Eastern Front, her Axis allies – Hungary, Romania and Bulgaria – were happy enough to be Berlin's friends. However, the Wehrmacht defeat at Stalingrad in early 1943 was a turning point in their relations with Germany.

In Hungary, with the approach of the Red Army in late 1943, Regent Admiral Horthy decided to try to broker a peace deal with the Soviets (cautious approaches through the Vatican and intermediaries had begun in the winter of 1943). Hitler was well aware of Hungary's position, and therefore ordered the occupation of the country in March 1944, although this did not prevent Horthy from maintaining contact with the Soviets. On October 15, 1944, Horthy dismissed the pro-German cabinet and announced that he had signed an armistice with the USSR. This resulted in Horthy and his son being seized by the Germans and the regent being forced to agree to the establishment of a German puppet government, under the pro-German Dome Sztojay, in March 1944 (Horthy died in exile in Portugal in 1967).

The approach of the Red Army towards Bulgaria in 1944 prompted Premier Dobri Bozhilov to speed up negotiations with the Western Allies while trying to avoid German occupation. Bulgaria had never declared war on the USSR, but that did not stop her from being invaded by the Red Army. Bozhilov failed in his entreaties to the West, as did his successor Ivan Bagrianov. In fact, on September 8, 1944, Premier Konstantin Muraviev was forced to declare war on Germany because the Red Army was on Bulgarian soil.

Romania was viewed by Berlin as of more importance than Bulgaria and Hungary because of its Ploesti oil fields, which were crucial to the German war effort. Romania made significant contributions to the effort on the Eastern Front, but by late 1943 Romanian dictator Ion Antonescu was using his ambassador to Turkey, Alexandru Cretzianu, as an intermediary with the Western Allies to seek a way out of the war. In addition, King Michael and royalist army officers formed a National Democratic Bloc with the same intention, although their efforts were separate from Antonescu's. The Red Army victory at Jassy on August 20, 1944, and attendant heavy Romanian losses, brought matters to a head. Three days later Michael announced on national radio that Romania had switched sides. Antonescu was arrested, and after the war was executed after being held in Moscow's Lubianka prison for two years.

▼ ***Blindfolded members of the Polish Home Army are escorted by German officers to discuss surrender terms. The uprising in Warsaw resulted in 200,000 civilian dead.***

envelopment of its right flank by the Soviet 126th Light Rifle Corps, an enemy breakthrough towards Luostari and Petsamo, and an envelopment on its left flank by naval infantry. Indeed, German positions along the Srednii Isthmus are battered by a 47,000-round, 90-minute artillery barrage. Following this Soviet naval infantry attack and break through the German lines. To the south, the 126th Light Rifle Corps is now west of Luostari, having marched over 72km (45 miles) in 72 hours. Meanwhile, the Soviet 127th Light Rifle Corps crosses the River Petsamo. There is fierce fighting between the Soviet 131st Rifle Corps and the German 6th Mountain Division along the Russian Road.

LITHUANIA, *LAND WAR*
The Soviet Fifty-First Army captures Palanga, thus cutting off the German Sixteenth and Eighteenth Armies in the Kurland Peninsula. The Forty-Third and Fifth Guards Tank Armies are at Memel as the Second Guards Army advances towards Tilsit.

LATVIA, *LAND WAR*
The Germans have some success at Riga when they repulse an assault by the 1st, 2nd and 3rd Baltic Fronts, allowing the Eighteenth Army to escape to Kurland before the Soviets pierce the defences.

HUNGARY, *LAND WAR*
The Soviet Fortieth Army forces the German Eighth and Hungarian Second Armies back from Cluj as the Sixth Tank Army advances to Debrecen, where it is counterattacked and partly encircled.

YUGOSLAVIA, *LAND WAR*
The Soviet Fifty-Seventh Army captures Petrovac.

▼ ***Infantry of the 2nd Ukrainian Front in Hungary. Army Group South fought with great skill as it pulled back – by October 20 the Soviets had lost 500 tanks in Hungary.***

OCTOBER 12

LATVIA, *LAND WAR*
The German Eighteenth Army is having difficulty holding the Riga–Tukums line.

HUNGARY, *LAND WAR*
The Soviet Seventh Guards Army captures Oradea while, at Debrecen, the Soviet Sixth Tank Army launches a counterattack that frees its trapped units.

YUGOSLAVIA, *LAND WAR*
The Soviet Fifty-Seventh Army, 4th Guards Mechanized Corps, plus the Yugoslav I and XIV Corps, are nearing Belgrade, where Army Group F has 57,000 troops inside and around the city. The partisans and Soviet Forty-Sixth Army capture Subotica.

OCTOBER 13

FINLAND, *LAND WAR*
The German 163rd Infantry Division launches a counterattack to the north and west of Luostari (which is now in Soviet hands) as the 2nd Mountain Division digs in between Luostari and Petsamo along Arctic Ocean Highway.

OCTOBER 14

YUGOSLAVIA, *LAND WAR*
As Soviet and Yugoslav forces battle their way into Belgrade, the Yugoslav XII Corps severs all roads south of the River Sava, thus severing the Germans' line of retreat.

OCTOBER 15

FINLAND, *LAND WAR*
The Soviet Fourteenth Army takes the Petsamo region, forcing the Germans to retreat to Norway.

LAVTIA, *LAND WAR*
The Soviet Sixty-Seventh Army captures Riga.

OCTOBER 16

LATVIA, *LAND WAR*
The Soviet Sixth Guards Army assaults Skrunda and the Fifty-First Army at Libau as the Red Army attempts to reduce the Kurland Pocket. The attacks make few gains.

EAST PRUSSIA, *LAND WAR*
The Third Panzer Army is attacked by the Soviet Second Guards, Fifth and Eleventh Guards Armies as the Soviets attempt to reach the River Niemen. The Third Panzer's southern flank is pushed back 10km (6 miles).

YUGOSLAVIA, *LAND WAR*
House-to-house fighting rages in Belgrade as Soviet and Yugoslav forces advance.

HUNGARY, *POLITICS*
Admiral Horthy announces on national radio that he thinks Germany is on the verge of defeat, which prompts Hitler to order his arrest. An élite commando unit led by Otto Skorzeny enters Budapest and seizes Horthy. The pro-Nazi Arrow Cross regime is installed as the new government.

OCTOBER 18

FINLAND, *LAND WAR*
The second phase of the Soviet Petsamo-Kirkenes Offensive begins with attacks by the 99th and 131st Rifle Corps towards the Norwegian border. The 24th Rifle Division crosses the border and penetrates 5km (3.1 miles) into German positions.

OCTOBER 19

NORWAY, *LAND WAR*
The Soviet Fourteenth Army launches an attack from Petsamo against the German XIX Mountain Corps.

EAST PRUSSIA, *LAND WAR*
The Soviet Fifth, Eleventh Guards, Thirty-First and Thirty-Ninth Armies break though the lines of the Third Panzer Army, forcing it to withdraw.

HUNGARY, *LAND WAR*
The Soviet Sixth Tank Army breaks into Debrecen.

YUGOSLAVIA, *LAND WAR*
An attempt to relieve Belgrade by Army Group F is defeated with heavy German losses. Inside the city the defenders are nearing annihilation.

OCTOBER 20

HUNGARY, *LAND WAR*
Debrecen falls to the Soviet Sixth Tank Army and Group Pliev.

YUGOSLAVIA, *LAND WAR*
The Belgrade garrison is wiped out: 15,000 are dead and 9000 made prisoner. Soviet losses are 4400 killed and 14,500 wounded. Yugoslav losses are unknown.

OCTOBER 21

FINLAND, *LAND WAR*
The Soviet 99th Rifle Corps attempts to reach the Norwegian border between

◀ *Troops of the German Twentieth Mountain Army in northern Finland on their way to the Norwegian border. The German retreat from Finland never turned into a rout.*

Rova and Salmiiarvi but is held up by strong German resistance. It reaches the border by the evening of the 22nd. Meanwhile, the 126th Light Rifle Corps reaches the main road leading north from Akhmalakhti to Kirkenes but is then forced to halt due to ammunition and food shortages.

The Soviet 31st and 127th Rifle Corps are closing in on Nikel. However, an assault by German troops allows 1000 of their comrades in the Nikel area to withdraw and escape the Soviet trap. In fact, the Germans are pulling back from Nikel, Akhmalakhti and Salmiiarvi.

OCTOBER 22

NORWAY, *LAND WAR*
Nikel has fallen to the Soviet 367th Rifle Division. The second phase of the Soviet offensive has forced the German XIX Mountain Corps to withdraw to Kirkenes, and the 163rd Infantry and 3rd Mountain Divisions to withdraw southwest towards Nautsi and Ivalo.

EAST PRUSSIA, *LAND WAR*
The Third Panzer Army launches a counterattack around Gumbinnen, which inflicts heavy losses on the Eleventh Guards Army and halts the Soviet advance.

YUGOSLAVIA, *LAND WAR*
The Soviet Fifty-Seventh Army captures Zemun as it advances from Belgrade.

OCTOBER 24

NORWAY, *LAND WAR*
The Soviet 10th Guards Rifle Division (131st Rifle Corps) is only 10km (6.25 miles) south of Kirkenes, fighting its way through a series of iron ore mines.

OCTOBER 25

NORWAY, *LAND WAR*
Units of the Soviet 99th Rifle Corps are fighting their way into Kirkenes from the south as the 131st Rifle Corps closes in from the southeast. The city falls into Soviet hands in the afternoon.

HUNGARY, *LAND WAR*
III Panzer Corps recaptures Nyireghaza, thus creating an escape route for the German Eighth Army.

OCTOBER 27

NORWAY, *LAND WAR*
The 83rd Rifle Division (31st Rifle Corps) drives German defenders from Nautsi.

OCTOBER 28

NORWAY, *LAND WAR*
The Germans order the evacuation of the population of Finnmark east of Lyngen. All houses and installations are to be destroyed to deny their use to the Soviets.

POLAND, *ATROCITIES*
The last transport of Jews to Auschwitz are gassed (2000 from Theresianstadt).

▲ *A Red Army M1938 120mm mortar on the outskirts of Budapest. This regimental-level mortar was an excellent weapon, and was directly copied by the Germans.*

OCTOBER 29

HUNGARY, *LAND WAR*
The Soviet Budapest Offensive begins. The Forty-Sixth Army attacks the Hungarian Third Army at Kecskemet, and the Seventh Guards Army breaks through the German Sixth Army. Meanwhile, the German Eighth Army breaks out of the Nyireghaza salient.

KEY WEAPONS

SU-152

Nicknamed *Zvierboy* (animal killer), the Soviet SU-152 tank destroyer was built at the Uralmash factory in Chelyabinsk and initially designated the KV-14 (the KV-1 chassis was the basis of the vehicle). The design and development had been very quick: the prototypes were completed in a record 25 days, and barely a month after the Red Army had captured its first German Tiger tank and the Russians had worked out the best gun/vehicle combination to knock it out. The first 12 SU-152s saw action at Kursk in July 1943 and were quite successful at destroying German Tigers and Panthers (an additional nine arrived as reinforcements during the battle). The cartridge and shell for the 152mm L/32 howitzer were loaded separately, thus the rate of fire was only two to three rounds per minute. Each vehicle carried an explosive charge to destroy the howitzer and engine if it had to be abandoned or was likely to be captured. The SU-152 was also used as an assault tank as well as a tank destroyer.

Weight: 45,500kg (100,100lb)
Crew: 5
Engine: 600hp W-2K 12-cylinder diesel
Speed: 43kmh (27mph)
Range: 330km (206 miles)
Length: 8.95m (29.3ft)
Width: 3.25m (10.6ft)
Height: 2.45m (8ft)
Armament: 1 x 152mm howitzer
Ammunition: 20 rounds
Armour: front (maximum): 75mm (2.95in); side: 60mm (2.36in)

NOVEMBER 3

HUNGARY, *LAND WAR*

The Soviet Forty-Sixth Army, having brushed aside the 22nd SS Cavalry Division, enters the outer defences of Budapest. A German counterattack against the army fails.

NOVEMBER 4

HUNGARY, *LAND WAR*

The Soviet Forty-Sixth Army penetrates into the suburbs of Budapest but then grinds to a halt. The Germans have deployed III Panzer Corps near the city; IV Panzer Corps at Jaszbereny; and LVII Panzer Corps around Cegled and Szolnok. Both latter locations are soon captured by the Soviet Seventh Guards Army.

NOVEMBER 5

FINLAND, *LAND WAR*

A detachment from the Soviet 31st Rifle Corps makes contact with Finnish troops at Ivalo as German forces in the area retreat into Norway. In two weeks the 31st Rifle Corps has advanced a total of 150km (94 miles).

NOVEMBER 6

USSR, *ARMED FORCES*

British ships deliver to Murmansk 9907 former Soviet prisoners who had fought for the German Army and were captured in France. They will each receive six years' exile - surprisingly lenient considering the Red Army's harsh penal code.

NOVEMBER 7

HUNGARY, *LAND WAR*

The Soviet Fifty-Seventh Army crosses the River Danube near Batina and Apatin as the Fourth Guards Army heads for Lakes Velencei and Balaton.

NOVEMBER 8

HUNGARY, *ATROCITIES*

Deportations of Jews from Hungary resume, organized by the Germans and members of the Arrow Cross government. Some 70,000 Jews are marched from Budapest towards the Austrian border.

▲ ***Troops and vehicles of the 13th Panzer Division, part of the garrison of Budapest. Only 60 percent of the division was in Budapest – 7255 men and 24 tanks.***

NOVEMBER 13

GREECE, *LAND WAR*

The Bulgarian First Army ejects Army Group E from Skopje although, as most Axis forces have left Greece, this does not trap the army group.

NOVEMBER 18

HUNGARY, *LAND WAR*

The third attempt by the Soviet Forty-Sixth Army to establish a bridgehead on the west bank of the River Danube fails.

NOVEMBER 21

HUNGARY, *LAND WAR*

The Soviet Forty-Sixth Army finally establishes a bridgehead on the Danube, on Csepel Island, and begins ferrying units across the river.

ALBANIA, *PARTISAN WAR*

Partisans capture Tirana and Durazza.

NOVEMBER 24

ESTONIA, *LAND WAR*

The Soviet Eighth Army clears Yezel Island of enemy forces, thus bringing to an end the campaign in the Moonzund Islands. Since the middle of September, the various Soviet fronts in the northern theatre have suffered the following losses: Leningrad Front, 6000 killed and 22,500 wounded; 1st Baltic Front, 24,000 killed and 79,000 wounded; 2nd Baltic Front, 15,000 killed and 58,000 wounded; and 3rd Baltic Front, 11,800 killed and 43,000 wounded.

NOVEMBER 26

HUNGARY, *LAND WAR*

Soviet gains continue apace, with the Sixth Guards Tank Army capturing Hatvan.

DECEMBER 2

HUNGARY, *LAND WAR*

With Budapest and the Hungarian oil fields at Nagykanitza under threat, the Second Panzer Army is deployed south of Lake Balaton. The German Sixth Army is deployed to the north between the lake and Hatvan, with the German Eighth Army farther north near Miskolc.

DECEMBER 5

HUNGARY, *LAND WAR*

The 2nd Ukrainian Front's Sixth Guards Tank, Seventh Guards and Forty-Sixth Armies and Group Pliev launch an attack from northeast of Budapest. The Soviets suffer massive losses but grind forward.

DECEMBER 9

HUNGARY, *LAND WAR*

The Soviets are closing in on Budapest, with the Forty-Sixth Army taking Ercsi,

◀ ***Soviet infantry on the outskirts of Budapest. To capture the city the Red Army amassed no less than 15 artillery or mortar brigades and regiments.***

◀ German Tiger tanks in Hungary in late December. By the end of 1944 the Germans and Hungarians had 60,000 troops in the Budapest area; the Red Army had 110,000 men.

the Forty-Sixth and Fourth Guards Armies linking up near Lake Velencei and the Sixth Guards Tank Army reaching the River Danube at Vac, which then repulses a counterattack by the Feldherrnhalle and 13th Panzer Divisions.

DECEMBER 13

HUNGARY, *LAND WAR*

The Soviet Seventh Guards Army is only 10km (6 miles) north of Budapest.

DECEMBER 20

HUNGARY, *LAND WAR*

The Soviet Sixth Guards Army reaches the River Hron as the Seventh Guards Army nears Esztergom, to be halted by German counterattacks. The Germans also manage to slow the advance of the 3rd Ukrainian Front south of Budapest.

DECEMBER 23

HUNGARY, *LAND WAR*

The noose tightens around Budapest: the Soviet Fourth Guards and Forty-Sixth Armies are nearing Esztergom, brushing aside an attack by the 8th Panzer Division, and have cut roads and railway lines west out of the city.

DECEMBER 27

HUNGARY, *LAND WAR*

The Soviets capture Gran, encircling German and Hungarian units in the grandly titled "Fortress Budapest". The garrison comprises the Hungarian I Corps: 10th Infantry Division, 12th Infantry Division, 1st Armoured Division (parts of), Hussar Division (parts of), Group Billnitzer (remnants of four assault gun battalions), 1st Parachute Battalion, Budapest Watch Battalion, five Royal Gendarmerie battalions, Budapest air defence units, three engineer battalions, the Budapest University Assault Battalion, the Royal Life Guard Battalion, an Arrow Cross unit (1500 troops) and the Budapest police. German units comprise XI SS Mountain Corps, 8th SS Cavalry Division, 22nd SS Cavalry Division, 13th Panzer Division, Feldherrnhalle Division, 271st Infantry Division, Flak Regiment 12, 4th SS Police Regiment and four infantry battalions. Altogether this force is 188,000 strong. An impressive number, but many are of dubious combat quality, especially the Hungarian units.

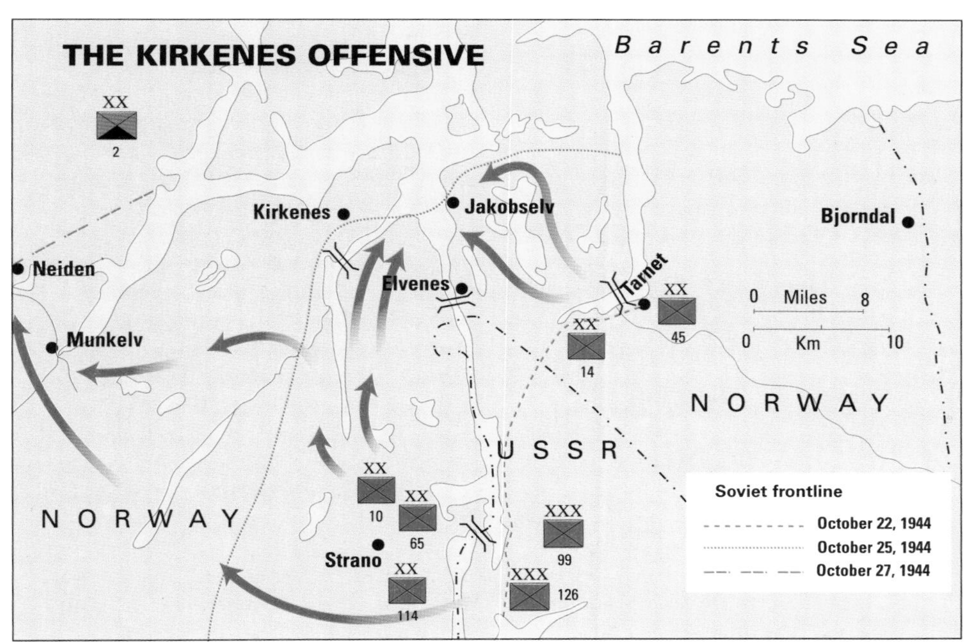

DECEMBER 29

HUNGARY, *LAND WAR*

The battle for Budapest is raging as the Soviets batter the Pest and Buda districts of the city. The Soviets offer surrender terms to Axis troops in both districts, an offer that results in the Pest emissary being shot by the Germans and the Buda emissary being killed by Red Army artillery fire while making his way back to friendly lines.

DECEMBER 30

HUNGARY, *LAND WAR*

Red Army artillery (100 guns) commences a massive barrage against Pest, accompanied by infantry assaults of the 2nd Ukrainian Front.

DECEMBER 31

HUNGARY, *LAND WAR*

The Germans manage to halt the Soviet advance into Pest, though Budapest continues to be shelled incessantly.

The first five months of 1945 witnessed the Red Army break the will and strength of the Wehrmacht to bring about the destruction of the Third Reich and an end to World War II in Europe. The price was high, especially during the Battle of Berlin, where the Germans fought with a desperate courage, reinforced by the knowledge that they would receive little mercy at the hands of the vengeful Russians. The cost of capturing the "lair of the fascist beast" was over 80,000 Red Army dead.

◀ *Twice Hero of the Soviet Union, Marshal Georgi Zhukov was the commander of the 1st Belorussian Front in early 1945 and earmarked to lead the drive on Berlin.*

JANUARY 1

HUNGARY, *LAND WAR*
The Hungarian 10th and 11th Divisions are forced to withdraw from parts of Pest.

USSR, *STRATEGY*
With 11,500,000 troops under its command, the Stavka begins the new year with the resolution and resources to bring the war on the Eastern Front to an end. The 2nd Belorussian (881,000 troops) and 3rd Belorussian (708,000 troops) Fronts will strike into East Prussia and Pomerania to attack Army Group Centre. The 1st Belorussian (1,028,000 troops) and 1st Ukrainian (1,083,000 troops) Fronts will annihilate Army Group A, advance to the Oder and Neisse Rivers and then capture Pomerania and Silesia.

JANUARY 2

SLOVAKIA, *LAND WAR*
In a bid to relieve Budapest, IV SS Panzer Corps launches an assault from Komarno against the 4th Guards Army, which drives the Soviets back 32km (20 miles).

JANUARY 6

HUNGARY, *LAND WAR*
The Soviet Sixth Guards Tank and Seventh Guards Armies attack along the River Hron to establish a bridgehead. The 22nd SS Cavalry Division abandons Soroksar in the Pest bridgehead.

JANUARY 8

HUNGARY, *LAND WAR*
After only a day, a counterattack by III Panzer Corps grinds to a halt. The Soviet Sixth Guards Tank Army advances towards Komarom on the Danube to engage and then wipe out LVII Panzer Corps.

◀ *The citizens of Warsaw celebrate freedom from the Nazi yoke. Unfortunately for the Poles, they were about to endure over 40 years of Soviet oppression.*

JANUARY 11

HUNGARY, *LAND WAR*

III Panzer Corps can go no farther, having been fought to a standstill. At Budapest the Soviets make further gains in Pest.

JANUARY 12

POLAND, *LAND WAR*

In response to Churchill's request to relieve pressure on the Western Allies being attacked in the Ardennes, Stalin opens the Soviet Vistula-Oder Offensive today. The 1st Ukrainian Front (Third Guards, Fourth Guards Tank, Fifth Guards, Sixth, Thirteenth, Twenty-First, Fifty-Second, Fifty-Ninth and Sixtieth Armies) launches a devastating attack against the German Fourth Panzer and Seventeenth Armies, which are soon reeling. The Soviet Fourth Tank Army is then fed into the attack, its tanks nearing Kielce.

HUNGARY, *LAND WAR*

IV SS Panzer Corps is within 19km (12 miles) of Budapest, but is then ordered to pull back.

GERMANY, *ARMED FORCES*

Fuel shortages are crippling the army's mobility. Units are increasingly using horses to move supplies and tow artillery pieces. There are currently 1,136,318 horses on the books of the Wehrmacht, of which 923,679 are on active service.

JANUARY 13

EAST PRUSSIA, *LAND WAR*

The Soviet 3rd Belorussian Front (Second Guards, Fifth, Eleventh Guards, Twentieth, Thirty-First and Thirty-Ninth Armies) opens its offensive and runs into strong enemy resistance around Kattenau.

POLAND, *LAND WAR*

The 1st Ukrainian Front's Fifty-Ninth Army is nearing Krakow, although German resistance is stiffening. After defeating a counterattack by XXIV Panzer Corps at Chmielnik in a bruising battle, the Fourth Tank Army continues to advance.

XXXXVIII Panzer Corps is shattered by assaults by the Third Guards Tank, Fifth Guards and Fifty-Second Armies.

JANUARY 14

EAST PRUSSIA, *LAND WAR*

The Third Panzer Army's 5th Panzer Division retakes Kattenau. The 2nd Belorussian Front (Second Shock, Third, Fifth Guards Tank, Forty-Eighth, Forty-Ninth, Fiftieth, Sixty-Fifth and Seventieth Armies) attacks from the River Narew, spearheaded by the Second Shock, Third and Forty-Eighth Armies. But falling snow negates Soviet air superiority.

POLAND, *LAND WAR*

The 1st Belorussian (Polish First, First Guards Tank, Third Shock, Fifth Shock, Eighth Guards, Thirty-Third, Forty-Seventh and Sixty-Ninth Armies) and 2nd Belorussian Fronts launch attacks from the Pulawy and Magnuszew bridgeheads. The Soviets achieve immediate success: the Fifth Shock, Eighth Guards and Sixty-Ninth Armies defeat a counterattack by the 19th and 25th Panzer Divisions (LVI Panzer Corps) and then sweep around Warsaw. From Pulawy the Soviet Third, Fifth Shock and Eighth Guards Armies shatter VIII and LVI Panzer Corps. The 1st Ukrainian Front has ripped open the German line at Baranow, allowing the Third Guards and Thirteenth Armies to advance unimpeded. Hitler is forced to deploy the *Grossdeutschland* Panzer Corps from Army Group Centre to Army Group A.

SLOVAKIA, *LAND WAR*

The Soviet Twenty-Seventh Army captures Lunenec in Slovakia, but lacks additional forces for exploitation purposes.

JANUARY 15

POLAND, *LAND WAR*

The 2nd Belorussian Front, supported by the Fourth Air Army, has ripped apart the German Second Army on the Narew, incurring heavy casualties. To the south, the Soviet Eighth Guards Army advances towards Radom, and the First Guards Army to Lodz and Posen. The Polish First and Forty-Seventh Armies are enveloping Warsaw while, at Kielce, XXXXII Corps is annihilated by the Soviet Third Guards and Thirteenth Armies.

JANUARY 16

POLAND, *LAND WAR*

German forces in Poland are facing catastrophe: XXIV Panzer Corps struggles to break out of Kielce; parts of XXXXVI Panzer Corps are now trapped in Warsaw; and the capture of Czestochowa by the

▼ *Soviet IS-2 Joseph Stalin heavy tanks in East Prussia. Armed with a 122mm gun, the IS-2 was designed to support breakthrough operations rather than tank-versus-tank combat.*

JANUARY 17

▶ ***In January SS chief Himmler (second from right) became the commander of Army Group Vistula. His attempt at a field campaign was largely disastrous.***

Third Guards Tank, Fifth Guards and Fifty-Second Armies has put the northern flank of the Seventeenth Army in danger.

GERMANY, *ARMED FORCES*
Hitler dismisses General Josef Harpe as commander of Army Group A, replacing him with Ferdinand Schörner. General Lothar Rendulic assumes command of Army Group North.

JANUARY 17

POLAND, *LAND WAR*
The Red Army captures what is left of Warsaw as the Third Guards Tank and Fifth Guards Armies near Krakow. Zawiercie falls to the Fifty-Second Army, and Radomsko to the Third Guards Army.

HUNGARY, *LAND WAR*
IV SS Panzer Corps deploys to attack the Fourth Guards and Twenty-Sixth Armies between Lakes Balaton and Velencei.

JANUARY 18

EAST PRUSSIA, *LAND WAR*
The Forty-Third Army pushes back the Third Panzer Army towards Königsberg.

POLAND, *LAND WAR*
The *Grossdeutschland* Panzer Corps has engaged the First Guards Tank Army near Lodz, and the remnants of XXIV Panzer and XXXXII Corps are retreating west. The Soviet Fourth Guards Tank, Fifty-Ninth and Sixtieth Armies are threatening Krakow and the German Seventeenth Army with encirclement.

HUNGARY, *LAND WAR*
Pest falls to the Red Army as IV SS Panzer Corps tries to relieve the city.

POLAND, *ATROCITIES*
In sub-zero temperatures, the Nazis evacuate more than 50,000 prisoners from Auschwitz west towards Germany. Many thousands will die from starvation or hypothermia in the march to other camps; others will be shot when they fail to keep up. Most of the survivors will end up in other concentration camps, such as Bergen-Belsen, Buchenwald and Dachau.

JANUARY 19

POLAND, *LAND WAR*
The Soviet momentum is gathering pace as the Fifth Guards Tank Army takes Mlawa, the Eighth Guards Army takes Lodz; the Fifty-Ninth Tarnow and Krakow is abandoned by the Seventeenth Army.

HUNGARY, *LAND WAR*
IV SS Panzer Corps reaches the Danube at Dunapentele and then advances north towards Budapest. The Soviet Twenty-Seventh Army is ordered from north of Budapest to block its march.

JANUARY 21

EAST PRUSSIA, *LAND WAR*
Tannenberg is evacuated by the Germans as the Second Shock Army threatens to cut off the German Second, Fourth and Third Panzer Armies in East Prussia. Gumbinnen is captured by the Soviet Twenty-Eighth Army. The entire civilian population of East Prussia is fleeing west.

JANUARY 22

EAST PRUSSIA, *LAND WAR*
The Soviet Forty-Eighth Army captures Allenstein; and the Fifth Guards Tank, Deutsch Eylau.

POLAND, *LAND WAR*
The Soviet Third Shock Army encircles Bromberg as Gneizno falls to the Second Guards Tank Army. The lead units of the Fifth Guards Army reach the River Oder, quickly establishing a bridgehead, and the Fourth Tank Army crosses the river at Goeben. Also nearing the river is the *Grossdeutschland* Panzer Corps and the remnants of XXIV Panzer Corps, which are conducting a fighting withdrawal.

HUNGARY, *LAND WAR*
IV SS Panzer Corps is battling the Fourth Guards Army as the German Sixth Army captures Szekesfehervar.

JANUARY 23

EAST PRUSSIA, *LAND WAR*
The Fifth Guards Tank Army is driving towards Elbing on the Baltic, thus threatening to cut off Wehrmacht forces in East Prussia.

KEY PERSONALITIES

ALEKSANDR VASILEVSKY

Born in 1895, Vasilevsky was a captain in the Russian Civil War and thereafter was involved in the Red Army's combat training. During the 1930s, he rose rapidly: he entered the General Staff Academy in 1936; became the first deputy of operations from 1939 to May 1940; and headed the operations directorate from June 1941. During the Russo-German War, Vasilevsky spent his time on attachment to various fronts and coordinating multi-front actions, becoming Chief of the General Staff in June 1942. In February 1943, Vasilevsky was promoted to marshal of the USSR. From June to August 1944 he was coordinating the operations of the 1st Baltic and 3rd Belorussia Fronts. Earmarked for command of Soviet forces in the Far East, Vasilevsky was forced to take command of the 3rd Belorussian Front in February 1945 when its commander was killed. However, after the end of the war in Europe, he led the offensive against the Japanese – Operation August Storm – in August 1945. He became defence minister in 1949 and then first deputy minister of defence until his retirement in December 1957. He died in 1977.

EAST PRUSSIA, *SEA WAR*
The Kriegsmarine begins the evacuation of thousands of civilian refugees from East Prussia and the Danzig area.
POLAND, *LAND WAR*
The Soviet Twenty-First Army reaches the Oder near Oppeln, and the Thirteenth Army engages in heavy combat at Steinau as it struggles to create a bridgehead.
HUNGARY, *LAND WAR*
IV SS Panzer Corps' attack is being contained by the 3rd Ukrainian Front. The Soviet Romanian Fourth and Fortieth Armies (2nd Ukrainian Front) launch an assault against the German Eighth Army along the Slovak-Hungarian border.

JANUARY 24

EAST PRUSSIA, *LAND WAR*
The Soviet Fifth Guards Tank Army captures Elbing, thus cutting off all or parts of the German Second, Third Panzer and Fourth Armies – 400,000 troops. Hitler forbids any retreat west.
POLAND, *LAND WAR*
The Soviet Sixtieth Army captures Gleiwitz, and the First Guards Tank Army cuts off the German garrison in Posen.
HUNGARY, *LAND WAR*
IV SS Panzer Corps' attack grinds to a halt 32km (20 miles) short of Budapest due to logistical problems and the resistance of the Soviet Fourth Guards Army.

JANUARY 26

EAST PRUSSIA, *LAND WAR*
The Soviet Second Shock Army assumes control of Marienburg, although the Forty-Eighth Army around Elbing is encountering stiff resistance from the German Fourth Army.
POLAND, *LAND WAR*
The Soviet Third Shock Army takes Bromberg as 100,000 German troops of the Seventeenth Army are threatened by encirclement in Silesia. Inside Posen, 60,000 German troops and Volkssturm are holding off attacks by the Eighth Guards Army.
GERMANY, *ARMED FORCES*
The OKW renames its army groups: Army Group North, trapped in Kurland, becomes Army Group Kurland; Army Group Centre, isolated in East Prussia, is now Army Group North; and Army Group A is renamed Army Group Centre. There is also the newly raised Army Group Vistula, comprising the Second and Eleventh Armies and commanded by the head of the SS, Heinrich Himmler.

JANUARY 27

EAST PRUSSIA, *LAND WAR*
The Soviet Forty-Third Army captures Memel after a fierce battle. The German Fourth Army launches an attack aimed at linking up with the Second Army on the west bank of the Vistula at Marienburg. However, Soviet ground and air power are soon inflicting heavy casualties on the German divisions.
POLAND, *LAND WAR*
The German Seventeenth Army falls back out of the Kattowice Pocket, and the Red Army takes possession of Upper Silesia. The 1st Ukrainian Front is now near Breslau. The Red Army liberates Auschwitz and finds 600 corpses of prisoners whom the Germans had murdered several hours before they fled, plus 7650 ill prisoners who survived because the Germans fled too hastily to force them to join the forced marches west.
HUNGARY, *LAND WAR*
The German Sixth Army recaptures Szekesfehervar but IV SS Panzer Corps is now on the defensive, being assaulted by the 3rd Ukrainian Front.

JANUARY 28

EAST PRUSSIA, *LAND WAR*
The German Fourth Army continues to be pummelled by heavy Soviet firepower around Wormditt.
POLAND, *LAND WAR*
The 1st Ukrainian Front takes Katowice and Leszno.

▲ ***The Red Army in East Prussia. As usual, massive firepower was deployed. The 3rd Belorussian Front fired 120,000 artillery rounds on January 13 alone.***

GERMANY, *STRATEGY*
Berliners are ordered to work on the digging of anti-tank ditches.

JANUARY 31

EAST PRUSSIA, *LAND WAR*
Heilsberg and Freidland fall to the Soviets.
GERMANY, *LAND WAR*
The Second Guards Tank Army is now in Zehden, only 96km (60 miles) from Berlin. The Soviet Fifth Shock and Eighth Guards Armies are also on the Oder, but have been halted by resistance. A unit of the Soviet Fifth Shock Army, commanded by Colonel Khariton Episenko, occupies Kienitz. At the railway station the station master asks Episenko if he is going to allow the Berlin train to leave. Episenko replies: "I am sorry, station master, but that is impossible, the passenger service to Berlin will undergo a short interruption – let's say until the end of the war."
BALTIC, *SEA WAR*
The German liner *Wilhelm Gustav*, which is filled with civilian refugees from East Prussia, is sunk by the Soviet submarine *S13* off the Hela Peninsula. More than 7000 people drown.

▼ ***The ruins of Warsaw following the retreat of German forces. Before they left, the Nazis had blown up large areas of the city.***

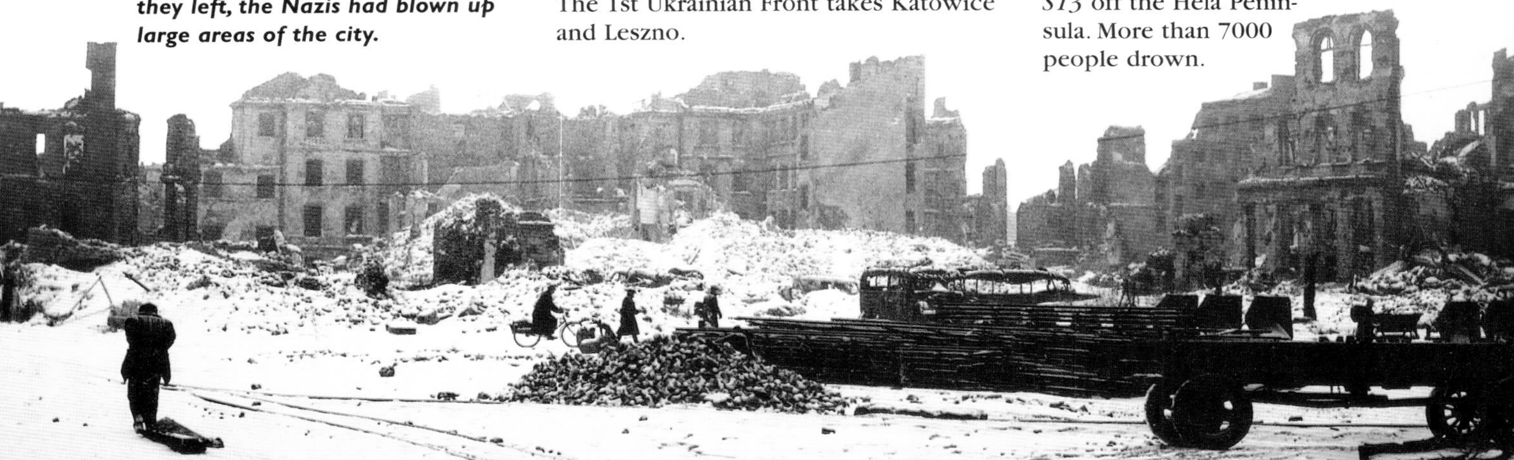

FEBRUARY 1

GERMANY, *LAND WAR*
An attack by V SS Mountain Corps against the First Guards Tank Army at Kunersdorf fails; Soviet forces then counterattack and force the Germans back.

FEBRUARY 2

GERMANY, *LAND WAR*
The Soviet Eighth Guards Army is crossing the River Oder as the First Guards Tank Army assaults Küstrin. The German Ninth Army is engaging both formations.

FEBRUARY 3

ESTONIA, *LAND WAR*
In the Kurland Pocket, the 2nd Baltic Front is attacking German defences at Libau.

EAST PRUSSIA, *LAND WAR*
The Second Guards and Thirty-First Armies capture Landsberg and Bartenstein.

POLAND, *LAND WAR*
Army Group Vistula cannot hold Soviet attacks towards the Baltic, despite the efforts of the Second and Eleventh Armies.

GERMANY, *LAND WAR*
At Küstrin, the Soviet Sixth Guards Army captures Ohlau and Brieg on the River Oder. To date the 1st Belorussian Front has lost 17,000 killed and 60,000 wounded, and the 1st Ukrainian Front 26,000 killed and 89,000 wounded.

FEBRUARY 7

POLAND, *LAND WAR*
The First Guards Tank, Second Guards Tank, Third Shock, Forty-Seventh and Sixty-First Armies of the 1st Belorussian Front (359,000 troops) and the whole 2nd Belorussian Front (560,000 troops) are now battering Army Group Vistula and lancing through its lines.

FEBRUARY 8

POLAND, *LAND WAR*
The 1st Ukrainian Front launches the Lower Silesian Offensive from the Oder north and south of Breslau. At first the infantry and armour find it heavy going due to a thaw. The German Seventeenth Army defends well but, eventually, the Fifty-Fourth Army breaks through at Steinau.

FEBRUARY 10

EAST PRUSSIA, *LAND WAR*
The 3rd Belorussian Front attacks the German Fourth Army near Heilsberg.

GERMANY, *LAND WAR*
The 2nd Belorussian Front opens the East Pomeranian Offensive towards Neustettin.

FEBRUARY 11

EAST PRUSSIA, *LAND WAR*
The Soviet Forty-Eighth Army captures Wormditt.

GERMANY, *LAND WAR*
The 1st Ukrainian Front forces the German Seventeenth Army back from the River Oder to the River Neisse. Glogau and 18,000 German troops have now been encircled.

HUNGARY, *LAND WAR*
The garrison of Buda attempts to break out, but the 28,000 troops suffer greatly at the hands of Soviet firepower.

▲ German prisoners of war trudge into Soviet captivity. Despite the hopeless situation, most German units retained good combat cohesion in 1945.

USSR, *DIPLOMACY*
The Yalta Conference opens in the Crimea, attended by Churchill, Stalin and Roosevelt. Stalin demands a strong, pro-communist government in Poland to guarantee the future security of the USSR. As the Red Army controls most of Eastern Europe, the British and Americans have little choice but to agree. The conference also confirms the decision to form a United Nations organization. Also agreed is the future division of Germany. Roosevelt's decision that the capture of Berlin is not a prime US objective will ensure that the Red Army will be the first to reach the city.

FEBRUARY 12

HUNGARY, *LAND WAR*
The breakout from Buda costs the Germans 12,000 killed or captured.

▼ T-34s of Zhukov's 1st Belorussian Front drive into Germany. Zhukov's Vistula Offensive cost the Red Army 1267 tanks and assault guns destroyed.

ARMED FORCES

SOVIET TANK ARMIES

By mid-1943, the Red Army fielded so-called tank armies to combat the German panzer corps. The creation of the first two armies – the Third and Fifth – was ordered on May 25, 1942. In theory each tank army was made up of two tank corps, one mechanized corps and supporting units – a strength of 560 tanks and 45,000 men, though some were larger. In January 1945, for example, the Third Guards Tank Army had 670 tanks, 43,400 troops, 254 assault guns, 24 BM-13 rocket launchers and 368 artillery pieces.

A tank corps in January 1943 was made up of three tank brigades, a motorized rifle brigade, a mortar battalion and various support units. The assault guns were usually grouped in their own units. Thus, a tank brigade had up to 65 tanks, giving a tank corps up to 230 tanks. The assault guns were grouped into heavy, medium and light regiments. Thus, the heavy units comprised 12 SU-152s, the medium units 16 SU-122s and 1 T-34 tank, and the light regiments were composed of 21 SU-76s or 16 SU-85s and 1 T-34 tank. The regiments made up of SU-152s were usually assigned to armies for breakthrough operations.

▲ ***Red Army troops fighting in Königsberg. The garrison consisted of five depleted divisions, but it still took the Soviets four months to capture the city.***

BALTIC, *SEA WAR*
To date the Kriegsmarine has evacuated 374,000 refugees from East Prussia.

FEBRUARY 13

HUNGARY, *LAND WAR*
The German defence of Budapest ends, with German and Hungarian losses standing at 138,000 captured and 50,000 killed. It is another catastrophe for the Wehrmacht. The Soviet 2nd Ukrainian Front has lost 35,000 killed and 130,000 wounded, and the 3rd Ukrainian Front 45,000 killed and 109,000 wounded.

GERMANY, *AIR WAR*
In response to a specific Soviet request for bombing German communications, and in particular with regard to the Berlin–Leipzig–Dresden railway complex, US and British bombers attack Dresden. The Western Allied air authorities have decided that the bombing of the city will fulfil strategic objectives of mutual importance to the Allies and the Soviets, and will satisfy the specific Soviet request presented to the Allies by General Antonov, Deputy Chief of the Soviet General Staff, to "paralyze the junctions of Berlin and Leipzig". More than 100,000 civilians will be killed in the air raids.

FEBRUARY 14

POLAND, *LAND WAR*
The Soviet Fifth Guards and Third Guards Armies link up near Breslau, trapping 80,000 civilians and 35,000 German troops inside the city.

FEBRUARY 15

EAST PRUSSIA, *LAND WAR*
The Soviet Forty-Ninth and Sixty-Fifth Armies push back the German Fourth Army 16km (10 miles).

GERMANY, *LAND WAR*
The Germans launch Operation Sonnenwende, an attempt to destroy the spearheads of the 1st Belorussian Front in Pomerania. The attacking Eleventh SS Panzer Army is divided into three groups: Central Group – III SS Panzer Corps; Western Group – XXIX Panzer Corps; Eastern Group – *Führer* Grenadier Division, 163rd and 281st Infantry Divisions. Only III SS Panzer Corps makes any gains.

▶ ***Germany's last hope – the Volkssturm. It was composed of males between 16 and 60 who were not in the armed forces but were still capable of bearing arms.***

▲ ***By 1945 the Soviets had air superiority over the Eastern Front, making German vehicular movement risky. This truck has been camouflaged against air attack.***

FEBRUARY 18

POLAND, *LAND WAR*
The Eleventh SS Panzer Army has been halted at Stargard. On the River Bobr the *Grossdeutschland* and XXIV Panzer Corps continue to fight the Soviet Third Guards Tank, Fourth Tank and Fifty-Second Armies.

HUNGARY, *LAND WAR*
I SS Panzer Corps pushes the Seventh Guards Army back across the River Hron.

FEBRUARY 20

EAST PRUSSIA, *LAND WAR*
The Germans have reopened a route out of Königsberg, allowing 100,000 civilians to flee west to Pillau, although they have to run the gauntlet of Soviet artillery and ground-attack aircraft as they do so.

POLAND, *LAND WAR*
The defenders of Breslau attempt to break out but are stopped by the Soviet Sixth Army, suffering heavy losses.

HUNGARY, *LAND WAR*
I SS Panzer Corps continues to pressure the Seventh Guards Army in the Hron bridgehead, and the German Sixth Army attacks the 3rd Ukrainian Front between Lakes Balaton and Velencei. The German Eighth Army around Esztergom is attacked by the Soviet Forty-Sixth Army.

FEBRUARY 23

POLAND, *LAND WAR*
The last pockets of the Posen garrison are reduced by the Soviet Eighth Guards Army, 12,000 German troops have been taken prisoner.

HUNGARY, *LAND WAR*
As the Soviet Seventh Guards Army abandons its Hron bridgehead, the Sixth SS Panzer Army deploys for its offensive against Soviet forces on the Danube's west bank to secure the Hungarian oil fields.

FEBRUARY 25

GERMANY, *LAND WAR*
The Soviet Nineteenth Army (2nd Belorussian Front) has advanced 48km (30 miles) towards Koslin, threatening Danzig and the German Second Army with encirclement.

▲ ***German prisoners under Red Army escort in an east German town. On the left is a knocked-out Panzer IV/70(V) tank destroyer, armed with a 75mm gun.***

FEBRUARY 27

YUGOSLAVIA, *LAND WAR*
Army Group E wrests control of the road to Sarajevo from partisans, thus safeguarding the army group's southern flank.

FEBRUARY 28

GERMANY, *LAND WAR*
Neustettin and Prechlau have fallen to the Soviet Nineteenth Army.

MARCH 1

GERMANY, *LAND WAR*
The First Guards Tank, Second Guards Tank, Third Shock, Forty-Seventh and Sixty-First Armies launch a fresh attack into Pomerania, hitting the junction of the German III and X SS Corps. The Soviet Third Guards Tank Army defeats a counterattack by XXIV Panzer Corps near Lauban.

MARCH 2

GERMANY, *LAND WAR*
The 1st Belorussian Front's offensive is lancing through the German lines, with the First Guards Tank Army approaching Kolberg, the Second Guards Tank nearing Stettin and the Polish First Army threatening the left flank of X SS Corps.

MARCH 4

GERMANY, *LAND WAR*
The Soviet First Guards Army and Polish First Army have reached the Baltic, X SS Corps is being degraded at Dramberg and the Soviet Sixty-First Army has captured

DECISIVE MOMENT

LEND-LEASE AID

Lend-Lease aid as provided to the USSR by Britain and the United States did not influence the outcome of the war on the Eastern Front – without it, the Red Army would still have been victorious. This was because the Soviet Union was also able to galvanize its vast industrial resources to produce tanks, artillery and small arms on a scale that Germany could not match. For example, in 1943 Soviet factories built 24,000 tanks and assault guns compared with only 9500 in Germany. The following year the Germans produced 17,000 tanks and assault guns, but the Russians built 29,000 armoured fighting vehicles. On the battlefield Red Army losses in tanks were huge. In 1943 and 1944 it lost 23,000, compared with 7500 German tanks lost in 1943 and 7600 in 1944. This made little impact on frontline tank strength because of Soviet industrial capacity. That said, without any aid from the West, the Soviet Union would have taken longer to defeat Nazi Germany, and would have suffered many more casualties doing so. Between 1943 and 1945, Western aid, specifically trucks, rail engines and rail wagons, allowed the Red Army to maintain the momentum of its offensives by transporting troops and supplies to reinforce breakthrough armies, thus denying the Germans time to organize fresh defence lines and escape encirclements. The Allies provided the Soviets with the following Lend-Lease aid:

Armoured vehicles: 12,161
Guns and mortars: 9600
Combat aircraft: 18,303
Aircraft engines: 14,902
Trucks and jeeps: 312,600
Explosives: 330,997 tonnes (325,784 tons)
Locomotives: 1860
Rail cars: 11,181
Field telephones: 422,000
Foodstuffs: 4,350,420 tonnes (4,281,910 tons)
Oil: 2,640,584 tonnes (2,599,000 tons)
Boots: 15,000,000 pairs

Stargard. At Lauban, XXIV Panzer Corps is still attacking the Third Guards Tank Army.

MARCH 5

GERMANY, *LAND WAR*
The Soviet Nineteenth Army captures Koslin as X SS Corps tries to break out to the west. XXIV Panzer Corps recaptures Lauban and forces the Third Guards Tank Army back. Colonel von Luck (25th Panzer Division) is witness to Red Army atrocities around Lauban: "For all of us, a terribly depressing experience was to stay forever in our minds. In the villages we recovered, we ourselves saw for the first time how the Russians had rampaged in the past weeks. Never in my life shall I forget the sight of the maltreated, violated women who came to meet us, screaming or completely apathetic. Neither old women nor girls, who were still children, were spared; the houses were plundered, old men were shot."

MARCH 6

GERMANY, *LAND WAR*
Grudziadz is captured by the Soviet Sixty-Fifth Army, and Belgard by the Soviet Third Shock and Polish First Armies.

HUNGARY, *LAND WAR*
The last German offensive of the war, Operation Spring Awakening, begins. The German forces comprise the Sixth SS Panzer Army (I and II SS Panzer Corps and III Panzer Corps), Sixth Army (IV SS Panzer Corps and Hungarian VIII Corps) and Second Panzer Army (XXXXIV and LXVII Corps) – 430,000 troops, 5600 artillery pieces and 880 tanks and assault guns, supported by 850 fuel-starved

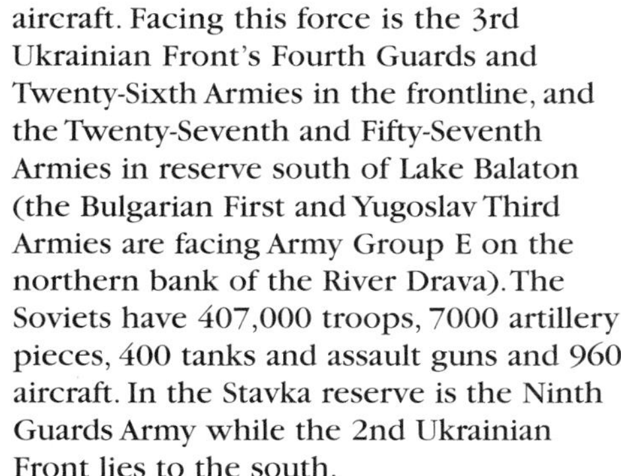

aircraft. Facing this force is the 3rd Ukrainian Front's Fourth Guards and Twenty-Sixth Armies in the frontline, and the Twenty-Seventh and Fifty-Seventh Armies in reserve south of Lake Balaton (the Bulgarian First and Yugoslav Third Armies are facing Army Group E on the northern bank of the River Drava). The Soviets have 407,000 troops, 7000 artillery pieces, 400 tanks and assault guns and 960 aircraft. In the Stavka reserve is the Ninth Guards Army while the 2nd Ukrainian Front lies to the south.

The German plan is to recapture Budapest by breaking through the junction of the Fourth Guards and Twenty-Sixth Armies, thereafter annihilating the 2nd and 3rd Ukrainian Fronts trapped on the west bank of the River Danube – a totally unrealistic plan given Wehrmacht resources and the strength of the Soviet fronts. Due to the water-logged ground, the offensive gets off to a slow start, and II SS Panzer Corps even fails to reach its jump-off position.

MARCH 7

HUNGARY, *LAND WAR*
II SS Panzer Corps joins the attack, hitting the Soviet Twenty-Sixth Army north of Lake Balaton, although the Soviets manage to hold the panzers. The German Second Panzer Army and Army Group E join the offensive, the former making some gains against the Fifty-Seventh Army, but Army Group E is largely contained on the Drava.

MARCH 8

HUNGARY, *LAND WAR*
Spring Awakening is faltering, with II SS Panzer Corps being held by the Twenty-Sixth Army and the Second Panzer Army by the Fifty-Seventh Army.

MARCH 9

GERMANY, *LAND WAR*
The Soviet Second Shock Army captures Marienburg.

HUNGARY, *LAND WAR*
There are now more than 600 panzers committed against the Soviet Fourth Guards and Twenty-Sixth Armies, but still the Germans can make little progress. To compound their problems, the Soviets are feeding the Sixth Guards Tank and Twenty-Seventh Armies into the line as reinforcements. On the Drava, the Yugoslav Third Army goes over to the offensive against Army Group E.

USSR, *STRATEGY*
The Stavka is already planning a counteroffensive in Hungary, using

▼ ***The tired face of the Wehrmacht in 1945. By this time German units were understrength, but some Soviet divisions were also depleted by the fighting, up to 50 percent in some formations.***

the 2nd and 3rd Ukrainian Fronts to attack the Sixth SS Panzer Army and Hungarian Third Army and capture Vienna.

MARCH 12

HUNGARY, *LAND WAR*
Operation Spring Awakening peters out in the face of fuel shortages, Soviet resistance and water-logged terrain. However, Hitler orders a resumption of the attack.

MARCH 13

EAST PRUSSIA, *LAND WAR*
The 3rd Belorussian Front launches an offensive against the German Fourth Army holed up in Heiligenbeil, Königsberg and Samland.
GERMANY, *LAND WAR*
The Polish First Army begins the destruction of the garrison of Kolberg.

MARCH 14

HUNGARY, *LAND WAR*
The Sixth SS Panzer Army renews its offensive against the Soviet Twenty-Seventh Army but makes no headway.

MARCH 15

GERMANY, *LAND WAR*
The Soviet Second Shock, Forty-Ninth, Sixty-Ninth and Seventieth Armies are fighting in the suburbs of Gotenhafen and Danzig, while at Kolberg Polish troops are battling their way through the streets. The Soviet Upper Silesian Offensive begins as the 1st Ukrainian Front attacks from Oppeln with its Fourth Tank, Twenty-First, Fifty-Ninth and Sixtieth Armies.
HUNGARY, *LAND WAR*
Spring Awakening has ended with German losses of 500 tanks and assault guns, 300 artillery pieces and more than 40,000 troops – the Wehrmacht's last operational reserves.

MARCH 16

HUNGARY, *LAND WAR*
The Soviet 3rd Ukrainian Front (536,000 troops) opens the Vienna Offensive, with the Fourth and Ninth Guards Armies attacking the weakened German Sixth Army west of Lake Balaton. Nevertheless, the Soviets find enemy resistance is initially strong.

▲ These German soldiers are building an anti-tank position in East Prussia. Note the 88mm Panzerschreck ("tank terror") anti-tank weapon on the right.

MARCH 17

HUNGARY, *LAND WAR*
The commitment of the Soviet Forty-Sixth Army (100,000 troops) to the Vienna Offensive shatters the Hungarian Third Army. The Sixth SS Panzer Army is also struggling to hold off the Twenty-Sixth and Twenty-Seventh Armies. To the south, Army Group E abandons its bridgeheads on the Drava.

MARCH 18

GERMANY, *LAND WAR*
Kolberg falls to the Polish First Army.

MARCH 19

GERMANY, *LAND WAR*
The Soviet Second Guards and Forty-Seventh Armies reach the River Oder at Altdamm, and in Silesia the Fourth Tank and Fifty-Ninth Armies have linked up and encircled the *Hermann Göring* Panzer Corps near Oppeln, also shattering the southern flank of the Seventeenth Army.
HUNGARY, *LAND WAR*
The Soviet Sixth Guards Tank Army joins the Vienna Offensive, a move that endangers the Sixth SS Panzer Army. Its commander, "Sepp" Dietrich, orders an immediate withdrawal.
GERMANY, *STRATEGY*
Hitler issues the decree on Demolitions on Reich Territory in response to the Soviets and Western Allies entering the Reich. It states: "It is a mistake to think that transport and communication

▼ Fleeing the "Bolshevik horde". German civilians board a train to avoid capture by the Red Army. Soviet aircraft strafed refugees as a matter of course.

facilities, industrial establishments and supply depots, which have not been destroyed, or have only been temporarily put out of action, can be used again for our own ends when the lost territory has been recovered. The enemy will leave us nothing but scorched earth when he withdraws, without paying the slightest regard to the population. I therefore order: all military transport and communication facilities, industrial establishments and supply depots, as well as anything else of value within Reich territory, which could in any way be used by the enemy immediately or within the foreseeable future for the prosecution of the war, will be destroyed." Albert Speer, Armaments Minister, is appalled and will secretly refuse to implement this directive.

MARCH 20

GERMANY, *LAND WAR*
The *Hermann Göring* Panzer Corps is wiped out at Oppeln: 30,000 killed and 15,000 taken prisoner.

MARCH 21

GERMANY, *LAND WAR*
The remnants of the German Third Panzer Army isolated on the east bank of the River Oder are liquidated near Altdamm: 40,000 killed and 12,000 captured.

HUNGARY, *LAND WAR*
As Soviet forces advance, the German Sixth Army is fighting to prevent the encirclement of the Sixth SS Panzer Army around Lake Balaton.

MARCH 22

EAST PRUSSIA, *LAND WAR*
The Soviet Forty-Ninth Army reaches the Baltic near Zoppot, effectively isolating Danzig from Gotenhafen, and the German Fourth Army is isolated at Heiligenbeil.

GERMANY, *LAND WAR*
The Soviet Fifth Shock and Eighth Guards Armies link up at Golzow, encircling 2000 German troops in Küstrin.

HUNGARY, *LAND WAR*
The German Sixth Army is overrun by the Soviet Fourth, Sixth Guards Tank and Ninth Guards Armies, trapping the Sixth SS Panzer Army. Dietrich orders his units to fight their way out to the west.

MARCH 24

SLOVAKIA, *LAND WAR*
The 4th Ukrainian Front launches an offensive to capture the Moravska Ostrava industrial area, the First Guards, Eighteenth and Thirty-Eighth Armies hitting the First Panzer Army.

HUNGARY, *LAND WAR*
The Soviet Fourth Guards Army captures Mor and Kisber. To the south the Second Panzer Army is assaulted by the Soviet Fifty-Seventh Army, and the German formation is now in danger of being encircled by the Fifty-Seventh and Twenty-Seventh Armies.

▶ Troops of Schörner's Army Group Centre in Silesia. The weapon in the background is a 50mm Flugzeug Abwehr Kanon Flak 41, its barrel depressed to engage Soviet tanks.

MARCH 25

EAST PRUSSIA, *LAND WAR*
Heiligenbeil falls to the 3rd Belorussian Front, although the Germans continue to fight on a strip of land on the coast.

HUNGARY, *LAND WAR*
The 2nd Ukrainian Front launches its Seventh Guards, Fortieth, Fifty-Third and Romanian First and Fourth Armies at the River Hron defences, pushing the German Eighth Army back as it establishes a bridgehead.

MARCH 27

EAST PRUSSIA, *LAND WAR*
The heartland of Prussian militarism is falling to the Red Army: the remnants of the Fourth Army are annihilated, the Soviet Nineteenth Army takes Gotenhafen, and the Second Shock and Nineteenth Armies break into Danzig.

GERMANY, *LAND WAR*
A counterattack by a weakened German Ninth Army to relieve Küstrin fails and incurs 8000 casualties.

MARCH 28

EAST PRUSSIA, *LAND WAR*
The battle to hold the Heiligenbeil Pocket has cost the German Fourth Army 93,000 killed, 47,000 wounded and 605 tanks, 3600 artillery pieces, 1400 mortars and 130 aircraft destroyed.

MARCH 29

GERMANY, *LAND WAR*
Küstrin falls to the Soviet Fifth Shock and Eighth Guards Armies. The commander of the Küstrin garrison, SS Lieutenant-General Rheinefarth, leads a breakout at the head of 1600 troops just before midnight. He and his men reach German lines, only for him to be arrested on the orders of Hitler.

HUNGARY, *LAND WAR*
The northern flank of the Second Panzer Army is encircled by the Soviet Twenty-Seventh and Fifty-Seventh Armies south of Lake Balaton.

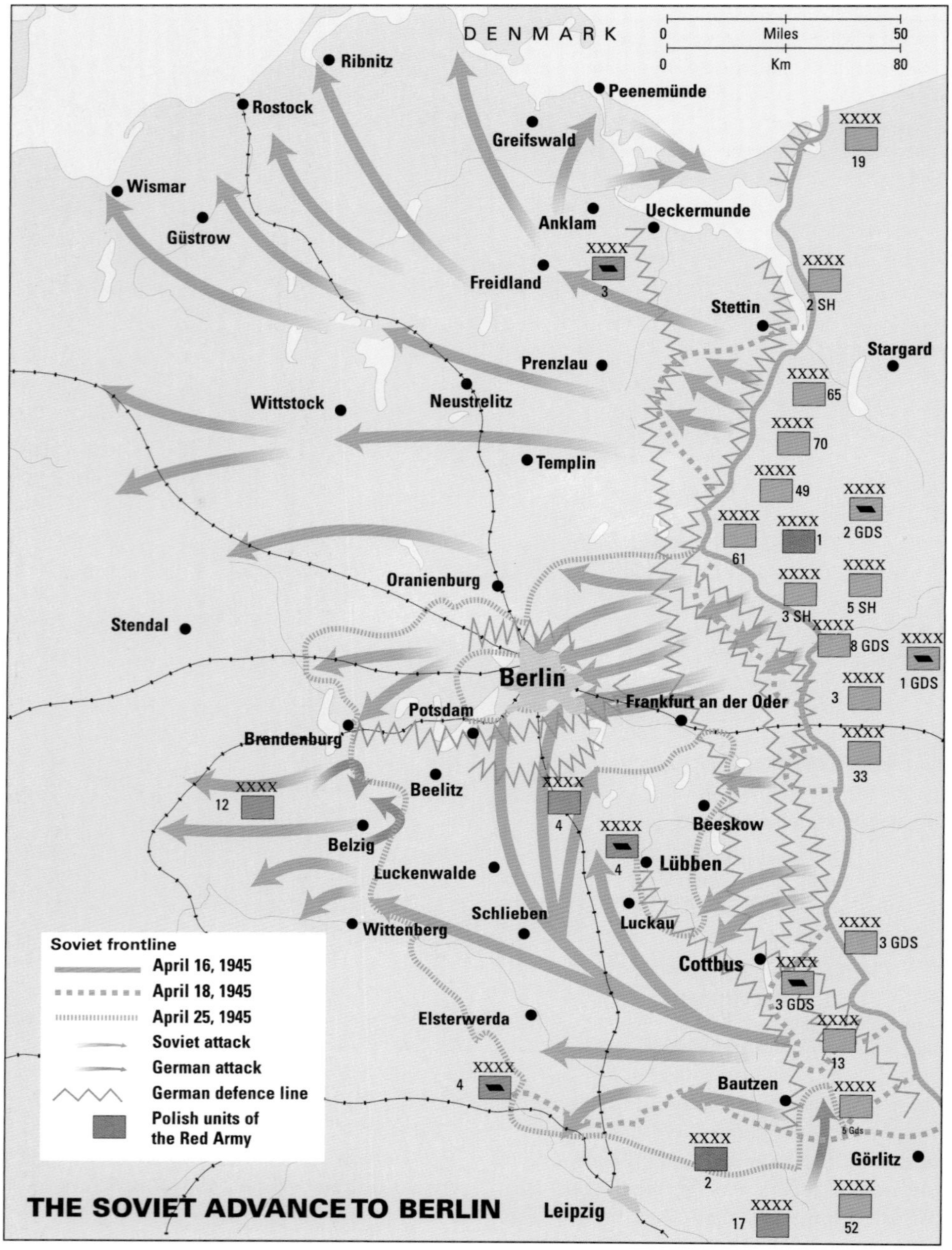

THE SOVIET ADVANCE TO BERLIN

Soviet frontline
April 16, 1945
April 18, 1945
April 25, 1945
Soviet attack
German attack
German defence line
Polish units of the Red Army

MARCH 30

EAST PRUSSIA, *LAND WAR*
The Second Shock Army mops up in Danzig, capturing 10,000 prisoners.

APRIL 1

GERMANY, *LAND WAR*
Glogau falls to the 1st Ukrainian Front's Thirteenth Army.

HUNGARY, *LAND WAR*
The Soviet Sixth Guards Tank Army captures Sopron after a short engagement.

APRIL 2

HUNGARY, *LAND WAR*
The Fifty-Seventh Army captures the Nagykanitza oil fields.

APRIL 3

SLOVAKIA, *LAND WAR*
The Soviet Seventh Guards Army is shelling the defences of Bratislava.

◀ A German machine-gun team. One soldier, Karl-Hermann Tams, wrote in March that "the feeling among us young soldiers could still be described as confident".

APRIL 4

EAST PRUSSIA, *LAND WAR*

The final reduction of Königsberg begins as the Soviet Eleventh Guards, Thirty-Ninth, Forty-Eighth and Fiftieth Armies probe the perimeter defences.

SLOVAKIA, *LAND WAR*

The Seventh Guards Army takes Bratislava.

APRIL 6

EAST PRUSSIA, *LAND WAR*

The offensive against Königsberg begins, the 3rd Belorussian Front deploying 138,000 troops against the 35,000 of the garrison. Overhead, the Soviet First and Fifteenth Air Armies pound the city as the Soviets break into the suburbs.

AUSTRIA, *LAND WAR*

The defence of Vienna begins as the 2nd and 3rd Belorussian Fronts launch their offensive. Defended doggedly by the Sixth SS Panzer Army, the Fourth Guards and Sixth Guards Tank Armies suffer heavy casualties as they attack.

APRIL 9

EAST PRUSSIA, *LAND WAR*

The commander of Königsberg, General Lasch, surrenders. German losses are 42,000 troops and 25,000 civilians killed and 92,000 troops captured. Hitler sentences Lasch to death *in absentia* and orders the arrest of his family and relatives.

APRIL 11

AUSTRIA, *LAND WAR*

The 3rd Ukrainian Front's Twenty-Seventh Army is nearing Graz. Inside Vienna, the Parliament building and City Hall are captured by the Fourth Guards Army.

▲ ***Soviet artillery firing during the Berlin Offensive. On each kilometre of front the Red Army was able to deploy 260 artillery pieces to support the advance.***

APRIL 13

AUSTRIA, *LAND WAR*

The Battle of Vienna is over. In a month German forces in Hungary and Austria have lost 134,000 troops captured. The 3rd Ukrainian Front has lost 32,000 killed and 106,000 wounded in the same period.

APRIL 16

GERMANY, *LAND WAR*

The Soviet Berlin Offensive begins. For this assault the Soviets have amassed 2.5 million troops, 41,000 artillery pieces, 6200 tanks and assault guns, 100,000 motor vehicles and 7200 aircraft, divided between the 1st Belorussian, 2nd Belorussian and 1st Ukrainian Fronts. Facing this host is Army Group Vistula (Third Panzer and Ninth Armies with LVI Panzer Corps in reserve – 200,000 troops, 750 tanks and assault guns and 1500 artillery pieces) and the northern flank of Army Group Centre (Fourth Panzer Army – 100,000 troops and 200 tanks and assault guns).

The 1st Belorussian Front (Polish First, First Guards Tank, Second Guards Tank, Third, Third Shock, Fifth Shock, Eighth Guards, Thirty-Third, Forty-Seventh, Sixty-First and Sixty-Ninth Armies) launches its initial attack against the Seelow Heights, but the Germans have anticipated this move and withdrawn some way back, thus the Soviet artillery "punches air", and Zhukov's tactics of using searchlights to aid the attack actually illuminates the attackers. As the Eighth Guards Army struggles forward, Zhukov commits the First Guards Tank and Second Guards Tank Armies, which creates chaos. Although the Soviets inch forward, they lose many tanks.

The 1st Ukrainian Front (Polish Second, Third Guards, Third Guards Tank, Fourth Guards Tank, Fifth Guards, Thirteenth, Twenty-Eighth and Fifty-Second Armies), at the River Neisse, has more success, establishing a bridgehead.

GERMANY, *STRATEGY*

Hitler issues his order of the day regarding the new Soviet offensive against Berlin:

▼ ***Berliners outside the Anhalter station. There was a bunker next to the station, which held up to 12,000 people, though in appalling sanitary conditions.***

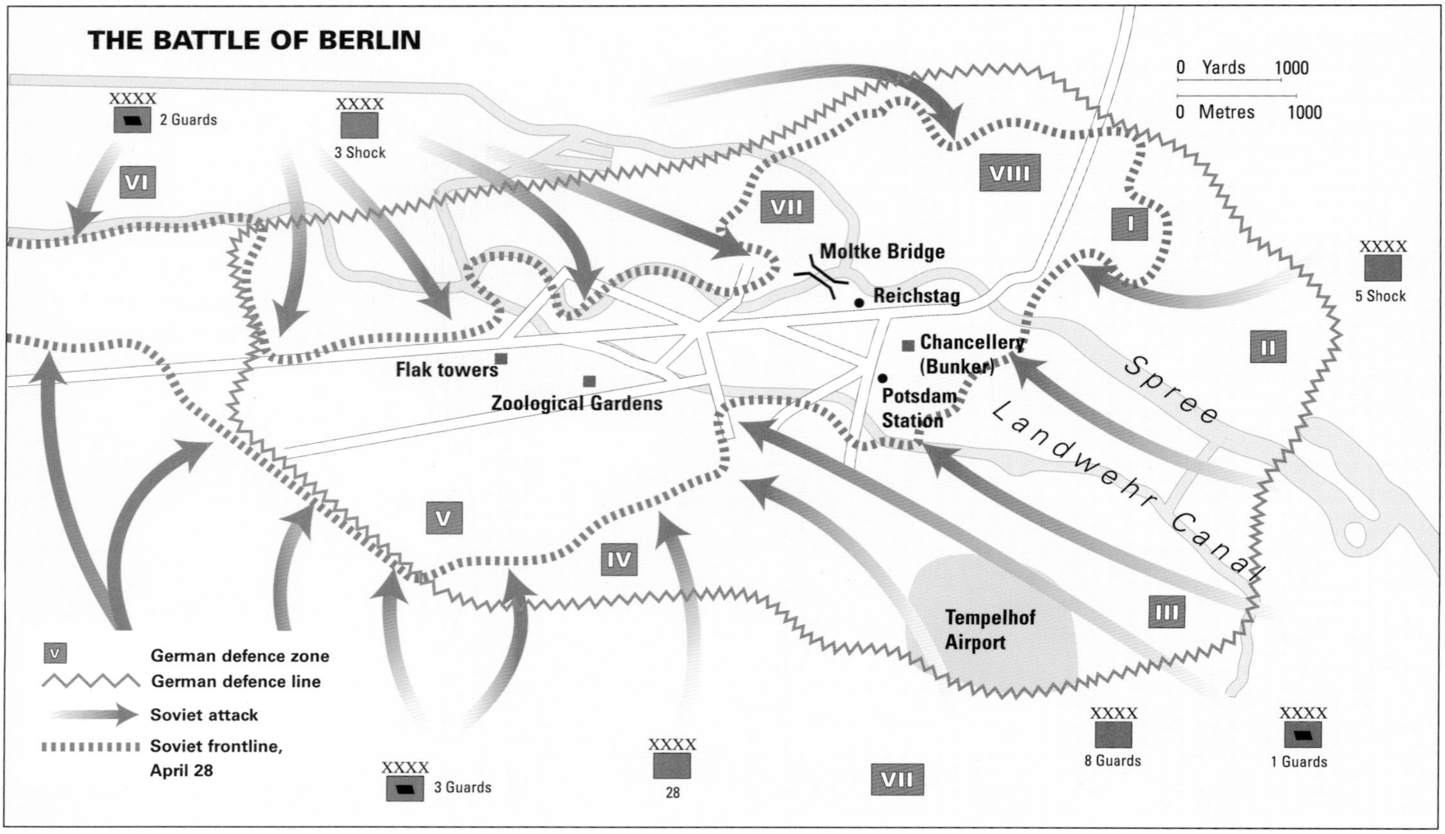

THE BATTLE OF BERLIN

0 Yards 1000
0 Metres 1000
XXXX 2 Guards
XXXX 3 Shock
XXXX 5 Shock
VI
VII
VIII
I
II
III
IV
V
Moltke Bridge
Reichstag
Chancellery (Bunker)
Potsdam Station
Flak towers
Zoological Gardens
Spree
Landwehr Canal
Tempelhof Airport
German defence zone
German defence line
Soviet attack
Soviet frontline, April 28
XXXX 3 Guards
XXXX 28
VII
XXXX 8 Guards
XXXX 1 Guards

"For the last time our deadly enemies, the Jewish Bolsheviks, have launched their massive forces to the attack. Their aim is to reduce Germany to ruins and to exterminate our peoples ... If every soldier on the Eastern front does his duty in the days and weeks which lie ahead, the last assault of Asia will crumple, just as the invasion by our enemies in the West will finally fail, in spite of everything."

APRIL 17

GERMANY, *LAND WAR*

Although the Soviet Eighth Guards Army captures Seelow late in the afternoon, the German Ninth Army retires to another defence line. The Soviets have suffered heavy casualties. The 1st Ukrainian Front is across the Neisse and has pushed back the Fourth Panzer Army. Its Third Guards Tank and Fourth Tank Armies are now heading towards Zossen and Potsdam.

APRIL 18

GERMANY, *LAND WAR*

The German Ninth Army has been shattered. The commitment of LVI Panzer Corps cannot hold up the Soviet advance, and soon the First Guards Tank and Eighth Guards Armies are powering towards Berlin. To the north the Soviet Third, Fifth Shock and Forty-Seventh Armies are also advancing. Meanwhile, Spremberg and Cottbus are encircled by the Soviet Fifth Guards and Third Guards Armies, respectively.

APRIL 20

GERMANY, *LAND WAR*

The artillery of the 1st Belorussian Front is shelling Berlin's eastern suburbs. Juterbog, the main Wehrmacht armaments depot, is captured by the Fourth Guards Tank Army. The Fourth Panzer Army is being broken apart at Cottbus by the Fifth Guards Army. The 2nd Belorussian Front (Second Shock, Forty-Ninth, Sixty-Fifth and Seventieth Armies) joins the offensive, its objective being to reach the Baltic and sever the Western Allied drive into Denmark. The defending Third Panzer Army is hit by artillery and aerial bombs but still defends stoutly. To date the Red Army has lost 2800 tanks in the Berlin Offensive.

▶ ***Red Army Katyushas unleash their rockets against the Reichstag in Berlin. The Soviets wanted to capture the Reichstag in time for Moscow's May Day parade.***

▲ ***Red Army troops in front of the shot-pummelled Reichstag. The final assault on the building was made by the 150th Rifle Division, backed up by tanks.***

April 21

GERMANY, *LAND WAR*

The noose tightens around Berlin: the Soviet Third Shock Army is fighting in the northeastern suburbs, the Fifth Shock is entering the eastern suburbs, the First Polish and Sixty-First Armies are fighting near Eberswalde, and the Second Guards Tank and Forty-Seventh Armies are across the main autobahn north of the city. To the south the Third Guards Army captures Zossen, cutting off a force of 200,000 troops of the Ninth and half of the Fourth Panzer Army from Berlin. This formation is then attacked by the Soviet Twenty-Eighth, Thirty-Third and Sixty-Ninth Armies.

USSR, *DIPLOMACY*

A Mutual Assistance Pact is signed in Moscow between the USSR and the Polish Government based in Lublin.

April 22

GERMANY, *LAND WAR*

The Soviet Second Tank Army fights its way into Berlin's northwest Hennigsdorf suburb, and the Third Guards Tank and Twenty-Eighth Armies reach the Teltow Canal in the south of the city. Hitler announces he will stay in the Berlin.

April 23

GERMANY, *LAND WAR*

The Sixty-Ninth Army captures Frankfurt and the Third Guards Army takes Cottbus. A counterattack by the weakened Fourth Panzer Army causes the Polish Second and Soviet Fifty-Second Armies some initial discomfort.

CZECHOSLOVAKIA, *LAND WAR*

The Soviet Sixth Guards and Fifty-Third Armies assault Brno, shattering the German Eighth Army.

▼ ***Soviet artillery and tanks in front of Himmler's Ministry of the Interior in Berlin, near the Moltke Bridge.***

April 24

GERMANY, *LAND WAR*

There is heavy fighting throughout Berlin. At Potsdam the Fourth Guards Tank Army is endeavouring to link up with the Forty-Seventh Army. To the south of the city the Fourth Panzer Army's counterattack has been halted by the Polish Second and Fifty-Second Armies. A relief attack by the German Twelfth Army initially throws the Soviet Fourth Guards Tank and Thirteenth Armies off balance.

April 25

EAST PRUSSIA, *LAND WAR*

Pillau falls to the 3rd Belorussian Front, which has suffered 89,400 killed and 332,000 wounded since January.

GERMANY, *LAND WAR*

The Soviet Fourth Guards Tank and Forty-Seventh Armies link up at Potsdam. The Fifth Guards Army has reached the River Elbe at Torgau, splitting Germany in two.

April 26

GERMANY, *LAND WAR*

The Moabitt and Neukölln districts of Berlin fall to the Red Army, as does

▼ ***Hitler (right) with his adjutant, Julius Schaub, in the ruins of the Reich Chancellery. On Hitler's orders Schaub left Berlin and flew to southern Germany.***

▲ ***Russians (left) and Americans (right) in Germany. The Soviets took a dim view of such meetings, ordering commanders not to divulge any plans to the Americans.***

Tempelhof airfield. Stettin is captured by the Sixty-Fifth Army, and the Thirteenth Army continues to inflict heavy casualties on the German Twelfth Army.

APRIL 27

GERMANY, *LAND WAR*
The German Third Panzer Army falls apart and its remnants flee west. In Berlin, Potsdam falls to the Soviets. Outside the city the Frankfurt-Guben Group is wiped out in the Halbe Pocket, and the Fourth Panzer and Ninth Armies disintegrate.

APRIL 28

GERMANY, *LAND WAR*
Soviet troops are now just 1.6km (1 mile) from Hitler's bunker below the Chancellery. By evening the Soviets are across the Potsdammer Bridge and are fighting in the Ministry of Internal Affairs.

APRIL 29

GERMANY, *LAND WAR*
The Soviet Third Shock Army captures the Moltke Bridge. Around the Reichstag, the German LVI Panzer Corps is almost out of ammunition. Hitler orders the troops to fight to the last man and bullet. The Führer dictates his last political testament, in which he states: "I die with a joyful heart in the awareness of the immeasurable deeds and achievements of our soldiers at the front, of our women at home, and achievements of our peasants and workers, and the contribution, unique in history, of our youth, which bears my name."

The German Twelfth Army launches a desperate attack at Belzig against the Soviet Fourth Guards Tank Army, which recaptures Potsdam and allows the survivors of the Halbe Pocket to escape west. The Third Panzer Army is in full retreat west.

▼ ***The Red Banner flies over the Reichstag, symbolizing the end of Hitler's Third Reich and the Red Army's victory over the German Army.***

MORAVIA, *LAND WAR*
German defences in the country are now beginning to fall apart as the Soviet Thirty-Eighth and First Guards Armies continue to advance.

APRIL 30

GERMANY, *LAND WAR*
Troops of the Soviet Third Shock Army engage SS soldiers in a vicious room-by-room fight for the Reichstag. Hitler and Eva Braun commit suicide, and their bodies are cremated.

MAY 1

GERMANY, *LAND WAR*
The Soviets capture the Reichstag, the 5000 defenders suffering 50 percent losses. General Krebs, Chief of the General Staff, asks the Soviets for terms, but Stalin wants unconditional surrender and so the fighting goes on. However, the Germans are out of ammunition and they begin surrendering anyway.

YUGOSLAVIA, *LAND WAR*
Tito's partisans link up with the 2nd New Zealand Division at Montefalcone, thus cutting off the 150,000 troops of Army Group E in Croatia and Slovenia.

CZECHOSLOVAKIA, *PARTISAN WAR*
The citizens of Prague revolt against the German occupiers.

GERMANY, *POLITICS*
Admiral Dönitz, following the death of Hitler, assumes his duties as the new German

head of state. He orders the utmost resistance in the East, where thousands of civilians are fleeing from the Red Army

▲ *The Red Army victory parade in Moscow. Shown here are some of the 98,300 tanks and self-propelled guns produced by the Soviets in World War II.*

MAY 2

GERMANY, *LAND WAR*
General Weidling, commander of the Berlin garrison, surrenders. The Battle of Berlin has cost the Germans 500,000 killed and captured; Soviet losses are 81,000 killed and 272,000 wounded. Josef Goebbels and his wife Magda commit suicide, but not before killing their six children. General Krebs also kills himself.

MAY 6

GERMANY, *LAND WAR*
Breslau surrenders to the Soviet Sixth Army, the 40,000-strong garrison having suffered 30,000 killed.
CZECHOSLOVAKIA, *LAND WAR*
The Soviets launch the Prague Offensive with the 1st Ukrainian, 2nd Ukrainian, 3rd Ukrainian and 4th Ukrainian Fronts - more than two million Soviet and Polish troops against Army Group Centre. The 1st Ukrainian Front attacks the Fourth Panzer and Seventeenth Armies and is soon in the rear of the German Seventh Army. The 4th Ukrainian Front shatters the First Panzer Army, and the 2nd Ukrainian Front cuts through the Eighth Army.
YUGOSLAVIA, *LAND WAR*
The German XCVII Corps, part of Army Group E, surrenders to the Yugoslav Fourth Army.

MAY 8

ESTONIA, *LAND WAR*
Army Group Kurland - 189,000 troops - begins to lay down its arms.
GERMANY, *LAND WAR*
The Soviet Fifth Guards Army captures the ruins of Dresden, as the 4th Ukrainian Front takes Olomouc.

MAY 9

CZECHOSLOVAKIA, *LAND WAR*
The Soviet Third and Fourth Guards Tank Armies are fighting inside Prague, isolating the German First Panzer and Seventeenth Armies. The German Eighth Army has been largely annihilated.

MAY 10

CZECHOSLOVAKIA, *LAND WAR*
Germans in Prague begin to surrender. The Soviets have lost 10,800 killed.

MAY 14

GERMANY, *LAND WAR*
The majority of German troops in Germany have now surrendered, with 150,000 laying down their arms in East Prussia today.

MAY 15

YUGOSLAVIA, *LAND WAR*
The troops of Army Group E - 150,000 in total - surrender at Slovenigradesk.

MAY 19

CZECHOSLOVAKIA, *LAND WAR*
The Red Army annihilates the last pocket of German Army resistance in Bohemia. The war on the Eastern Front is over.

DECISIVE MOMENT

RAPE AND PILLAGE IN BERLIN

When the Soviets reached Berlin, they embarked on an orgy of looting and rape. Why? First, the German Army had committed enormous atrocities in the Soviet Union, including the deliberate massacre of civilians. Many Soviet troops had seen at first hand the results of German policies when they liberated concentration camps. Soviet propaganda and political commissars stressed continually that the Red Army was fighting "fascist beasts", who deserved no mercy for the crimes they had committed on Soviet soil. This had the effect of further infuriating soldiers who were already thirsting for vengeance. Although the frontline Soviet troops were generally well disciplined, many Red Army soldiers, especially in support units, came from areas of crushing poverty, particularly those from Siberia and the Asiatic republics. When they got to Germany, they were determined to take what they could. Finally, the searing experience of combat on the Eastern Front made many Red Army soldiers "live for the moment", indulging themselves whenever they had the opportunity (privates, NCOs and junior officers were, for the most part, young men in their physical and sexual prime).

The pattern of behaviour among Red Army soldiers in Berlin and other German towns, even after the end of hostilities, was as follows: sober soldiers would invariably relieve civilians at gunpoint of any valuables they had (watches were particularly sought after) once they entered a town; the soldiers and their officers would then get drunk and embark on a hunt for women of any age. Those found would be raped, often gang-raped. German women soon learnt to hide during the "hunting hours" of the evening. In Berlin, the Red Army was soon out of control, and an estimated 100,000 German women were raped by Soviet soldiers, including the wives and daughters of German communists.

CONCLUSION

"When we flew into Russia, in 1945, I did not see a house standing between the western borders of the country and the area around Moscow. Through this overrun region, Marshal Zhukov told me, so many numbers of women, children and old men had been killed that the Russian Government would never be able to estimate the total." (General Dwight Eisenhower).

When the Germans retreated from the Ukraine in late 1943 and early 1944, they conducted a scorched earth policy to deny supplies and shelter to the advancing Red Army. In the process they destroyed more than 28,000 villages and 714 cities and towns, leaving 10,000,000 people without shelter. They also wiped out 16,000 industrial enterprises, more than 200,000 industrial production sites, 27,910 collective and 872 state farms, 1300 machine and tractor stations, and 32,930 schools.

The scale of the losses inflicted on the USSR during the war is difficult to comprehend. It is reckoned that 35 million Russians lost their lives during the four-year Russo-German War (with a further 35 million Soviet citizens wounded, both civilian and military), although this figure may include those killed by Stalin before the war and also deaths from exposure, malnutrition and disease in the months immediately after (when millions of Russians were without shelter). Through such sacrifices had the Soviets destroyed the Wehrmacht's capability on the Eastern Front, and thereby achieved victory in Europe. Of the Allies, it was the USSR that made the greatest contribution to the defeat of the Third Reich (of the total German armed forces losses of 13,488,000 in World War II, 80 percent – 10,758,000 – were suffered on the Eastern Front). How was this possible?

Stalin's USSR was a totalitarian state that mirrored many of the features of Nazi Germany. Above all, in both systems the individual existed only to serve the interests of the state. As such, it was better equipped to engage in a form of barbaric warfare than the Western democracies. In addition, in the 1930s Stalin had developed a "personality cult" around himself, which paid dividends during the war. People looked to him for leadership, seeing him as the physical embodiment of Soviet resistance. He in turn demanded, and largely received, great sacrifices from his people. Of course the organs of state repression, the Gulag and NKVD, meant that the USSR could be transformed relatively easily into a vast war factory following the German invasion, with seemingly impossible production quotas and inhumanly long shifts, without dissent. But it would be wrong to attribute the efforts of the Soviet people solely to intimidation. Among both workers and soldiers there was a burning desire to defeat the fascist invaders, both to liberate Mother Russia and to avenge Nazi atrocities. Workers made superhuman efforts to produce guns, tanks and aircraft, and existed on meagre rations without complaint while doing so. There was an immense national drive to victory.

The war saw the gradual evolution of the Red Army from an ineptly led "beached whale" into an effective all-arms force expertly commanded, albeit possessing a harsh code of discipline and a doctrine that accepted high battlefield losses as a matter of course. The ability of the Red Army's regiments and divisions to absorb heavy losses, yet still carry on fighting, saved the USSR in 1941 and led to victory in 1945. The huge Soviet manpower pool made such losses bearable (in a military sense). For example, in 1941 there were 45 million men aged between 20 and 59, compared with only 25 million Germans of comparable age. This meant that, throughout 1943 and 1944, notwithstanding losses, the Red Army was able to maintain a strength of just over six million troops on the Eastern Front. In comparison, the German Army was down to 2.5 million men by the end of October 1944.

Allied to the Russian fighting spirit was the USSR's massive industrial capacity. For example, in 1942 Soviet industry in the Urals built 25,000 aircraft and 25,000 tanks for the war effort. Against such capacity the Nazis had no answer, and they thus lost the war of production. By this time, Stalin was giving his commanders greater leeway than earlier in the war, as they had proved themselves adept at handling large formations. In this he differed from Hitler who, as the war went on, increasingly micro-managed operations, thus emasculating his commanders. There is no doubt that the Führer hastened the German defeat in Russia by making a series of catastrophic decisions, such as refusing to allow the Sixth Army to withdraw from Stalingrad in late 1942 and delaying the Kursk Offensive in 1943.

On May 9, 1945, the Wehrmacht High Command announced in its last report that the armed forces had laid down their weapons and that "the German Wehrmacht was, in the end, honourably defeated by overwhelming superior forces". In fact, superior Red Army numbers had been combined with economic strength and Russian national will to defeat the Germans. As Hitler stated in 1943: "In this war there will be neither victors nor vanquished, but only survivors and annihilated."

BIBLIOGRAPHY

Adair, Paul. *Hitler's Greatest Defeat: The Collapse of Army Group Centre, June 1944.* London: Cassell military, 2000.

Ailsby, Christopher. *SS: Hell on the Eastern Front: The Waffen-SS War in Russia, 1941–45.* Staplehurst: Spellmount, 1998.

Applebaum, Anne. Gulag: *A History of the Soviet Camps.* London: Penguin Books, 2004.

Beevor, Antony. *Stalingrad.* London: Penguin Books, 1999.

Beevor, Antony. *Berlin: The Downfall, 1945.* London: Penguin Books, 2003.

Bonn, Keith E. *Slaughterhouse: The Handbook of the Eastern Front.* Bedford: Aberjona, 2004.

Butler, Rupert, *Hitler's Jackals.* Barnsley: Pen and Sword Books, 1998.

Carell, Paul. *Scorched Earth.* New York: Ballantine, 1971.

Clark, Alan. *Barbarossa: The Russian German Conflict, 1941–45.* London: Cassell military, 2001.

Command Magazine (editor). *Hitler's Army: The Evolution and Structure of German Forces 1933–1945.* New York: Da Capo Press, 2003.

Cooper, Matthew. *The German Army 1933–1945.* Chelsea: Scarborough House, 1997.

Corti, Eugenio. *Few Returned: The Diary of Twenty-Eight Days on the Russian Front, Winter, 1942–43.* Columbia: University of Missouri Press, 1997.

Davies, W. J. K. *German Army Handbook, 1939–45.* Hersham: Ian Allan, 1973.

Duffy, Christopher. *Red Storm on the Reich.* New York: Da Capo Press, 1993.

Dupuy, Trevor N. *A Genius for War: The German Army & General Staff, 1807–1945.* London: Macdonald and Jane's, 1977.

Erickson, John. *The Road to Stalingrad.* New York: Harper & Row, 1976.

Erickson, John. *The Road to Berlin.* London: Cassell military, 2003.

Fey, Will. *Armor Battles of the Waffen-SS 1943–45.* Mechanicsburg: Stackpole Books, 2004.

Glantz, David. *The Siege of Leningrad 1941–1944: 900 Days of Terror.* Staplehurst: Spellmont, 2001.

Glantz, David M., and House, Jonathon. *When Titans Clashed: How the Red Army Stopped Hitler.* Lawrence: University of Kansas Press, 1995.

Glantz, David, and House, Jonathan. *The Battle of Kursk.* London: Ian Allan, 1999.

Guderian, Heinz (transl. Christopher Duffy). *Achtung-Panzer!* London: Arms & Armour, 1992.

Guderian, Heinz. *Panzer Leader.* London: Joseph, 1952.

Haupt, Werner. *Army Group South: The Wehrmacht in Russia, 1941–1945.* Atglen: Schiffer Publishing, 1997.

Heiber, Helmut. *Hitler and His Generals: Military Conferences 1942–1945.* New York: Enigma Books, 2003.

Hitler, Adolf. *Hitler's Table Talk,* London: Weidenfeld & Nicolson, 1953.

Hooton, Edward R. *Phoenix Triumphant: The Rise and Rise of the Luftwaffe.* London: Weidenfeld & Nicholson, 1996.

Hooton, Edward R. *Eagle in Flames: The Fall of the Luftwaffe.* London: Weidenfeld & Nicholson, 1997.

Kershaw, Ian. *Hitler, 1889–1936: Hubris.* London: Penguin Books, 2001.

Kershaw, Ian. *Hitler 1936–1945: Nemesis.* London: Penguin Books, 2001.

Knappe, Siegfried. *Soldat: Reflections of a German Soldier, 1936–1949.* London: Bantam Doubleday Dell Publishing Group, 1993.

Kurowski, Franz. *Bridgehead Kurland.* Manitoba: JJ Fedorowicz, 2002.

Liddell Hart, B.H. *The Other Side of the Hill.* London: Pan, 1999.

Lucas, James. *The Last Days of the Reich.* London: Cassell military, 2000.

Lucas, James. *Das Reich: The Military Role of the 2nd SS Division.* London: Cassell military, 1999.

Lucas, James. *The German Army Handbook 1939–1945.* Stroud: Sutton Publishing, 2002.

Lucas, James. *Grossdeutschland.* London: MacDonald and Jane's, 1978.

Lucas, James. *War on the Eastern Front: The German Soldier in Russia 1941–45.* London: Greenhill, 1979.

Lucas, James. *Hitler's Commanders: German Bravery in the Field, 1939–1945.* London: Weidenfeld & Nicholson, 2000.

Lucas, James, and Cooper, Matthew. *Hitler's Elite: Leibstandarte SS.* London: Macdonald, 1975.

Luck, Colonel Hans von. *Panzer Commander: The Memoirs of Hans von Luck.* Westport: Praeger, 1989.

McCarthy, Peter, and Syron, Mike. *Panzerkrieg: A History of the German Tank Division in World War II.* London: Constable and Robinson, 2003.

Macksey, Kenneth. *From Triumph to Disaster: Fatal Flaws of German Generalship, from Moltke to Guderian.* London: Greenhill Books, 1996.

Manstein, Erich von. *Lost Victories.* Chicago: H. Regency Co., 1958.

Megargee, Geoffrey P. *Inside Hitler's High Command.* Lawrence: University of Kansas Press, 2002.

Mellenthin, F.W. von. *Panzer Battles 1939–45: A Study in the Employment of Armor.* London: Cassell, 1955.

Munoz, Antonio, and Romanko, Dr Oleg V. *Hitler's White Russians: Collaboration, Extermination, and Anti-Partisan Warfare in Byelorussia, 1941–1944.* Bayside: Europa Books Inc., 2003.

Newton, Steven H. *German Battle Tactics on the Russian Front 1941–45.* Atglen, PA: Schiffer, 1994.

Nipe, George. *Decision in the Ukraine.* Manitoba: JJ Fedorowicz, 1996.

Overy, Richard. *Russia's War.* London: Penguin Books, 1999.

Overy, Richard. *Why the Allies Won.* London: Pimlico, 1996.

Padfield, Peter. *Himmler: Reichsfuhrer-SS.* London: Weidenfeld & Nicholson, 2001.

Pleshakov, Constantine. *Stalin's Folly. The Secret History of the German Invasion of Russia, June 1941.* London: Weidenfeld & Nicolson, 2005.

Quarrie, Bruce. *Hitler's Teutonic Knights: SS Panzers in Action.* Yeovil: Patrick Stephens, 1988.

Reynolds, Michael. *Men of Steel.* Staplehurst: Spellmont, 1999.

Reynolds, Michael. *Sons of the Reich: The History of II SS Panzer Corps.* Staplehurst: Spellmont, 2002.

Ripley, Tim. *SS Steel Storm: Waffen-SS Panzer Battles on the Eastern Front, 1943–1945.* Staplehurst: Spellmont, 2000.

Ryan, Cornelius. *The Last Battle.* London: Collins, 1973.

Salisbury, Harrison E. *The 900 Days.* New York: Da Capo Press, 1985.

Seaton, Albert. *The Battle for Moscow.* Staplehurst: Spellmont, 1993.

Stein, George H. *The Waffen-SS: Hitler's Elite Guard at War, 1939–1945.* Ithaca: Cornell University Press, 1984.

Stolfi, R.H.S. *Hitler's Panzers East: World War II Reinterpreted.* Norman: University of Oklahoma Press, 1993.

Sydnor, Charles. *Soldiers of Destruction: The SS Death's Head Division, 1933–1945.* Princeton,: Princeton University Press, 1977.

Taylor, Brian. *Barbarossa to Berlin: A Chronology of the Campaigns on the Eastern Front 1941 to 1945. Volume 1: The Long Drive East, 22 June 1941 to 18 November 1942.* Staplehurst: Spellmont, 2004.

Taylor, Brian. *Barbarossa to Berlin: A Chronology of the Campaigns on the Eastern Front 1941 to 1945. Vol ume 2: November 1942 to May 1945.* Staplehurst: Spellmont, 2004.

Tsouras, Peter G. *Fighting in Hell: the German Ordeal on the Eastern Front.* London: Ivy Books , 1998.

Ungvary, Krisztian. *Battle for Budapest: 100 Days in World War II.* London: I.B. Tauris, 2004.

Werth, Alexander. *Russia at War, 1941–1945.* New York: Carroll & Graf Publishing, 2001.

Wilbeck, Christopher. *Sledgehammers: Strengths and Flaws of Tiger Tank Battalions in World War II.* Bedford: Aberjona, 2004.

Zaloga, Steven J., and Ness, Leland S. *The Red Army Handbook, 1939–1945.* Stroud: Sutton Publishing, 1998.

Italic page numbers refer to illustrations

A

- Anglo-Polish Agreement of Mutual Assistance (1939) 9-10
- Antonescu, Ion *19*, 21, 23, 26, 46, 162, 167
- Attica, Operation 103
- Auschwitz 174, *174-5*
- Austria 180, 183
- Autumn Journey, Operation 131

B

- B-4 Model 1931 howitzer *11*
- Babi Yar 59, *59*, 134
- Bagration, Operation 151-9
- Baltic Offensive 164-5
- Bamberg, Operation 80
- Barbarossa, Operation 24-5, 31-55
- Barvenkovo Pocket 77, 84-7
- Belgrade 165, 168
- Belorussia 25, 151-3
- Beowulf, Operation 56-7
- Berezina, River 41, 42, 155-6
- Beria, Lavrenti 11, 41, 147
- Berlin 51-2, 153, 175-87
- Bialystok 38, 40, 42, 123, 133-4, 160
- Birdsong, Operation 88
- Blitzkrieg 10, 18, 23, 33, 139
- Blücher, Operation 93
- Blue, Operation 74, *88*, 89, 90-4
- Bock, Field Marshal von *31*, 47, 68, 70, 76, 93
- Brauchitsch, Field Marshal Walter von 19, 21, 26-7, 29, 69, *69*, 71
- Brest-Litovsk 38, 41, 158
- Brody Pocket 157, 158
- Bryansk 58, 60-3, 79, 88, 131, 136
- Bucharest 162, 163, *163*
- Budapest 169-75, *170-1*, 177, 179
- Budenny, Marshal Semyon 45, 50, 52, 57, 59
- Bug, River 11, 38, 47, 148, 157
- Bukrin 137, 139-40
- Bulgaria 19, 21-2, 27, 141, 161, 164, 167
- Bulgarian units 167, 170
- Bustard, Operation 84

C

- Caucasus 64, 74, 82, 89-115, 138
- Cherkassy Pocket 140, 142, *144*, 145-7
- Chir, River 105-9
- Cholm 50, 77, 78, 84, 119
- Chuikov, General Vasily 101, 103, 104
- Churchill, Winston 97, 141, *143*, 167, 176
- Citadel, Operation 120, *121*, 122, 123, 124-30
- commissars *29*, 30, 47, 104
- convoys 55, 92, *93*
- Crimea 58-9, 62-6, 71-85, 88-93, 97, 136-40, 150
- Czechoslovakia 10, 142, 186-7

D

- Danube, River 170, 172, 174
- Danzig 8, 175, 178, 181, 182
- Debrecen Offensive 166, 168
- Degtaryev machine gun *87*
- Demyansk 75, 76, 78-81, 83, 96-7, 115, 117
- Desna, River 52, 54, 57, 131, 137
- Dnepropetrovsk 54, 137-9
- Dnieper, River 40-1, 45-53, 58, 60, 84-5, 135-45
- Dniester, River 43, 46, 148-50
- Don, River 92-4, 96-107, 125
- Donbas 50, 63, 70, 133
- Donets, River 25, 30-1, 70, 90, 92, 114-19, 130-2
- Dornier Do 17 *47*
- Dresden 177
- Dvina, River 38-41, 44, 55, 153-4, 156, 160

E

- East Prussia 173-8, 180, *180*, 182-3
- Edelweiss, Operation 94
- Einsatzgruppen 45, 46, 48, *67*, 68, 83
- Eremenko, General Andrei 41, 60
- Estonia
  - German invasion and occupation 43, 45, 47-50, 56-7
  - Nazi-Soviet Non-Aggression Treaty 9
  - Soviet advance 159, 162-3, 165, 170, 176, 187
  - Soviet occupation 12, 18-19

F

- Feodosia 64, 72-3, 74, 76
- FH 36 howitzer *28*
- Fieseler Fi 156 Storch *86-7*
- Finland
  - Barbarossa 31, 38-45, 47-57
  - German strategy 24, 25, 49
  - German troops in 21-2, *56*
  - Nazi-Soviet Non-Aggression Treaty 9
  - peace negotiations 148, 153, 160, 163-6
  - Soviet advance 152, 157-9, 166-70
  - Winter War 12-13, *12-13*, 14-17
- Finnish units 42, 53, 62, 83, 85, 86
- First Moscow Conference 97
- flamethrowers *148*
- Flugzeug Abwehr Kanon Flak 41 *181*
- Frantic, Operation 152
- Freissner, Field Marshal 155, 161-2, 165

G

- German Army
  - infantry divisions 18
  - order of battle 31-3
  - panzer divisions 31, 121
  - panzergrenadier divisions 139
  - tactics 23, 76, 125
  - Volkssturm *177*
  - women 153
- German-Polish Non-Aggression Pact (1934) 8
- Germany
  - Pact of Steel 8-9
  - Poland 8, 10
  - Soviet advance into 176-87
  - treaties with USSR 9, 11, 15
- Gersdorff, Colonel Freiherr Rudolf von 30, 115
- Goebbels, Josef 116, *116*, 187
- Gomel 48, 50, 53-4, 138, 140
- Göring, Hermann 107, 113
- Great Britain
  - Allied conference 97, 139, 141, 167, 176
  - Greece 22, 29
  - Hitler's strategy 21
  - Poland 9-10
  - treaties with USSR 45, 86
- Greece 22, *23*, 28-9, 36, 167, 170
- Grozny 53, 94, 98, 99
- Guderian, General Heinz 16, 37, *73*
  - dismissal 70, 72
  - General Staff 158
  - initial invasion 39
  - Moscow 56, 58, 66, 68
  - Poland 11
  - Smolensk 47

H

- Halder, General Franz 19, *19*, 21, 23, 26-7, 48, 103
- Harnack, Arvid von 30, 115
- Hausser, Paul 115, 128, 129
- He 111 bombers *25*
- hedgehog tactics 76, 107
- Heiligenbeil Pocket 181-2
- Heinkel He 111 47
- Heron, Operation 94
- Himmler, Heinrich 45, 93, 123, *174*, 175
- Hitler, Adolf 16, *16*, *19*
  - Allied invasion of Italy 130
  - assumes command of Eastern Front 71-2
  - Bagration 154, 155, 156
  - Battle of Berlin 183-4, 185, *185*
  - Caucasus (Blue) 93-4, 109
  - directives 30, 47, 49, 51-2, 53, 69, 82, 93-4
  - Finland 88
  - Greece 22, 28-9
  - Guderian 37
  - Hungary 149, 168
  - Italy 9
  - July Plot 157
  - Königsberg 183
  - Kursk 120, 122, 123, 128, 131
  - Leningrad 56, *82-3*
  - Moscow 56, 58, 68
  - Nazi-Soviet Non-Aggression Treaty 8, 9
  - "no retreat" order 70
  - partisans 108-9
  - Poland 8
  - retreat from Lithuania 166
  - scorched earth policy 180-1
  - Spring Awakening 180
  - Stalingrad 98-9, 109, 111, 113
  - strategy 19-21, 22, 23-5, 26-7, *29*
  - suicide 186
  - Ukraine 149
  - Waffen-SS 121
  - Winter War 17
  - Yugoslavia 28
- Horthy, Admiral Nicholas 22-3, *22*, 163, 167, 168
- Hoth, Colonel-General Hermann 109, 124
- Hummel self-propelled heavy howitzers 31, *156-7*
- Hungarian troops 91, 111-12, 164, 165, 168-9, 180
- Hungary
  - Barbarossa 39, 41
  - German occupation 148-9
  - Jews 170
  - Soviet advance 163-6, 168-82
  - Transylvania 19, 21
  - Tripartite Pact 22-3

I

- Ie IG 18 infantry gun *38*
- Ilmen, Lake 44, 46, 49, 53, 61, 77
- Ilyushin II-4 51
- Ilyushin IL-2 165, *165*
- infantry
  - German divisions 18
  - German order of battle 31-3
  - Red Army order of battle 33-7
  - Red Army rifle divisions 33
- IS-2 Joseph Stalin heavy tanks *173*
- Iskra, Operation 111
- Istra 65, 66-7, 69, 70
- Italian units 83, 91, 98, *107*, 108-9, *109*, *110*
- Italy 8-9, 22, *23*
- Izyum 82, 86, 113, 117, 131

J

- Japan 9, 10, 29
- Junkers Ju 52 78, *79*, 84
- Junkers Ju 87 Stukas *24-5*, *32-3*, *98*, *108*, *136*
- Junkers Ju 87G-1 131, *131*
- Junkers Ju 88 40, 47

K

- Kalinin 61-2, 63, 68, 70-1
- Kamenets 55, 149, 150
- Karelian Isthmus 12, 14-15, 17, 43-5, 152, 157
- Kastenga 83, 86
- Katyn Massacre 11, 120, *120*
- Katyusha rocket launcher 53, *53*, *184*
- Keitel, Field Marshal Wilhelm 23, *29*, 30, 48, 91, 105
- Kerch 65, 72, 74, 79-85, 93, 140, 150
- Kharkov 53, 62, 63, 74-7, 84-7, 114-19, 132-6

Kiev 20, 25, 42-5, 47, 49-59, 123, 140-1
Kirkenes Offensive 166-9, *171*
Kirponos, General Mikhail 38, 39, 40-1, 44-5, 48, 58
Kleist, Field Marshal Ewald von 48, 69, 86, 88, *88*, 149
Kluge, Field Marshal Günther von 41, 70
Konev, Ivan 20, 61, 122, *122*, 156-7
Königsberg *177*, 178, 180, 183
Krakow 118-19, 173, 174
Krasnograd 76, 85, 117
Krivoi Rog 139, 140, 145, 147
Kuban, River 96, 98, 114-15, 122-3, 136-7
Küchler, General Georg von 75, 77, 145, *145*
Kurland Pocket 168, 175, 176
Kursk 74, 85, 114-15, 120-30, 134
Kutuzov, Operation 131
KV-1 tank 37, 40, *40*

L

Ladoga, Lake 49, 50-1, 56, 70, 112
Latvia
- German invasion and occupation 43, 45, *45*
- Nazi-Soviet Non-Aggression Treaty 9
- Soviet advance 156, 158-61, 164-6, 168
- Soviet occupation 12, 18-19

Lebensraum 7, 8, 16, 19, 28
Leeb, Field Marshal von *29*, *31*, 55, 70, 75
le FH 18 howitzer 112, 124
Lend-Lease Aid 20, 73, 178
Leningrad 93, *98*, 99
- German advance on 43, 46, 48, 50, 52-4
- German assault 54, 55-8, 62, 64, 69-72
- German strategy 25, 26-7, 49, 51-2, 82
- Road of Life *66*
- Soviet breakthrough 76, *110-11*, 111-13, 131, 145, *149*

Leningrad Offensive 145
Lindemann, Georg 149, 155
List, Field Marshal Wilhelm 57, 101
Lithuania
- German claims on 26
- German invasion and occupation 43, 45, 48, 68
- Nazi-Soviet Non-Aggression Treaty 9
- Soviet advance 156, 158-9, 166-7, 168
- Soviet occupation 12, 18-19

Little Saturn, Operation 108, 108-9
Litvak, Junior Lieutenant Lydia 132
Lodz 160, 174
Lublin 157, 158
Lucy Spy Ring 30, 115
Luftwaffe
- attack on US bases 153
- Barbarossa 38, 40
- Blitzkrieg 23
- Kharkov 117
- Leningrad 56
- losses 68
- Moscow 47-8
- order of battle 32-3
- Poland 10
- Stalingrad *98*, 99, *103*, 114
- strategy 24, 25, 49

Luga, River 43, 44-5, 48, *48*, 52, 146
Lvov 38, 40-2, *43*, 48, 156-8, *158-9*
Lyuban 83, *83*, 145
Lyutezh 137-8, 140

M

Maikop 53, 97
Malaya Vyshera 64, 66, 68
Malinovsky, Marshal Rodion 162
Maly Trostenets 84
Mannerheim, Field Marshal Carl *11*, 12, 55, 62, 88, 160
Manstein, Field Marshal Erich von 16, *115*, *119*, 135
- Cherkassy Pocket 145
- Crimea 58, 73, 88, 92
- Demyansk 100
- Kharkov 116-19, 131, 132, 134
- Kiev 140-1
- Kursk *125*
- relieved of command 149
- Romanians *24*
- Stalingrad 106, 108, 109

Marita, Operation (Greece) 23, 28-9, 36
Mars, Operation 107, 111-12
Maxim Model 1910 machine gun *10*
Memel 166, 168, 175
Meretskov, General Kirill 12, 14, 20, 71
MG34 machine gun *42*
MG42 machine gun *118*, 129, *129*
Mga 55, 56, 131, 133, 134, *143*, 145
MI938 mortar *169*
Minsk 39, 40-1, 44, 123, 153, 156
Mius, River 66-8, 70, 92, 116-17, 130-3, 135
Model, General Walther 107, 147, *147*
- Bagration 155
- Kursk 124, 129
- Leningrad 145
- Orel 131
- Ukraine 149

Model 1891/130 rifles *47*
Model 1937 anti-tank gun *128*
Mogilev 153, 154, 155
Molotov, Vyacheslav 11, 22, 26, 38, 41, 86-7, 139
Mongolia 9, 10
Moscow
- bombing of 47-8
- German advance on 16
- German strategy 25, 26-7, 52
- Operation Typhoon 16, 37, 56-68
- Soviet counteroffensive 68-71

Moscow, Treaty of (1940) *15*, 17
motorcycles *52*
Mozhaisk 60, 62, 75, *75*, 77
MP38/40 submachine gun 34, *34*
Munich, Operation 80
Murmansk 40, 41, 56, 58, 166-7
Mussolini, Benito 9, 22, 131

N

Narva, River 49, 146, 158
Nazi-Soviet Non-Aggression Treaty (1939) 8, 9, 11
Nebelwerfer 41 rocket launcher *140*
Neva, River 98, 131
Nevel 138, 140, 142, 143
Norway *16-17*, 17-18, 25, 168-70
Novgorod 52, *54*, 145
Novorossisk 101, 114, 137

O

Oboyan 74, 126-7, 129-30
Oder, River 174-5, 176, 180-1
Odessa 46, 50, 59, 62, 150
Oranienbaum Pocket 57, 58
Orel 60, 130, 131, 132, 134
Orsha 46, 53, 153, 154
Ostrov 41, 43, 158
OT-26A tanks *18*

P

Pact of Steel (1939) 8-9
Pak 35/36 anti-tank gun *100*
Pak 38 anti-tank gun *44*
Pak 40 anti-tank gun *146*
Pak 43/1 L/71 gun *147*
Palanga 168
Panzer 35(t) *23*, *44*
Panzer 38(t) *41*
panzer divisions 31, 121
Panzer II *46*
Panzer III *28*, *46*, *61*, *63*, *80-1*, *118*, *122*, *127-9*
Panzer IV 31, *36*, 43, *43*, *178-9*
Panzer V Panther 31, 122, *122-3*, 126, *126*, *154*
panzergrenadier divisions 139
Panzerkeil 125
Panzerschreck *180*
partisans 41
- Bagration 152
- Belorussia *143*
- German operations against 80-1, 88
- Hitler 108-9
- Slovakia 163
- Soviet 87, 154
- Tehran Conference 141
- Warsaw Uprising 160-1, *160-1*, *162*, 163-6
- Yugoslavia 57, 83, 112, *112-13*, 168, 186

Paulus, Field Marshal Friedrich 25, *100*, 103, 106-13, *106*, *113*, 130
Pe-2 134
Perekop Isthmus 58-9, 62, 139, 140
Pervomaisk 48, 49, 50
Petlyakov Pe-8s 51
Ploesti area 21, 151, 161, 163
Poland
- atrocities 45, 48, 120, 160
- German invasion and occupation 8, 9, 10
- Katyn Massacre 120, *120*
- Nazi-Soviet Non-Aggression Treaty 9
- pact with Britain 9-10
- Soviet advance 157-8, 160, *162*, 163-5, 173-8
- Soviet invasion and occupation 11-12, *18*
- Warsaw Uprising 160-1, *160-1*, 162, 163-6
- Yalta Conference 176

Polish troops 114, 158, 165, 180
Pomerania 177, 178
Potsdam 184, 185, 186
PPSh-41 submachine gun 39, *39*
Pripet Marshes 23, 24, 25, 43, 50
Prut, River 42, 149-50, 162
Psel, River 128, 129-30
Pskov 42, 44, 76, 158
PTRD anti-tank rifle *79*, *164-5*

R

Red Army
- cavalry *136*
- combat effectiveness 37-8
- Great Purge 10, 20, 37
- order of battle 33-7
- rifle divisions 33
- tactics 37
- tank armies 176
- women *151*, 153

Red Orchestra 30, 115
Reichenau, Walter von 67, 76
Reinhard, Operation 93
Rendulic, General Luthar 164, 167, 174
Ribbentrop, Joachim von 8-9, *8-9*, 11
Riga 40, 41, *45*, 67, 123, 159-60, 165-8
Ring, Operation 111
Rokossovsky, General Konstantin 20, 103, 110-11, 125, 161, *161*
Romania
- German Military Mission 21, *21*, 23
- German strategy 24
- Iron Guard rebellion 26
- politics 21
- Soviet claims on 19
- Soviet invasion 149, 161-3, 164, 167
- Tripartite Pact 23
- US bombing 151, 152

Romanian troops 42, 46, 50, 58-9, 62, 84, 88-9, 106-9, 161-5, 175
Roosevelt, F.D.R. 141, *143*, 176
Rosenberg, Alfred *26*, 28
Roslavl 48, 50, 55, 59, 88, 123
Rostov 61, 64-7, 93-4, 115, *116*
Rundstedt, Field Marshal von *30*, 66-7, *67*
Rzhev 75-9, 95, 96, 98, 107, 117-19

S

Saturn, Operation 106, 108
Schörner, Ferdinand 149, 174
Schwerpunkt 23
SdKfz 10 half-track *51*
SdKfz 251/10 *100*
Second Moscow Conference 167
Sevastopol 65, 71-3, 77, 79, 82,

84, 88-93, 151
Silesia 180-1, *181*
Simferopol 64, 70, 150
Sinyavino 57, 62, 98, *112*
Slovakia 11, 23, 39, 163, 182-3
Smolensk 45, 46-50, 56-7, 77, 132-7
Soviet Union
- evacuation of industry 60
- invasion of Poland 11-12
- Iran 54
- Japan 29
- Mongolia 9, 10
- occupation of Baltic States 18-19
- Stalin 20
- treaties with Britain 45, 86
- treaties with Germany 9, 11, 15
- Winter War 12-13, *12-13*, 14-17

Soviet-German Treaty of Friendship (1939) 11
Soviet-Japanese Neutrality Pact (1941) 29
Soviet-Yugoslav Non-Aggression Treaty (1941) 28
Spanish troops 61, *61*, 138
spies 30, 115
Spring Awakening, Operation 179-80, *181*
Stalin, Joseph 20, *20*
- atrocities 147
- Barbarossa 42
- Finland 12, 14
- German surrender 186
- Kursk salient 120
- Leningrad 57
- Moscow 71, 74-5
- Nazi-Soviet Non-Aggression Treaty 8, *8*, 9
- Order No 227 95
- partisans 154
- Polish troops 114
- purges 10
- Second Moscow Conference 167
- spies 115
- Stalingrad 99
- Tehran Conference 141, *143*
- Yalta Conference 176

Stalin, Lieutenant Yakov 120
Stalingrad 16, 74, 92-114
Stalino 62, *62*, 115, 136
Staraya Russa 50, 75, 76-7, 78, 80, 146
StuG III SdKfz 142 assault guns *62*, *114*, *120-1*
SU-76 self-propelled gun 132, *132*
SU-152 heavy assault gun *158*
SU-152 tank destroyer 169, *169*
Suomussalmi, Battle of (1939) 13, *13*, 14
SVT-40 automatic rifle *50*

T

T-26 tank *13*, *75*
T-34 tank 37, 40, 85, *85*, *117*, *130-1*, *134-5*, *148-9*, *176*
T-34/85 *159*
T-40 Light Tanks *81*
tactics 23
- hedgehogs 76
- *Panzerkeil* 125
- Red Army 37

Tallinn 53-4, 55, 165
Tarnopol 148, 149, 150-1
Tehran Conference 141, *143*
Tiger tank 31, 105, *105*, 122, *125*, *130-1*, *171*
Tikhvin 64-9
Timoshenko, Marshal Semyon *15*, 85
- Barbarossa 40-5, 57
- Barvenkovo 86
- Belgorod 74
- Stalingrad 93
- Winter War 14

Tripartite Pact (1940) 22-3, 27
Turkey 31, 70, 141
Typhoon, Operation 37, 56, 58, 59-68, *63*, *64-5*, 70

U

Uman 47-9, *48-9*, 50, *51*, 144, 148
United States of America 87, 139, 151, 152
Uranus, Operation 104-5, 106-7, *107*, 109

V

Vasilevsky, Aleksandr 174, *174*
Vatutin, General Nikolay 20, 104-5, 115, 128, *128*, 129, 130, 132
Velikiye Luki 46, 48-9, 53-4, 78, 80-1, 107-11
Velizh 77, 78-9, 81
Vienna 180, 183
Viipuri 16, 17, 54-5, 152
Vilnius 39, 156, 159
Vinnitsa 47, 59, 144, 149
Vistula, River 158, 159, 174-5
Vitebsk 43-5, 61, 78, 80-1, 153, 154
Volga, River 48, 75, 93, 99, 101-6
Volkhov, River 49, 53-7, 61-2, 65, 69-70, 75, 77, 80, 87, 91, 100, 111, 131
Vyazma 58, 60-2, 75, 78, 119

W

Waffen-SS 31-3, 121
Warsaw
- liberation *172-3*
- Soviet advance 159, 160, 164-5, 173-4, *175*
- Uprising 160-1, *160-1*, *162*, 163-6
- Warsaw Ghetto uprising 120-1, 122-3

Weiss, Operation 112, *112-13*
Weserubung, Operation 17-18
Wilhelm Gustav 175
Wilhelm, Operation 89
Winter Storm, Operation 108, 108-9
Winter War *11*, 12-13, 14-17
women 153

Y

Yak-9 *100*
Yalta Conference 20, 176
Yartsevo 46, 47, 48
Yelnya 48, 55, 56, 80, 135
Yugoslav units 168
Yugoslavia
- German invasion of 28-9, 36
- partisans 57, 83, 112, *112-13*
- Second Moscow Conference 167
- Soviet advance 167, 168, 178, 186, 187
- Tripartite Pact 27-8

Z

Zeitzler, Kurt 103, 158
Zhitomir 42, 44, 45, 140-1, *142*, 143
Zhukov, Marshal Georgi 55, 164, *164*, *172*
- Bagration 153
- Berlin Offensive 183
- Kursk 120, 123
- Leningrad 57, 58
- Mars 107, 112
- Mongolia 9
- Moscow 60-1, 64-5, 66-8
- Moscow Offensive 74-5
- Olenino 79
- rivalry with Konev 122
- Stalin 20, 49

Zis-3 divisional gun *50*

PICTURE CREDITS

All images from The Robert Hunt Library except the following:

History in the Making: 18, 21tr, 21b, 28tl, 50tr, 61tr, 84tr, 136br, 137b, 138tr, 138bl, 139tl, 140/141, 140bl, 141b, 152br, 155br, 163tl, 164/165, 166bl, 170tr, 171t, 178/179, 179bl, 180tr.

Nik Cornish: 10bl, 11br, 14bl, 20, 23br, 49br, 53tr, 56tr, 100m, 132tl, 132bm, 134/135, 134tl, 142bl, 144tr, 144bl, 148tl, 154/155, 168/169, 168bl, 169tr, 174bl, 178tl, 182.